ECHOES OF
BLOSSOM PEAK

*Cowboys, Horsemen, and
History of Three Rivers*

" Happy Trails "

Earl A. McKee Jr.

Earl A. McKee Jr.

In Loving Memory

EARL A. McKEE, SR.
EARL A. McKEE, III

CONTENTS

FOREWORD

〇‴‴〇

The colorful narrative in this book offers a picturesque slice of the history of Three Rivers and the rugged Sierra Nevada–through the eyes and ears and experiences of Earl McKee, Jr.

With amazing recall, Earl relates the colorful history told to him by his family and many other old timers. The stories begin in the mid-1800s with the disappearance of the Yokuts river villages and the arrival of the white pioneers.

Earl grew up in a family whose experiences, all generations, especially Earl's, come to life in his writing. He loved all these great old timers and friends, feelings he clearly conveys in this history. Those who know Earl would say the same about him: "I love that man."

Whether you grew up here and can relate immediately to the writing, the story on these pages will quickly draw you into the unique personalities and scenic panoramas of Three Rivers and the Sierra.

It all began and continues in the shadows and stories of Blossom Peak.

–Bobbie McDowall

ACKNOWLEDGEMENTS

This book came about as a result of friends and acquaintances over the years who would say, "Why don't you write a book about your lifetime around Three Rivers before you're gone?" I can remember back when I was much younger listening to old-time story-tellers—cowboys and characters I knew—and saying the same thing to them!

Well, along came a friend one day by the name of Carol Nadine (Post) McGrew whom I have known since she was a young girl growing up here in Three Rivers. She is a direct descendant of the Alles family, one of the earliest settlers here in 1887. Carol came in and sat down and said to me, Earl, I think you need to write a book and I would love to help make that happen. All you have to do is sit down and tell your life's memories, I'll transcribe them the way you tell them and we'll go from there. That was about a year ago since we started and what a great experience it has been working with Carol on this book. Her tenacity and determination is extraordinary, not only typing but documenting background and dates. She has done a mountain of work—the size of Blossom Peak—and this book would never have been possible without her. I can't thank her enough.

My thanks are due also to my friend and classmate years ago in grade school through high school, Dan B. Busby who helped enlighten me with the facts about early happenings on South Fork.

For proofreading and great ideas concerning the book, my thanks go to my classmate Roberta (Bobbie) McDowall, daughter of one of my favorite families, Archie and Mary McDowall. Her father, Archie is a character I worked with in the Sierra mountains a good part of my youth.

Thanks also to Terry L. Ommen, author and local historian, for his kind words of approval and encouragement and for giving me hope in the outcome of this book. His suggestions about content and structure were most helpful.

Others who assisted and deserve a big thank-you are: Frances Florio for proofreading; Robert Cochran and Paul Boley for map illustrations; and Jeremy Cormier for photo restoration and cover design.

Of course, my most heartfelt words of appreciation go to my dear wife, Gaynor, my loving partner and best friend for sixty-two plus years, who was constant in her encouragement and assistance in retrieving family records and reminding me of stories—especially funny ones—to include in the book.

Blossom Peak, center, Three Rivers landmark where my family settled in 1902. Photo January 2013.

AUTHOR'S COLLECTION.

X

'Neath The Watchful Eye of Blossom Peak,
The Place That I Call Home

In the morning as I step outside, before the streaks of dawn,
I've planned to catch a horse to ride, yet to other things I'm drawn.
High above is the Constellation, with the Dipper pointing North,
I know this is God's creation, while this world is spinning forth.

The morning star lights up the East and the starlit sky is awesome.
Silhouetted as the lights increase, stands her majesty, Mount Blossom.
This mountain is the very same one, where the Indians gazed in wonder
As their children climbed when they were young, like me when I was
younger.

She greeted all the pioneers, as they entered this peaceful valley.
What tales she heard, if she had ears, from their camp fires as they'd rally.
Only God knows how many eagles reared their eaglets from her crest;
Still her granite face stands regal, while they soar 'round Blossom's breast.

I've seen plenty of this earthly world, viewed its splendor and mystique;
I've watched the Sierra scenes unfurl, but my pick's still Blossom Peak.
Like a sailboat's mast, in a line of peaks where her thermals please the
hawk,
Her black north face with its snow white streaks paint what I call Gas
Pump Rock.

She's the hub of "Old Three Rivers," where my folks settled here below
In this old house, built and delivered, over one hundred years ago.
I've lived all my life in this old house; it's the place where I was born,
Married sixty-two years to my loving spouse, here forever our love was
sworn.

She's my love of life and she'll always be, so artistic and born a trainer
With her hand in mine she stands by me, my precious partner, Gaynor.
Our children, Linda, Chearl and Earl, they all grew up here too.
They've felt this mountain top's breeze swirl and saw her awesome view.

Like a milestone pointing heavenly, she'll know when my life's complete.
With my family I'll spend eternity resting peacefully at her feet.
And she's watching, listening as I speak, ever mindful where I roam,
'Neath the watchful eye of Blossom Peak, the place that I call home.

Earl A. McKee, Jr.

INTRODUCTION

༼ᐤᐤᐤᐤᐤ༽

I was born in the house I live in just over 81 years ago. From my front step I look up at Blossom Peak, a rugged sentinel that watches over our beautiful valley. On the backside of Blossom Peak over another range of hills was our South Fork Ranch, and further east another eleven miles is the trail we took to summer pasture at Cahoon Meadow. In the opposite direction about a mile to the West of my place we forded the river at Forrest Homer's ranch to move the cattle to and from our ranch in Greasy Cove. To the northeast about 25 miles is the expanse of the Sierra Nevada and Sequoia National Park, where our horse corrals and packing business was headquartered.

The distinctive pyramid-shaped Blossom Peak looks out through the gap to Lime Kiln. A scattered cover of oak trees grows out of fractured rock and erosion exposes her granite shoulders a little more each year. There is an aura about Blossom Peak that must have beckoned the early pioneers to settle close to her, and later choose her lower slope above my house for their final resting place.

From my horse corrals I enjoy the early sunrise putting a first glint of light on Blossom Peak. This is where my Grandfather Frank Finch chose to build his home in 1902 on 160 acres, a prime quarter section of gently sloping property fronting the then main road and extending north and west to the river.

The narrow road that goes by the front of my house was once the main road to Giant Forest and Mineral King and was called the Mineral King Road. The first post office for Three Rivers was established south-west and across the road from where my house stands today. Years later it was moved up the road a half mile to the general store at the "Y" known as Phipps Store or Alles Corner. It then moved later another half-mile to the Britten general store; then another half-mile to a store by the North Fork bridge and in more recent history a mile west to the newest town center.

In 1915, my parents, Earl A. and Edna Finch McKee, bought a house on land adjoining the Finch property and that is where I was born and have lived my life. With my dad's cattle ranches and his backcountry packing business, our time was divided between Three Rivers and Giant Forest. Every kid should experience the backcountry. It would make better men and women if they could spend time among 2000-year old giant redwood trees, and ride over rocky passes above the timberline. It puts life in perspective when you learn how to live in the dirt, build a campfire, work with animals and make things. As kids we shared hard work, hearty laughs, played and sang music everywhere. Still do.

In a small community you learn to be a good neighbor. In the cattle business it has always been our custom to help each other gather cattle, brand, or whatever needs to be done. Just a couple of weeks ago I was on my horse at 5 o'clock in the morning to help gather cattle for my friends on South Fork and we didn't finish the day until 5 o'clock that evening. They needed me the next day because the cattle trucks were coming in, but I had to call them at 4 a.m. to cancel out because my horse was stiff and tired.

I think 80 is the new 50 because I am busier than ever. Some of the members of our high school class of 1949 still meet once a month for dinner and, as I told them recently, I am so lucky to be healthy and of course that luck has cost me a lot of money for new parts and maintenance. I've collected photos, clippings, recordings, and stories from a lot of people for a long time. In my packing days I used to trade cassettes with Bart Ross on which we each recorded stories about our packing experiences. Over the years people have given me old photographs and artifacts discovered in trunks and cupboards. I have a computer full of photos of gravestones from around the county. This isn't meant to be morbid; the information on headstones is very useful as a quick reference about dates and events.

Not long ago a guy in Oregon found some old negatives in the attic of a house he bought there. He was able to identify a sign in one picture that read "Blossom Peak" and with the help of the Internet he found Three Rivers, made contact with someone who contacted me, and he mailed the old photos to me.

Three Rivers is the "Gateway to the Sequoias," located in the foothills of the Sierra, about 35 miles east of Visalia, California. This book has a slice of history about Three Rivers, a lot of colorful stories from old timers that go way back, and many years of life experiences on the ranch, on the road, and in the backcountry. I've been gifted with a good memory that still works and I need to write this down before I go up the hill.

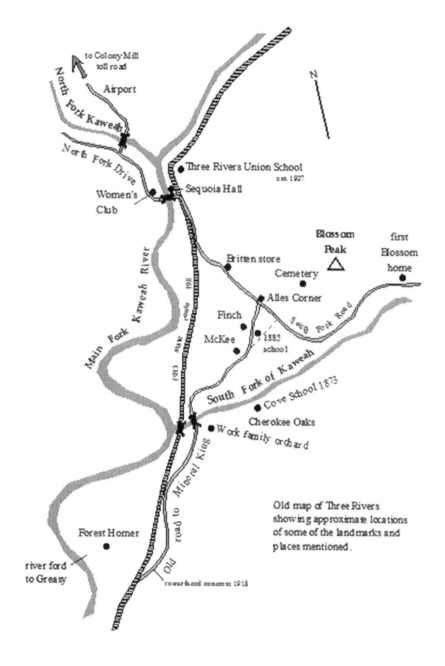

Old map of Three Rivers showing approximate locations of some of the landmarks and places mentioned.

TRAIL TO THREE RIVERS

ⓒⓘⓘⓘⓞ

The cover photo was taken about 1885 looking east at Blossom Peak. The wagon road going easterly was the original and only road going to Mineral King. On the far right is the Three Rivers livery barn where they shod and changed teams before heading up to the timber and Mineral King mines where gold was discovered in 1867. Tom Phipps, packer, horse trader and son of early settlers, told me the small cabin beside the road (center) is where travelers and muleskinners might purchase a bit of liquid power before they tackled the big pull up the mountains. The McKee home where I was born was built in 1910 by a Mr. Underwood a few feet to the left of the larger house at the center of the photo, and the first schoolhouse built in Old Three Rivers was to the left of the big oak tree. A cultivated apple orchard not yet leafed out is in the foreground.

Another photograph of this road and Blossom Peak was taken in 1903 from my Grandfather Finch's porch of the U.S. Cavalry riding by from patrol duty in Sequoia National Park. The Finches had moved to their place in Three Rivers in 1902. In 1913, my parents homesteaded 320 acres in Three Rivers. When the McKees and Finches arrived in

California, both families first settled in Lime Kiln, downstream from Three Rivers about eleven miles to the west, and farmed citrus and cattle.

Lime Kiln was named for the limestone deposit discovered by William Cozzins in 1859. He found what he thought was an inexhaustible deposit of limestone about fifteen miles east of Visalia, California, at the edge of the foothills of the Sierra Nevada. Cozzins built a small processing plant and delivered the first load of lime to Visalia in 1860. Prior to that, lime came by ox team from Stockton. Ten years later Congress approved a post office to serve Lime Kiln and appointed I. D. Mullinex (1844-1930) the first postmaster on July 14, 1879. You see the Mullinex name in early Three Rivers history. Lime Kiln was renamed Lemon Cove some twenty years later.

This photo of the U.S. Cavalry riding from Giant Forest was taken by my grandmother Rhoda Finch from the porch of their house in 1903. Blossom Peak is in the background. Note the tall redwood picket fence—you see miles of them in all the old photographs. Philip and Grace Alles' home is to the right.

AUTHOR'S COLLECTION.

Nora Pogue Montgomery wrote a wonderful book, *Early Days of Lemon Cove*, published in 1966, in which she described the community's history where she was born in 1883 and lived her life of over 100 years. It is of interest to me because Nora tells about the citrus ranching endeavors of both my Finch and McKee grandparents in the early days, and the fact that the McKee side of the family was related to Nora's family, the Pogues.

The 1888 *Business Directory of Tulare County, California*, listed fifty-seven businesses in Lime Kiln, the majority, as you would expect, were farmers and stockmen. Among the farmers were J. W. C. Pogue, W. A. McKee, S. A. D. McKee; a teamster, George W. Swanson; and hog raisers, H. D. Tharp and Norton Tharp.

Nora Pogue Montgomery's father was James William Center (J. W. C.) Pogue who first arrived in Tulare County in 1862 and in 1877 planted the first citrus in this area—20 orange and lemon trees to be exact. Over the next decade, he expanded his citrus orchards to 6,000 acres. J. W. C. Pogue, in partnership with C. W. Crocker and W. B. Wallace of San Francisco, bought up 10,000 acres of railroad land around Lemon Cove which was first planted to winter wheat that grew as high as the horses' backs. Pogue diversified to sheep, then to hogs, and then converted all the acreage to citrus farming. In 1896, five and ten-acre parcels were sold off to a dozen or so individuals for the specific purpose of citrus orchard plantings. S. A. D. McKee bought and planted one such parcel (he later sold it to J. E. Pogue). Marcellus Brown planted 10 acres. His wife was Eliza J. Pogue, daughter of John Pogue, a half-brother of J. W. C. Pogue. After Eliza died in 1902, Marcellus Brown moved with his nine children to Lemon Cove from their previous home near Mt. Pinos. I knew three of his sons: Marcellus Brown Jr. with whom I worked in Sequoia National Park; Rennie Brown who served as our Constable; and a hero of mine, Onis Imus Brown.

Along with expanding his citrus industry, in 1894 J. W. C. Pogue set aside 15 acres for a town center and named it Lemon Cove. It was laid out between two sharp S curves. The most notable landmark in Lemon Cove was and is the J. W. C. Pogue Hotel built in 1879 to serve as their family residence and a hotel. Nora Pogue Montgomery, the Pogue's youngest child, was born at the residence. It was later bequeathed to her and in 1936 she donated the building to the Lemon Cove Women's

Club. The beautiful structure fronts on Highway 198 and is the site of the Club activities to this day. Today Lemon Cove is surrounded by even larger citrus ranches.

The relation of the Pogues to my McKee family is best described by the inscription in a copy of the *Pogue Memoirs* compiled by Eva Pogue, daughter of J. W. C. Pogue.

"Given to Earl Alfred McKee, great-great-great grandson of John Pogue of Virginia. Great-great grandson of John and Nancy Pogue of East Tennessee. Great grandson of John and Lydia Jones Pogue of East Tennessee. Grandson of Nancy Pogue McKee and John McKee of East Tennessee. Son of William Alfred McKee and Mary Jane Maddy of Missouri. Given by Eva Pogue Kirkman, your 1/2 first cousin once removed, and Jonathan Grant Kirkman. December 1945."

The J. W. C. Pogue family tree included his half-sister named Nancy Pogue. Nancy Pogue married John McKee on February 15, 1842 in Greene, Tennessee, and they had one son, William McKee, born July 1845. John McKee was a soldier in Missouri during the Civil War. At some point, John McKee married a second time to Martha (known familiarly as "Aunt Martha" to residents of Lemon Cove) and together they had four children: Dee, Caroline, Mark, and Cecil. This family, including John's first son William McKee, lived on Dry Creek about 1880. Martha McKee was the nurse in attendance when Nora Pogue was born in 1883. Neighboring landowners were the Bequettes, Hammonds, S. G. Nye, Thomas Davis, and Ragles. Caroline and Cecil McKee married Bequette boys. John McKee died about 1892, and his widow, Martha McKee, went to live with her oldest son, Dee, at his orange ranch.

William McKee's brother-in-law Lou Bequette, John Rice and Frank Finch were Lemon Cove's ". . . most noted fiddlers, playing at celebrations and contests, and so enjoyed it that it was easier to get them started than it was to get them to stop" (Nora Pogue Montgomery, *Early Days in Lemon Cove*, 1966).

William McKee rented the J. W. C. Pogue house on Dry Creek where my father was born. In the early 1900s, William McKee planted orange groves and built a home in Lemon Cove but he later sold out and moved to Naranjo, east of Woodlake. William and Mary McKee had five children: Ernest, Lena, Maud, Stella, and Earl A. McKee. Miss Maud McKee and Mrs. Stella McKee Britten were charter members of the Lemon

Cove Presbyterian Church in 1907. Ernest McKee played on the 1906 Lemon Cove Baseball team, was later a mountain guide, an explorer in the Sierra, and noted horseman.

In 1900, Frank Finch and Rhoda Rice Finch were residing in Iowa and had been hearing about the expanding citrus business in Lemon Cove from his brothers-in-law who had arrived here a decade earlier. He answered an advertisement in a national newspaper, probably the Police Gazette, for an orange orchard for sale in Lemon Cove, California, and decided to move West. Frank Finch arrived in Lemon Cove, California in 1900, with a satchel containing about $5000 in gold coin to establish himself as an orange grower. Nora Montgomery describes Finch's 80-acre property as "the Knolls." It extended from the site of the old Earlibest Packing House at the Woodlake turnoff from Highway 198, east to the foothills. In 1913, J. E. Pogue built and operated that packing house—his middle name was Early.

Frank Finch sent for his wife Rhoda and their children, Jesse, age 9; Edna, 8; Loren, 5; and Zola, 2, who came by train to their new home in Lemon Cove. The orange property had a house toward the foothills that served as their family residence for two years. By 1915 Frank Finch was one of the Lemon Cove partners in the newly formed Sequoia Citrus Association. Among the partners were four investors from Three Rivers–James Pierce, Fred Savage, Jason Barton, and Joe Carter.

In August 1983, my mother and I were invited to the grand celebration of the 100th birthday of Nora Pogue Montgomery at the Lemon Cove Women's Club House, the beautiful home Nora was born in. I was asked to sing. I sang for Nora's funeral the following April 1984.

Lime Kiln Hill forms part of the earthen Terminus Dam built in 1960 across the Kaweah River and old limestone mines are still visible on the downstream side. The Kaweah River carries the snowmelt from the Sierra and is one of the steepest rivers on the continent. The Sierra drainage flows through several deep canyons into the Middle (Main) Fork of the Kaweah–Marble Fork, North Fork and South Fork, as well as several creeks. Pioneers settled up each Fork but wagon roads did not cross the rough ridges canyon to canyon. The North Fork and South Fork feed into the Middle Fork in the shadow of Blossom Peak, a dozen miles upstream from Lime Kiln Hill.

Grandparents Frank and Rhoda Finch

My grandfather Frank Finch loved the oak-covered foothills of Three Rivers at the foot of the magnificent high Sierra range, a scenic wonder especially to someone from the Iowa prairies.

Frank Finch and his twin, Fred, were born in 1867 to Jessie and Grace Finch who had two other children, a boy and a girl. The family resided in the wilds of Cherokee, Iowa. My great grandfather Jessie Finch was widowed twice before his marriage to Grace, and was the father of twelve children and seven stepchildren. In 1854 they made the twenty-seven day journey by wagon from Delaware County, Ohio to Cedar County, Iowa. When Jessie Finch arrived in Iowa he recalled the country was very wild; there was an abundance of horse thieves as well as vigilantes ready to hang the horse thieves. Jessie also wrote in his personal history that "Wild Oat money"–counterfeit–was sowed so thick "we never could tell when we went to bed if the money would be good the next day." Their farm produce had to be hauled 45 miles to Davenport, Iowa by wagon. There were no railroads in the state. The neighbors hauled lumber from Davenport to build a school and church with their own money and hired the first teacher at a salary of 75 cents a week, which Jessie paid. Jessie Finch died in July 26, 1906. Grace died a year later.

My grandmother Rhoda Mary Rice Finch was one of eleven children of James Nicholas Rice and Mary A. Williams Rice of Cherokee, Iowa. James Nicholas Rice was born April 25, 1836; he was a well-respected and generous man who lived by the Golden Rule. James and his brothers were huntsmen, and part of their business was collecting wild animals–buffalo, elk, deer, antelope, white swans, cranes, and beaver–for Central Park, New York City. His brother, William C. Rice tamed and shipped wild animals to the zoological gardens of Europe, but his handwritten family history doesn't tell us how he managed to transport exotic specimens from the Plains to the Eastern ports. William C. was the last commercial gunner, which meant he was hired to furnish game to hotels and estates and such; he hunted the untouched prairies of Minnesota, the Dakotas, Nebraska, Kansas, and Oklahoma. My grandparents came from very strong stock.

A sister of James Nicholas Rice, Clementine Rice and her husband Charles Marx, moved from Iowa to Lemon Cove with their two children, Cora and Jacob in 1884 or 1885, fifteen years before her niece–my grandmother–Rhoda Rice Finch arrived. Clementine's brother, John Rice and family followed two years later in 1886. Charles Marx and John Rice had large orange groves east of Lime Kiln Hill–now in the Kaweah Lake bottom.

Two years after purchasing his orchard in Lemon Cove, Frank Finch bought 160 acres in Three Rivers. The property has a picturesque view of Blossom Peak and extends from what we now call South Fork Drive (the road through Old Three Rivers, known in 1900 as Mineral King Road) north to encompass part of what is now the golf course, to the river and west past the former Indian restaurant. He built their home by the road to face east to Blossom Peak. He planted a small orange grove which depended on ditch water; in drought years water had to be hauled by wagon to keep the trees alive. There was already an established apple orchard. Mr. Finch drove a team back and forth to Lemon Cove to take care of his citrus business there.

When I was a kid, the Finches kept a small herd of cattle as well as a milk cow on the home place. This kept the grass down in the summer and provided beef for the locker. In the summer when feed was scarce, neighbors would combine herds and take them to the mountains, often times to River Valley which is to the east of Hospital Rock between Bear Paw and Redwood Meadow. I remember Grandfather's pair of white Percheron horses; he used them in his groves in Lemon Cove, they had big feet, could go through mud, pull a wagon or a sled when it was too wet. He kept the team because he said his tractor might break down or get stuck in mud, but the horses would always be there, rain or shine.

After the new grammar school was built on the main road, Frank Finch bought the old school property and remodeled it for their home where they lived out their lives. After my grandparents died, their original house and property was sold in 1956 to a doctor in Southern California. I bought that land back in about 2000 and it adjoins my horse ranch.

Earl A. McKee, Sr.

My father, Earl Alfred McKee Sr., was born January 13, 1891 on the Pogue property that was later bought by Fred Ward and known as the Ward Ranch on Dry Creek. He attended school at Naranjo through grade nine. My dad first packed a party into the back country when he was fifteen years old and by the time he was twenty years old, he had his own pack stock–horses and mules–and guided trips into the High Sierra every summer. He took on a partner, Clarence Britten, in the packing business. Clarence was a half-brother of Harry Britten, my dad's brother-in-law. My dad also had a team of horses to haul freight to Giant Forest by way of the old Colony Mill Road. In winter, dad hired out his mules for plowing, and took care of his mother's cattle.

My dad is on the horse in front of the Naranjo School. It was known as Lime School until c. 1900 when it was renamed Naranjo for a variety of orange tree grown locally. Photo c. 1904.
AUTHOR'S COLLECTION.

In 1912, accompanied by friends and family, Earl McKee and Edna Finch rode the electric train to Fresno to be married. Afterwards, they departed from Three Rivers on horseback with a pack mule for their honeymoon in the backcountry.

My dad homesteaded 320 acres in 1913, up the hillside from the old road that runs parallel to Highway 198 east of Slick Rock. He and my mother traveled by horse and buggy drawn by his remarkable horse, Joker. In the winter, they both packed oranges in Lemon Cove. (My dad always kept a journal—pack trips, horses and mules bought, expenses, supplies, income, etc.; in the winters he wrote the number of boxes of oranges they each packed–for example, one day in December,

1923, he tallied 53, my mother 56, for which they were paid ten cents per box.) They moved into Grandfather Finch's old place in Lemon Cove where their first child, Blanche, was born April 11, 1915, then moved to the homestead shortly after. My dad built a cabin not far from a spring with wood stove and candles, no electricity or plumbing of course. The flat area was planted to winter barley and fenced to meet homestead requirements. After Blanche was born, two children died in infancy; then Earleen was born in 1927 and I was their last-born four years later.

Earl A. McKee, Sr. and his bride, Edna Finch McKee, pictured at the start of their honeymoon pack trip to Willow Meadow. My mother is riding Joker. Photo 1912.

AUTHOR'S COLLECTION.

The house that I was born in, and in which I have lived my entire life, was purchased by my dad from a Mr. Underwood who built the single-walled house. We've added to the house and remodeled it a few times. This was part of pioneer Ira Blossom's property that Sam Kelley acquired; the acreage took in both sides of the road over to the South Fork river.

Kelley's house was not far from where ours was built. My parents moved into the Underwood house shortly after they'd proved their homestead. By that time my dad was contracting for pack trips with clients in Visalia, Fresno, San Francisco, and New York.

My dad registered his stock brand, "Bar-O on the hip"; it had a very early registration number, in the 5,100s. It was admired by others because it meant "bar none–the best." Sometime in the late 1930s, the annual registration fee and form was lost in the mail and the next thing my dad knew, someone else had claimed his brand. He was furious. He had to go to "Bar-O on the rib." In the 1970s, I found that Bar-O on the hip was lapsed, so I called the Brand office and asked do you take a credit card? I don't want to let this get away again. Since then my brand is the same as my dad's: Bar-O on the hip.

A July 1917 article in the local paper reported that "Earl McKee is packing the Eastman party [of Eastman-Kodak] through the mountains. His assistants are Jesse Finch, E. McKee, Steve Hector, D. McBride and Kenneth Savage." Before my dad acquired the concession at Giant Forest, many pack trips started right where I live now, in the apple orchard out back. Our neighboring cattle rancher Forrest Homer packed for my dad in the old days and told about one trip that left our front yard with 65 head of horses and mules heading for Kern River. They camped at Potwisha the first night, a popular campground four miles inside the Ash Mountain entrance to Sequoia National Park (SNP), about 2100 feet elevation, near Marble Falls.

My dad was packing a party from the Huntington Lake area and I was born on the day they came out. One of the dudes congratulated my dad and insisted he accept a $100 tip to open a bank account at Security Pacific Bank for his new son. So you could say I banked at Security Pacific from the day I was born until it was sold to Bank of America.

Three Rivers

Across the road from where I live was the site of the old livery stable and barn where the freight wagons from Visalia and Lemon Cove would change teams on their way to Mineral King. The first post office was located across the road and about 200 yards southwest of my home, this according to Jason Barton, an early pioneer and resident of note.

The December 29, 1879 *Los Angeles Herald* listed new post offices across the country that Congress had approved including one for Three Rivers, California, Laura E. Grove appointed as postmistress. Some subsequent postmaster appointments were in the newspapers: Francis

N. Grove, December 30, 1880; Samuel W. Kelly, April 18, 1881; Henry Y. Alles, February 11, 1895; Catherine C. Clayton, September 16, 1898. August 7, 1903, Rhoda Finch took over the position after Mrs. Clayton resigned. Abram Dinkins was appointed June 29, 1907; Noel Britten, October 20, 1909; Nellie A. Britten, July 8, 1935.

Several old timers said that at one time the postmaster position was held by a man who did not sort the mail; instead he dumped the mail bag on a table for patrons to paw through because this postmaster could not read or write. The monthly mail reports were filled out for him by I. D. Mullinex who had been the postmaster in Lime Kiln. At a Pioneer Dinner in 1938, Henry Alles told a similar story, that the mail was brought up the canyon once a week and the postmaster dumped it into a box on his front porch and told people to hunt their own mail. Henry was appointed postmaster in 1895, and said he went down to the post office and ". . . moved it [the post office] to his place in a barley sack." An 1887 Three Rivers news brief published in the Visalia paper said, "There is a lot of mail in the post office for Wm. Hill and C. Allen that has been there a long time."

The 1880 U.S. Census for Three Rivers section, counted on July 5, 1880, lists Laura Grove, age 23, occupation postmistress, born in Pennsylvania, and her brother Francis Grove, age 21, also from Pennsylvania. (He was appointed postmaster in 1880.) Rather mysterious is the fact that not far from the location of the first post office is the grave of a Henry Grove, relationship to Laura and Francis unknown. Grace Alles, whose father was I. D. Mullinex, was on the Three Rivers Cemetery board with me for many years, and told me a relative of Henry Grove arrived here from Pennsylvania in October 1915 and placed a headstone in the Three Rivers Cemetery for Mr. Grove but did not relocate the grave. Mr. Grove was born January 8, 1847 and died May 18, 1880. Just an interesting historical aside. I guess he is still out there in my pasture somewhere.

At a Pioneer Dinner, Bob Barton made the distinction between the early settlers on the flats of Horse Creek, and the first pioneers to settle in the canyons of Three Rivers: ". . .Ira Blossom was the next. The Blossoms for whom Blossom Peak was named. He moved on the South Fork before there was any road of course into Three Rivers, brought his household equipment, probably not much, but a stove at least, in over Big Oak Flat from the Tharp Ranch on a sled, had a large family, settled there and planted the first apple trees in Three Rivers, and took out a ditch to irrigate the apple orchard. The ditch is still being used. [Ira settled] just about across the road from where Curt Siodmak lives now. And then, about the same time, Hopkins Work with a very large family moved in right down at the mouth of the South Fork about where Dr. Weaver and George Brooks live now. . . .He was completely flooded out in the big flood of 1867 and 1868. His farm, he had planted an apple orchard and had taken out a ditch there [the Work family]. . .The Blossom and the Work, I believe were the first settlers this side of Tharp."

The Work property was later part of the Carter homestead that took in what is now the Cherokee Oaks subdivision. The Cove school was built on the big flat area where the first community rodeos were held. We crossed the river to play there when we were kids.

Kids in Three Rivers

My earliest childhood memory is strumming my ukulele and singing. My Grandmother Finch arranged to have a movie made of the Pioneer Dinner at the Woman's Club House in 1933. In the final scene, I perform a song. I was two.

Earl A. McKee, age 4, on the ranch.

My dad was a good friend and customer of Mr. Jack Iseman of Goldstein & Iseman Market–G&I–in Visalia, because Iseman put up all the pack orders for the backcountry trips. G&I celebrated a grand opening of some sort and invited my dad to bring me down to sing. I was three years old and I vaguely remember that performance; I was always strumming a ukulele and singing "Pop Goes The Weasel" but there I sang "Every Night When Ida Comes Home." Apparently my version was "when Idy come home." When I was four years old, I sang "Home on the Range" and "Pop Goes the Weasel" at the annual Pioneers Dinner.

When I was two, I tried to sing at the evening wedding of my sister Blanche to Lee Maloy celebrated under the big China Berry tree in the front yard of our home. The flower girl in the procession was my sister, Earleen, and the soloist was Norma Lovering, daughter of South Fork rancher Whisperin' Bob Lovering, (and mother of Gaynor, who became my wife). Norma had a beautiful soprano voice. When she began her solo, I figured I better run up there and sing too. I made a scene when Grandfather Finch held on to me, and cried louder when he carried me up the road out of earshot because I was so mad that they wouldn't let me sing at my sister's wedding.

My parents and grandparents were active in the community. Frank Finch served on the county grand jury. Social activities were card parties of Pedro and Bridge, playing horseshoes, and dances. Mr. Finch and his neighbor Philip Alles played serious horseshoes and I can remember seeing four ringers on a post. Some of the dances were held at the Sequoia Hall in Three Rivers and us kids were put to bed on the stage or under hinged tables on the walls while the adults danced the night away.

Grandfather Finch played the fiddle in fiddling contests and won the state fiddling championship in Sacramento the year I was born. He also played fiddle in the Poison Oak Orchestra of local fame. My mother taught me to play the piano; from my Grandfather Finch I learned to second on piano while he sawed the fiddle, and when I was in fourth grade, I sat in for Ben Hardin on piano for the orchestra. Grandfather taught me chords to play guitar as well as simple hoe-down fiddling. My sisters, Blanche and Earleen, both sang. I accompanied my sisters on the violin for a hymn at Easter Sunrise Service when I was twelve. In the winter we played and sang around the wood stove and in summer we played music in the mountains around the campfire. When I was older, I loved classical music and listened to Mario Lanza and old Caruso records. There was always music around.

I grew up next door to my cousin, Sherman Finch. We shot our BB guns and by the time we were ten years old, our parents taught us to shoot .22 rifles. No one thought anything about a 10 year old having a .22 then. I remember like it was yesterday, Sherman and I out there, we shot a couple of quail, skinned them and cooked them on an open fire, really roughing it. We imagined ourselves as real tough mountain men, just like our great-grandparents in Iowa.

A rite of passage was the climb to the top of Blossom Peak. Just like my mother, Della, and Floyd Carter did when they were kids, we'd hike to the top and holler out over the canyon so our parents would know we were okay.

I started school at Three Rivers Union School in 1937. Mrs. Mary McDowall was the principal and there were two other teachers. Average daily attendance that year was 81. Mary McDowall was hired as a teacher of 3rd, 4th, and 5th grades in November 1930. In 1940 she was appointed principal. She retired as principal in May 1968.

Rena Ogilvie prepared a hand-written chart of the schools around Three Rivers, with the name of the principal/teacher, number of additional teachers, and average daily attendance for each year of operation. The Cove School was established in 1873 in present-day Cherokee Oaks area with average attendance of 15 the first year. The Oak Flat School east of Horse Creek opened in 1881 with one teacher and 7 students. Also in 1881, Sulfur Springs school, named for springs on the east side of Highway 198 on the Middle Fork, opened with one teacher and average attendance of 16. It burned and was rebuilt across the road; after that building also burned, a new school was built on A.G. Ogilvie property on the north side of the Middle Fork. Cinnamon Creek school on South Fork opened about 1886, burned, and was never replaced.

In 1885, the Cove schoolhouse was dismantled and hauled from Cherokee Oaks, across the South Fork, to Old Three Rivers drive where it was rebuilt. It was a rough clapboard, unpainted affair located next door to the Phil and Grace Alles place, across from my Grandfather Finch's. It was called Three Rivers School. In 1906, Oak Flat school was merged with Three Rivers School.

My mother and her brothers Loren and Jesse, attended that school along with Floyd Carter, Della Carter, and Clarence Britten.

In 1914 a new schoolhouse was built to replace the old clapboard one. School continued there until 1927 when all the elementary schools were combined into the new Three Rivers Union School at its present site on the main road.

My cousin Sherman Finch (r.) and me with our rifles in front of my house. We were about 10 years old. Photo 1941.

AUTHOR'S COLLECTION.

My dad used his mule team to do some grading around this new schoolhouse. In 1935, the steep hillside in back of the school was graded into four large terraces to make playgrounds and ball fields. In 1939 the school cafeteria opened to provide hot lunches for the kids. Effie Fry was the cook.

Johnny Britten attended the school across from the Finch place. He said he had several teachers, but they didn't last very long because teachers found it was pretty rough living in the mountains. Ord Loverin remembered two of his teachers at Sulfur Spring school, Professor W. F. Dean and Emma Purdy. Professor Dean was a well-respected teacher and an active member of the community. Dean sold his home and apple orchard in 1930 and moved to Oklahoma to live with his nephew. Ord said the kids were really ornery. The boys would put water snakes in the teacher's desk, and sometimes a kid would grab the school marm in a bear hug when she tried to discipline the class. Once, Kenneth "Skinny" Savage distracted the teacher while all the kids climbed out the window.

15

To put an end to the fistfights between boys and girls, one teacher divided the playground into boys side and girls side.

Johnny Britten also told about trapping when he was a youngster: "Leighton Hicks was one of my classmates. He was my buddy and he and I caught most of the skunks and pretty near everybody's cats in Three Rivers and some of the dogs . . . trying to make a living."

When I was a kid in grammar school I decided I could be a mountain man and make money as a trapper. I trapped over in the South Fork river bottom where Cherokee Oaks subdivision is now. All that land was part of Floyd Carter's family homestead, and before that the Work family's apple orchard. My mother said if I was going to run traps, I had to get up early before school to check them, because "you're not going to let those animals stay in those traps all day." My mother knew all about trapping; her grandfather and uncles were professional trappers in Iowa. I'd come back from the trap line and my mother could smell me before I got to the door and she'd make me leave my clothes outside. I remember my schoolmates Forest Busby and Dan Busby trapped also, and when we rode the school bus in the mornings we would excitedly compare catches, "What'd you get?" "What'd you get this morning?" I remember one time having maybe five or six skunks. I would make a shingle that fit the hide and fasten it on wrong side out and it would cure for a long time. Then I would ship the furs, mostly skunks and raccoons, to various companies. I was paid $2.50 for each skunk fur, quite a nice price in those days.

One thing about living in Three Rivers, there are a lot of bridges and you were liable to be stranded during heavy rains. I watched the big wooden bridge that spanned the Kaweah to North Fork wash away in 1937. Debris piled against the bridge and water was going over the top. Orlen (Baldy) Loverin and Fred Gim were trying to get home to North Fork so they ignored the warning to stop and headed across just seconds before the bridge gave way. Their car was almost to the other side when the bridge broke loose and swung around and headed downstream. They dove off the far end and managed to get to the bank. I can still remember their car sitting on the bridge as it turned slowly like a big ship and about where the river drops off toward Old Twenty (a swimming hole) the bridge slowly rolled over. Later their car was dragged out of the sand flat on a sled and, for some odd reason, it was abandoned near the bus barn at our school. It was an object of curiosity for us kids but if they caught us there, Fred Ogilvie, our custodian, would give us a swat, with a stern look but a hidden gleam in his eye. He kept all the kids in line, made them act civilized. There was never a better man in the world than Fred Ogilvie.

My dad taught me horsemanship as soon as I could sit on a horse. Back when I was a kid, during World War II, we didn't use the truck to drive around as much due to shortage of fuel. Instead, we just rode horses from home down to Slick Rock and took the trail over Rayme Gap to Greasy Cove, about a 2-1/2 hour ride, or up South Fork. Gas was rationed and my dad just had a rattle-trap truck in the old days with hand-made wood racks that would shake and sway. So we rode. Now days, it is so easy to haul the horses as far as you can and then ride. Well, horses need to be ridden, to go on the trail climbing through rocks, opening gates, to get a sense that they are going some place.

At age 11, I decided to raise pigs. Carl Sweeney, who worked for my dad at Giant Forest corrals, took me along to a livestock auction in Tulare where he bought a hog. I saw what grown hogs were selling for, and when some shoats came across the block I thought it would be a great idea to buy those little pigs and raise them to sell. My dad was a cattleman. There would be no pig raising on the Bar O. He told Carl to take those pigs on home with him. Carl probably was not surprised, just made an exaggerated huff and hauled all the pigs to his place.

My dad raised most of the horses for his riding and packing concession and on the off-season he helped to organize a riding group for fun, the Three Rivers Range Riders. My dad had a lot of deer hides he was given on hunting pack trips. These he had tanned and sewn into matching white deerskin chinks for all the riders. (Chinks are like short chaps that extend just below the knee. They are good for branding because they protect the upper leg from the rope when working in the saddle, and on the ground.)

The riders were: my dad and mother, sister Earleen and me, Johnny and Thelma Britten, Forrest and Marjorie Homer, Ted and Maricia Bartlett, Darren Carter, Floyd and Helen Carter, Byron and Della Allen, Joe and Dot Carmichael, my sister Blanche and husband Lee Maloy, and their kids Leroy, Billy and Virginia. Billy could ride like a little wart when he was a tyke, and Virginia was about a year old so she rode with her

17

mother. We all wore matching maroon color cowboy shirts, most of which were sewn by Blanche, who was an expert seamstress. The horses had white deerskin brow bands. We looked really sharp. The Three Rivers Range Riders rode in many valley parades and won a blue ribbon at Visalia in 1942.

After we quit riding in parades, our group was renamed The Do Nothing Club and we gathered for annual summer picnics and outings. The picnics were usually at the Three Rivers airport, or sometimes at the Apple House. One time we went to Shaver Lake to the cabin of Roy and Lillian Richards of Visalia.

GIANT FOREST

Giant Forest History

Giant Forest was named by John Muir in 1875. Stockmen from Three Rivers vicinity staked out claims there for summer grazing areas as early as the 1860s. Lumbermen sized it up for the timber and conservationists looked to save the big trees. The editor of the *Visalia Delta*, George W. Stewart, led a group of Valley citizens that lobbied congress to preserve this unique forest of giant redwoods.

In 1885, a group of people arrived in Visalia and filed upon 42 quarter-sections under the Timber and Stone Act of 1878 for lands adjacent to Giant Forest and upper Kaweah River. They formed the Kaweah Cooperative Colony with a plan to move to the mountains and produce lumber for sale in Visalia. The giant sequoias would be carefully preserved and only pine and fir trees cut. To this end, construction of a wagon road to their timberlands was started in 1886. Two hundred Colony men worked for four years to complete twenty miles of road that started from the North Fork at 1500 feet elevation and climbed to 5000 feet, eight miles short of Giant Forest. Officially it was the Giant Forest Wagon and Toll Road but it was commonly known as the Colony Mill Road. When the members submitted their proofs and payment for their land certificates, bureaucratic interference stopped the process and eventually all claims were declared null and void. The legal wrangles between the government and the Colony were reported coast-to-coast.

The congressional bill to create Sequoia National Park (SNP) was signed by President Benjamin Harrison on September 25, 1890, but Giant Forest was not in the new Park's boundaries. A week later, however, the area of Giant Forest was put into SNP by means of a rider tacked on to the bill that established Yosemite National Park.

After the creation of Sequoia National Park in 1890, the federal government assigned protection of the new Park lands to the United States Army. Units of the U. S. Cavalry were rotated out of the Presidio in San Francisco to Giant Forest and Mineral King to guard against poachers, unlawful grazing, and logging. It was a 16-day, 325-mile trek for the cavalry, stock and supplies. Enforcement wasn't always uniform. For example, in 1894, the commander of the 58 men in Troop B was later charged and disciplined for selling his troop's rations and horse feed to hunters, allowing illegal hunting, fishing, cattle and sheep grazing for a bribe of a bottle of whiskey while his men and stock went hungry. Army officers acted as Park superintendents from 1890 until 1914 when the first civilian superintendent, Walter Fry, was appointed. From the *San Francisco Call*: "Soldiers Finish 300 Mile Ride. Troop A, First Cavalry, Arrives Dusty and Tired From Sequoia Park." From the *Los Angeles Herald*, August 27, 1898: "Visalia–A detachment of the Utah voluntary cavalry, under command of Lieut. Smith, arrived here this morning en route to patrol the Sequoia National Park."

John Grunigen told about the time in 1896 that he, his brother Armin, and a friend named Bill took a trip to Giant Forest from Three Rivers. They rode up the North Fork, camped at Colony Mill, and the next day rode over to the army outpost at Halstead Meadow. This is how John told it:

"We thought we'd go by the camp and leave our arms . . . we didn't have many, but we knew we weren't allowed to take guns in, so we went in there and the sergeant said, 'You got any arms with you?' 'Yes,' we said, 'we came by to leave them with you.' 'OK. The corporal will escort you through.' So we started off in Halstead Meadow and went right down to Marble Fork, just above where the bridge is now, and when we got to the river, there was a nice big buck on the other side of the river. And the soldier jumped off his horse and – bam! bam! bam! bam! He missed that buck! We thought that was funny, we had to leave our guns and then they shoot–and miss!"

The hand-built Giant Forest Wagon and Toll Road became the property of the new national Park which, along with the loss of their land claims, led to the dissolution of the Colony. So the government got a free road into the Park that the army continued to work on to reach Giant Forest whenever Washington provided money. The last eight miles had to be routed through heavy forest on rough terrain and was slow going. Captain Charles Young and his Buffalo Soldiers were transferred to Giant Forest from San Francisco in 1903 and under Captain Young's leadership completed the final several miles into Giant Forest and Moro Rock in record time. They built more miles of road in one season than the army had in five, for which Captain Young was honored.

This is the road we used when I was a kid to herd the horses and pack stock to Giant Forest each summer. In 1913 automobiles were allowed into the Park on Colony Mill Road and my dad's sister Stella and husband Harry Britten who was a ranger lived at the Cedar Creek Ranger Station and checked the cars through–the toll was $5.00, a pretty big sum for that time, but it was set high to pay for future road improvements.

My grandfather Frank Finch received a handwritten invitation to the big picnic celebration of the road's completion to Giant Forest held

on November 11, 1903. The dedication photograph shows a crowd, including Captain Charles Young, Bill Swanson holding a shovel, Frank Finch, Phillip Alles, John Grunigen, and the Buffalo Soldiers. Recently in 2011-12, a bill to commemorate the work of the Buffalo Soldiers in the national Parks was introduced into Congress.

Grandfather Finch's souvenir from the 1903 dedication of the completed road to Giant Forest. "We sat beneath the redwood shade, After the forest road was made, And took our feast from boxes laid On well-worn shovel, pick and spade."

AUTHOR'S COLLECTION.

The first forest rangers of Sequoia National Park were: Ernest Britten (1900-1905); Lew Davis (1901-1909/1924-1929); Charles W. Blossom (1901-1916); Harry Britten (1902-1903/1906-1915). Harry Britten, married to my dad's sister, Stella, was a nephew of Ernest Britten, Sr. In 1905 the Rangers were officially designated Park Rangers; Ernest Britten transferred in that year to the Forest Rangers.

Stephen Mather (1867-1930) was appointed Assistant to the Secretary of the Interior in 1914 where he lobbied for a more professional, standardized management of federal Parks. The National Park Service (NPS) was created in 1916, and Mather was appointed its director. Stephen Mather was originally the sales manager for Pacific Coast Borax Company and coined its identity "Twenty Mule Team Borax." He became very wealthy with his own borax mines which enabled him to purchase and donate several private forest lands to the Park.

In 1903 the redwood trees were counted. *The Mt. Whitney Journal* reported that "Forest Ranger Ernest Britten, on duty in the Sequoia National Park, assisted by Corporals Smith and Mosby of Troop I, Ninth U.S. Cavalry, made an accurate count of the sequoia trees in the north half of the northwest quarter of Section 6, Township 16 south, Range 30 east, Mt. Diablo Base and meridian. The count embraced all trees in this 80-acre tract in the giant forest having a diameter of not less than 2 feet. The trees were tagged as counted, and the result was verified by a recount. A total of 185 trees was found, and of this number about 160 were not less than 10 feet in diameter. If these large trees are equally numerous in all parts of the giant forest—and the tract chosen did not appear to be an exceptional one—there are 6500 sequoias of great size in this splendid body of timber."

John Broder homesteaded on South Fork; Onis Brown showed me the place on what later became part of the Wells Ranch. In 1898 an attorney from San Francisco hired Broder to pack his party into Giant Forest to look for available timberland. When he was paid $600 for the trip, Broder decided this might be a good business to get into, so the next year he formed a partnership with Ralph Hopping called Broder & Hopping. Their base was Giant Forest, with a camp and three tents to begin with. Two years later their pack station had 85 horses and pack stock, 10 tents and a cook house. They were deep in debt when Broder died in 1907; the following year the outfit was sold at a Sheriff's sale. There were two other owners until 1924 when Ord Loverin bought the outfit. Five years later he sold it to my dad.

Broder bought ads in the city papers, for example, the *San Francisco Call* advertisement, August 28, 1906: "GIANT FOREST: The Biggest of the Big Trees. The grandest of Mountain Scenery. Good fishing, mountain climbing and perfect climate in September. Only 39 miles staging;

fine Government road. Good accommodations. Sierra Camp. Address: Broder & Hopping, Three Rivers, Tulare County."

Colonel John R. White was appointed superintendent of Sequoia National Park in 1920, and served until January 1, 1939. My dad and Colonel White were good friends and the Colonel personally okayed the contract for my dad to operate the Giant Forest pack station. Some improvements were made at that time, the old corrals and buildings at Muir Gap were removed, and an area between Sherman tree and Wolverton on the old Lodgepole road was cleared for separate corrals for our packing stock and the government stock.

The Colonel was born in England, educated at Oxford, joined the American army in 1899, was stationed in The Philippines, and later fought in World War I. After retirement he wanted to work outdoors and was hired as a ranger in the new Grand Canyon National Park a year before his appointment to Sequoia. His passion was to preserve this natural treasure for future generations, keep it as undisturbed as possible, yet accommodating and accessible for the enjoyment of all. Commercial interests wanted large developments for hotels and resorts; the small lodge and little tent cabins and beautiful picnic areas reflected Colonel White's philosophy of gentle treatment of the forest.

In the late 1930s the Roosevelt CCC program (Civilian Conservation Corp.) established five camps in Sequoia with 35 army officers, 60 park supervisors and 1096 enrolled young men whose energy Colonel White tried to steer to projects to fit his vision for the Park. The CCCs made lasting improvements to roads and facilities. A permanent mess hall to accommodate 100 men was built in 1937 at Red Fir, four miles beyond Lodgepole.

The commissioner of fish and game saw the new park as a fine place to transplant species. In August 1911, 150 state-raised, full-grown turkeys were carefully crated and shipped to Sequoia National Park and liberated in the same spot as a previous year's shipment; they thrived. Not so successful was the transfer of elk herds, many of which died of exhaustion trying to outrun the herders, but it was reported as a success because a three mile, very high fence had been built to contain them.

Growing up in Giant Forest

My parents bought the riding corrals concession in Giant Forest and the Wolverton Pack Station from Ord Loverin in 1929, before I came along. Before I was weaned I spent my first summer in Giant Forest in our little cabin at Hazelwood across from Giant Forest lodge, where we lived every summer until I was in high school.

No relics remain of the old Giant Forest village that I remember. It was a picturesque little neighborhood carefully tucked in among the giant groves of redwoods bordering meadows and streams. There were some 600 campsites, including cabins and tent cabins in Giant Forest, Lodgepole and Dorst Creek. This forest of the largest, oldest trees on earth was our playground, the backcountry trails our classroom. George Mauger, Park concessionaire, ran a great facility at Giant Forest with a store, a lodge, service station, coffee shop, curio shop and even a small hospital staffed with a resident doctor. In the mid-1920s, our neighbor, Floyd Carter, brought his dairy cows to supply milk to the campers at Giant Forest. The cows were pastured in Crescent Meadow. Byron Allen had the meat concession, operated a meat market at the store, and kept his beef cattle at Cabin Meadow. The barracks, corrals, and mess hall built by the U.S. Army and CCCs were still in use when I was a kid.

George Mauger also had the concession for the Bear Paw Meadow camp, a four-hour trip east from Crescent Meadow on the High Sierra Trail. We packed all the supplies to Bear Paw for forty years, and guided horseback rides there for people who didn't want to hike.

Giant Forest, elevation 6500 feet, is a wonder of the world enjoyed by thousands of visitors who, back then, could camp among the giant sequoias, hear echoes through the canyons, behold the majesty of cliffs and meadows, cook in the open air, be entertained by the wildlife and gather around big bonfires every night for songs, dancing and skits. Giant Forest, under the direction of Colonel John R. White, was fun.

Every evening at the roaring bonfire, little dots of light appeared through the trees as park guests made their way with flashlights to the amphitheater for singing and entertainment. We were ornery little kids, we'd run across the road to the campfire, and like all kids trying to get attention, we'd make fun of their songs and sing our made-up words at the top of our lungs. I remember George Mauger running us off and scaring the heck out of me.

A favorite of the campfire crowd was the silhouette pantomime performed behind a white curtain, the scene an operating room where surgeons pulled all manner of ridiculous objects out of the patient—giant sausages, hoses, or horseshoes.

Carl Sweeney worked summers at the Giant Forest corrals for my dad, entertaining the dudes and taking them out on guided trips by horseback to Alta Peak and Four Lakes. That's what Carl was good at— he was always at the campfire in the evenings getting business, inviting vacationers to sign up for horseback rides. Carl was real vaudeville in

a cowboy hat; people would ask for his autograph like he was a star. In the evenings around the campfires, Carl and some of the other guys at the pack station would put on skits. In one, Carl played the bad guy running from the posse into the night. He was rigged with a hidden harness hooked to a line attached to the stage backdrop. The posse thundered out of the dark into center stage, holding a rope with a hangman's noose around Carl's neck. He was yanked out of the saddle by the unseen harness line and hung there, doing his comic spiel: "By the way, while I'm hanging around, tomorrow we are having an all-day ride to Alta Peak so be sure and sign up at the corrals.

This is me on Buster in front of a giant Redwood at Giant Forest. I was four years old. Photo 1935.

AUTHOR'S COLLECTION.

Carl published a little book of poetry in 1940 called *Poems That Show 'em I Know 'em,* and signed himself C. E. Sweeney, Poet Lariat of the Mountains. He was a great fan of Robert Service and the famed "Klondike Gold Mining Days." Carl used to recite Service's poems like "The Shooting of Dan McGrew" or "The Cremation of Sam McGee." In fact, he helped me memorize these two poems when I was about 10 years old and I recited "The Shooting of Dan McGrew" in front of my fourth grade class, verbatim, from memory. My teacher, Mary McDowall, was flabbergasted! Of course, she was from Alberta, Canada and Robert Service was one of her heroes too, and she did not stop me. I had to change the word "damn" to "dern" but I said the word "hell." She let me know I should have changed that word also. I loved Mary McDowall and I think the feelings were mutual.

In the early and mid-1940s, Floyd Brown was employed by the Park as a Ranger during summers in Giant Forest. He led the singing at the campfire and his deep voice carried through the trees. He was personable and friendly with all the visitors and an excellent master of ceremonies. He and his wife relocated to Three Rivers next door to their close friends, the Pusateris.

Another evening activity at Giant Forest was dancing at the recreation hall at Sunset Rock. Sam and Juanita Pusateri, also a Southern California couple, worked at Giant Forest at the same time the Browns did. Sam was a Ranger, and he and Juanita also taught ballroom dancing at the hall. Gaynor and I danced a million miles there. Sam and Juanita demonstrated all the different dances, rhumba, waltz, fox trot, to make an evening of laughter and fun. They were just good and wonderful people.

As kids, we spent every summer running barefoot at the corrals in Giant Forest—my cousins Sherman Finch, Don Britten, and my sister's kids, Leroy and Billy Maloy, and me. We learned to ride as soon as we could sit on a horse. We rode and packed burros—we called them jackasses—as well as horses and mules. Don Britten, my second cousin, was just a year older than me, and we were really close. Until college, he came out to spend every summer with us. His father, Clyde Britten, who packed for my dad when he was young, was also a cowboy for the Gill Ranch in his younger days. Don's grandparents were Harry and Stella McKee Britten, my dad's sister.

Every spring, my dad took us to Giant Forest as soon as the snow was gone and school was out to get ready for the tourists. So the last of May we'd try to get the horses up there and sometimes even as early as the first of May, depending if it was a dry year and open. Timing was important to have horses ready when the vacationers started arriving and wanted to go horseback riding.

We trailed (herded) the horses and mules to Giant Forest each spring by way of the North Fork road. We stopped for the night at

Shorty Hengst's place and put the stock up in his rock corral, then got up at 4 a.m. to take them on up the old Colony Mill road to Giant Forest. It was a pretty ride up the old road into the park. We came out at Pinewood Camp that had tent cabins for rent. This concession was run by Iva Tingley, our next-door neighbor here in Three Rivers, who bought uncle Jesse Finch's house. From our corrals across from the lodge, it is about a mile to Pinewood, which is located out on a point. The Marble Fork Trail came out right there, and we brought the stock up on an old dozer road almost to Sherman Tree, then across to the trail to the Wolverton corral.

My dad's riding horses were kept at the corrals in Giant Forest and the pack stock over at the Wolverton pack station. Regulations allowed only pack or riding animals within the Park. One year we got permission from Colonel White to bring our cow to Wolverton to provide milk for us kids. When we drove up at the park entrance, the ranger heard "moos" and demanded to know what we were hauling into the Park. I remember an old timer's cow story: after Mineral King and Hockett Meadows became part of the Park, no cattle were allowed on Park land, just pack stock. Mont Barton said he just put special-built pack saddles on his two milk cows and brought them up to Hockett in the string of mules.

Corral cleaning was our first job as little kids. Every morning before daybreak a chunk of wood hit the tent to wake us up and we hustled out early to rake the corrals before the horses were fed, because if the hay wasn't exactly how they wanted it, the horses would throw some out of the mangers and the corral had to be clean so they would eat it off the ground. We'd use heavy rakes, we'd pile the horse manure, then we used a finish rake with narrow tines so it looked spic and span, and everything was hauled away before the corral opened for business. We were right across from the Giant Forest lodge and there was a reason to keep it spic and span–Colonel White! Like in the army, he would come over to make inspections, but we never had any demerits. We used sheep dip also because a lot of horses urinate in the same place, it is a habit of some horses, but not all, so we used the sheep dip and that would make everything smell clean and sterile.

The horse manure was trucked out on Deer Ridge along the road going to General Sherman tree. We drove on an old trail and just scattered the manure on the hillside. We always laughed about the spectacular growth of those young redwoods; people never knew why those trees grew greener and larger than anywhere else.

One day my cousin Sherman Finch, nephew Leroy Maloy and I were at the stables and Leroy was fiddling around with a lariat, tossing it at one thing and another. He was just a fuzzy-haired little kid a few years younger than me. There was a big buck nearby, very tame because we fed the deer, and Leroy threw the rope and it settled over the buck's horns. The deer went wild, jerked the rope out of Leroy's hands and disappeared over the ridge. And here came the Chief Ranger, Irv Kerr, who looked us up and down, and finally said, "Well, I'm thinking somebody from here could be responsible. A while ago a big buck jumped off the bank over there and he had this rope dragging off his horns. The buck hit a car and was killed. Would that be anybody here?" Leroy quickly piped up, "Oh, No!" and I remember Irv had a knowing look on his face, because I think he knew enough about our family he would suspect Leroy because Leroy would try anything.

Alta Peak, elevation 11,000 ft. Snow pattern is in the shape of an elephant. Near the elephant's eye is where we lost a horse on a moonlight ride out of Giant Forest with the dudes. Photo winter, 2012.

The horses for rent had to be bomb-proof, suitable for the inexperienced riders, although when you asked, invariably the dude would insist "Oh, yes, I am an excellent rider," but after the test ride around the corral, you knew they couldn't ride for sour grapes. So you would ask them to please step off and try another horse.

The moonlight ride to Alta Peak was very popular with the tourists. When Carl Sweeney was guiding, if someone asked where Mt. Whitney was, he would point to some mountain or other and exclaim "There it is!" because he didn't know either. (Mt. Whitney can be seen from Alta Peak, but not from Moro Rock.) About where the elephant's eye is on Alta Peak is where we lost a horse one night. It was a moonlight ride and the saddle turned on one of the horses, pinched it, so it bucked. The rider slid off, but the horse lost its footing and rolled down off the trail, pretty steep there, hit a tree and was killed instantly. The lady rider was led out on a guide's horse. Don Britten and I went back the next day to get the saddle. It was a good horse, named Conejo, a big bay. This happened about 1948. I was 17.

On horseback from Giant Forest to Wolverton was a ride of an hour and a half. The ride from Wolverton to Pear Lake was spectacular, the trail climbs up by Four Lakes and around the Watch Tower. Some riders would scream and get off their horse because it is a straight drop down 2,000 feet to Tokopah Valley, a pretty scary spot. But the trail was wide and you couldn't beat a horse off of it. I remember guiding folks and they'd squeeze their eyes shut and lean way over from the edge and I'd tell them, "Open your eyes, you're going to hit your head on the bank. If I was going to go off the edge there, I'd want to see where I was going!" A nice ride was to Twin Lakes, about six miles, and we'd take a mule with all the fishing gear for the guests, a good all-day trip. We had a lot of fun there.

It was 1949 when I guided a day trip for a couple that turned out to be Michael O'Shea and Virginia Mayo, the Hollywood actress. She looked the part of an aloof movie star, big sunglasses, rode along with clothes half on, not saying a word. Michael, on the other hand, was talkative and it turned out he was a friend of Monty Montana, the famous trick roper and entertainer who rode in sixty Pasadena Rose Parades. His act was headlined at the 1935 Visalia Rodeo. Montana's most famous rope trick was in 1953 when he roped President Eisenhower in his inaugural parade in Washington D. C. The Secret Service was not amused. At any rate, Michael said his friend Monty taught trick roping at Riata Ranch in Exeter for Tommy Maier, the owner and a former Hollywood cowboy himself. Tommy brought in experts like Monty Montana to coach his riders, The Riata Ranch Cowboy Girls. That's where I later met Monty Montana.

You don't want the horses standing around eating hay without making a little money, so if business was slow, we had permission from Colonel White to turn the horses out at Willow Meadow up from Lodgepole on the Kings River trail. There was a fenced meadow with all kinds of good feed. There'd always be several bell mares. I learned to track horses there because the fence didn't go into the peaks and sometimes the horses would climb up and around the end and head back toward Tokapah, or over Cahoon Gap and drop down into Clover Creek, and some of them would just keep going down into the Rowell Meadow country. One time I rode for a couple of days looking for horses that we needed for a pack trip coming up. Finally I asked Forrest Homer to come along and on a hunch took a truck over to Big Meadows where we rode out and found them and hauled them back. They had traveled about 15 miles from home.

Every visitor to Giant Forest had a bear story. Sorted garbage from the village was dumped at the bear pits about a mile away. Of course every bear in the country went off and told his friends and soon there were more bears than garbage. It was entertaining to watch because the bears were tame and posed for photographs and could be coaxed to eat from the hand of a foolish tourist. In 1939, a seven year old bear, Goofy, created a lot of excitement when she brought her quadruplet cubs to the feeding area. Colonel White installed a bathtub especially for the bears–bears love to play in water–and a redwood grandstand afforded a nice viewing area. One day Sherman, Leroy and I were pretty close, watching the bears splash when they got in a scuffle and one bear chased another right at us. We hit the ground and got soaked when the old wet bear jumped right over us.

The over abundance of bears prompted Colonel White to install an incinerator and eliminate the bear pit right in the middle of the summer. Waiting until the end of the season would have been smarter. It was just poor timing for the bears to have their food source disappear suddenly so they invaded the campsites in search of the daily buffet they had become accustomed to.

Old Bake, my dad's old dog was kept tied to the table inside the cabin at night. One time he started barking, so Lee Maloy got up and let Bake outside where he treed a bear cub. Lee was standing there hollering "go get him" and said he felt something funny at his back pocket and heard a kind of "woof." He about jumped out of his skin when he turned around and there was mother bear sniffing his pockets. Lee grabbed a milk bottle from the porch and threw it to scare her away. The bottle bounced off of the bear, hit his car, and cracked the windshield.

One year we arrived to find that a bear had spent its winter hibernation inside our cabin. What a terrible mess that was to clean. We often saw the results of curious, hungry bears going after food in parked cars. One I remember was a touring car, the kind with slats and canvas roof. The bear had climbed into the front seat, the door shut behind him, and after he finished off the picnic basket, backed up and sat on the horn. That bear tore through the roof like you'd opened a can.

Years later when I was shoeing horses for the Park, I took my family for a picnic at the campground near the old cabin where I grew up at Hazelwood. We were enjoying fried chicken and watermelon when a little cub came near us and the kids were scared to death– Bear! a Bear!– Earl was four years old. The cub looked so thin and poorly I thought he was an orphan. I shoed the cub up a tree where he started crying, and I should have been thinking a little more clearly, because across the meadow an old bear was making her way around toward us. I grabbed a limb and went out to meet her, ran at her and threw the branch in front of her but she didn't pause, she was going to her cub and I was in the way, not a good place to be. I ran and hollered to get everything in the car, mama bear is coming. I reached the car just as mother bear jumped on the table to eat up the remnants of our picnic.

Another Road to Giant Forest

Until 1925 the Colony Mill Road from North Fork was the only way into Giant Forest from any direction, a narrow, often washed out, dusty wagon road. One army officer called it a "pack trail." There were only intermittent wide spots wagons could pass so bells were used to warn other travelers of an approaching wagon. When a stage driver to Giant

Forest heard bells ahead in the distance, for example, he'd pull to the very edge or even off of the road at the next wide spot and wait to let the 6 or 8-mule freight wagon edge by on the inside with a bare inch to spare from the jagged rocks. Freight wagon drivers were known by their particular bell tones and drivers would inform passing wagons who else was coming down the road and about when they'd likely meet. When automobiles were permitted into the Park starting in 1913, most of Colony Mill Road was too narrow for more traffic of cars and wagon teams to pass, so travel was restricted to one-way. Going uphill, cars were allowed to leave Kaweah from 4 a.m. to 1 p.m., and could depart from Giant Forest between 3 p.m. and 5 p.m. All of the army officers and park superintendents stressed the need for a new road to Giant Forest: " . . . travel up hill at a snail-like pace through stifling dust does not appeal to the modern traveler."

The Mt. Whitney Power Company was granted permission in 1907 to build a wagon road from Three Rivers to Hospital Rock to access a new flume and Power House No. 3 under construction. The first proposed route for a new road to Giant Forest was to build up the mountain from the power company road at Hospital Rock. This new road was initially designed as one-way, one lane, going up. The Colony Mill Road would be the one-way exit going down. This 1920 plan said, "When both roads are completed a system of one-way traffic will make it possible to travel faster and with less risk." For three years the work progressed on a narrow one-lane road until some official visitors from Washington D. C. concluded that the one-way idea was unworkable, so the curves and switchbacks had to be blasted out wider to make space for two lanes and two-way traffic. Thank goodness for someone's better vision.

For the first time, landscape architect-engineers had the final word on all Park road construction proposals. The highway was designed to "lie lightly on the landscape." There were several surveys for the best route, some east of Moro Rock, some west of Moro Rock; the west one on Deer Ridge was selected. From Hospital Rock to Giant Forest, the road climbs 3600 feet in ten miles, has 23 switchbacks, two S curves, 200 other curves. This road was opened to the public in 1926, without guardrails, curbs or fences. It was named the Generals Highway by Colonel White, for the two largest Giant Sequoia trees, General Sherman, in Sequoia National Park, and General Grant in Kings Canyon National Park. The section of highway connecting Giant Forest to General Grant was built later and dedicated June 23, 1935.

ON TOP OF THE WORLD

⟨⟨⟨⟨⟨⟨⟨⟩⟩⟩⟩⟩⟩⟩

The McKee Pack Station

Away from civilization; no phones, no work, no worry, no noise, no hurry. Just twenty-five miles from my ranch lies one gateway to 700 miles of alpine trails that crisscross nature's spectacular granite masterpiece whose rugged beauty rivals that of the Alps. The Sierra is a great granite uplift stretching 400 miles from Shasta to Tehachapi. The highest part of the Sierra features dozens of snow capped peaks topping 11,000 feet, and the deepest river gorges in the country. The tallest mountain in the continental USA, Mt. Whitney, at 14,494 feet elevation, is just to the east of us. What you need to do now is log on to Google Earth and fly over this wonderland. Unless you are young and fit and can get a permit, that's about the only way you are going to see this rugged backcountry of Sequoia-Kings Canyon National Park.

This is where my dad mapped out special itineraries for his clients to marvel at these stunning vistas from horseback—range after range of granite spires and dramatic rainbow-hued ridges, boulder-strewn 13,000 foot mountain passes, lakes in all different colors, lush meadows, river gorges and gentle valleys, all carved by glaciers over time measured in eons. It is another world; once you ride into it, the compass of your soul is drawn there forever.

My dad was an expert horseman and packer who had an encyclopedic knowledge of the Sierra trails. His horses and mules were mountain-trained. All this, coupled with a sense of humor and common sense, had the dudes saying at the end of the trip, "Goodbye, Earl. See you next year!"

The Trails

Trails are the threshold to the Sierra splendor and trail crews keep the doors open. Several main trails traverse the four directions, and the experienced guide knows shortcuts and side trips to hundreds of secluded lakes and meadows.

The High Sierra Trail and Twin Lakes Trail are main trails that we used from our Giant Forest pack station to connect to the vast back country, to the top of Mount Whitney, or the stock could be trucked over to Cedar Grove in Kings Canyon to depart on the Roads End Trail through 3000 to 5000-foot canyon walls into the South Fork and Middle Fork of the Kings, through Paradise Valley, Simpson Meadow, for example, up canyons and over high passes to hundreds of creeks, lakes and valleys. There were trips to or out of Yosemite National Park and some that started from the Eastern Sierra out of Bishop, Independence, and other pack stations.

The Twin Lakes Trail goes north from Giant Forest into Kings Canyon National Park, connects with a maze of other trails, and reaches Cedar Grove. Work on the High Sierra Trail was begun in 1928 to connect Crescent Meadow in Giant Forest across the Great Western Divide to Mt. Whitney, a trail 70 miles long, the first trail built for the public's use. As the crow flies, it is about 26 miles from Giant Forest to Mt. Whitney.

John Grunigen and Jim Livingston built the High Sierra Trail from 1928 to 1932; the most spectacular section of trail, frequently photographed, was blasted out of the side of precipitous granite bluffs that plunge down to River Valley as well as Hamilton Lake, a trail wide enough to turn a string of mules around. That is a story for later.

As soon as mountain passes were melted enough for trail crews to reach their territory, work was started to repair damage from the winter storms, remove fallen trees, dislodge boulders, blast and widen trails, or chop steps across snow fields. The packers would be out on the trails as soon as possible; the dudes were anxious to explore the backcountry.

Elite Pack Trips

My dad traveled to San Francisco to call on clients to arrange pack trips. Many were arranged by mail with clients in New York and Los Angeles. Some of my dad's 'elite' clients from the beginning were the

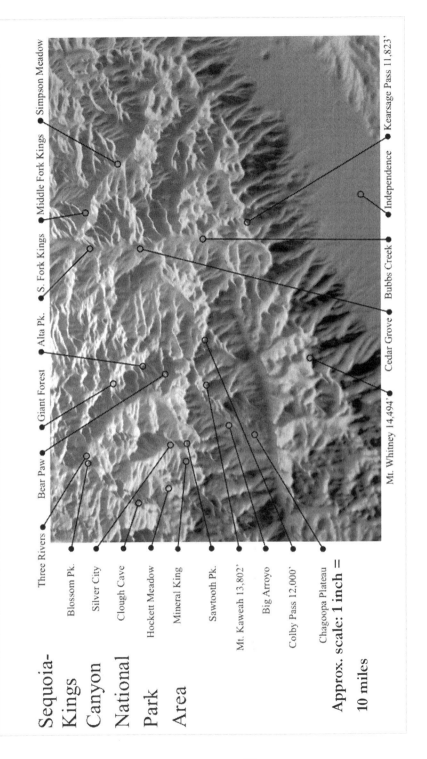

Sequoia-
Kings
Canyon
National
Park
Area

Approx. scale: 1 inch =
10 miles

W. P. Fullers, William Crocker, the Don Tressiders, Walter Haas, Dean Whitter and George Eastman. Dean Whitter's nephew, Lt. Jean Whitter worked for my dad for two summers at Giant Forest (he died in WWII on the USS San Francisco).

My dad was a guest of W. P. Fuller, Jr. at his home in San Francisco every winter to plan their annual pack trip with maps and suggestions. The Fullers–the W. P. Fuller Paint Company–packed into the mountains with our family for thirty-two seasons. Mr. Fuller was a brilliant man, slightly crippled by polio when he was young and he rode with a brace on one leg; his left arm was atrophied so he rode right-handed.

Mr. Fuller would refer my dad to the elite of San Francisco enterprise and give him tips for his sales call; "you might have to wait on him a little more" for example. My dad stayed at the Fuller's home and many years later when I was their guest, Mr. Fuller told me that my dad always liked to take a walk in the morning around their estate, down a little canyon, over to the home of their gardener, and suggested I do the same. I visited the gardener and we talked a long time because he remembered my dad and was quite fond of him.

A news brief from Three Rivers dated August 5, 1936 describes a Fuller pack trip: "Earl McKee left yesterday with his helpers for Yosemite to take out the W. P. Fuller party. With him were Ernest J. Britten, Onis Brown, Alan Savage and Walter Pratt. Jesse Finch of this place took one of the three truck loads of horses, mules, pack outfit and provisions which had to be shipped over to meet the party." In 1937, the Fuller party arrived in their private airplane at the Three Rivers airport and motored to Giant Forest to begin their annual pack trip. Two years prior, the Fuller party of eleven flew to Bishop where my dad, four packers and one cook met them with 40 head of stock for a five-week high Sierra excursion.

Here are a few other interesting trips my dad mentioned in 1937 and 1938. One of the most lavishly outfitted parties was Walter Haas, president of Levi Strauss, his wife, three children and two friends– a party of seven which required 37 head of stock and four packers to haul all their personal tables, chairs, Coleman lanterns, and over-stuffed beds–it was described as one of the most complete camping outfits ever taken into the Sierra–looked as if they had bought out the Emporium. The two-week outing left from Giant Forest to Bear Paw

Meadow, Kaweah Gap, Nine Lake Basin, to a base camp at Big Arroyo from which my dad took the guests on guided day trips. Alan Savage, E. J. Britten, and Jim Kindred were his packers. Another trip that made news, was a more unusual one in 1937 for Professor Donald S. Mackey, his wife and four children and another professor; this trip was guided by E. J. Britten for my dad from Giant Forest through Kings River country. All the dudes walked, instead of riding a horse, except the young daughter. The following year they also walked on their pack trip. Following a twenty-day pack trip into the Paradise Valley country for C. F. Lamont, partner of J. Pierpont Morgan of San Francisco in July 1938, my dad went out a few days later with a party of ten doctors and two dentists from the Bay Area into the Kings River country on a twelve-day trip.

Dudes around the dinner table at Cloudy Canyon. Burl Hyde, Visalia businessman (left front); Bert Nice, packer, looking at camera with cigarette; my dad Earl McKee, Sr. extreme right. Photo 1928.

AUTHOR'S COLLECTION.

Orval Overall, vice president of Security Bank, booked annual deer hunting trips for his party into the Kings with my dad. My dad referred to him privately as Orval Overbritches. Orval was a former star pitcher for the Chicago Cubs in 1905. Orval's father was Dan G. Overall of Visalia, one of the founding partners of Kaweah Lemon Company in Lemon Cove in 1892.

W. P. Fuller, Jr. and William C. Crocker (of Crocker Bank) families had a close relationship, both being prominent businessmen in San Francisco. Both were Special Members of the Burlingame Country Club in 1924. Both families enjoyed summer pack trips into the Sierra as our clients. The Crockers went for three weeks each summer and preferred to go earlier in the season. The Fullers went for a month each summer toward the fall, and most of the time coordinated their trips so wherever the Crockers came out, the Fullers would hook up and go from there. There were some places it was not possible to connect the Crocker and Fuller trips, so we would have to dead-head the stock, but most of the time they worked together nicely. Don Tressider, then President of Stanford University, also went with us—he was married to Mary Tressider, who was a Curry, (Curry Company owned the concessions in Yosemite) and he preferred to go out of Yosemite. The Fullers and the Crockers were our bread and butter for years.

In 1961, three personal invitations arrived, addressed to my mother, Edna B. McKee; to my brother-in-law and sister, Lee and Blanche Maloy; and to my wife Gaynor and me, inviting us to attend the 50th wedding anniversary of W. P. and Adaline Fuller at the old Crocker Mansion on the grounds of the exclusive Burlingame Country Club. We were seated with Mr. and Mrs. Fuller and family in front of a large stage in a huge ballroom. After a magnificent dinner, their three sons, W. P. Fuller III, George Fuller and John Fuller, took the stage and sang several comical tunes they used to sing around the campfires and a couple of bawdy songs as well. It was all great fun and laughter. As they came off the stage, "Parmer" (W. P. the Third) grabbed a Martin guitar from under the stage, came straight toward me and said, "Earl, get up there and sing us a couple of songs!" I sang two songs, the first one that I haven't thought of in years was called "Fifty Years From Now." It was an old tune written by Haywire Mac—Haywire Mac was a stage name of Lloyd McClintock who sang novelty songs and wrote the Bum Song, "Hallelujah I'm a Bum," and many others. Then I sang the old comical tune, "Life Gets Tedious, Don't It." The songs brought on more fun and laughter. The rest of the evening was a storybook experience, and although it's been 50 years since that night, I will never forget the thrill of being there. Seems just like yesterday. Mr. Fuller loved to sit around the campfire and sing. He had several tunes that he was famous for and always sang, and other tunes we sang together.

A noted author, Kathleen Norris of San Francisco, who went on several backcountry trips, produced a promotional brochure for my dad's packing business. At least two of her novels were made into movies: *My Best Girl*, and *Manhattan Love Song*. In October, 1936, this was written about the husband of Mrs. Norris: "Outstanding because of the large equipage for so small a party was the trip taken into the Kings River country by Charles G. Norris, author husband of Kathleen Norris, his son, Frank Norris, and secretary, McClellan. Fifteen big pack mules, making 22 head of stock, three packers and a cook, were taken for the party of three. Eleven guns and 100 pounds of ammunition were carried. Norris bagged one deer, his son two, and his secretary two. McKee accompanied this trip personally, with Onis Brown, Walter Pratt and Alan Savage as helpers."

In 1922, my dad packed the distinguished naturalists Mr. Stephen Mather and Mr. Francis P. Farquhar on official business to the backcountry. Mr. Farquhar was an early director of the Sierra Club and author of many books on Sequoia National Park, its names, history, and species.

George Eastman was another elite client. I have Mr. Eastman's letter to my dad dated March 30, 1917 in which he says Mr. William E. Colby had recommended my dad to him as a competent guide, and went on to outline the trip he had in mind. William Colby was the first secretary of the Sierra Club in 1900, led members into the backcountry, served as a director for 49 years. George Eastman was an inventor, primarily of cameras, but he also designed a folding camp kitchen he wanted to bring along to use, and then promote it to other packers. He was a highly organized and principled individual who gave away millions of dollars to charity. He loved to cook. Milton Savage taped an interview with me in which he told me about his dad, Kenneth Savage, going out as the cook for my dad with the Eastman party. He said he only cooked for the crew because Mr. Eastman brought along his own personal chef.

Stupendous scenery at Big Bird Lake, a climb up from of the south end of Deadman Canyon, to the west. Lush meadows splashed with brilliant wildflowers border the trail through Deadman. Black granite slopes glisten under cascading streams. Photo c. 1930.

AUTHOR'S COLLECTION.

It was such a wonderful surprise when the W. P. Fuller's daughter, Adaline Jessup, looked me up at the Sacramento Jubilee jazz festival not too long ago. We had just finished playing our set and a lady called to me from the walkway and said, "Earl?" It was Adaline. Such a surprise. She asked for my address because she had put together some movies taken of everyone on all the Fuller pack trips and wanted to send me a copy.

Learning to Pack

Nineteen forty-three, I was twelve years old when I first went out on an "elite" pack trip with my dad. He let me go as a flunky, and I helped my dad pack the lunch mule. It was one of the trips with William Crocker, of Crocker Bank; Onis Brown and Skinny Kirk were the packers. On moving days, my dad would lead out with the dudes and the lunch mule before the packers got the string on the trail. When you're packing, you're going to take a long trip, maybe a month out, so you have a planned itinerary: so many hours to camp, stay all night and maybe lay over a day or two, then pack up and move on, so you come out at your clients' ride-out point on schedule.

The following summer, 1944, I packed my first string of mules, five of them, for my dad on another elite trip with the Crockers. I was 13, it was during the War and it was hard to find packers because everyone was in the army. I remember I had five old mules in my string—you'd call them 'dinks,' now you'd call them old gentle mules, but they were really dinks. I can even remember the names of those mules, or at least some of them. There was Old Bim and Star; there was Harding, named after President Harding—in those days mules were named after anybody controversial, and one of them was, well you don't say that word anymore, but can we print it? N_ Nice was his name, he was coal black and my dad bought him from Bert Nice. Heart was the name of another mule, a black mule that had an almost perfect heart in the middle of his forehead.

Onis Brown and Skinny Kirk were packers on that trip; they were both too old for the Service. There was a total of 15 or 16 mules, and the dudes and packers rode horseback.

I have great respect for mules. The mules you had trouble with were the young ones, they'd kick the gloves right out of your pocket. Mules are very smart, smarter than horses. Most people don't know this. There is a saying, "Smart as a mule." Mules are more intelligent than a horse mainly because of their breeding. The burro side came from the desert, Andalusia, Spain. The Spaniards brought both burros and horses to America. The native American Indians did not have horses until the white man imported them.

Packing my first mules, I had been around packers long enough to know how to lift the kyacks on the mules and you'd run the rope through the ears of the kyack to the ground, then the mules would think they were tied and would stand still. There was a learning system here. You'd have to know how, not to just pull the rope tight, but to go around the pack boxes and lift on the corners a little bit when you're tying the diamond hitch then get behind and check to see that the kyacks were level, because if one side was higher than the other, it could slip and turn a little after a long day's ride even though you had weighed them so each side was the same weight. The load would be topped off to make a nice square pack, maybe with chair covers, or a small folded bed or small tarp. Then the manty (a canvas top cover) would cover the load, a 5' x 7' would just cover the kyack and small top pack and would not hang much below the bottom of the pack boxes on either side. You could tuck the ends around; I didn't like to tuck them behind the corners because I thought it would be better to let more air in there, and tucked corners might rub the mule's shoulder. These are all the things you have to learn.

Hunting Horses

When we made camp, all the animals were turned loose at night and as a rule they don't go far away. If you know anything about stock, you don't want to camp next to a meadow that has been grazed off because the stock will roam until they find something to eat and if it is cold they might move on another four or five miles. We knew all of the little canyons where feed was plentiful and the stock could fill up and wouldn't want to leave.

On the pack trips, to help locate the horses and mules the next morning, you needed a bell mare, a mare that all the mules love and try to stay close to. You'd keep the mules with her all the time. I've had as many as three bells because there might be one little group of mules that wouldn't stay with the main bell mare and so another mare would be belled, and maybe there would be a loner that just wanted to go off somewhere and stand in the sun. But generally there were no more than two bells.

I'd get up before daylight, take a nosebag of oats, a bridle and flashlight, start looking down the trail and listening. I could track and tell where a horse went through and when. You listen for the bells, and keep tracking. The old timers used to caution us to beware of the "river bell" because if you're listening for bells and you're walking along a stream, you actually swear you hear a bell. It is your imagination taking tones out of the river noise, and because the bells will be a brief ding-a-ling, you stop and listen and think you've found them when they are actually five miles away. A steady bell sound means they are moving.

I've had a couple of real long hunts. One time we were camped at Cardinal Lake, which is the west side of Mather Pass (named for Stephen Mather). We camped at Cardinal Lake, the last pasture in Deer Cove and we turned the horses and mules loose up the canyon. Jim Kindred and I got up very early and figured that when the stock got cold they must have travelled, but they did not pass by our camp during the night, so that meant they probably headed up to a Pass above us. All of the tracks were going up; they'd fed around the meadows and when it got cold they went up the trail and over the Pass. We tracked them through Mather

Pass to the other side which is above timberline and drops down into the South Fork, a long ways. We couldn't see them. We started down and finally could see a bit of dust about four miles away and we really started hot-footing it. Old Jim could walk really fast, I don't think he ever weighed over 145 pounds, and man-for-man he was the toughest guy I ever knew. We finally caught them in the timber and headed back. I rode the bell mare and Old Jim rode one he could herd with, up and over the Pass, back down to Cardinal Lake. Then we had to pack up, so we didn't leave camp until about 1 o'clock. We wound up taking the string back over the same trail and through the same Pass because that was the direction the party had planned to go that day.

It was September, in Upper Basin the headwaters of the South Fork of the Kings River, high elevation and cold and it snowed during the night, cleared, then froze. It was a moving day so I had to get up at 4 a.m. to start hunting the horses, because on a cold night they will travel and if they get going the wrong way, I might have to walk half a day to find them. Our cook, Archie McDowall, knew I had to be up, so he was up earlier to make coffee and some breakfast. He was puttering around the kitchen, he made a little hotcake batter, and I heard the 'put-put-put-put' of the spoon hitting the bowl as he stirred the batter; then he got the coffee ready, but he was acting distant and wouldn't say anything to me while we were building up the fire, acting like he didn't want to talk or something. Finally, I said, "Archie, what the hell's the matter with you?" He turned around and muttered, "I put my teeth in my water cup last night and they froze solid!" The porcelain cup was on the stove and he was waiting for his dentures to thaw. He was terribly embarrassed without his teeth, being English and very proper.

Some of the high country had drift fences, like on Kern River where the drift fences were built across the canyon so the horses could only go so far when loose. It was fairly flat in the Kern River and a long way going down hill, so we relied a lot on the drift fences there. The same was true at Simpson Meadow in the Kings. In the chapter about pleasure pack trips is a story of hunting horses through the night.

Stock in the Sierra
In 1950 I was out in the backcountry for 62 days before I got to a road somewhere. (I always thought the guys at the pack station were trying to keep me away from this young lady I was going with, but I fooled

them–I married her the following December.) We left Cedar Grove with the Adams party and went to Blaney Meadows up beyond Florence Lake. We returned to Florence Lake to pick up the Crocker party and packed them to Yosemite, San Joaquin and up and over Lyell Pass, Lyell Glacier, Tuolomne and Glacier Point, where I went down and helped shove the fire off the bluff, an evening ritual for the tourists, because we were camped nearby. We were hooking up with the Fuller Party the next day. We packed those mules up with fresh loads and headed back with the Fullers over Isberg Pass, down to Rainbow Falls, hit the John Muir Trail and back-tracked clear to Jackass Meadow at Florence Lake. The Fullers departed for home. Then we picked up a hunting party and took them deer hunting in country we'd never been before. It was a successful hunt, up Singer Creek.

It was getting late, the first part of October, so Leroy Whitney, Jim Kindred and I brought all that stock, about 40 head, back to Giant Forest, a total of 75 miles in three days. We just kept going and whenever we could jog in those flats we did. But you didn't do too much jogging because the horses were saddled, of course, with whatever else could be tied on, and jogging a long time, the saddle blanket will work out and slip and then the saddle turns and all hell breaks loose. You had to watch all of them constantly. The first day we went to Evolution, the next day we rode to Muir Pass, down by Grouse Meadow, through Simpson Meadow to Granite Basin, that's a long ways. The next day we covered the 30 miles from Granite to Giant Forest.

My dad had Colonel White's permission to run horses on park lands in the winter; he needed range land, and the Park was trying to keep fire hazard down, so it was beneficial to both. The horses were pastured over on the west boundary of Sheep Creek and Cow Creek, and on South Fork and Bald Mountain. They'd stay away from the trailheads and just winter there. If there was a heavy snow, my dad would have to go up to get them, and one year in a severe snowstorm, he went in to dig out several head of horses. It was so cold he wrapped his boots in gunnysacks and still suffered near frost-bite. Cows come down in a storm, but horses go up, and those horses got up on the ridge and were standing in belly-deep snow when he dug them out.

DUDES AROUND THE CAMPFIRE

⟨∞⟩

My dad always told George Mauger that he provided the dudes with all the comforts of home—white tablecloths, meals served on china, privacy screens for sleeping, beds rolled out and pumped up—and hot and cold running water! Hot and cold running water—we run it to you, a bucket in each hand. We always laughed about his story around the campfire.

We called our elite customers "dudes" and they knew we called them dudes and they were dudes. But good folks. At night we all sat around the campfire and told stories. The Crockers always had a time to meet around the fire, right before supper or immediately after supper to relax and tell stories and talk about the day. There would be six or eight people in their party. The Crockers expected a little more attention than the Fullers because they were perhaps more accustomed to the deference accorded the very wealthy. William Crocker owned Crocker National Bank that was created and given to him by his father Charles Crocker who partnered with Leland Stanford to make immense fortunes building the railroads. Lots of people hated railroad people because they wrote their own deals with the government and the government gave them every other section (640 acres) of land plus $48,000 per mile as payment for building the railroads. It is history; there are many books about it.

On the 1945 Crocker trip, I was a big kid of 14. We were camped at Paradise on the South Fork of the Kings. In the party was Gertrude Perot (we pronounced it "parrot"), the future Mrs. Bill Crocker. We'd gone out to gather the horses early and were starting to saddle up, when my dad says, "You'd better come with me, we're going down to the river." Gertrude Perot's bed was set up right beside the river, and there beside her bed was an empty pint whiskey bottle, but no Gertrude. My dad said we'd better take a walk down the river because if she went in, we're going to find her down there somewhere. That part of the river is rough and goes down into Mist Falls, just boiling white water.

The Fuller party at Bubbs Creek, one of many Alpine meadows ideal for a layover for two or three days to enjoy fishing and day trips. Photo c. 1930.
AUTHOR'S COLLECTION.

Ellen (Helen) Russell, Bill Crocker's sister, was angry and everyone was upset because Gertrude did not come to breakfast.

So we hiked the river and down about a quarter of a mile we could hear someone singing. Pretty soon we found her; she was standing on a wet rock out in the river, singing, drunk as a hoot owl. All she had on was a slip that was wet from the frothing water and plastered to her body. I had to hang on to a tree to support my dad so he could climb on a rock where he could reach across and get her hand. The rock was slippery; if she fell it would be certain drowning. We got her off the rock and my dad took his Levi jumper to put around her. She kept singing and stumbling along barefoot; we had to carry her up some of the rough places to get to the big smooth rocks where she could walk. We got her back to camp, whereupon Mrs. Russell declared, "Well, we are not leaving today. We will leave tomorrow." Gertrude was in bad shape, hung over all day, and very lucky she had not drowned. We had to turn the horses loose again and re-do everything the next morning.

Paradise is famous for rattlesnakes. It is just snake heaven and I camped there with the Fullers and killed two or three rattlers in camp and around the camp. You never know when you are sleeping there if a snake will crawl up in your bed at night. They're not there to bother you, they smell you as they flick their tongue and crawl away.

So later that year (1945) on the Fuller trip at the same camp site at Paradise, I set up the throne–a little folding toilet—that Mr. Fuller used because of his leg brace. I put little ducks (a little pyramid of three small flat rocks for a trail marker) on the rock, made a barricade for privacy, and put a can of ashes beside it. I stomped the shovel into the ground to dig a small hole, turned it over, and I'd stomped it right into a yellow jacket nest. They swarmed out of there and hit me with their stingers. I took off running. Mr. Fuller got a kick out of that. I told Mr. Fuller that he would have to wait until dark before I set up his throne. After the yellow jackets calmed down, I retrieved the toilet and set it up in another location. That would have been something, poor Mr. Fuller would have sat on his throne, disturbed the yellow jackets and been stung all over his rear end. That would make for a painful day in the saddle.

The Fuller party was full of fun, especially in the evening when they'd have cocktail hour and of course we were too young to drink but they invited everyone to come around the campfire to talk about the day, sing, and perform skits they wrote. Mr. Fuller had a good voice, a sense of rhythm and he could sing songs that nobody knew, kind of novelty songs. His favorite song was called "Mike McCarty's Wake." He'd act it out and sing it with a brogue, it was very funny, and he invited everyone to join in. I'd get up and sing with Mr. Fuller once in a while or recite a poem. Mr. Fuller told me he was in San Francisco to attend the performance of Caruso at the opera house in 1906 when the earthquake struck and he said it threw him out of bed. He looked out his hotel window on Union Square and saw Caruso in the Square trying to help people in the midst of the mayhem.

A friend of the Fullers who later married into the family was Bruce Jessup, M.D., a graduate of Stanford Medical School. He was a diabetic all of his life, his insulin was always carefully protected in the packs. His specialty was Pediatrics.

At the end of each Fuller trip, everyone, no matter who, had to get up and perform something. It made for a memorable evening. We all knew the performance was coming and some of the guys would start brushing up on a poem. I remember a couple of newly hired cowboys were really worried about what they were going to sing on the last night.

Archie McDowall, our camp cook who Mr. Fuller always requested, liked to perform also; he'd sing with a funny vibrato, like this: huh, huh, huh; it was a diaphragm vibrato and it was comical to watch because Archie was English with an English accent and he was a showman. He performed at many functions around Three Rivers because he liked to be on stage. For the final "talent" night, Archie decided he would write a poem about everybody on the trip, some little thing they did. Mr. Fuller was always writing. He had reams of paper, just writing stuff constantly, you could see in his eyes that his mind was going full speed all the time. He was a very smart guy. He saw Archie writing, and asked, "What are you doing, Archie?" "Well, I just thought, you know, the last night out we all do something and I am writing a little poetry about each person." So pretty soon, Mr. Fuller comes back and says, "You know, Archie, I want to write mine." A few days later, getting toward the end of the trip, Mr. Fuller gave Archie a little poem to read as if he had written it. I don't remember the first part of it, "da da da, da da da. . .may his life be ever rich" and the rhyming line: "Here's to Old Man Fuller, the Dirty, Foul-mouthed Son of a Bitch." Archie looked at that and shook his head, 'Oh NO, I can't read that!" "Yes, you can and you will! Don't you worry about this, you don't say anything other than you wrote it!"

Of course at the performance, Mrs. Fuller almost fell out of her chair laughing, and everyone roared. It was maybe ten years later on another trip that Mr. Fuller told me that the poem Archie read was one of the funniest things, everybody always laughed about that, and Mr. Fuller said he never, ever told Li who really wrote it. "Li" was a nickname joke for his wife, Adaline—Ada-li-ne.

Not long ago I ran across the 1910 engagement announcement in a San Francisco newspaper for W. P. Fuller, Jr. and Adaline Wright. Their wedding took place February 21, 1911 in Pasadena, where Adaline's family resided. Both were graduates of Stanford University with the class of 1910, both had been very active in literary and performing arts, starring in the University productions–in onethey had the lead rolls–as well as society plays. This bit of information gave me a new appreciation for their laugh-filled skits and songs around the campfires. They loved to entertain and amuse their audiences.

Earl A. McKee, Sr. getting the gear together for a deer hunting pack trip with the Orval Overall party up the Kings River Canyon. Photo c. 1930.
AUTHOR'S COLLECTION.

Mr. and Mrs. Fuller started going on pack trips with my father in 1929, and their three sons, Parmer, George, and John kinda grew up every summer on those trips. All three sons were in the Service during WWII so could not go out for the full month during the war years. The Fuller sons loved to sing their favorite bawdy songs; one was a poem by Ogden Nash set to music, "Four Prominent Bastards," which they also sang at their parents' 50th Wedding Anniversary party. Look it up, it really suits the times.

It was about 1948 when I guided a small party over to Big Arroyo. I had Bert Nice as cook and Jim Kindred packing. The head dude was a professional photographer whose equipment was packed on the lunch mule. Jim went on ahead to prepare camp and I guided the party. It was the slowest ride I have ever been on because he wanted to shoot every picturesque panorama, which meant I packed, unpacked and packed that mule a hundred times to get his gear. He was old school, and at the camp he used flares to illuminate the night scenes. Our first night camp was set up at Bear Paw Meadow and we didn't get there until 9 p.m. Jim was so worried, he was coming back to look for us.

On the return ride, we were going slow so we decided to camp at Alta Meadows. Since we knew the deer would be ravenous for salt and apt to chew up our saddle rigging looking for salt, we stacked all the saddles together, put out some salt and I slept by the saddles. Jim had to sleep near the trail to keep the stock from going on home to Wolverton because we were so close. Bert slept some distance below the trail in his "kitchen" beside the kyacks stacked like shelves to hold the food.

All night I was up scaring deer away from the saddles. Every once in a while I'd hear Bert yell at something down there and I yelled occasionally. Along about two or three o'clock in the morning I heard someone yell and then the damnedest crash. Sounded like somebody had set off a charge down there, pots and pans crashing and banging. I yelled, "You all right, Bert?" and pretty soon he hollered back, "I just b-b-bit a bear!" Bert stuttered when he was excited.

Later Bert told us what happened. Apparently an old doe had been nosing around camp, looking for salt, lettuce, or anything Bert had inside the pack boxes stacked in his kitchen, and he had scared her off several times—the yelling I'd heard. Well this time, Bert heard a noise and when he reared up with his mouth open to yell at the doe, he got a mouthful of hair off a bear's ribs. It seems the old bear, being tourist-wise and not afraid to come in close to camp, was standing across Bert's bed with his nose in the kyacks when Bert raised up.

That old bear was scared a lot more than Bert. He laid a stream of bear scat across Bert's bed and left camp right through the wall of pack boxes and kitchen implements, creating the explosion I'd heard. Always after that we referred to the time "Bert Bit the Bear."

Bert Nice was two years ahead of me at Woodlake High School. His father, Hubert Nice, Sr. packed for my dad in the 1920s, and had come to Three Rivers in 1918 with his father who was a physician. They lived at the site of the Spotts Cider Mill. Bert Jr. died in 1969, Bert Sr. died in 1973.

My dad told about the time he was camped with his elite party at Bear Paw Meadow on the return from Tamarack Lake and a bear stole the meat out of the pack. So the second trip of the season when they camped there, my dad had a big side of bacon and swore that the bear wasn't going to get this bacon because he was going to put it under his pillow. When he woke up early the next morning, the bacon was gone and not far away was all the shredded bacon wrapping. I guess the bear wanted to make sure they would know who did it because he left his calling card beside my dad's bed.

Walt Pratt and Elmer McKee packed for my dad on one of the early Fuller trips when Mr. Fuller brought his own chef—a small Chinese fellow named Norman Ju. Little Norman Ju was unfamiliar with the mountains, so Walt Pratt took pleasure in tormenting him. On a travel day when Mr. Ju would be riding his horse along in an open area, Walt and Elmer would gallop wide open up behind him and swoop by on either side causing his horse to take off. Poor Mr. Ju couldn't ride that well.

They camped at Paradise, an area known for rattlesnakes. I know exactly the camp, my dad showed it to me one time. Elmer McKee was on this trip and was a prankster like Walt; there were two or three other packers with the Fuller party and his Chinese cook.

Crossing a snowfield over Mather Pass on an elite pack trip. Everyone dismounted and the horses and mules were sent across loose. Photo c. 1930.

That night they sat around the campfire and told rattlesnake stories. One of the culprits pretended to go off to relieve himself and put a hair rope under Norman Ju's blanket in his sleeping bag, hooked it on to a lash rope, and strung the lash rope clear across to where the packers were sleeping. After hearing all those snake stories, Norman Ju went to bed. Walt waited until everything was quiet, but not so long that Norman would be asleep, then pulled that rope out real slow like it was crawling under him. The little guy went crazy, screaming in Chinese. Of course the pranksters yanked that rope away and took it apart so there was no evidence of who might have done what. My dad demanded to know who scared the man. Oh, no. No one knew anything about it. My dad said whoever did this is fired. These things were unacceptable. Mr. Fuller and my dad worked out the problem. Mr. Fuller brought Norman Ju on one more pack trip the following year.

During the Korean War, Lee Maloy took the Crocker party into Granite Basin and had been out a few days when my sister, Blanche Maloy, got an emergency call at the Giant Forest pack station from the military; they needed to get word to a general who was traveling with the Crockers to return to Washington on the double. I was sent immediately to find the general. There was only one horse available at the corrals, named Van, and he was unshod, so to speed up my departure, Milton Savage helped me shoe him—we did two corners at once—I was on the right front while Milton was on the left rear, then we switched. We had him shod in thirty minutes as he stood on two feet. He was a fine horse.

I hauled Van and a mule to Cedar Grove and left out of Copper Creek on the Kings River Trail for the long ride trying to catch up to the Crocker party. I hoped they had laid over in Granite Basin. This area between the South and Middle Forks of the Kings River is a massive granite ridge with ribs that extend and surround many lake basins. Van was a good mountain horse, and we rode into the night, so black I couldn't see his ears, but he knew the trail and we just kept going. I could barely see the outline of rocks, but Van could see and that's what mattered. I arrived in the Basin and heard a bell off to the left which gave me hope that the Crockers were camped somewhere in the Basin. We were getting close to the lake when Van stopped and would not move. I kicked him and he didn't budge. Then I realized he was standing next to their mule line.

One of thousands of glacial lakes in the Sierra with talus-covered shoreline. Bunch grass was plentiful for the horses on the rocky slopes. Camps were always located near water–lake, stream, or river–to provide "hot and cold running water" to the guests: "We run it to them, a bucket in each hand," was my dad's favorite campfire joke. Photo c. 1935.

AUTHOR'S COLLECTION.

Jim Kindred was startled awake and sprang up with "Who's there! Who's there!" We decided not to disturb the dudes at that hour. After early breakfast, we took two horses for the general and his wife and I led them out to Cedar Grove so he could hurry back to the war.

One heavy snow year in the early 1960s, Lee Maloy was laid up with an ulcer, so I was the guide for Peter McBean, his very English wife, and their two children. Peter McBean was a cattleman whose range included the area around Magic Mountain in Southern California; McBean Parkway off I-5 is named for him. McBean's guests on the trip were Peter Folger, of Folger Coffee, and his two kids, Abigail and Jock-o.

The packers were Dickie Homer who is Forrest Homer's stepson, Leroy Maloy, another one or two young fellows, and Les Salmon was the cook.

Peter Folger always had a cup of our cowboy coffee with us because Mrs. McBean insisted the dude's coffee be expresso, a jolt of caffeine that you could stir like pudding. Peter Folger couldn't drink his own coffee! Mr. McBean just drank hot chocolate. Mrs. McBean was a lovely lady with a delightful British accent: "Plenty of grawss for the hawss."

The first thing the four kids did was to hide Mr. McBean's new battery-operated shaver, and Abigail Folger confided their prank to me and made me promise to keep the secret. It wasn't easy because Mr. McBean started to cast a suspicious eye on the packers. On the last day, the kids had their fun and returned the shaver to their bearded dad.

Abigail Folger was one of the victims in the Sharon Tate murders in August 1969.

We were in Marion Lake Basin and set to go over an old sheep trail Lee Maloy had used back in 1946, a short cut from Marion Lake, over the mountain to State Lakes and Horseshoe Lake. It was very rough and we had a couple of wrecks with mules there, none hurt, but one mule was upside down so we had to unpack it to get it on its feet. There was a pass—a chute—that makes about three switchbacks that wash out. It's a dirt trail so we spent two days shoveling and raking until we could get to the chute. The chute ends at the lake and it looks like there is no way out, but we made a trail through the willows along the lake edge. The next day we scouted a way to get to Whitter Pass (named for the Dean Whitter party when Lee took them through ten years before). We didn't tell anyone about the short cut, didn't put any ducks out, because Marion Lake had the best fishing anywhere. It was a snowfield up to the Pass so we dug stairs one day and rode over it the next and came out at Horseshoe Lake and on out.

In the 1940s, the W. P. Fuller, Jr. party was camped out near Bear Paw Meadow. Lee Maloy was the guide. Mrs. Fuller had as her guest Mrs. Herbert Hoover, former First Lady of the United States. Mr. Fuller had served as a legal secretary to Herbert Hoover when he was president (1929-1933) and continued to exchange personal notes and cards with Hoover the rest of his life. One evening in the high mountains, Mr. Fuller showed me a birthday card and note addressed to Adaline from President Hoover, signed simply "Herbert."

Mrs. Hoover and Mrs. Fuller shared a tent. During the night a bear came into camp and was tearing into the packs next to which Lee had positioned his bedroll to guard against such wild intruders. Lee grabbed a camp tool at hand and whacked the bear and yelled. The bear took off running straight at Mrs. Hoover's tent. Oh, my God! Lee was wide-eyed, expecting disaster. At the last minute the bear veered away into the forest.

Jim O'Brien, an attorney and later partner of W. P. Fuller, Jr., went on all the Fuller pack trips after he completed his service in WWII. Jim had traveled with General Eisenhower, knew him really well, told us a lot of stories, not being boastful, just very interesting. Jim was also an attorney for Standard Oil and had an oil tanker named for him. He flew all over the U.S. when it was really something to have lunch in New York City and dinner at his home in San Francisco. Fuller paint brand was later changed to Fuller-O'Brien Paints.

We were camped at Thunder Lake, 12,000 feet elevation. Jim loved to sing around the campfire, he and Archie would sing old songs, a favorite was "The Rose of Tralee," an Irish ditty. Sometimes I'd be part of a quartet of close harmony and we'd sing a little tag ending, "Star of the East, Shining on the Cookhouse Door," but change a word (cookhouse to s—house) to surprise our listeners for a laugh. That evening everyone had a nightcap or two and went to bed except Jim and me. I was standing by the table eating some peaches when Jim walked by, tripped, and grabbed at me as he fell. I landed on top of him, knocked the air out of him; he scared me to death–he wasn't breathing, his mouth open like a silent gasp. I ran for Parmer to help me; about then Jim raised up and asked what are you doing, Earl? When Parmer saw that everyone was okay, he growled why don't you two drunks go to bed.

Two weeks prior to the Fuller 50th wedding anniversary party, Jim O'Brien invited Gaynor, my mother, and me to a pack trip reunion party at his home in the Bay Area. We enjoyed the party at the O'Brien home where I sang lots of songs. I realized later that the Fuller sons and O'Brien had used the reunion to work out a program for the big 50th event, including my guitar numbers.

Camp Cooks in the Back Country

The cook was paid more than any other crew member because he worked harder than anyone else. It was a tough job to keep the stove going, water heating, prep and cook for a half dozen or more hungry dudes plus crew. The cook usually started work before daylight. My dad had several cooks: Kenneth 'Skinny' Savage who was Milton Savage's dad; Alan Savage, Sr. was a good cook; a guy named Scotty was a good cook. Archie McDowall cooked all the later years.

Archie McDowall was a favorite of Mr. Fuller. My dad carefully planned the itineraries and menus to pamper the dudes. My dad provided a special touch to his high country dining room–the main course was served on hot dinner plates, really nice for supper at 11,000 feet. My dad and Archie came up with the idea to heat the china in water in the big pressure cooker. Notice I said china–the dudes' dishes were china, not pottery or tin. I remember that pressure cooker. It was still around when Lee sold the outfit to DeCarteret, and I'll bet Lee retained it. No one uses them anymore. It was tall, had a lid with handles that screwed down

and pressure release ball that would blow off if it got too high. You'd watch the ball and if started bouncing, you needed to set it off the heat. It was used every day, set next to the stove, to heat the plates for dinner.

On a pleasure trip with the guys, I'm cooking bacon for breakfast. Note the sheepherder stove and the tall square cans of water heating behind it. Photo c. 1990.

AUTHOR'S COLLECTION.

The backcountry kitchen appliances, utensils and ingredients of course were transported on mules, and each mule had a specialty. The egg and whiskey mule was a very important mule; you wanted the gentlest mule, easy to catch anywhere if he got in a wreck, no bucking even if he got in the yellow jackets. The eggs were packed in a honeycomb-like cardboard divider inside a 5-gallon bucket, one layer of eggs alternated with a layer of barley poured over it, continuing to the top.

The grain, potato and horseshoes mule was generally a young beginner mule; if he was ornery or ran into something, he couldn't do much damage to his load. We packed mule shoes #2s and #3s so on lay-over days, mules needing it could be re-shod. The china plates were packed in the big round pressure cooker with cardboard separators. The help used different plates. Mr. and Mrs. Fuller brought their own favorite camp plates, "Geraldine," a divided aluminum plate, the bottom half had a 1-1/2 inch space with a cap to be filled with hot water. The flatware–knives, forks, spoons–was rolled up in a utensil bag with sewn pockets and a flap. All the flatware and dishes stayed clean and dust-free. The kitchen utensil bag was canvas with sewn pockets; there might be a second one just for butcher knives. These were rolled up and tied for transport. At camp, the utensil bag was wrapped around a tree and tied, real handy for the cook. We always had folding tables, or roll up tables that you can't find anymore. I still have a roll-up table in the barn.

It took one mule to pack the stove and the "black" utensils–pots, tongs, etc. that are blackened in the cooking fire. The stove was what people called a sheepherder stove; it is built in two halves that can be packed, half on one side, half on the other. This kind of stove generally weighed about 80 pounds. When the two parts were fit together it made a cooking surface about 24" x 30." I have an old one that my dad had, and I wish that thing could talk because it has been all over the mountains. Inside a stove half, the dutch oven, pliers in a bag, tongs, the 45-degree angle stovepipe connector, were packed. The stovepipe was packed on top, a rake and shovel on one side, and an ax on the other. The load would hang close to the mule, not too tall, and about eighty pounds on each side.

Old Gus, a buckskin mule, was the most exceptional mule. My dad bought Gus from Gus Harwood who used to play harmonica in Print Stokes band once in a while. Old Gus packed Archie's kitchen boxes. Archie McDowall, the cook, always had to throw in something else at the last minute until sometimes the boxes would weigh 100 pounds, 100 pounds a side. You needed the swamper to help pick them up. Gus was 16 hands high, big, powerful and a master at judging his clearance between trees. Those kitchen boxes extended way out like a "wide load" but Gus never scraped them. He'd go down the trail, loose, and if two pine trees looked too close together, he would stop, look and then go around.

On one of the Crocker trips we were packing down in French Canyon that is on the San Joaquin River in north Kings Canyon. We had come over Muir Pass, through Evolution Lake and San Joaquin to Blaney Meadows and up Piute Creek. We hadn't gone very far up Piute when we encountered a boulder field where the trail went through a tunnel-like opening between two huge boulders leaning across; the opening was large enough for the average-sized mules to get through, but not tall Gus with the wide kitchen boxes. He looked at that overhang above the trail, he looked to the right and to the left and there was nothing but boulders. So Gus went up and looked at it again, then he got down on his knees and squatted and slid through there and never scraped a box. He knew if he got down low enough his load would clear. I was riding about two mules behind Gus. I saw it. I'd give anything for a movie of that.

Just ahead of this was a swinging bridge, very primitive construction of cables and timbers. We were traveling with a big party, broken up in little groups so each packer had several mules in front of him so he could keep an eye on the packs. We sent the mules across, one at a time, because if that bridge started swinging, you'd have a serious wreck. It took a couple of hours to get everybody across.

The Grub List was usually filled by G&I Market (Goldstein & Iseman) in Visalia. My dad really liked the way Jack Iseman put up the pack order. Jack even supplied paraffin-dipped flour sacks to keep moisture out of anything water could damage. Other cotton sacks were reused as kitchen towels when they became empty. Jack understood how to supply the packer's pantry. G&I even baked a special order 25th anniversary cake to fit in a kyack for a party of fourteen going out from another pack station.

My dad always raised a few sheep at the home place because he liked lamb. The day before a pack trip going out of Cedar Grove, he'd butcher a lamb to take along. The dudes liked lamb chops; the best way to cook all the cuts of lamb was to fry over a hot fire. The fresh-butchered sheep was wrapped in a cotton sack to hang out in the cold night just like they did deer meat. On a rare occasion when opportunity presented itself in the backcountry, the cook might find venison in the sheep bag. Deer ribs resembled sheep ribs if anyone asked.

Early in the trip we served steaks; the meat was packed in dry ice. Ham was on the menu, and one of my favorites was corned beef and cabbage. It is especially delicious in the cold crisp air of the backcountry. Archie made lots of salads. He started out with two gunnysacks full of head lettuce; the rule for lettuce was, never let it get wet and never let it be in the sun. To serve, the outer leaves were peeled off and the lettuce was put in the cold stream to chill, then torn and tossed in salad. Tomatoes were wrapped individually in newspaper and packed in a kyack box. Canned provisions such as beans, corn, peas, peaches were mainstays.

The lunch mule was packed with a little coffee pot for heating water for coffee or tea, all kinds of goodies for lunch, loaves of bread, crackers, melba toast maybe, jams, jelly, peanut butter, fruit, and tasty trail hors devourers. The dudes and the lunch mule left camp first ahead of the packers who had to break down camp and pack the mules. We kept a distance of an hour or so between the dudes and the pack string so the mules couldn't crowd the riders trying to get close to one of the bell mares.

Dinner service at 10,000 feet on a Fuller party trip. In the kitchen is Mr. Fuller's personal chef, Norman Ju, (l) and my dad. Photo c. 1935.

AUTHOR'S COLLECTION.

Setting Camp

My dad knew the mountains and the best campsites. He had permission from Colonel White to camp in little out-of-the-way canyons, picturesque for the dudes with lush feed for the stock. We avoided any area that was over-camped where horses had trampled the grass, or pawed holes indicating that somebody did not know what they were doing. We had camps that only we knew about and would not tell anybody where we were going. When the party moved on, all trace of the trail and camp was erased. Once in a while a ranger would happen upon our camp and exclaim that he didn't know this camp was there and we would say, well please forget it, would you?

My dad and his horse on a backcountry pack trip. Photo c. 1920.
AUTHOR'S COLLECTION.

Month-long trips, like the Fullers, we would re-supply in the middle of the trip–for example, at Middle Fork over Bishop to South Lake, we'd send a string of mules over for another half-ton of food resupplied from Bishop.

An itinerary through Florence Lake, the resupply would come from the end of the road at Florence Lake. This was more economical for the dudes because of the per diem fee for each animal; 12 mules resupplied halfway was less than 24 mules packing all the groceries for the whole month.

We chopped wood for the stove every day. We packed an ax, a small drag saw with a handle on each end that was small and flexible and easy to tie over a pack. Most of our trips were up around 10,000 feet, between 9,500 and 11,000 and that is the best source for good wood. It was always the cleanest high in the granite where there is less dust. Foxtail pines that were dead or with dead branches were the best for the fire because the wood has cured standing up and is full of pitch. It looks kind of yellow. We would use a lash rope—the rope that the packs are tied on with which is about forty feet in length fastened to a 30-inch cinch with a knob on one end—to break dead limbs from the tree. I would bundle several branches 4 to 5 feet long with a lash rope and carry it to camp on my back, then saw it—or more often than not just hit the dry limb on a rock to break into stove lengths. Some limbs were left long to make the big evening campfire.

When we made camp the crew really hustled, quickly unloading the mules, unsaddling the horses, getting wood. The mules were washed down every day. The kyacks were lined up so they could be covered with the manties, with our beds right next to the kyacks in case there was a bear around or the deer came in to lick the latigos looking for salt. The camp cook tied up his horse and started grabbing the kitchen mules to unpack and get the stove going, water on to heat, and retrieve the groceries for dinner. It was quite a procedure. Of course we set up the camp tables with white tablecloths, chairs, and the dudes' sleeping areas with windbreaks. We waited on the dudes hand and foot, that was our job.

Tearing down camp meant leaving the area so no one would ever find the campsite, could not see you had ever been there—leave no trace. The stove was disassembled, soot knocked off and burned with anything else burnable, then we made sure everything was out by spreading the fire real thin and pouring buckets of water over the ground where the stove was. It would bubble under the ground, it was so hot, maybe bubble 20 minutes. You wanted to make sure there wasn't old buried wood underneath the soil that might ignite. In those days most everyone smoked, so all the cigarette butts were collected and burned. Even the divots made by the horses were covered and smoothed. We didn't leave a trace.

Camp Clinic

We always packed first-aid kits. I remember W. P. Fuller, Jr. brought along his personal physician, Doc Johnson, of Stanford on several trips.

I was working on the Fuller trip one summer, about 1952, when we crossed trails with old Ben Loverin and George Whitfield working on trail crew. George was really sick with chills and chest congestion and asked me if Doc Johnson might have a shot of penicillin he could give him and sure enough Doc made a trail call and fixed up old George. George was a man's man, a good packer and good hand. He used to shoe horses at the racetracks.

Lee Maloy was guiding the Crocker party on their annual pack trip, this time out of Cedar Grove leading over to Roaring River. Lee hadn't been feeling well and on the first day out he was in pain and at camp he had to lie down, unable to help with anything. His son, Leroy, was working that trip and was really worried, told his dad to go back out and see a doctor. Lee refused, insisted he would be fine in the morning. After everyone was asleep that night, Leroy took a flashlight, rope, and his saddle down the trail, caught his horse and rode to Cedar Grove, several hours ride downhill from their camp. He phoned Doc Jakes–Harry Jakes, M.D.–in Exeter.

Doc Jakes was our doctor, too. He made house calls in his classic two-door green MG convertible; once at a call to our home, he decided an ambulance was too slow so he carried Gaynor to his MG and sped off to the hospital, 25 miles away. No house call was too far for Doc Jakes; he loved the mountains and had spent time in the high country on call.

Doc immediately got his boots and bag and drove to Cedar Grove, about 100 miles and 2-1/2 hours distant, over the Grant Grove Crest (6500 feet elevation) and down 2000 feet into the Kings River gorge. Leroy borrowed a horse from the Cedar Grove pack station for the Doc and they rode back to camp, arriving in early morning when folks were just starting to get up.

Lee argued with the Doc when he was told that it was imperative for him to get to a hospital because he had a serious abdominal condition. Finally Doc threatened a citizen arrest to force Lee to go. It turned out that Lee had suffered a perforated ulcer that required surgery and a long convalescence. He couldn't go anywhere for the rest of the summer. Leroy and Archie and the other packers continued on with the dudes.

I know Doc Jakes was called to the mountains several times, once to treat a young boy who had been playing in the rocks at Hamilton Lake where a boulder tipped and rolled onto him. There were enough adults to extricate him, and one hiked out to Bear Paw to phone for a doctor. It was nightfall when Doc Jakes and his escorts made their way on the High Sierra Trail along the bluffs toward Hamilton, a distance of about sixteen miles from Giant Forest. Doc was wearing a fancy wristwatch with an alarm that went off unexpectedly. The alarm made a high buzz which to the horses sounded like a little rattlesnake. His horse jumped and shied all over the trail, didn't buck though, and Doc stayed on.

The story had a good ending. A helicopter was called to pick up the injured boy. Doc demanded to go with his patient even though the pilot insisted the chopper couldn't make it with that much weight in the thin air. The doc prevailed and it landed safely at a hospital in the Valley.

In the daylight, Doc Jakes saw the trail where his horse acted up–it was along the bluffs where you look straight down hundreds of feet to the tops of towering pines. He could only exclaim, "God Almighty!"

On the first day of the Fuller trip, I was the guide in place of Lee Maloy, who was in the hospital at the time, so I was nursemaid to the dudes. Jim Kindred took my place as packer. I put the dudes on their horses every morning and took them and the lunch mule out ahead of the packers who had to break down the camp. We stopped in Tent Meadow beside a beautiful little stream to enjoy a light lunch and watch the pack train go by on their way to set up at the next campsite. My horse was tied to a tree and when I walked by he kicked me full length, that steel shoe hit just off center of my shin bone; if it had hit square the bone would have broken in two. I was even wearing chaps. Doc Johnson administered first aid and gave me a shot. My leg turned black and left me hobbling around the rest of the trip.

This trip had a series of small emergencies. After many trips with us, Mr. Fuller was acquainted with Jim Kindred and insisted that Jim's wife, Lucille, join them on this one. The Fullers were seasoned backcountry riders, but poor Lucille was not. High country trails are cut into steep granite cliffs, they skirt precipices, wind through giant boulder fields, go over 13,000 foot mountain passes that seem to drop off into thin air, and Lucille was scared the whole time, crying and scared. Doc Johnson gave her sleeping pills at night. I was hobbling around trying to ease Lucille's terror, and finally told Jim that we really needed to trade places so he could be nursemaid and stay close to his wife because the first day she cried all the way and we hadn't got to the rough stuff yet. In exchange I would pack his string of mean mules.

Jim was packing bronc mules. He had a way with bronc mules and didn't want anyone else messing with them. Lee bought those mules from Ray Buckman. I remember them. There was Chili, Dynamite, Soup Bone, Nanny, and Old Rube. They were all 9-iron mules from Jim Pogue's ranch, branded with his 9 on the hip, never been handled much and were pretty rough to handle.

Dynamite was dynamite; Nanny was a kicker, Jim didn't shoe her because she'd break a new lash rope trying to kick at him. The first time I started to put a saddle on Old Rube, he tried to jump over the mule line. Chili was really head shy and you never looked her in the eye or got near her head. Jim said, ah, here's how it's done: when brushing or saddling, you can't be forward of her shoulder. It was tricky to reach over with the breast collar and flip it around so you could catch it without reaching under her neck. But I did it. Once Chili was saddled, she would stand with the rope down like she was tied while you packed her. Lydabelle Wylie, Bill Wylie's wife, was a talented Western artist and sculptor who used Chili as a model for her bronze mule sculptures, which she titled "Chili."

After a couple of days, Jim's mules and I got along fine. We went over Forester Pass, 13,000 feet, and when you come over the top, your horse looks straight down about 1000 feet into a lake. Lucille survived it with Jim close by for her.

One move was down South Fork of the Kings and no one had been down the South Fork for about 25 or 30 years. Leroy Maloy and Dickie Homer were packers and the four of us worked on that trail. It was early on a moving day and I was hunting horses with Leroy and Dickie. They were just young fellows off looking around and I kept yelling at them to hurry up because we had to catch the horses. They started hollering to come back. They had found two square cans, 12" x 18" or so, that turned out to be survival cans, probably parachuted before the pilots bailed out of a WWII P40 that was running out of fuel. (The pilots were rescued.) The plane crashed in the next drainage over. Inside each can was a fold-up rifle and 200 or so rounds of ammunition along with a machete with a big heavy blade. We used the machetes to cut willows out of the old trail down to Muro Blanco that goes into Paradise Canyon.

We worked on the trail for several days and then took the dudes down. Jim asked me to come ahead with him to help him get the ladies and Mr. Fuller through the talus (fields of rocks). Rock with a shiny surface meant it was slick and will tumble a horse. Lucille was riding the gentlest horse, Dixie mare, and before I could warn her not to let her horse step on that shiny rock, she did and–shew-bang–the horse fell out from under her and Lucille hit the rock on her rear end and bounced. I bailed off to help but she cussed and cried that she was just scared. We didn't go a quarter of a mile further when I could see Jim in the lead yelling and waving his hat. I galloped up to him and I don't know what had happened, but one of the horses, Sandy, a good mountain horse, was on her side on the willows half under a boulder overhang. Her rider, Mae Goodin, was further under the rock. The horse was thrashing trying to get up, but luckily the boulder protected Mae from flying hooves. I held the horse's head while Jim unbuckled the saddle and we just pulled the horse off of the gal. Mae was just sitting in the saddle tucked up underneath that boulder. Mr. Fuller rode over and handed Mae a flask of whiskey and said, "How about a little courage!" There was one more really bad place where we made everyone get off and walk, then we sent the horses through one at a time. After that it was a nice ride into Paradise.

A PACK TRIP CUT SHORT

⟨〰〰〰⟩

In 1946, I packed several trips with my dad and the last one of the season in September, was the trip my world changed.

This 18-day trip out of Florence Lake to Cedar Grove was with the W. P. Fuller, Jr. party, with guests Dr. and Mrs. Bruce Jessup, the John Fullers, the Don Tressiders and James Brady. We met Lee Maloy and the Dean Whitter party when they came over the shortcut to Marion Lake. Lee had a layover day so both parties camped apart in the beautiful little meadows. Across the lake, a white granite wall rises out of the deep clear water. The fishing was good. From there the Fuller party continued over Cartridge pass, over Pinchot and down to Woods Creek Junction where my sister Blanche McKee and Jim Kindred met us with a resupply string from Giant Forest. I said goodbye to my dad there on the 9th of September and rode out with Blanche and Jim and the empty mules in order to get home in time to start high school. It was my sophomore year; I was 15 years old.

Four days later, on the 13th of September, my dad died. They called it a heart attack, but I think it was a massive stroke. He died in Sixty Lake Basin up over the hill from Rae Lakes, which goes into the South Fork of the Kings.

Before we went out on that pack trip, we had hauled some cattle over to Ward Ranch and my dad, Joe Chinowth, and I drove the cows up from there to Greasy Cove. Joe and my dad were close friends, grew up together and traded help on the ranch for years. My dad was riding a tough horse; he liked to ride thoroughbred type horses. We were half way up into Greasy when his horse started bucking, bucked off the road and down the bank. My dad rode him all the way to the bottom, but the horse planted his feet and my dad was thrown head first into the hillside. He was knocked out a bit and it took a long time for him to get his bearings. Afterwards he had a pain in his back. We all thought later that something must have happened right there. About ten days later, just before we left Marion Lake Basin, we were pulling a mule line and my dad was pulling on it and the rope broke, he fell over backwards, hit a rock, chuckled a bit, and said, "You know, I wish I'd a fell down and hit that rock sooner, because that thing in my back quit hurting."

The day before he died, he was hiking around camp at 11,000 feet elevation. The night before he died he had a pain up the back of his head, and he told the guys he had a terrible headache that night and did not sleep well. The next morning he was joking around the campfire before the dudes got up, it was just the packers there making fun of each other the way they always do, and my dad was just walking over to the packs, and Loren Finch was there and so were Walt Pratt, Harry Hughes, and Archie McDowall. They said it looked to them like he sort of stubbed his toe. He fell over, didn't put his hands out to break his fall. He was gone before he hit the ground. They were right there and rolled him over immediately and said he fell on one side and never knew what hit him. Never breathed anymore, everything was instant, whatever it was. . . .

They had two more days to go on the trip, and of course didn't want to ride with a body, so Walt Pratt rode to Cedar Grove where he called home, and then called for permission from the Park Service to pack my dad out without a coroner examination first. Now days they'd fly a coroner in there. But they used common sense and granted permission. They just put him in a sleeping bag and put it over a mule, it was Old Gus that packed him out. Mr. and Mrs. W. P. Fuller, Jr. and the Tressiders came off the pack trip in time to attend my dad's funeral at the Hadley Chapel in Visalia. The Honor Guard was the Tulare County Sheriff's Posse, of which my dad was a member.

My mother called some people to help at the pack station. She formed a partnership with her son-in-law, Lee Maloy, who was married to my sister, Blanche. Lee Maloy and my mother ran the pack station as a partnership while I was in high school and through the one year I attended Fresno State. My mother booked the trips with my dad's clients. The McKee-Maloy Company continued to reach all the famous spots in the high country—the Kings River canyon, the Kern, the San Joaquin, Muir Pass, and Mount Whitney.

I packed during the next five summers when I could, still had to work the cattle ranch, worked every minute, took over the ranch and everything my dad had done.

I remember after my dad died Johnny Britten came down to see Mother and he said to me, "Well, Earl, looks like you're going to have a big job here and I'll help you whenever you need help."

RUNNING THE RANCH

ᏬᎳᎵᎵᎧ

My dad was a very honest, down-to-earth, outgoing guy who was comfortable talking to anyone. He was never boastful, never drank much, but he enjoyed smoking Bull Durham, and a cigar once in a while. He was never ashamed to be a cowboy or a hillbilly—he was Earl McKee. He was the guy I always wanted to be like.

My dad bought his first herd of cows with $1,000 borrowed from Duncan McDuffie. His first deeded cattle ranch was their 1913 homestead of 320 acres on the northeast side of the hill just east of Slick Rock on the Kaweah River which he improved with a cabin, fencing, and some dry grain farming. Eight years later, he bought the South Fork Ranch in three parcels from ranchers Bill Canfield, Roy Stevenson, and Billy Lewis of Woodlake. My dad was one of those guys who could put things together. The ranch joined Britten Cove at the head of the canyon and it went south to the Loverings and all across the mountains. It joined the BLM (Bureau of Land Management) holdings which we leased going up on Horn Mountain, so it covered 3000 acres or so. A lot of it was very rough at the upper end, the cattle couldn't cross the mountain top because of dense Chamese and Blue brush.

The packing business was good, even in the depression, and right afterward in about 1937, my dad bought Greasy Cove in a foreclosure from a bank. The bank encouraged him also to buy another bigger, very fine ranch nearby, but he had already borrowed more money than he'd ever borrowed in his life. The entrance to the Greasy Cove ranch was across Dry Creek (called Lime Kiln Creek in 1892) in the vicinity of where my dad was born and where his mother, Mary Jane McKee owned a parcel and not far from his uncle S. A. McKee's acreage. Surrounding his mother's place was a checkerboard of large holdings owned by Thomas Davis I, S. G. Nye, J. W. C. Pogue, the Ragles, and the Bequettes.

My dad, Earl McKee, Sr. with his white-faced cattle at Greasy Cove Ranch. Photo 1940s.

AUTHOR'S COLLECTION.

The cattle business improved and he was able to pay off the loan on Greasy in just a few years. He grew winter grain on 160 acres below Lemon Cove to supply feed for his packing stock and cattle. My dad had good cattle, a herd of about 250 cows that the two ranches of 5000 acres could support. He sold cattle to the William McDuffie ranch in Mendocino County, and Jesse Finch hauled his cattle to buyers in Los Angeles County.

True Friends and Mentors

My dad died in 1946. Lee Maloy helped my mother and me on the ranch while I finished high school and one year at Fresno State. I was 19 years old when I took over the cattle ranch full-time.

Several cowmen, who I count as my heroes, gave of their time and wisdom as I strove to follow the example of my father's success as a cattleman and a human being. It was a good time to be in the cattle business and to know all those fine cattlemen here and in the Valley–Johnny Britten, Bill Wylie, Forrest Homer, Thomas H. Davis II, Adolph Gill, Herman Colpien, and Axel Anderson.

A year after my dad died, I went to see Axel Anderson to buy two steers for my high school FFA project. Axel drove me out in his field and I looked over the stock and made my selections. He concurred that those were good choices. I had to break the steers to lead and gentle them–they had been raised wild and free–to prepare them for the FFA stock show at the Cow Palace in San Francisco.

Axel Anderson was a turkey farmer before he was a cattleman. He also raised grain. The mural covering one side of the building next to Bank of America in Exeter, California, is rendered from a photograph of Axel's 14-horse harvesting team; Axel is driving the team. Axel owned 5000 acres in Grouse Valley off of upper South Fork, Three Rivers, where he took his turkeys in the summer. The turkeys were raised in Yokohl. Before a road was built from South Fork into Grouse, the turkeys were herded up over the head of Yokohl Valley into Grouse, but sometimes the turkeys were herded home by way of South Fork. My mother remembered big flocks of noisy turkeys ambling down the road past our house. Turkey dogs were used to keep the herd together. The gathering pens and later turkey loading chutes were built right next to Ace Peck's place in Grouse.

My uncle Jesse Finch hauled about twenty-five head of our high school FFA stock entries to the big show at the Cow Palace. I remember my classmates Dave Wilson, Alan Savage, Bob Curtis, and Hap Baker had show animals. Bob Curtis had a Vanderhoof Hereford Ranch polled steer that graded higher than any of ours. Hap Baker showed a black steer that he hadn't worked with near enough to get him gentle. Inside the Cow Palace pens, Hap was trying to put the halter on when his steer took off through an open door to the top of the stairs inside the big arena. The wall around the upper level was opaque glass. That steer was running around the top of the stadium and we were all afraid it would try to bust through the glass and fall several stories to his death outside. It was a heck of a time trying to calm that steer. A bunch of guys eased him real quietly down the stairs–a steer doesn't like to go downstairs but we got him down–then had to run him through the food court over to the pens where we roped him and put his halter on. I knew how to braid rope and had made an extra long show rope for one of my steers that was a bit jumpy. Hap borrowed my long rope to show his steer but even with two other guys on the rope it tried to wipe out the ring.

Johnny Britten

My closest neighbor was Johnny Britten who I knew all my life and was a dear friend of mine. Johnny helped me a bunch. He took the best care of his cows, fed them more hay than any of us did ours, he spent a lot of money to keep them in winter feed so they'd have healthy calves. At one point he rigged a cable and basket from Cobble Lodge across the Kaweah River to deliver cottonseed cake to his steers so they could stay on pasture to get ready for market. He was a fine cowman and rode great horses; he was an excellent roper, but usually had someone else work the gate. We enjoyed each other's company.

Johnny Britten's father was Ernest John Britten (1862-1943), one of the first two rangers in Sequoia National Park. Johnny was almost related to Ord Loverin–Ord married Johnny's half-sister, Maud Britten. Maud was a cousin to my uncle Harry Britten, my dad's brother-in-law. In 1939, Johnny bought the triangular property between the old road and new state highway (where Three Rivers Mercantile is today) with an orange grove, barns and home for his family. He could tell some great stories. Johnny spent a lot of time in the Park with his dad and used to run cattle over in Cahoon and Hockett Meadows before Forrest Homer did. If I lost any cattle in those mountains, Johnny could tell me where they'd likely be in all that country.

We'd help each other over on South Fork–our ranches shared a 2-1/2 mile fence–and talked about everything and faced some problems together. When he was a kid, Johnny worked for Byron Allen, driving about 200 head of cattle up the North Fork road into the mountains. He said it was quite a chore getting the cattle through the traffic control gate at Colony Mill Road when the Park limited traffic to one-way–going up hill toward Giant Forest, they could only use the road from 4 a.m. to 1 p.m. You can imagine trying to hold cattle at the gate for hours in line. The road was narrow and rough and in summer the cattle would get hot and tired.

Johnny died December 22, 1995, and I sang at his funeral. I really missed seeing and talking to him.

Johnny Britten roping off of Old Doc. Photo c.1990.

Bill Wylie

I could call on my neighbor Bill Wylie any time of the day or night. Bill and his family moved to Three Rivers in 1946 from Cuyama, California where he was raised. His family had oil property near Taft that made it possible for Bill to buy out Byron Allen's ranch and become a cattleman. I remember the first time I saw Bill Wylie, he was looking for some of his horses that got out–he soon learned that Byron didn't fix fences. He was a faithful friend, the most faithful cowboy to me. We did a lot of things together, he helped at all the brandings, helped on the cattle drives, and came along on pack trips to the back country. He had a great sense of humor. I'd call him at three o'clock in the morning for help gathering cattle at daybreak, and ask, "What're you doing awake?" and he'd growl, "Well, if it wasn't for some s.o.b. calling me up, I'd be asleep."

We served together on the cemetery board, went deer hunting in Colorado, he helped me build fences. He wasn't a flashy cowboy, he became a good roper and took care of his cattle. He ran Black Angus for several years until he decided there wasn't enough money in it, so he leased the ranch to Carter Arnett, Lee Maloy and Ray Pinnell who ran feeder cattle purchased from Gill Cattle Co. Wylie sold the Cherokee ranch to Cy Vaughn's dad. Cy was just a young guy and didn't know sic 'em about cattle, but he learned fast. We all traded help and had a lot of fun working together. Wylie eventually sold the rest of his rangeland to Walter Wells and it became part of the Wells Ranch.

I remember paying a visit to Bill just after his son, James, died of an abdominal aneurysm when visiting in Three Rivers one Christmas. I met Bill in his yard and pulled him into an embrace and he cried. Even though his little dog knew me so well, it bared its teeth and bit my leg. I told Bill to please call off your dog, the little s.o.b. is chewing off my leg. We laughed through tears.

My good friend Bill Wylie at the Tom Davis branding at Antelope Valley, always the best event at the beautiful Davis ranch. Photo 1975.

AUTHOR'S COLLECTION.

Bill was in his 90s when he died, almost blind from glaucoma. He'd tell me, "Earl, I can only see a hazy shadow, but I know you by your voice." His wife, Lydabelle, had stage IV cancer, Bill couldn't drive and the pain of shingles was unrelenting, so Bill made a decision to check out early, a shock but not a surprise to me. His ashes are scattered on Blossom Peak. Wherever Bill is now, he knows that I love him.

Forrest Homer

Forrest Homer was our neighbor on Greasy Cove ranch–our property shared a two-mile fence–his ranch stretched on both sides of the Middle Fork of the Kaweah River and his ranch house sat back from the highway. Forrest knew my dad, and watched me grow up. After my dad was gone, Forrest came by to see me a lot and we'd talk horses or cattle. Forrest won many first-place cash prizes and trophies at annual livestock shows all over the state in stock horse class, parade show outfit, and team roping. He traveled out of state to purchase horses from breeders in the Midwest and Arizona.

Forrest Homer was related to the first cattleman in this area–his great-grandfather was Hale Tharp. Hale and Chloe Tharp had two children, Norton and Fannie, both of whom were born before the Tharps arrived in Horse Creek flats above Lemon Cove in 1856. Fannie Tharp married Bernard Mehrten in 1885 and they had three children: Dave, and twins Jimmy and Tillie. Tillie (Mehrten) and Thomas Homer were Forrest Homer's parents. Thomas Homer's brother was Truman Homer, father of Caryl Homer. The Truman Homer ranch on Dry Creek was handed down to Caryl, and his cousins Forrest and Ed. Caryl Homer was a good man, slow and deliberate and unlike his cousin, Forrest, had a quiet mouth. Getting a little off-track here but Truman Homer married Alice Rice, a distant cousin to the Rice clan and therefore one several times removed from me.

Everyone knew when Forrest was on his way over to visit because he was one of the worst drivers, he would drag the clutch, especially on his old International truck, when he'd shift and the pitch would scream higher and higher. He wore out a lot of clutches. We'd talk about horses and I respected him for his knowledge and he, in turn, liked the way I broke horses. We helped each other gathering and moving cattle from the time I was a youngster riding with my dad.

Forrest was one of the most outspoken men I've ever heard; I probably was Forrest's closest friend, got along better with him than anyone because I'd cuss him sometimes about the way he insulted people. Odd, but many times he was right, he was just out of line to say it the way he did. He had no couth - he was often loud and impolite, but he held the attention of his audience. We testified at one of the county supervisor meetings about the county trapper. A paper shuffler down at the courthouse decided to save money and eliminate the services of the county trapper. Cattlemen needed the trapper because the area was overrun with coyotes that kill baby calves. Forrest got up and told them how the hog ate the cabbage and received applause when he finished. He sounded pretty level-headed when he locked horns with the county agent. The trapper was contracted for several more years. Another citizen who had an issue coming before the supervisors was so impressed he pleaded with Forrest to be his presenter.

I valued Forrest's cow sense. He grew up helping Byron Allen take cows up to Silver City and passed on to me his knowledge about handling cows, about letting them rest, giving a cow time to find her calf, don't push them hard on a long drive, things like that. Forrest was a real friend. He was an excellent judge of horseflesh and a skillful horseman.

Thomas H. Davis, II

A cowman whose advice I valued was Thomas Davis II who was my neighbor up Dry Creek at our Greasy Cove ranch. His father, Thomas Houston Davis, Sr. bought a beautiful ranch in Antelope Valley, by Woodlake, about the year my dad was born, along with land adjoining my Grandmother McKee's little ranch on Dry Creek, some of Greasy Cove and above to Mankin Flat. About 1900, Thomas Sr. went to Mexico to buy cattle and drove them hundreds of miles up here. He married the daughter of a neighboring rancher named Nye and ran two brands–JJ (a J up and J down so no matter how you turned it, it was right); and NI.

Thomas Davis II (Tommy) ran the ranch when I worked with him. His cattle wintered in Antelope and Dry Creek. I'd help him bring them through Greasy Cove every year headed to Mankin Flat. He had some of the best black cows around. He managed his herd a lot differently than anyone else–he let his cattle grow, had ample year-round feed, and sold them as 3-year old steers, average weight was 1250 pounds, the prettiest steers. He sold his cattle to Shannon Ranch mostly, because Shannon had contact with hotel markets that wanted those big T-bones that measured a foot across. Now days people don't want steaks that big.

Tommy ran his JJ cattle over on the Woodlake foothills with the big W on the slope overlooking town, and the NI cattle on Dry Creek. It all had to be kept separate to divide the proceeds among the heirs, siblings and half-siblings. Tommy had two sons, Thomas Houston III, and Gary.

Thomas Davis II was such a fine cowboy, a good cowman, ran an exceptional cattle operation. He always came to my branding and I always went to his down in Antelope Valley. He always rode a good horse that could watch a gate and was really good at parting cattle out. I always admired his ability and tried to emulate him. He team roped at the Three Rivers airport arena and over at Richard Ayer's Shady Acres in Lindcove where Lee Maloy, Forrest Homer, and I also roped.

Tommy was an excellent steer tripper at competitions in Wyoming, Texas and New Mexico. Steer tripping, also called steer tying, uses bigger steers, about 600 pounds now, come out of the box and just one cowboy ropes the horns, brings the rope over the hip and above the hock as he rides past it, then turns about 45 degrees and the steer is flipped, the cowboy steps off his horse, and the horse drags the steer to the cowboy who bends down, ties the front feet together and throws his hands in the air for time. Tommy had some stout horses he trained especially for this event, trained them to pull by hitching them to railroad ties, had a certain yell, "he-yar" when he stepped off and the horse knew what that meant–pull, pull and keep pulling. I watched the event in Laramie when I was there for a horse sale. When the cowboy throws that trip they call it "wiping his ass–roped his horns and wiped his ass."

I sang at the funeral of my friend, Thomas H. Davis II. It wasn't easy.

These men were all true friends and advisors to me in the cattle business. I was nineteen years old when I took over our ranch operation in partnership with my mother. My mother was not a hands-on cow person, but we talked over the major decisions. I had grown up with cattle; if I wasn't in school, I was on a horse helping my dad somewhere.

I built up our herd to about 500 mother cows and that is a full time job, buying bulls, looking after the cows, weaning the calves. I weaned calves at the home place and all the neighbors knew when I weaned calves–they didn't sleep too good with cows and calves bawling all night.

During the five years I worked summers for the Park, starting in 1957, I worked twelve days for the Park, and four days off to tend to the ranch. The minute I'd get home I had to start packing salt, check all the pastures, repair water problems and tend to a hundred details. And a couple of those years, the Park let me off early so I could pack the annual W. P. Fuller, Jr. trip.

I was always partial to the Hereford white-faced cattle. They've got more scale, smoother cattle, and a little bigger. But by the time I sold out, I had all Angus. They've bred these black cattle until they're big; the black cows are now superior to anything we've ever had.

Managing the Rangeland

There is a lot of calculating on how and when to move your cattle; hopefully, you can move cow-calf pairs to the mountain pastures before it quits raining so the grass will grow up behind them, then when you come back, you'll have some feed. Even having several ranches, if there was a bad year, no rain, I'd rent permanent pasture in the valley so the cows would raise nice fat calves to be weaned and sold as yearlings. Joe Correia, a good man who ran a small feedlot and also owned rangeland in Auckland, rented irrigated pasture to me west of Goshen. Joe's son, Gary, still works cattle. I usually bought 100 tons of alfalfa hay to feed every year to ensure healthy calving. I remember one drought year I had to buy 250 tons of alfalfa.

Nineteen seventy-six was a drought year. Rainfall for the whole year was less than seven inches and it was so far apart it didn't make much difference. Several of the springs on the range dried up. We ran out of feed. Everyone was scrambling for feed. Forrest Homer, his brother Ed, and I found a section of land up on the Pitt River in Bieber, California. Actually, Johnny Britten had it leased and agreed to sublet it to us. I had 150 cows and calves; Forrest had the same, and Ed had 100 pair—a total of 400 pair in DeCarteret's cattle transports. It was just under 500 miles from Three Rivers, a long haul, Forrest and I were in my pickup pulling a trailer with two horses so we had to stop often for them to rest. I did all the driving because Forrest was a terrible driver, one of those who talked the whole time and had to look at you, not at the road, while he talked and waved his arms for emphasis. I couldn't rest a second if he was behind the wheel. I'd turn on the radio to try to listen to music and Forrest would reach over and turn it down so he could talk, or just talk louder. I only wish I could have taped some of the old stories he told.

Of course, in the fall we had to truck the cattle home. I had planned to sell my calves there instead of bringing them home, which I did.

Forrest remembered the last big drought back in 1924. That same year was the largest outbreak of Hoof and Mouth disease in California and the west. A lot of cattle were lost, and there were quarantines everywhere. The control point into Three Rivers was manned around the clock where all vehicles and foot traffic had to go through a sheep dip. My dad worked swing shift at the control from 6 p.m. to midnight during quarantine. Sheep dip was used for everything. In the early 1920s, my mother raised small flocks of turkeys to sell at Thanksgiving. One time they got lice and my dad was advised by someone to use sheep dip. Well, my dad took each turkey and dipped it quick—in and out. They all died, killed every one of them, because he dipped them headfirst. But by god it killed the lice.

I've seen wet years when the grass was exceptionally tall. I think it was 1958 when it rained and rained and I went over to Greasy to help Dofflemyer. I was riding up a long ridge on that red soil and the wild oats had grown so high that my horse couldn't see where he was going and he'd get panicky and start lunging. I'd heard my dad and the old timers talk about the good years when the oats were so high you could tie them in a knot over the saddle horn. It was true. I had to get off my horse, knock down the grass and lead him because he didn't want to walk blind. The dog trailed in the track because he couldn't see anywhere either. When we got higher up in the rocky country the grass was shorter.

That reminds me of a Ben Harris story. Ben was known as the "greatest liar in the Sierra" and had a story for everything. He was talking about good years and bad years and said the best he'd ever seen was when the wild oats were as high as the oak trees and a lot of cattle were lost because they couldn't see their way out to find water. And further down on the plains, thousands of cattle were killed because they got into that high grass and a big windstorm came, knocked the grass over, and smothered the cows. (There's more about Ben Harris later.)

I was friends with Frank and Myrl Atwood, orange growers in Lemon Cove. About 1910, as a young girl, Myrl lived near the Sulfur Springs school in Three Rivers; her stepfather was A. G. Ogilvie who was employed in Lemon Cove planting the first orange orchards, and Myrl's half-brother was Fred Ogilvie, our school custodian and bus driver, son-in-law of Grace and Phil Alles. In the 1970s I leased one of Myrl's ranches, a 320, to run cattle down on North Ben Maddox in Visalia. Myrl offered me the sweet deal of a lifetime for me to buy that ranch–she really wanted me to have it–but I didn't take her offer and that is at the top of my list of most backward decisions I've ever made.

Bulls

We had about 15 to 20 head of bulls scattered around the ranches. I had cows in Greasy, on South Fork, and some at Lemon Cove. Sometimes I'd have to buy a young bull and let him grow up there. They need to be cared for so you don't lose track of them in their first year. On the ranches there is a lot of rough country, and sometimes cows and bulls will hide in that brush country. You just hope the bulls are breeding. We had a place at Lemon Cove where I kept the bulls in the early days to fatten them up, get them in good shape. They were always turned out the first of April. Nowadays the cowmen want them out in January for calves in September. We ran ours four months behind that schedule to produce winter calves because we were in the granite country where winters are colder.

Every year we bought bulls, often from Clay Dalton and his son Keith up in Madera. Forrest Homer and I attended bull sales at the Cow Palace. I bought a lot of cattle from Gladys Cooper in Tipton. She and her husband, Frank Cooper, a brother of Old Cutch–Forrest (Forrie) Cooper–whose son was Forrest and the third one is Forrest–they are all called Forrie.

I'd visit the Coopers and we'd talk music as well as bulls. I always admired the beautiful Steinway concert grand piano in the Cooper's living room. Gladys Cooper was an accomplished pianist and Frank sang like Caruso, a tenor with a magnificent voice. Frank Cooper sang all over the Valley and San Francisco, including at the dedication of the new steel bridge in Three Rivers in 1939.

It was 1939 and I was just a kid the first time I heard Frank Cooper sing. My parents and I were part of a large contingent of Three Rivers folks at the Hotel California in Fresno to celebrate the final go-ahead to build Friant Dam. Frank Cooper came out on the balcony and sang a song, like "Danny Boy;" everyone was spell-bound and near tears. Gladys accompanied him on the piano. The same program featured Three Rivers square dancers with the Poison Oak Orchestra, as well as solos by my sisters, Blanche Maloy and Earleen McKee.

Gladys had a good eye for cattle and bought Chandler bulls out of Oregon. Frank exhibited prize-winning cattle at the Hereford shows. One year I bought six bulls from them. I always bought pure-bred bulls to raise commercial cattle, to keep building good blood lines, changing for the better. Pardon my French, but one criterion in selecting a bull is the size of the testicles, you want a bull with big balls, because the data show they are better breeders. Now there are computerized records of the performance of every animal–rate of gain, rib eye measurements, weight-per-day-of-age, etc. to help breed smoothness, size and bone, and each bull has a score, the highest scored bulls go through the sales ring first.

I used to take all my bulls down to the Colpien feedlot, to what we called "put the lead back in their pencil"–another old saying of Ray Pinnell's–feed the bulls up in the fall so they were big, virile guys to go out and fight and scatter out and try to whip each other come breeding season. You turned your bulls out on the range, they're fat and they hate each other, ready to fight over all the cows and that is exactly what would scatter the herd–run one bull out of the canyon over into another cove. You don't think about it, but that's how the herd was divided up and scattered.

I spent my entire working life–55 years–just raising cattle. I have fond memories of the melodic tones of a dozen cowbells in my herd echoing up the canyon as we rode along the South Fork in the shade of the Sycamores–clink-a-clink-a, clink-a-clink-a, driving cattle to the mountains and every trip was a different story. You learn a lot about life following a bunch of cows.

An Award and a Poem

About ten years ago, I was gratified to be recognized by the Tulare County Cattlemen's Association as outstanding cattleman of the year. I had been a member of the Association for more than 40 years. John Dofflemyer, a rancher on Dry Creek, presented the award and recited a poem he had written about me years before. I think the poem better describes my father because he taught me how to live life.

A Poem by John Dofflemyer

Robert Frost never built a fence between a neighbor as fine as mine, who shared more than his cow sense on both sides of the line.

He helped a shaggy-headed kid, whose ignorance could fill a book; and kept his impatience mostly hid, 'less I took a second look.

And then he knew, I knew the pain and like a son, he worked with me and tell a joke to keep me sane; so frustrat'd I couldn't see.

In time, I'd be workin' the gate, he damn sure had me lookin' sharp workin' round my each mistake! the cattle, easy to part.

Whenever I call, he'll be there, savin' most of his work for last, he helped me ship 'em on Easter, a drought year gone past.

A slick calf could cause discussion, he'd always argue it was mine; I'd debate for his possession, losin' most of the time.

And when he'd weigh out justice, you'd find his thumb upon the scale but on your side of the balance, your logic to no avail.

So before you go buildin' fences and stretchin' brand new barbed wire, there's one gone b'yond common senses, and made Bobby Frost a liar.

If you'd ever find a pattern cut that'd be suitable for me, reckon you'd be hard pressed to put, usin' other than Earl McKee.

John Dofflemyer continues to raise cattle on the beautiful Dofflemyer Ranch on Dry Creek that his family acquired about the time my dad bought our Greasy Cove ranch. John spent his summers during college in the 1960s packing mules in the Sierra backcountry. He is now known the world over for his award winning Cowboy poetry, as publisher of *Dry Crik Review*, and author of many books of Cowboy poems including *Uneven Green*, *Hung Out to Dry*, and *Poems from Dry Creek* that earned the 2008 Western Heritage Wrangler Award by the National Cowboy & Western Heritage Museum, Oklahoma City, OK.

Earl A. McKee, III. Photo 1980.

EARL III

My son, Earl, was 26 years old when he died of liver cancer. That is not supposed to happen to a young person. He was treated at Stanford Children's Hospital, where everything was tried – surgical resection of the tumor, chemotherapy, and sometimes it seemed to work. He fought it for about 2-1/2 years.

Earl III–everyone called him Little Earl, like they used to call me when I was a kid because my dad's name was Earl–grew up helping me a lot and just being there, like me and my dad. (Here, I will just call him Earl.) His love for the ranch, horses, pack trips, and nature was the subject of poetry he wrote during his short life. Times were a little different with my son, of course, because of the modern changes. Earl helped me on the ranch, working on corrals, gathering cattle. He learned to shoe, but his life was busy with school and sports so there wasn't as much time for ranch work as I had when his age. My father was in the packing business, I grew up in the packing business, but we sold out of the packing business before Earl came along. Earl A. McKee III was born November 21, 1957.

Earl did go to work for the Park on a trail crew in the summers. The first year he worked in Roaring River. Ralph Whass was the trail boss who had the crew do some packing, so my boy got some of the packing experience that his father and grandfather had. It was the second year, about 1980, on the trail crew that an accident happened that might have led to the cancer. There is no way to prove it, it just drives your mind into "what if" circles. The crew was building a bridge on the Middle Fork of the Kings around Simpson Meadow. The Park allowed, at that time, trees to be cut for stringers across to support the bridge. (In the old days that is what they did–not now.) They were putting the decking and handrails on and that's when the accident happened. Earl was below in the riverbed when a 5-gallon bucket of creosote on the platform above was knocked over and it poured onto his head, into his mouth and covered his face where he could barely breathe. It does not wash off, it is toxic, a carcinogen, and burns. He was taken by helicopter to a Fresno hospital where he was hospitalized for several days. His face was burned and peeled.

I knew from first-hand experience how badly creosote burns. I was trying to apply creosote at my corral with an old Hudson sprayer that plugged up. I beat on it, turned it around to look at the nozzle and the thing went off and hit me right in the face–just like it got Earl only it was just a spray not five gallons of suffocating oil. I jumped in the horse trough and put my head under water, but that didn't work because oil won't wash off. My face peeled.

My boy graduated from Woodlake High School and College of the Sequoias. He excelled in sports–basketball, swimming, skiing, football; on the COS football team he set a record for the longest touchdown return–caught the ball in the end zone and returned it for a touchdown, 100 yards plus. In high school and college Earl was in band and choir.

Right out of high school Earl went to Porterville and trained for the Hot Shots, the fire jumping teams that are dropped from helicopters– they'd fly low and jump in close to the fire–jump, hit, and roll–to fight forest fires all over the state. It is an elite bunch, all athletes and runners, they ran five miles a day to train. He was in the prime of his life.

Earl A. McKee, III at age two, holding the reins to Joe.

Earl transferred to Humboldt State where he was busy with sports and music along with his Forestry major. There he met a lovely young lady and they planned to marry. In his third year at Humboldt he was seen by a young doctor at the Clinic, a graduate of Stanford University Medical School, who suspected a liver abnormality. When we got the news, it was impossible to sleep, so we drove all night to be with him for diagnostic procedures. When we arrived, Earl tried to reassure us: "I'm OK now, but last night you wouldn't have wanted to be here." Like anybody, when it hits you that something is wrong, it is tough.

The physician at the Humboldt clinic ran the diagnostics and told us there was definitely a liver tumor and he suspected it was malignant, the worst news you are not prepared for. The doctor's first choice for referral was to a liver transplant specialist on the East Coast; however, his other choice was another Stanford doctor he believed was the best on the West Coast, a Dr. Pinto whose office was in San Francisco. There, in Dr. Pinto's office, I sat next to Earl when Dr. Pinto told him, "You may die."

I asked Dr. Pinto if he knew another Stanford doctor, Bruce Jessup. He looked at me with such surprise that I would know Dr. Jessup. Oh, yes, Dr. Pinto was well acquainted with Dr. Jessup, he was the doctor who had provided funds and a room in his own home to a young fellow whose passion was to become a doctor but who could not afford medical school–that young man was Dr. Pinto. Dr. Pinto came to be one of the best liver specialists in the country.

I knew Bruce Jessup from the W. P. Fuller pack trips–he was a good friend of the Fullers and married into the family. Years before, I had called Dr. Jessup to see our tiny daughter who had been diagnosed with an irreversible disease. Dr. Jessup knew first hand the course of disease because his brother had succumbed to it. He was able to prescribe a brand new treatment and our daughter was cured. Again, Dr. Jessup came to our side when Earl became ill.

One year I got a call from Dr. Jessup asking what I was going to be doing in the next month or so, because he was going on a pack trip out of Wawona in Yosemite, be gone for a week, and invited us to go along as guests, he was buying and we weren't allowed to pay for anything. My wife Gaynor and I enjoyed being guests for a change. The O'Brien part of what later became Fuller O'Brien Paints was on that trip also–Jim O'Brien. Jim had been on many of the Fuller trips when I was packing.

During the cancer treatment–when Earl had a shunt in–we planned a family pack trip to Simpson Meadow country, afraid it might be our last one together. It was. We were going out for about ten days, and I had invited Jimmy Rivers to go along. Earl, Jimmy and I had our guitars. Old Ray Pinnell was along, too.

Jimmy Rivers was a world-class guitar player whom I met at the Sacramento Jubilee jazz festival some years before. Jimmy was from Oklahoma and first got into playing music on the circuit in Las Vegas. His day job was for a company that installed and serviced refrigeration units for big grocery chains like Safeway. He lived in El Dorado and ran the California Hayride, a live TV country music show out of Stockton, for ten or eleven years and he played in bands up there and knew all the musicians in the Western music industry–this was early television in the

1960s. He talked about Johnny Cash, Buck Owens, Bob Nolan, Bob Wills and all those guys.

Jimmy was acquainted with cancer; his first wife had died of a brain tumor and after that he quit music altogether for a time. When working in Sacramento, a friend invited him to the Sacramento Jubilee jazz festival. Whoever heard of an electric guitar in a traditional jazz band? Our High Sierra Jazz Band played at all the Jubilees and that's when I met Jimmy when he jammed with us. His guitar playing blew everyone off the stage. The Fulton Street Jazz Band hired him and he proved to be the main attraction, everyone wanted to hear Jimmy. He'd sit out in front and play the guitar and never look at it, the music just ran out of his fingers. He took a liking to Earl and started coming to Three Rivers to visit when Earl was sick.

I have a cassette tape we made on the Simpson pack trip of Earl singing and the three of us playing guitars, and you can hear the river in the background close to our camp. Earl had studied with a guitarist, Gary Olenslager of Three Rivers, who taught him Flamenco style fingering. John Denver was Earl's hero and he could sing Denver's songbook. Earl had a good voice. That was 1982. At one point, in his home recording studio, Jimmy Rivers made a recording of Earl singing an old Jimmy Rogers tune.

Earl loved the mountains; his spirit was as pure as the crisp mountain air. With poetry he painted pictures of his soul. A poem he wrote December 25, 1976 is included in the chapter of poetry.

Jimmy wanted to be near Earl and started coming down to visit him in Three Rivers, and the first thing you know, he was helping with all our projects. I bought a big mobile home for Earl. He and his fiancee, Linda Murray, planned to get married, it was just one of those sad stories that he couldn't because of the cancer–there was no way out, you know. So we installed his mobile home on a knoll on the home place and Jimmy helped us build a big redwood deck all around it. I brought in a dozer to excavate several big ponds because he wanted to raise catfish. Jimmy stayed down here because he loved Earl, they just got along so well and Jimmy wanted to be close to him during his illness. Jimmy sort of became like family and brought a co-worker along to help. This guy, a little Japanese fellow, was a good sport and he would come by to lend a hand whenever he was in the area.

When Earl was undergoing treatment at the Stanford Lane hospital which was part of the Presbyterian Hospital in San Francisco, Jimmy Rivers and his second wife, Maria, came over to be with Earl. Maria was a pretty Spanish spitfire, so nice and lots of fun to be around.

Earl was a fine guy. This is not supposed to happen, but it does. You cry all the tears you can cry until there are no more. You can make yourself sick because you cannot change anything—fact is, it is what it is, and you have to suffer for that. Losing him was so devastating to us all. The tragedy brought us much closer together as a family. All those wonderful memories, all the fun, laughter and tears we shared with Earl growing up together gave us renewed compassion, strength, and love for his life. His spirit and strength is still evident to me every day as I see the many things we built together around this ranch.

My boy tried so hard to stay alive. He died in my arms. You never forget these things.

MC KEE RANCHES

ᏜᎲᎲᎧᎲ

Greasy Cove

I have a lot of memories working cattle with my boy in Greasy Cove. Greasy Creek drains into Lake Kaweah at the north end of Terminus Dam, that last canyon is Greasy. I can tell you every rock and ravine of that property from the days riding with my dad and doing tractor work, brushing, and building roads with my boy.

Edgar Linnell, (1870-1951) of Exeter, liked to hunt quail in Greasy with his friend, Bud Sherman, former county sheriff, so I gave Ed a key. We rode together and he told me some history of the place. It used to be called Greasy's Cove, named for Bill Greasy who lived at the east end, about a half mile south from the sulfur spring house, but right on the creek. He had a cabin and planted fig trees that still grow there. We found some old stove pieces at the site. The 1892 survey map showed nine farm houses in the Greasy Cove area.

The house by the sulfur spring above Greasy's cabin was still standing in 1960. Sulfur Peak, 3200' elevation, is 1-1/2 miles northwest of the house. J. E. Monroe lived there in the 1890s; it was described as having beautiful gardens near the spring. The spring water smelled of sulfur, but when left to air over night it was sweet. Loren Finch called it the Huntley House because he remembered Fat Huntley who lived there. My dad said the Sweeney brothers from down in the swamps had run it when he bought the place. We stayed there off and on when gathering cattle. The story goes that the house was an alternate hideout for the train robbers Sontag and Evans. My dad told me his father, William McKee, was trusted by the train robbers to pack supplies to their hideouts.

We found two or three chimneys and old logs left of other cabins in Greasy. One daughter of Edgar and Louise Linnell married my cousin

Clyde Britten, son of Stella McKee and Harry Britten. Another Linnell daughter married the grandson of J. W. C. Pogue of Lemon Cove, so Edgar had spent many years riding those hills when it was owned by Pogue. Pogue bought sections of land that encompass Greasy from his wife's cousin, Calvin Blair. In 1877, Pogue took his ten thousand sheep - wooly mowers - through Greasy Cove on the way over the mountain to summer pasture on North Fork.

Not many people knew how beautiful and what excellent cow country Greasy Cove is because it was hard to get to. You have to ford either Dry Creek or the Kaweah River to get on the old wagon road. If the water is high, you just don't go. You really needed to be young and tough to get your cattle in and out of Greasy in those days, plus it was a long ways to market.

The first wagon road to Greasy came up the west bank of the Kaweah River, forded Dry Creek at the flats across from Terminus Beach then north through the gap now blocked by the dam. It was graded for mule wagons as far as Section 17, (the Schrimsher property in 1892) not far from the sulfur spring.

My dad and I drove the lower part of the old road for years. After the road crossed Greasy Creek, it graded south on a new road built by the WPA about 1938 nearly a mile where it makes a switchback pretty high on the steep mountainside, then back to the north two or three miles to the ranch land. About 1952, I hauled a heavy load of heifers, probably 15 or 16, should have left one off, but the weather wasn't too hot and the truck was chugging along. My old neighbor Floyd "Peanuts" Carter was with me. We got out to the point, coming to the hairpin turn, Floyd was looking over his shoulder straight down the cliff edge, nervous: "Pretty steep off here, isn't it, Earl?" I said yeah. I had the truck in grandma gear, couldn't go any lower, but still had gears. I could tell Floyd was afraid we weren't going to make it. "You know, Earl, maybe I'd better get out here." It was scary, especially to a lot of old timers who really didn't trust machinery. "Well, Floyd, if you think I'm going off the edge here, maybe both of us ought to get out." He looked kinda funny and then laughed. It was about three miles further to the corrals where we unloaded. Floyd never wanted to go back to Greasy.

Today from that hairpin turn you'd look right down on the dam. When the dam was built the road was rerouted higher on the north side of the mountain up Greasy Creek.

My dad bought Greasy in 1937–Sections 7, 9, 17, 19 and part of section 8–3000 acres in all. A year later Lee Maloy and Jim Kindred built concrete water troughs, double-sided forms, eight feet square with three-foot troughs. Everything had to be packed in on mules and horses from Terminus and about twenty-five mule-loads of sand were packed over the mountain from Ken Savage's place on the North Fork river. The next year, January of 1939, Lee and Jim camped at Greasy for six weeks to repair eleven miles of fence. I remember Clyde Britten, my dad, and I went hunting up there and had our lunch at the old sulfur spring house. Our corrals were nearby.

We'd gather in Section 17 and herd the cattle southeast a mile through Rayme Gap on the ridge and down the other side three miles or so to Forrest Homer's where we forded the Kaweah River on the way to summer pasture. In the fall we brought them back the same way.

Todd Dofflemyer was a successful grape farmer in Exeter, smart and frugal. He bought the ranch next to Greasy, the one the bank wanted my dad to buy at the same time he bought Greasy. It is a fine ranch with great feed where you could always bring off fat cattle to market. Todd's son, Robert Dofflemyer, managed the cattle ranch. He was a business cowboy who kept meticulous records and developed excellent stock. Joe Chinowth was the first foreman for Todd Dofflemyer when Robert served in WWII.

Joe Chinowth lived in the green house just off the Woodlake turnoff from Hwy. 198. Joe was a great guy, everybody liked Joe. He and my dad were really close. His family was from Visalia, lived at Chinowth Corner, where Chinowth Street is named for them. Joe's brother was the opposite, a horse trader who'd sell his mother a blind horse.

Joe rode an old black horse he called Leppy–Leppy means an orphan calf or colt. Joe and Leppy grew old together. Joe always rode Leppy when he and my dad traded help gathering and checking for strays, and they hunted together at Greasy. One year we were deer hunting up high in the sulfur spring section and I was way behind, Joe was in the middle, and my dad was in front on a jumpy colt. We got off the horses to head into the brush when Joe slipped and slid behind my dad's horse. That colt jumped and kicked Joe square on his leg and broke it. Poor Joe turned white as a sheet. We had to get him on a horse to bring him down those steep mountains. We lifted him up on his good leg side and got him in the saddle. He was in a cast for a long time.

Joe handled one of the most famous horses around, Old Mark, a real red sorrel owned by Gill Cattle Company. Old Mark was a famous steer tripper horse owned by Carl Arnold in north Texas in the 1930s. Arnold rode Old Mark and beat the world champion steer tripper, Bob Crosby. At Gill's, Old Mark stood at stud for twenty years, then Joe kept him near Emmett Gill's place for his last ten years. I owned the last colt by Old Mark, born in 1946 out of the same mare that had Parmer, and my dad got to see him. I trained him to be a great cow horse.

Joe had a stroke and couldn't get around. I visited with old Joe and his wife often during his later years. We'd talk about old times and he really perked up after our visits.

Joe and Elsie were married in Visalia on July 4, 1906 when the floodwaters were up to the horses' knees at the Court House and everywhere for a month. Joe died in 1962.

Harvey Learned McCants (1919-2001) was the second ranch foreman at Robert Dofflemyer's ranch neighboring Greasy and he came to some of our first brandings. Harvey was quite a character. We traded help a lot. He was a hard worker and liked to ride with me and he loved to talk. Harvey later moved to Yettem to go into the farm equipment business but I think the ranch days were the happiest time of his life.

I remember when Harvey helped at our branding in 1955, he had "no ass-atall," his pants sort of bagged, and that day his pants caught on something and ripped all the way down the back side. It started to rain and by the time we finished it was pouring. Our trucks were all parked in the field at the bottom of the hill and at day's end the road was too slick, so we left the rigs and came out on horseback. Harvey was so embarrassed because he had to ride all that way with his bare butt showing. We put the horses up for the night at the corral at Dry Creek road and found a phone to call for rides.

At his funeral, Harvey's friends remembered him as a man of few words. I had to get up and say, well, he wasn't always like that. Harvey was one of the talkingest cowboys I ever worked with. I wouldn't call him windy, but he sure liked to keep the air moving.

Clarence Holbrook was just a kid when he came to work for Bob Dofflemyer doing odd jobs at first. I met him when I took over our ranches in 1949. He was several years younger than I was. Clarence was always a good hand, he helped me a lot in the old days and if I still had cattle he would help me today.

Clarence learned about horses and got a real education from different trainers, including Harry Rose who was known for unusual training techniques. Clarence was interested in training and breeding cutting horses. He took his stud to the World Championship Reining Horse in Long Beach, California, and won. Clarence followed the cutting horse circuit for a number of years. He lives on Dry Creek and works with John Dofflemyer.

He was a good dog man also, still raises working cow dogs and goes to the Red Bluff dog sale every year. He is a dear friend and we worked together for a long time; he knew Forrest Homer and we reminisce about old Homer stories.

One time I was invited to a wedding at the Gary Davis ranch up on Mankin Flat and I drove there towing a horse trailer because I had to check on cattle at Greasy first and decided I had enough time to get to the wedding. Gary's dad, Tom Davis, was my old friend and advisor. I drove up to the south entrance to the Davis ranch but the combination to the gate lock had been changed so I couldn't get in and couldn't turn around. I unloaded my horse and rode up the ridge to another gate I knew about to get to the ranch. I thundered in to their celebration at a full gallop and let out a roar, "Hold it! Hold it!" right in the middle of their vows. Granddad Tom Davis said that really made his day; it could have only been more perfect if I would have had a pistol and rode in firing just when the preacher asked, ". . . if anyone objects, speak now . . ." bang!

Somebody reminded me the other day about the wrecks up Greasy. It was forty or fifty years ago and a long ways from a phone. It was a hot July day–112 degrees–and I was driving a truck with a twenty-foot bed loaded with heifers and a two-year old bull up the dirt road into Greasy Cove. I got within 200 feet of where I was going to turn around when the motor over-heated and vapor-locked, which meant I lost the vacuum brakes and started to roll backwards. I turned the truck to aim the rear duals into the bank, but it hit a hump and the truck flipped on its side. My window was smashed, my ear was in the dirt, so I crawled out of the passenger side. The heifers were dumped out and walked away, but the bull was lying inside. He looked dead. I jumped on his ribs–on his side, right behind his front legs–you might call it cowboy CPR–and he came to; he had been buried underneath the pile of cows and had the air knocked out of him. He got to his feet dizzy, stumbled and fell down, but finally his head cleared. Now to get back home. Of course this happened about as far back as was possible to go, and I had to walk clear to Dry Creek road, about 2 to 3 hours in that scorching sun. I caught a ride at Dry Creek and called Pat O'Connell–one of the most neighborly and best-liked guys in Three Rivers–who had the tow truck service. (Pat's son, Jay O'Connell, is the author of several books on local history here.) The next day Pat and I went back with his tow truck.

Branding in Greasy Cove. I am working the gate on my horse, Copper. Photo c. 1955.

AUTHOR'S COLLECTION.

Another rancher in Greasy was old man Ban Freeman from Hanford, California. He bought the old May place in Greasy and ran Holsteins up there–he ran just about anything, not really range cattle. Holsteins just stayed stacked up at the bottom of the hill, wouldn't climb up to graze. Ban was a tough old guy who thought my dad was

Number One. They were in lodge together and were good friends and neighbors. Ban Freeman's brother-in-law was Jesse Shackleford. Ban's son, Jess Freeman, farmed alfalfa in the valley and sold hay up here. One time Ban, his little grandson, and Shackleford were hauling a load of tall Holsteins in his old International short bed truck up the steep grade of Greasy road. Ban shifted down and missed a gear on the old transmission and couldn't grab another gear, the airbrakes quit, so the truck rolled backwards down hill. It was July, hotter than blazes, so the truck bed was full of "soup," cow sh-t, shall we say. (I remember Ban always placed emphasis on profane words.) The truck rolled over twice, the Holsteins tumbled out and ran off unhurt, but a tidal wave of soup sloshed through the cab. The little boy's arm was broken. After the long, arduous walk to Dry Creek Road, there was a little trouble flagging down someone to help because they were all covered head to toe with cow soup. Eventually someone took them to Exeter hospital and to the farm store to buy clean clothes.

Another wreck happened some years before that. I was using a short-coupled truck to haul some cows and calves up Greasy. Again, it was a very hot summer day when I was pulling a steep grade and the cows lost their footing and slid in the cow soup and piled up against the tailgate. The front end of the truck tipped up ten feet off the ground. I couldn't get the loading door open, so I took a fence post and baling wire to make a fulcrum to pull around the corner to release the latch on the loading gate. Out rolled the cows. Inside were two dead calves–one was lying with its head hanging over the tailgate. I ran up and jumped on its ribs and it started gasping for air; the other one started breathing after the same maneuver. Saved them both. This happened before I got to my property, and the cows and calves were running all over my neighbor's ranch. I needed to get them up to section 9 in Greasy, had to gather them up on foot and herd them up to my gate.

I used to see many magnificent Golden eagles in the trees along the bluffs in Greasy where they could just fall off into space and soar. One time I was riding fence high above the lake in a real rough area when I heard this prolonged screeching sound carried on the wind from the ridge. I rode over the hump to investigate and saw something not many people have seen in the wild at the end of the world–stretched out on a flat rock were two Golden eagles mating.

When range feed was low, every few days I hauled hay to feed at Greasy, a dozen bales of alfalfa on my flatbed one-ton. On the flats, I'd aim the wheels, position the steering wheel and tie it to the passenger door handle, then let the truck go in low gear while I pitched hay off the back. One time I had Gaynor's little dog, Sweetie Face, with me in the cab. It was excited, running side to side across the seat. The truck was headed for a tree so I jumped down only to discover the dog had locked both doors, so I ran alongside trying to find a rock to bust the window. Luckily the wind-wing hadn't been latched so I knocked it open and I got in and stopped the truck before the tree did.

One morning we were herding cattle from South Fork to Forrest Homer's where we crossed the Kaweah river to Greasy. My working cow dog, named Sam, was with me. From the Three Rivers home place we got on the road real early to get ahead of the commuters. We turned on to Highway 198, and the cows were strung along the road just past Kulik's Kaweah General Store, almost to the Cider Mill. Sam was eager and he started bearing down on the cows. When you start out you don't want your dog fighting the cow and cow fighting the dog because they're going fast enough, you don't want the dog to push them. It was a cool morning and Sam was anxious to work and kept trying to get in a fight with the cows and I would have to yell at him. I had just gotten after him when another cow turned and Sam tried to bite her nose. I hollered at the top of my lungs, "Sam! Get back, you son-of-a-bitch!" and I heard this car screech to a stop right beside me. I had been looking at the cows, didn't see the car. The windows were down, and the driver's face was beet red. It was Sam Pusateri, professor at College of Sequoias, on his way to work. He always joked that I was the only person who got away with calling him an s.o.b.

Forrest always appreciated my help in getting his cows across the river because I knew about that river. It was tricky in high water years, and I lost a horse there one time. To get the cattle across the river, you have to get them to step into the water first. When none of them wants to get in, you about tear the shoes off your horse to push the first little group into the river, holler, yell, pop them on the rear with the rope, whatever it takes to get them in. Once the cows see another going into the water, they will follow, so the herd has to be kept in little groups following close together and you can't let one turn away or they will all try to run back.

For a good many years, I had a cow worth her weight in gold because she always wanted to lead, to be first, and she wasn't afraid of water. Funny how some animals have memorable personalities. This cow would come down the hillside and run right at the river, just look across and swim out, and once one goes in, the others know it is okay and will follow. When Forrest Homer saw this cow leading the herd across the river, he said, "Earl, don't you ever sell that cow unless you sell her to me." She was in a load of cattle I bought one time up by Galt, California. She was brindle-colored, a beef cow but with brindle in her, might have been some Devonshire crossed with white-faced. I belled her. This cow came off of Greasy Cove and summered in Cahoon Meadow.

I took Parmer, my dad's great palomino stud, to Greasy in 1960 when he was twenty years old to let him graze with an old palomino mare in that nice cove. Parmer was born May 1, 1940 and named for W. Parmer Fuller, Jr. I fell heir to him after my dad died in 1946 and he was my favorite horse. Emmett Gill admired that horse and I let him run with Emmett's mares for several seasons. Emmett gave me one of Parmer's buckskin colts.

I went back to check on the horses, it was January 5, 1960–the date stuck in my head–and as soon as I drove up I had an eerie feeling something was wrong. I found Parmer laying in the shade of a tree, two days dead, puffed up, a buzzard sitting on him.

The cabin was weathered, the door was wired shut, but the downhill wall with a window had blown in during a windstorm, leaving about a six-foot opening. The cabin was built on a slope, the floor was two feet off the ground, one room sunken, another room sturdy. Inside the kitchen was an old rusty bedstead, a big, beautiful wood cook stove and a twenty-five gallon bucket full of empty fruit jars but buried at the bottom was a little bag of squirrel poison. How and why old Parmer had jumped up onto a wood floor and nosed around in the other room, I'll never understand. But it was evident that he'd dumped over the jars and eaten a couple of handfuls of poison grain and gone over to the oak tree and died.

I was so upset, I set fire to that cabin and burned it down on the spot! I eventually took a piece of Parmer home–his bleached hip bone; funny how that seemed important and comforting.

South Fork Ranch

South Fork Ranch was in the upper end of the cove on the backside of Blossom Peak. It was about 3000 acres, good for a nice little herd of 200 cows. In 1921, my dad bought the Lewis ranch which was a half of section 5, across from Byron Allen's old corrals, east over the top abutting Bob Lovering's place and the BLM that we leased; Section 32 from Roy Stevenson and Section 20 from Billy Canfield to the north. In 1947 Floyd Carter sold us one-half of section 29. A section is one mile square and contains 640 acres. It is foothill country west of Horn Mountain, with some huge rocky gulches clear down into Britten Cove. Rocks are piled high in ridges in some places.

I was just up there for several days in the spring of 2012 helping the guys gather their cattle and we started telling stories about the old days. One time in the early 1990s we were gathering; helping me were John Dofflemyer, Clarence Holbrook, Chucky Fry, and Don Pelham. I was in front on the bluff where exposed oak tree roots criss-crossed the trail, so I got off and led my horse through the tangle. It was a steep 15 feet off your stirrup to the bottom. That's where I stepped on a tough little poison oak bush for solid footing, but it was hanging over thin air and I went flying. I heard Chucky yell to watch out, my horse was coming down right behind me. I landed on granite, my horse cartwheeled over me and was fine, but I tore a big flap in my scalp that bled profusely. I asked the guys, could they just pick up the flap and look inside? Was my skull fractured? I was taken to the hospital for 40 stitches. Don said it was a good thing I hit on my head, otherwise I could have got hurt.

Troy Hall and his wife, Laura, lived on South Fork across the river from my ranch where they rented Dolph and Beulah Beam's old house. Dolph had the primary interest in the tungsten mine on the east side of Blossom Peak, west of my ranch land. Laura went the extra mile to care for Beulah during all the years after Dolph died. The Park Service hired Troy to help me when I was packing bridges. I met Laura for the first time one day after I rode by Dolph's pond and spotted one of the Hall's cows laying there with a serious condition of protruding uterus, what was commonly called a "womb out." So I rode over to the house and introduced myself and told her the cow needed attention. Laura knew about horses and cows and was fearless. She got her horse and we rode back to the cow and Laura did the old-timer's repair where the uterus is pushed back inside and wire stitches are sewn in to hold it. Laura was a sweet lady and a hard worker. She went to school to learn artificial insemination of horses and later she gave me her set of AQHA (American Quarter Horse Association) stud books to make my collection complete.

Troy and Laura raised a little of everything at their place, cattle, chickens, geese, and one time Troy bought a herd of hogs and turned them out across the river where I ran my cows. I was riding my stallion, Parmer, down from my ranch to the Beam place looking for some cattle. I loped toward a large bushy Live Oak tree surrounded by tall feed growing into the low branches. Hidden within this foliage was Troy's herd of hogs, napping. The approaching hoof beats startled the hogs. With loud huff-huff-huff noises they scattered right in front of my horse and Parmer swapped ends. When I picked myself up off the ground, I could feel Parmer's heart pounding, he was so scared. He had never seen or smelled a hog!

Another incident we laughed about was when Tommy Ray Welch was helping me. Tommy worked as a cowboy for Walt Seaborn whose wife, Peggy Wells, owned the former La Cuesta ranch on South Fork. We were after several wild cows that had grazed down on the Beam's land. We saw the cows run into a Live Oak thicket. Tommy was watching from the other side and didn't know I was in the world, and I didn't know he was in the world, so we came around right in front of the cows to head them off, and like two outfielders running for a fly ball, we collided—my big bay hit his horse at the shoulder, knocked his horse flat, ran right over him and Tommy went flying. After we realized that nothing was broken and could get air again, we sat and laughed, it was so funny.

One time we were gathering cattle on the South Fork ranch up in the big Live Oak Canyon that runs right up the face of Horn Mountain. On the north slope it is cool, there's a little water in the creek and when the Buckeyes are leafed out the sun never directly hits it. Chucky Fry, Clarence Holbrook and John Dofflemyer were helping me and we were scattered out through there. I told Chucky to ride in the direction of an old road and I would head down through some real brushy stuff. The brush got so thick it was almost impossible to ride through. I saw some bear prints. When I broke into this rather narrow little flat, my horse snorted and ahead was a bear, an old mother bear that went "woof" and she had a little cub. She slapped him up a tree, and I had to ride by that tree, it was the only way. I thought maybe she'd give ground to a horse, but she started snapping her teeth as a warning–to me, or telling her cub to stay put, I don't know. I couldn't get around her, so I had to turn around and crash back through the brush against the grain. When I got out on the hillside, just to put Chucky on edge a bit, I called to him to watch for a big mother bear and her cub that's kind of mad and headed his way.

Another time, Johnny Britten and I both suffered losses to our livestock on our South Fork ranches from a pack of dogs that were allowed to run loose by deadbeat owners in Alta Acres subdivision over the hill to the north. We called the county trapper who put out cage traps and after waiting a few weeks captured the alpha dog, a big police-type breed. This dog pack had killed one of Johnny's bulls, as well as a half dozen calves; even chewed the tail and ears off one of my calves–it did recover down at my home place.

There have been wild cows in the mountains since ranchers first took cattle to the high meadows in the 1860s. During fall gathering, one or two cows will hide or will be off in another canyon. Henry Icho, the last chief of the Wutchumna Yokuts, was skilled in gathering cattle in the rough mountain country and rode for several cattlemen who took their cattle up in the Sierra forest. Hudson Barton, Jeff Davis, Henry Scott, and Louis Broder, told author, Frank Latta, that Icho was always in demand to help bring wild cows out of the brush.

You needed a good dog to help you get those cows down through the brush, and you needed a place to hold them so you could haul them out, otherwise your dog worked his tail off just to see them get away again. There were cattle that would get away from you a few times, maybe they had a little Brahma or Devon blood, they were tough and knew how to hide. That's why I belled ten or twelve cows in my herds.

To trap wild cows, I made two pens using panels, with a cross fence, located across a little creek to furnish constant water, put two panels in a V shape, sticking into the large pen like a fly trap, the narrow end just shoulder width. The cows would go in to eat the hay placed inside the big pen and couldn't get out. Because there was water and hay it could be checked every few days and when a truckload of fifteen head or so was enclosed, we could load them and take them home. One time I had collected some wild stock of mine on a neighbor's place when a wild bull charged me. The bull was standing behind his cows in the corral, looked up and saw me on foot in the pen, and charged full speed. I knew I couldn't run fast enough, even though I was 15 years younger then, so I had no choice but to stand my ground. Just as we were almost eye-to-eye, I hit him in the face with a mighty swing of my cowboy hat. It distracted him long enough for me to escape but he plowed into the fence and broke some boards and a gate for which I had to reimburse my friend.

One year I lost a bull out of Cahoon Meadow, a Red Angus bull that I was worried about so I had belled him. A bull sometime behaves like a big buck. In the fall when all the cows are bred and there isn't much to do, it will wander off alone and won't follow the cows out when you gather. We couldn't find that red bull anywhere–searched from Hockett Meadow over to Horse Creek. Dave Wilson rode with me. We hauled the horses to Look Out Point on the road to Mineral King, then rode across the river and up through stands of redwoods at Eden Grove where we spotted a single set of tracks. We called and listened. Finally, on the backside of Homer's Nose, we heard a clank-clank, bang–probably the bull was hitting a fly–so I sent my dogs up the mountain probably a half-mile. The dogs brought the red bull out; we followed him to the road and down to Oak Grove where Craig Thorn had a small loading chute, loaded him up and went home.

Cahoon Meadow

I was about twenty years old when Forrest Homer wanted to form a partnership with me to buy 5500 deeded acres in Grouse Valley for $150,000, a big undertaking at the time. This was the Axel Anderson ranch in Grouse where he had run turkeys and then cattle. Axel sold it to Gill Ranch, but Gill decided that they didn't want brush country and put it on the market a year later. Bill Wylie was selling real estate then. I talked to Axel about the property and what sections were best for grazing and how it could be fenced. Forrest and I were ready to close the deal, but just as the papers were being prepared, Forrest must have had a meeting with himself because he did a sudden one-eighty and withdrew. He decided he wanted a meadow instead and the next year acquired a 51% interest from a Mr. Beaumont McClure in Cahoon Meadow, 320 acres with streams, lush feed, bordered by pines and redwoods outside the national park boundary. He ran cattle there for about fifteen years and I helped him take his herd up every spring. When his boy, Mehrten, bought a ranch in Oregon, Forrest didn't want to go to Cahoon anymore because he couldn't handle it alone, so he offered to rent it to me.

I rented Cahoon Meadow for summer pasture from Forrest Homer for seven or eight years, from 1969 to 1977. The eighth year, I couldn't take the cows in because Forrest was dickering with the Park for them to buy it.

I enjoyed going to Cahoon because it is so beautiful with some of the largest stands of fir trees I've ever seen, Douglas fir, red firs, big trees. The lush meadow fed by pretty little streams and no fences was a perfect place to summer a small herd. Forrest sometimes ran too many cows and locked horns with the Park people over it. He didn't get along with a lot of people really, but I knew him and I knew his bite. Once in a while I'd have to get a hold of his shirt collar and shake him a little, "Forrest, this is the way it is!" We traded help a lot. Forrest was a fine horseman, a knowledgeable cowman who fattened his cattle ahead of anyone else on his good range soil with early grass. We were always friends. He respected me and I respected him. He was without question the most outspoken man I have ever known. As cowmen, God knows we both miss each other to this day. He's been gone for 12 years.

Camping at Cahoon Meadow among the beautiful stands of fir trees during fall gathering. Photo early years.

AUTHOR'S COLLECTION.

The stand of enormous fir trees is one reason Forrest was able to get the price he wanted when he sold Cahoon. The Park made an offer that Forrest declined because he wanted about twice as much. So their agent pressured Forrest, asking, well who else would be willing to buy it? Forrest told them he already had timber men from Oregon looking at it. The agent countered that logging would not be possible because there was no road; Forrest said he already knew that they log with helicopters. It probably was all hooey, but the Park did prepare a bid and Forrest got his price.

Taking cattle to Cahoon Meadow, we would bring the herd up the South Fork road to a place my dad used to rent just outside the Park before Forrest Homer took it over. It was a place to put the cows for the night, then we'd get up real early and head up the road. At Clough's Cave a narrow foot bridge about five feet wide crosses the river. The cows did not like to walk on a narrow wooden bridge that vibrated under their hooves, high above roaring rapids. The trail to the bridge wasn't wide and if the cows wouldn't go across that bridge we would be backed up there for hours. I've been there helping Forrest with his cattle and seen them back off and fall into the river because we couldn't get them on that bridge.

In my herd, the famous brindle cow would push pass the other cows to get in front and trot right across that bridge, the other cows would see her and they would follow. What a time saver she was. She was belled so we could hear her bell far ahead on the trail because she knew she was going back to the meadow. She could smell that meadow in her head. I kept that old cow until she got so old she couldn't go anymore.

Once across the bridge, we stayed on the north side of the river on the trail used by the old timers until it crossed Cedar Creek. There the Park had built a hiking trail with long switchbacks to make the climb easier, good for hikers but not for cattle because the cows don't under-stand the concept of going way off one direction and when they look up there are cattle coming back the other way, so they will leave the trail and climb straight up. This tears up the switches. Cows have a different idea of climbing hillsides—just go up the most direct route. So at the end of the first switch we connected to the old trail going to Whiskey Log, a large blackened redwood log, burned out like Tharp's Log, deeply burned in a very hot forest fire one time, maybe 1000 years ago. Johnny Britten used to say his dad would hide whiskey in that log so if they were chased out of the mountains by a storm, they would have something there to warm them up. Above the log about 300 or 400 yards was a beautiful camp in the redwoods between the bluff and the river where we camped right in the trail so cows couldn't get by if they tried to go home in the night.

We would push the cattle beyond the campsite to Squirrel Creek and across into a natural pocket to leave them to drink and rest for the night, then we'd go back for a nice dinner. I took two mules, one with hay and the other with our sleeping bags and food for dinner and breakfast. The horses and mules were put on a picket line, fed and watered. Then we settled in for a nice steak or fresh fish dinner, maybe an ear of corn, a couple of drinks to enjoy by the fire. It was so easy this way, not like all the years Forrest took cattle to Cahoon. He drove them all the way up in one day so it would be 6:30 in the evening when we arrived at the meadow and then we had to turn around and ride three hours back out. Horses, dogs and guys would be exhausted. He never wanted to stay all night; maybe he was afraid of bears. I did this exactly once with my cattle the first year I rented the place, and never again.

The next morning we would leave the mules at camp and ride up to gather any stragglers and push them up the mountainside, an hour of steep climbing, before we got to the top (8200 feet elevation). The last mile you climb 2000 feet. Most of the time we didn't have anything to drive because in the night the cows remembered the meadows and they would take their calf and climb slowly up the trail.

We didn't have to ride all the way in to the meadow because the cows went ahead just like they were going home. Before we took the cows up, I would ride in and put salt out. There were no fences, but it was lush grazing with plenty of water so they didn't want to go anywhere else.

There were a lot of lessons to be learned in driving cattle to Cahoon Meadow. I would wean calves in September-October, and the next spring take about 65 pair up there—a pair is a cow and her calf—about 130 head, which was about the size herd allowed there. You soon learned you cannot hurry cows. When they are climbing, going to the high mountains, you have to stop and let them get some air once in a while, if they are slowing or their tongues are out, then you stop and yell to the other guys that we are stopping to let them cool.

My cow dogs were headers that went after any cows that broke off the trail. We would have at least four riders, and take a couple of mules. You travel in little bunches, each one taking a bunch of cows, just let them travel slow, and the last one brings the mules. There was often a cow that got separated from her calf, and she would head back through the bunch, bawling for her calf. You just made room for her to go by, and you might hear her bawling coming back again because she did not find him yet; but once she found her calf, it would be tired and walking with its head down, so everyone had to stop to rest. That was just part of it.

Going along, you holler a lot at the cows, "Heyo Hup! Heyo Hup!" Sounds like a half dog bark, and when the cows are moving along fine, you don't have to do anything, just ride at their pace.

In the fall, when we were gathering the cattle to come out, we'd stay at the old Cahoon Meadow cabin, a simple crudely-built shelter. What is interesting, the underside of the roof sheeting that rests on the rafters is full of signatures of early campers, the oldest one I believe was dated 1886. Many are Spanish names, written in charcoal or carved in the rafters. One was a captain, probably a Spanish officer. I don't know the history of that cabin but I hope it is still there.

Behind the cabin was an old log that hid a mountain of cans that had been thrown there by lazy or thoughtless people for eighty years. It was disgraceful. Just threw the cans out of sight behind the log. My boy, Earl, and I rode in there one day and I went on up to Hockett to look around for any of my cows that might have crawled over there. Earl said, "You know, dad, I'd like to kinda clean up around here." He didn't go into detail, but when I returned, he had dug a hole, deeper than he was tall, and worked all day and it still didn't hold all those cans. We tromped cans, they were rusty and corroded, with no food residue to interest the bears, but it wasn't enough. The next day Earl dug another hole and buried the remaining cans, and cleaned the area so there was no trace of litter. The proper way for can disposal was to burn them, then bag and take them to the trash barrel at the ranger station.

One year we brought the cattle out of Cahoon and the count wasn't right, there was a bunch of cows and quite a few yearlings that weren't there. I took Earl and went back to look for them when snow in the meadow was belly-deep on the horses. We stopped for lunch at the gap where the trail starts to descend. In the meadow, there were no tracks, and no signs of lion attacks. The next spring, Dave Wilson and I found my cows on Bald Mountain where they had spent the winter. The cows had tried to follow us out, but wouldn't cross that wooden bridge at Clough's Cave, so were on the mountain until we went back for them.

If I were in Cahoon Meadow alone for a few days, I would ride up to the Hockett ranger station and take a bottle of whiskey along for the ranger. His name was Hill. One time I visited and he asked me to stick around to have dinner. That meant I rode back in the dark, so dark I couldn't see the ears of my horse, but he was a good horse and would take me home exactly the way we came. Horses have an unbelievable sense of smell and eyesight.

We were talking at dinner and he told me, "You know, I've really got a problem bear." He explained that this problem bear was in Giant Forest and it was tearing things up over there, wasn't afraid of people, and was likely to hurt somebody. He told me the bear had been captured and hauled by helicopter to Cahoon and dumped in the meadow where my cows were. Well, I thought, that was very interesting. Later, I saw the chief ranger—we were good friends—and said, "Bob, I hear you've been dumping things over in my meadow." He kinda grinned. I told him there were only two reasons a guy would do that: one, he's trying to get me to leave the mountains, and you know that ain't going to happen; the other one is, nobody is going to see that bear again. He just laughed, because that is exactly what he was thinking. They were not allowed to shoot a bear, but figured I would to protect my stock. But I didn't. I think the bear beat them back to Giant Forest.

Quinn Cabin

Quinn cabin is the only surviving ranger station from the time Sequoia Park was administered by the U.S. Army. A Park Service registry listed the architect as Harry Britten. Harry was my dad's brother-in-law. It is a log cabin, but the logs are set vertically instead of the usual horizontal stacking. I have a handmade wood bench from that cabin with signatures on the underside of my dad, Earl McKee, his two sisters Maud and Stella, and Harry Britten, dated August 3, 1907. They signed in pencil. The bench was very well made using a foot adz and a saw, hand-hewn boards by someone who knew how to put the braces on each side. There is an interesting story on how I came to have that bench.

Grace Mullenix Alles and her sister Rose Vaughn worked at the lookout stations in the summers–Grace at Atwell's Mill, Rose at Cahoon Rock Lookout just above where I ran my cows. Grace and Rose were great walkers. They often took a couple of mules and headed out on their own, perhaps to Sand Meadow up to Hunter Creek, then over to Wet Meadows. The Quinn cabin was close to Wet Meadows. One day Grace and Rose were trying to reach an old insulator on a pole at the Quinn ranger station. Telephone lines had been strung through there to connect the ranger cabins in 1907 and I remember Lloyd Finch used to walk those lines over the mountains. There was one tough guy, Lloyd. He'd just climb down through rocks and rattlesnakes or climb a tree to check a line. Grace and Rose were searching for something to stand on to reach that insulator with a pole when they found a bench in Quinn cabin to use. The bench tipped over and that is when they noticed the signatures. Grace told me about that bench one evening at a cemetery board meeting that we both served on.

So I made mention to the Chief Ranger Pete Shuft that when new Park superintendents are assigned here, don't let anyone burn that cabin down in Quinn because there is a bench in there I would like to have. Not too long afterward, Roy Lee Davis, who was working at the Park, pulled in at my place and said he had a present for me from Pete. It was the bench.

Mystery Cabin

Not long ago a "mystery" log cabin was located somewhere around Wet Meadow by searchers or hikers, and a story and map in the local paper said no one seemed to know anything about it. Well, I knew about it so I wrote a letter of explanation.

That cabin should not have been a mystery. It was there a long time and I knew the fellow who built it. His name was Sam Brown and I met him. Bob Lovering and my dad knew him. Sam Brown was a trapper, like Shorty Lovelace was over in the Kings. My dad, Bob Lovering, and I took a couple of mules and rode in on a deer hunting trip in the fall of 1944, from Clough's Cave, up and over to Wet Meadow. We bagged two bucks. It was not in the Park then. Bob knew that Brown had little cabins in the area, and we stayed for a couple of nights in one of them, the one pictured in the paper. The roof has fallen in. But we were there more than 60 years ago. I don't know if they were related, but Onis Brown spent one winter with Sam Brown at his Wet Meadow cabin; both Onis and his brother Marcellus visited Sam at his trapping camp in Little Kern during the holidays in 1930. In the late '30s Sam was trapping in the Milk Ranch country above Three Rivers where Onis's son, Lewis, packed supplies to him.

I met trapper Sam Brown a few years later, about 1947. He lived a quarter of a mile from my house at the old cactus patch just north of where the Alles clan lived in Old Three Rivers. He rented the little one-room cabin from Frankie Welch. The reason I went to meet him started with a quail hunting trip with Loren Finch, Sherman Finch, and me up in Crowley Creek which is the North Fork of Sheep Creek (commonly called East Fork because the canyon runs East and West). Jim Kindred owned that 320 acres. Loren and Sherman were on one side of a draw and I was coming down the other and the dry sycamore leaves started rustling and an animal jumped out of the brush right at me. I hollered across at Loren that there's a black animal coming at me, looks like a big Pine Martin. What should I do? He was charging within a couple of yards of my feet. I didn't know if he was rabid or not; I shot. He was so close that the .20 gauge shotgun only made a 3/4 inch hole between his eyes. With tail and everything it was three feet, looked like a giant weasel, only black. Jess Carmichael, the state trapper who lived near the Mountain Oak Inn, could not identify the animal but said that he knew someone who could–Sam Brown. Sam offered to buy the animal for its hide, but I declined. I used to stop by from time to time to visit with him and that's when he told me that he trapped up in the Wet Meadows country and he built that cabin.

Shorty Lovelace Cabin

One pack trip in about 1960 we took our shortcut down to Marion Lake in Kings and I found one of Shorty Lovelace's cabins. He trapped all over the mountains in Kings country, and built about three dozen cabins including one at Doughtery, a large one at Woods Creek Junction below Rae Lakes, and a couple in Crowley Canyon and the one at Marion Lake. It was really hidden off the trail. His cabins were small log shelters, about five feet high by seven feet long, with a sloped shed roof and a stacked rock fire pit with a rock chimney in the corner. He'd stock them for trapping season and ski from one to the other and no one would see him until he came out with his furs in the spring. We were looking around there and I saw some boards among a rock pile. Sure enough they were stretcher boards for skins. The cabin was still standing in 1960.

Shorty Lovelace hung out in this area in the off-season and used to eat lunch at Searcy's on Houston Avenue in Visalia. After he sold the season's pelts, Shorty would have a couple of thousand dollars to live on. When my nephew, Billy Maloy, was making custom saddles at Visalia Saddlery, he used to see Shorty at lunch time. If you wanted to talk to Shorty, you needed to do it early because by noon he'd be slumped over at the bar talking and laughing to himself. Shorty told a story about skiing to his cabin at Marion Lake. He dug through snow to retrieve his stretchers and a hibernating rattlesnake bit his hand. He spent nine days in the cabin, delirious, feverish, but survived using snowpack and hooch. Shorty was born in Three Rivers in 1886 and attended all grades at Sulfur Spring school here. The 1900 U.S. Census for Three Rivers lists his parents Joseph W. and Helen Lovelace and sons Nathan, Walter (Shorty), Clay and Lee.

PACKING BRIDGES

꘎ꘜꘜꘌ꘏

1957

I worked for the Park for five summers, two specifically to pack steel bridges and three after that shoeing horses and mules and trucking stock. With the cattle up in summer pasture, it was possible to work both jobs–twelve straight days for the Park and four off to keep the ranch going.

In 1957, I was hired to pack steel for bridges (Bailey-type bridges built in sections) in the Park, packed in the crew, all the supplies, tools and equipment, then packed it all back out. That's before they used helicopters. I had to keep a logbook for the Park and tallied 2600 miles the first year packing bridges and even more the second year.

Bob Davis was a trail foreman for Sequoia Park in charge of the trail crews. Bob and his brother Joe lived across the road from us in Three Rivers and we grew up together. The Park Service didn't have any mules to pack steel, so Bob was sent to buy stock at Fort Carson, Colorado, where the U.S. Cavalry was decommissioning their mules. The Cavalry was going out of business, it was ten years after WWII, and it was selling horses and mules, thousands of them. Bob bought about 25 head of mules. Each mule was branded on the neck with a GI brand, a number, and its "personnel" record in a book with information about its behavior. These records were worthless; some mules were described as gentle and easy to pack but would kick your gloves out of your back pocket.

I was given my pick of the bunch, and I chose big stout mules to haul bridge materials. Some weren't broke and would try to kick your pants off. Others were terribly spoiled because army packers were just off the street and didn't know much about handling animals, just tied on the guns and ammo boxes and went, no knowledge to train or correct unacceptable mule behavior.

I more or less had to start over with the mules. Several of them I had to blindfold to get the saddle on, but I'd been raised with mules so I didn't have a problem. I packed most of them, learning which ones I wanted, which ones would pack the best, packing the heavy loads. Some were hard to shoe and there were a couple of young mules, big and stout but never had been packed, so I thought, heck, we'd just as well start out and all learn together.

In 1864, William H. Brewer, a member of the State of California Geological Survey party appointed by Josiah D. Whitney to map the entire state, wrote in this in his journal before his party left Visalia to explore the Kings Canyon: "Packing is an intricate art. To put a load of baggage on a mule and make it stay there, and at the same time not hurt the mule, is a great art." How true that is; not only art, but math, physics, and veterinary medicine, I'd say.

I wound up with some really cracker-jack mules and they learned to carry unwieldy materials. I could tell right away that several of them were real gentle and just sweethearts. All the mules were named, of course, after guys we knew in the Park. One mule, named Jerry, had to be blind-folded to pack him the first time. I packed grub on him the first time and oh, he was a bear! He was big, probably four years old and hadn't been handled much. I tied him up first, then had to tie up a hind foot and still couldn't get him packed that way, so had to blindfold him and finally got the pack on and I remember I thought I had it tied down tight. I pulled the blinds off before I turned him loose and that mule tore the corner out of the platform he was tied to and bucked. I mean he bucked every-thing off. These things happened in breaking mules, but Jerry turned out to be a really good mule.

You watched how the mule went down the trail–some traveled this way–rocking front to rear–and some traveled rocking side to side, and there's a place for that. For instance, I had a mule I named Hercules, after one of the Park employees, Herky Alcott. Hercules, famous Herky, walked down the trail and rocked front to back like his ears flopped forward and back, and he became the "generator" mule. We built a flat-top platform–a pack tree with the forks cut off and braces bolted to the saddle bars–with a grid of drilled holes so we could center the load. We always packed a Homelite generator for the air compressor and jack-hammer. The old timers said never put a rock on the side of a mule to balance the load. Depending on how the mule traveled, it seemed like the pack would want to slip to one side or another because all 140 pounds–the generator–was in one little pile. So we'd move that generator around on Herky to get it set right in the middle, and by golly we finally got it centered so Herky could pack that thing all day because he never swayed side to side. He packed the generator on all the bridge jobs in 1957 and 1958. Herky was also known for his genius at opening gates–he couldn't be left in a corral anywhere without wiring the gates shut because he could figure out how to undo a latch and let all the mules out, which he did many times.

We also packed wheelbarrows on the platform saddle. Loads packed on mules that rocked side to side would start to swing and slip, so on those mules I'd pack steel. We built wood boxes, cut concave to fit around the mule so it wouldn't rib the mule, with a lip on the outside on which to tie the steel.

A lot of packers liked the aluminum boxes used for foodstuffs. There's a pressure point right in the middle because the aluminum box is square and it won't give. They finally improved these by making them concave and these kind of boxes we used for all kinds of things–grub, packed sand, packed water.

If I was going out by myself, I'd take five or six mules, five is about the best. But when I was packing a lot of steel, I got a swamper (helper) and used ten mules. Troy Hall and Jim Harvey were two of my swampers. You can haul a lot of material with ten mules. You can't just hang 100 pounds on each side of a mule–it is too much dead weight so you shoot for 80 pounds. That's why I picked the big stout mules.

There was one big mule I broke to haul the decking timber. His name was Fritz, off his fat he'd weigh 1350 pounds, a real power house. The decking timber for the bridges was 4x12s x 8 feet long, and the boards extended out past his head. I tied a box hitch on there and lowered the front so he could see out and raise his head to turn. Fritz had to be blindfolded the first time I put the boards on him and when I turned him loose he ran across the trail and into the bank because he didn't know how to turn. He ran away a couple of times that day because he was afraid of the planks. But as I said before, mules are smart and can figure things out. Fritz thought that over, and he turned out to be one of the finest mules at judging his pack clearance, like at Bishop Pass where the switchback trail is chopped right out of the bluff. If one of his boards just touched anything, he would stop, back up, move his body over and go forward. He was a great mule, he packed an 80 pound plank and a 4x4 rail, or two 50 or 60 pound boards–over 100 pounds on each side, and hardly grunt all day. I packed a lot of material on Fritz in the next two years.

People don't think about a mule's trail sense when they are going on a pack trip, but the mules have to know something. You get pretty proud of your mules, you know, you go down the trail and even though they are not tied together they stay in line. I'd put the swamper in front, and I was in the back and I used a slingshot–pretty good with that. I'd find little round rocks from the river bottom and if a mule got out of line, tried to run out and roll, I'd yell his name just as I popped him on his rear end. It wasn't long until you yelled at one like that and he'd flop his ears a couple of times and get back in line and you could go anywhere with them.

The first bridge we worked on was back in from Hospital Rock, across the river on the old trail that went up to Paradise Peak and up toward Silver City. There was not a lot of material to pack there, some steel across the river. It was late spring and Lon Maxon was the boss of the bridge crew. But on this first bridge, all the trail crew foremen were supposed to work together. Well, they were all trail bosses so no one wanted to take orders from anyone. It was really funny. There was Skinny Kirk from Kern River; Ben Loverin from the Middle Fork of the Kings; Thad Morehead from Cliff Creek; Duck Brooks from the Middle Fork of the Kaweah; and Marcellus Brown who was running the trail crew at that time on the High Sierra Trail out of Giant Forest toward Kaweah Gap.

We packed cement, because where the trail crew couldn't get up the hill they had to pour cement footings. They needed sand to mix it, so I'd pack it on four of the gentlest mules. First, I'd put the manty across the mule's body, then the saddle and boxes, and lead the mule right down into the sand in a creek bottom, get a guy on each side counting shovels, and if you missed, the sand would just roll off. It wouldn't get under the saddle, and you didn't have to be an expert–if you missed a shovel here, just throw another one and the sand wouldn't get in the saddle blankets. We could also pack water in those aluminum boxes for a short distance, just drape a little canvas over the top but no more than 12 gallons a side, because then it's 100 pounds, dead weight. If the water leaked out the corners we just duct taped it. Then the water could be packed up the hillside and save someone walking to the creek and carrying small buckets by hand. They made a lot of cement that way.

I packed seven of those bridges: Hospital Rock to Paradise; Lower Buck Canyon; Giant Forest to Lone Pine Creek; Bishop Pass to Dusy Basin; Middle Fork of the Kaweah to River Valley; two from South Lake over Bishop Pass to Dusy Basin ('57) and LaConte Canyon ('58); and Mineral King to the Kern River over Franklin Pass.

The loads had to be weighed correctly to be the same on each side. All the steel had to be weighed, even if it looked the same size, there would be differences. All that had to be checked and the ends of the steel had to be wrapped in case one mule ran into another, bare steel would cut like a butcher knife. We got a pickup load of old army blankets and rags cut into pieces to wrap and wire the ends. The mules were loose because you can't keep the mules tied together with stuff sticking out the front. And if they are tied together, they'll want to drink somewhere and get their head down and if they ever get that lead over the steel, get too close to the next mule, you'll have a bloody mess.

The steel would be delivered to wherever we were packing from, or sometimes I would haul it there myself. I went home every other week to tend to the cattle ranch and they would send me down in the truck with a helper to load the order of steel and haul it up.

The third bridge I packed was from Giant Forest to Lone Pine Creek, between Bear Paw and Hamilton Lake. Bear Paw Meadow has tent cabins for hikers who come in from Crescent Meadow to stay overnight and go on to Hamilton Lake. It is a beautiful place with views to Hamilton Lake, Mt. Stuart and Eagle Scout and the Kaweah Peaks. This bridge was mainly for the hikers' convenience.

Lon Maxon was the trail boss on this one. There was a natural place up stream to ford the river, bedrock which is slick and the horses could lose their footing and fall. But in my opinion it should have been blasted and roughed up to make a good ford out of it. During high water it was dangerous and hikers were afraid of it, so Fred Walker who was head of trails then in 1957 decided a bridge should be built across the gorge further down.

The backcountry above timberline where trail crews worked a 700-mile network of high Sierra trails connecting Kings, Kaweah, and Kern River canyons. As soon as snow in the passes melted, crews like Ben Loverin's packed in to work all summer clearing avalanche debris and improving the trails. Photo c. 1930.

AUTHOR'S COLLECTION.

I packed Lon into Lower Lone Pine Creek. It is a little hell's canyon with no place to camp, but they pitched a camp below the crossing and started blasting a trail down into the gorge. The trail was built to the bridge site, and I started packing the steel and cable in from Giant Forest. Jim Harvey, a big old kid, swamped for me and became a good packer. He worked for 35 summer seasons in the Park. My swampers had to be Park employees or be approved by the Park administration. Lon put a highline across the gorge and hung the bridge from it. The bridge was 48 feet long and 153 feet above the river. Spooky. I had to pack a lot of cable. We'd take the required length of cable–several had to be real long ones that spanned the canyon–start rolling the coils, put a half-roll on one side of the mule and another same-sized coil on the other side, ideally 80 pounds on each side, then string it back to the next mule and do that same thing for all the mules. These mules would be tied together. You'd have to figure out the size of the coils, it would pack very close, so the packs seldom turned.

The highline was anchored and the bridge was hung off of it, then cross plank sections were built and pulled out and across as another section was added, and when the bridge was complete it was very tight and I had to "christen" it–ride my horse across it. I had the shakes a bit, but I had watched them building the bridge and tramping around on it and knew it was strong. I got on my horse and rode him across. You had to have a horse like I had that wasn't afraid of things like that, but even then he put both ears out flat when he looked down–a long 150 feet to the bottom. So I rode over and back and then hitched up a couple of mules just to satisfy the requirement that a pack string had to be led across the new bridge. I told Lon I was never going to lead the whole string across his new bridge because I could simply cross the creek just a short ways up stream. That bridge lasted exactly one year; an avalanche took it out. I have pictures of the bridge in the bottom of the gorge, east of Bear Paw camp.

Another bridge, that might still be there, I packed out of Mineral King to Big Arroyo and I'll tell about it in the Mineral King chapter.

Traveling Loose

In the early days, we all traveled loose, the mules were not tied together. Then Park regulations said a packer could take five mules but had to tie them together, and it got to be that everybody had to tie their mules together; then a packer was required to spot somebody. The rangers were against traveling loose because most of them were naturalists, not horse people, and could barely get on their horse, much less handle a pack string. Unless it was an old-school ranger, then they would not have a problem but old-school rangers didn't write the regulations. When I was packing for the Park, I told the suprintendent that mules packing steel cannot be tied together because if they run into each other the steel would slice them open, and I received permission to pack loose with steel.

Jim Kindred quit packing because of the Park regulation to keep mules tied together. He would not tie his mules together because a mule is much safer loose, and if you keep them in line and keep them together you wouldn't even know they were not tied together. Bureaucratic regulations. Jim was caught loose and was given a ticket. He appeared before the judge and told him, "I've never tied my mules together, and I'm old school, working in rough country trying not to kill my mules." Jim was fined $200 and he told the judge, "You've just wrote me off. I will no longer pack in these mountains." Jim did not pack again, he quit right then.

Being tied together is really not healthy for the mules; if one mule hurried around a switchback, and the next one is just doggin' along looking for grass to nibble on, he wouldn't make it around the turn, then he'd be yanked across, then he'd pull the next mule across and it would tear up the trail. Mules tied together are harder on trails than mules going loose because a loose mule can pick his own way. If you stop for water when they are all tied together, you have to ride out in the stream so all the mules can drink at once.

Trail Stories Packing Bridges

One of the stories I will never forget was on that first year going to Lower Buck Canyon. A granite boulder the size of a railroad car stood above the trail since the glaciers melted, sort of a landmark. It was raining that day when I went by that rock with my mules loaded with steel, wrenches, cables, compressors and jack hammers, headed for Buck Canyon. When I got to the job, we unloaded the mules, had lunch, and I rode back with the empty string about an hour and a half later. Came to that rock, but the rock was not there. It had tumbled on the trail, flattened two pine trees and rolled down into the canyon. No telling how many trees it crushed going down. I just suppose it might have been the vibrations of the mules walking along there just an hour earlier. Or maybe God just decided to turn that one loose. It was spooky.

The mules sensed it too. For the duration of the job when they got to where that boulder used to be they would snort and go around below that hole. Another time, I was packing a bridge to Lone Pine Creek and just past the bluffs a rattlesnake buzzed. Mules know that sound and they broke out of line, but with a swamper in back we got them back on the trail. I got off and it took some time but I killed the snake. On all the trips afterwards the mules would not walk where the snake was killed.

The same was true when a mule was hit by yellow jackets; he'd detour below the trail to avoid the place he was stung.

My folks always talked about Hamilton Lake, which is very close to that bridge suspended 150 feet above Lone Pine Creek. Just a few miles from Lone Pine Creek was an ice cave. My dad said they would stay at River Valley and hike up through the rocks to Hamilton Lake and fish for big rainbow trout. The catch was put in the ice cave until they were ready to pack out.

About 1955 or so we were having a mountain oyster feed at Bob Lovering's place on South Fork. Ord Loverin was there and started talking about Hamilton Lake. He was quite a storyteller and he and Bob Lovering were spiking each other's drinks all evening and they got a little louder and the stories got a little longer. Forrest Homer had invited a friend from Visalia who got pretty caught up in Ord's stories. Ord told about chasing lions with Jay Bruce, beating them off him with a rock, packing lions on horses and other tall tales and fish stories. Ord described the great big fish in Hamilton Lake; he said if those two-foot long trout would swim up to your hook, you'd move it "cause you didn't want to catch those little ones!" He got so tired from landing so many big fish, he said, he decided to put two hooks on the line so he'd catch two at a time and they'd fight each other until they gave out and be easier to land. After a bit, the flatlander guest finally said, "Gosh, fish like that, they must have fought like crazy!" And Ord said, "Fight, man! Why I've seen them jump right out on the bank and whip a coyote!"

Getting back to the trail stories, this one happened packing bridges, the third one in 1958 over Bishop Pass out of South Lake on the Bishop side. That is a spectacular pass and the trail is just chopped out of the bluff and as you're climbing up you can look right down off your stirrup and see the tops of all your loads coming up the mountain face of that bluff. You want to be sure your mules are broke when you go up there. Mine were. One sorrel mule named Corky, named for Corky Johnson a Park employee, was gentle and a character. I always packed short steel on him that didn't stick out past his head. The mules went loose and I was behind them to keep them in line with a pop from my slingshot.

We were on the top of Bishop Pass, about 11,000 feet, loaded with steel and there were some people at a little lake off to the left. It was rolling mountainside down to the lake and I could see a lady standing near the shore. The mules were walking like a bunch of schoolboys right down the trail when Corky suddenly cut out and ran straight toward the lady. She started hollering and running, ran into the water and jumped on a rock, and Corky chased after her along the bank. I thought what the heck is going on and rode over to cut him off, whipped his ass, and put him back on the trail. When I rode by, I saw what had set Corky off–the lady was carrying a great big Siamese cat! Corky had spotted that cat and was trying to see what the heck it was. Scared the poor woman to death. I apologized and told her that the mule wasn't after her, mules are just curious and they don't see many Siamese cats up here in the backcountry.

Nineteen fifty-eight was a heavy snow year that triggered avalanches through the backcountry. That year, Lon Maxon, Troy Hall, and I dead-headed the stock from Cedar Grove over Granite Pass down the Simpson and up the Middle Fork of the Kings headed to Grouse Meadow. Up toward Devil's Washbowl we encountered a snowfield that stretched to the river and completely buried our trail. We could see a hole out in the middle which told us that there was a creek bed below so we couldn't cross above or below that hole without a mule falling through.

We made a mule line a safe distance away in the snow, then probed around the hole with shovels to make sure it wouldn't cave. We carried plenty of dynamite so we set a charge and blew out one side. The snow was twenty feet deep to the creek bed. We shoveled a trail down to the creek bed and up the other side. Then we had to get the mules through. They were loose, we made them stay in line and led them down into the snow-walled passage. One old Jerry mule got down to the bottom and got scared in the big snow tunnel, ran into the hole and brayed and ran out the other side.

We continued up to Grouse Meadow and on the way there was a snow bridge across the Middle Fork of the Kings—an avalanche had completely filled the river canyon and made a snow bridge so huge you could have driven a train across.

Dudley Boothe operated the Rainbow Pack Station at South Lake and he packed sand up the north side of Bishop to put on the trail so we could get over the Pass and down the other side.

One day, packing over Dusy Basin, I was leading the generator mule, Herky, and got into a terrible lightning storm. All the mules could go loose except the generator mule because of the cost of the equipment he was packing. I was leading the generator mule and lightning hit a rock in front of me, always seemed like a hundred yards, but could have been a quarter of a mile away, but it threw dirt and brimstone everywhere and your hair would wiggle around. I got off my horse in a hurry, untied that mule and tried to get away from that steel. We had loads of steel and the dammed mules stuck tight to us, asses turned to the wind. It was a blinding blizzard to the point I couldn't see Troy Hall who was riding at the back end of the string that day. I searched back up the trail and thought maybe the lightning had killed him. When I found him, his eyes were as big as saucers and he said, "By Dog!"–he always said "By Dog"–"You know that dammed lightning just knocked my hat off!" I told him if lightning had knocked his hat off he would have been fried. But he stuck with his story until the day he died.

Pack train in the high country, resting the animals after a steep climb over Glenn Pass. Photo c. 1920.

AUTHOR'S COLLECTION.

We regrouped in a hurry and high-tailed the mules to a lower elevation. We were packing a bridge down there in LeConte Canyon so we camped at Little Pete Meadow on the Middle Fork near Muir Pass.

I packed a lot of dynamite and it was an unwritten law if you are packing caps, and you get in a lightning storm, you get those caps out of the packs and take them off the trail and hide them under a rock or something far enough away it wouldn't hurt anybody if they were set off by static electricity. You can go back for the caps later. On one bridge job I was going out to Bear Paw and a terrible lightning storm set fire to the trail right behind me, and I had several mule loads of dynamite and all these caps. I hid them under a log away from the trail. Another time in River Valley, I watched the lightning hit below me on the mountain. That wasn't a good feeling, you're up higher and the lightning is hitting below you, and your hair starts pulling and the hair on your hands stick up.

On the rocky trail to Mt. Whitney for a nice lunch on top of the United States. My dad's stock were mountain-trained, quiet-spirited, and well-shod to negotiate miles of rough trails such as this one. Photo c. 1920.
AUTHOR'S COLLECTION.

One fall we had come over Pinchot Pass on the way to Bench Lake, and it was snowing, cold, just sleet blowing in your face. It was above timberline and I ran onto some back packers sitting around a nice fire on a rock. The little dry white pine roots, full of pitch, make a hot fire. I had a pack turn–it was slipping–so I had to catch the mule to straighten the pack. I was riding Van, a horse that would stand with the reins down. I always rode with a split rein and my horses were trained to stand when I dropped the rein, so I could leave Van like he was tied up. I caught the mule and tied him to a rock to adjust the pack and when I got done I looked around and Van was gone. The guys were up there laughing. Van had quietly backed up that hill to stand near them, steam rolling off, enjoying the fire. Van was a terrific mountain horse that had been in the backcountry enough to know how good it felt to put your backside to the campfire on those cold nights.

I've had a lot of experiences packing and shoeing ornery mules. I shod mules and horses for the Park in 1960, '61 and '62. One old army mule was named Alma, after Alma Walker. To shoe her front foot, I had to tie it up and put a rope on the hind foot on the same side and tie it back to a pine tree. It wasn't tied tight, just so she knew it was anchored to something because if you were shoeing her front foot, she'd shift her weight over on the other side and reach up with the hind foot and knock your hat off. If you weren't watching she'd kick your brains out with a hind foot. She was something. Another Army mule named Charlie was supposed to have been real gentle and easy to pack and ride, but of course none of that was true. He was a mean one and a kicker. I had to tie up his foot to wash his back.

When I packed two bridges over Bishop Pass I stayed with Dudley Boothe who owned the Rainbow Pack Station in South Lake. Dud and his wife Alice and their three kids were the finest people in the world. Dudley's father, Ray Boothe, was the ranger in charge of construction of the John Muir Trail in 1915. Dudley's son, John, married Jill Kinmont, the Olympic skier who was paralyzed in a tragic accident while training in 1955. Her story was made into the movie *The Other Side of the Mountain*. Jill just passed away not long ago at the age of 75.

I had run into Ben Loverin along the trail somewhere and he told me he had one sore-footed mule that his packer couldn't shoe because he didn't know you-know-what. Ben said a Park shoer had tried to help the guy shoe two of his mules and put the shoes on so crooked that when the mules walked down the trail their tracks went crosswise.

So Ben wanted to send one of his crew over with the two problem mules for me to shoe at Dudley's place, because his guy couldn't do it. From his description I knew one was an army mule that I had packed and she was real gentle. The other one was Old Charlie, named after Charlie Hand, a mechanic up there in the Park at that time. I knew Old Charlie and he was a little difficult.

Ben's packer brought the two mules over and the Boothes invited him to stay for dinner. The guy said he used to be a bull rider and had been hooked or horned in the head. He had no manners at all, and his uncouth behavior seemed to prove out his story about a head injury. When we finished dinner he reached over, got a napkin and blew his nose on it, rolled it up, and put it in his plate. I yanked him out of his chair by the arm, hauled him outside and told him if you ever do that again I'm going to whip your ass. Where were you raised, in a damned barn?

I took old Charlie first to shoe because he looked like he'd kick; I knew he kicked when I had packed him before. I had to cross tie him, tie his foot under to one shoulder and put a rope on that one and pull out so I could shoe it, otherwise he would cow-kick you. Mules are always watching and aim their kicks. He was a smart son-of-a-gun, but I got his shoes on.

The other one they said was such a battle, I put a rope on a hind foot, stood out behind her and pulled her foot out in back and she just stood there with that foot out. I walked down the rope to the foot. I said to Ben's packer, did you ever try this? There was nothing wrong with that mule. They had been so afraid of her they tied her down. I shod her all the way around without ropes. I just put a rope around the foot, laid it on my knee and shod her. As soon as I shod those two "impossible" mules, we sent them back to Ben.

Shoeing Stock and Driving Truck

After I packed bridges, I drove truck and shoed stock for the Park for three seasons. I hauled stock to Cedar Grove or Mineral King many times, and picked up rangers and stock to bring back to headquarters, whatever Bob Davis, head of trails, needed. I drove truck anywhere they wanted.

Bob sent me with a load of mules to Florence Lake early one season. The backcountry hadn't opened up yet, but a trail crew with Thad Morehead was going in.

I took the Park's old Ford truck, really ran good, but the racks on the bed were made wrong. Someone used the minimum inside width measurement for the outside allowable width so it wasn't the full eight feet and the tails of those long mules got skinned. We stacked them, head to tail crosswise, and loaded the gentlest one last because he had to be pushed around the corner to get him to fit. I hauled eight mules.

Frank McDonald, a great little old guy from Woodlake, followed in the pickup. Frank packed summers for the Park, and ran a cobbler shop in Woodlake for years. He was an old cowboy from Oklahoma, bow-legged, used to ride broncs when he was young.

We stopped at Shaver Lake on Hwy. 168 to fill the truck and the guy asked where we were going. I told him we were headed to Florence Lake today. He shook his head, uh-uh, don't think so because the road hasn't been plowed over Kaiser Pass yet. Well it was getting late, I was clear up at Shaver and had to get those mules out of that truck, their asses all peeled. We found an old timer, an old packer who had known Ord Loverin and my dad in the old days and he put us all up for the night.

I got on the phone to Bob: "You did a lot of reconnaissance on this, didn't you, Bob? No? Well, we can't get in if the road isn't plowed." We loaded up the next morning and hauled the mules back to Ash Mountain.

Another Bob Davis story, we took a truckload of mules to Wishon. Bob was following in a pickup pulling a horse trailer and two horses. Bob knew a short cut. Well, it looked like a cutoff on the map and Bob might have thought he'd been on that road, but I don't think he had because he would have never gone that way a second time. The road was twisting and narrow with no way to turn around. If we met anyone, one of us would have to back up. One inside turn was so narrow I had to pull up, back up, to jockey the wheels over far enough to make it around. As it turned out, we didn't meet a soul and made it.

It was about 1957 when a lightning strike caused a fire between Paradise Peak and Redwood Meadow. (Redwood Meadow was purchased and donated to the national park by Steven Mather.) I was packing a bridge near Moro Creek, so I was sent with a truckload of mules to Mineral King to pack supplies to the fire line. About 200 prisoner trustees had been trailed to the fire from Atwell's Mill to fight fire. Frank McDonald came along and we left about quitting time from Ash Mountain.

We arrived in Mineral King about 9 o'clock at night, packed the stock and took the trail over Timber Gap, down Cliff Creek to Redwood Meadow. At breaking light that morning we could see smoke coming up the canyon. At Redwood Meadow there was a real nice redwood cabin and storage shed built by Clarence Fry and his crew back in the day when redwoods could be cut for Park use. The meadow was fenced for stock. There were K-rations stored in the cabin, so, as instructed, we packed up the mules with rations, all the shovels and rakes that would fit, and headed for the fire line. The mules were tired; we'd been on the trail all night.

We had to take a down-hill, round-about way to get past the burn, trying to keep the winds at our back so we wouldn't have to face the smoke. We got in a jam when the winds changed and fire was burning towards us. There were some big logs the mules had to jump, one mule sat back, a couple of lead ropes broke and we had a wreck, but finally got them through there, got up to the fire line and those mules were kicking because the duff was burning the hair off their fetlocks, didn't burn the flesh, just made a sssssss sound.

Before helicopters, the Park had some fixed-wing planes. Bob White was a crackerjack pilot and he was parachuting bundles of tools to the fire fighters. Of course, the 'chutes caught in the high branches so they had to cut down the trees to get the tools which wound up smashed under the falling limbs. Bob also tried to do water drops on the fire from the fixed wing–Bob would kick 5-gallon square cans of water out the door without a parachute, just shove them out with his foot. The cans of water were supposed to hit and burst open to help squelch the fire. I told him to stop dropping those cans because who was going to tell my mules to duck? Bob would message us with toilet paper–he could make a pinpoint drop right in front of us. He would put a note with our instructions–to go pick up more supplies, for example–on the end of a roll of toilet paper and let it stream down, he could get that TP to drop right in front of us.

We got back to the cabin late, turned the mules and horses out in the meadow, went inside and made a fire only to find there was no food. We'd packed it all out. The cupboards were empty except for one little package of pearl barley. There was nothing else to put with it so we cooked a big dinner of barley soup. The next morning we found a little cupboard on the backside of the cabin that held some K-rations, so we had breakfast, then called in for a food supply which Bob White dropped in the meadow that day.

We took the mules back to the fire line and packed 5-gallon cans of water all day for the crew to fill their canteens. We worked a couple of more days and then rode out to Mineral King and hauled it all home. From time to time I'd see old Frank McDonald–he'd shake his head a little as he talked–and he'd ask, "Say, Earl, have you had any pearl barley lately?"

MEN OF THE BACK COUNTRY

✺✺✺✺

APAs (American Pack Animals)

This is from a cassette recording of a Pioneer Night dinner, early 1960s. The emcee Richard Comb invited Ord Loverin to talk about the old days. After some perfunctory questions, Richard said, "Well, Ord, would you like to lie a little bit now, tell a tall story?" So Ord told the following:

"I know, I guess, did you read that in the *Republican*? That story about the pack train out of Mineral King in 1903? Well, we started with 60–12 packers, 60 mules, one cook and we left Mineral King and I think it was the 12th of May, 12th or 14th, right in the middle of May and we camped with that outfit right in Farewell Gap in about six or eight feet of snow that night. Couldn't get over. Next day we led the packs down on the other side, took the mules up the hill and got them down, and got to William Flat less than a mile the next day. That was 1903. We had 365 people in the party when they came in. And that's the year we chain harnessed them in Mineral King. You know what a chain harness is? Well, they all got to sleep in their sleeping bags in the flat there, all over the place, the ladies were over here and the gents were over on the other side, you get a bunch of chain harnesses and you start on down there with bells and chain harness and hollering, 'whoa! whoa!' Well, they all jumped up, didn't have flashlights, so didn't know where their beds are and neither do we! [laughs] There's no wood in Mineral King, so they built what fire they could, set up and went around there and looked for their beds, and even if one comes across his bed, he wouldn't know it, so we just had an awful time all night long. All night long. Ah, well, that's about how some of them go."

Mr. Comb: "1903?"

Ord: "Long time ago. Sixty years ago! Very few of them alive today."

Mr. Comb: "What kind of party was it?"

Ord: "Sierra Club. Old Bill Colby, Warren. . ."

Mr. Comb: "Do they still discard things as they went along, leave fishing poles?"

Ord: "Oh, yeah. They lost this, that and the other, you know. One of them didn't get this, one of them didn't get that this morning, and they–but as a rule they were pretty good."

Mr. Comb: "How long was the party out?"

Ord: "30 days."

Mr. Comb: "And there were 365 of them?"

Ord: "Yup."

My dad had a name for hikers–APAs, American Pack Animals–everybody in the mountains knew what an APA was. They were members of the Soharra club–Sierra Club–pardon the expression, but my dad had no love for them. You can see why. They were the biggest detriment to the mountains in those early days because they would walk and ride en masse, over 100 people on back country outings, looked like ants coming down the trail; they'd find a beautiful spot to camp where they discarded trash or items too heavy or unnecessary to carry any further. The Club's second annual outing in 1902 had 200 people, several tons of baggage including ping-pong games, gramophone, not to mention steel ranges and 15,000 pounds of food, all packed on mules. Sierra Club groups of over 100 people on horseback left a trail that was hard to miss. I would see groups of 100 crawling all over when I was packing bridges in the Bishop Pass country. They finally got smart and said what you pack in, you pack out. My dad had done that from the beginning. The APAs had, still have, an aversion to horses in the high country and would often show their dislike by purposely leaving the gates open on the drift fences. Large meadows like Simpson and on the Kern River had drift fences across the valleys so at night the horses could only graze so far. We had to sleep by the gates because APAs would come through at any time of night or day and let our stock out. The APAs roughed it in the high country, but they weren't as tough as they wished they were. On the other hand, our party would be sitting in comfortable folding chairs, cooking steaks, smelling the aroma of home cooking and fresh coffee; this seemed to engender resentment in the APAs toward these horse people. Even now they continue to work to get the horses off the high country trails.

Ray Banks of Visalia organized a meeting of people interested in the use of riding and packing livestock in the Sierra, to form an association of stock users. We met at the California Division of Forestry (CDF) Headquarters on Lovers Lane in Visalia. I suggested the name, High Sierra Stock Users Association, and on a majority vote it was so named, its purpose was to work with the Park on trail repair, fix drift fences, or any improvement project to help the government to maintain the Park. The Association has been renamed Backcountry Horsemen but is still the voice of reason to allow pack trips to the high country, a great benefit to folks like Mr. W. P. Fuller, Jr., for example, who rode with us on 32 annual trips, but did not hike because of the effects of polio. Ray Banks was the CDF unit commander at the time. He was also a great pilot and flight instructor, tragically killed in a plane crash trying to teach someone to fly.

In 1915, Mark Daniels, General Superintendent and Landscape Engineer of National Parks wrote of the wonders of Sequoia National Park: beauty to rival the Grand Canyon, the deepest canyons in the world, highest point in the United States and oldest and greatest living things on earth. The stunning Sierra was and is only accessible via pack trips. For this reason Daniels advocated the building of a system of lodging facilities and connecting roads for the public to visit this wonder of the natural world. His idea was to expand the park to include the Kings River and Kern Canyon ". . . across which a magnificent circuit of mountain inns covering the entire area, a chain of trails and series of roads that would make available to the tourists and public the finest stretch of mountains . . . ." The Park, in fact, was expanded to include Kings and Kern. Such a system to accommodate visitors was built across the Alps. Daniels suggested, why not here?

Trail Builders

My dad started packing to the backcountry when he was twenty years old. My dad always laughed that when he'd tell Onis Brown about a new place he'd discovered, Onis had already been there and knew a short cut! But my dad marked a trail on the east side where Onis hadn't been yet from the Big Arroyo to a point just short of the Kern-Kaweah chute, looking for a way to get across the Great Western Divide. Building a trail across the Divide would shorten the trail between Giant Forest and Mt. Whitney.

Ernest McKee and Onis Brown (on the buckskin horse) guided the Hutchison party over Colby Pass. They built trail up treacherous slopes and finally up a 1000-foot long chute to the pass. They crossed the pass on August 5, 1920. Photo 1920.

AUTHOR'S COLLECTION.

William Colby had observed what looked to be a saddle at the head of Cloud Canyon east of Whaleback, between Milestone and Triple Divide Peak and speculated that it might be possible to cross the Divide there. In August 1920 my dad's brother, Ernest McKee, and Onis Brown packed the J. S. Hutchinson party to find that pass. (Hutchinson wrote about this trip in the January, 1921 *Sierra Club Bulletin.*) A party of 13 people, 4 horses, 9 mules left Giant Forest, over J. O. Pass into Roaring River and over to the head of Cloud Canyon, building trail over treacherous, rocky steep slopes, and through vast talus mazes. Onis was asked if he could get the animals through—his classic reply was, "Ain't nothin' holdin' me back is there?" They built zigzag stairway trail up a forty-degree slope, had to use ropes on the animals to keep them from going over backwards or off into space. It is a great story about getting around an unnamed lake (since named Colby Lake) and building trail to get to the northeast side of Whaleback and finally clearing trail up 1000 feet in a 300-foot wide chute to the pass—the chute narrowed between steep walls, it was loose granite, gravel, sand, rocks, and boulders. The horses were brought up as the trail was built in 25, 50, and 100-foot segments. Tons and tons of rock was slid or rolled; they joked that the topographical maps would have to be redrawn after they moved so much mountain.

A monument was built at the top of the now-named Colby Pass:

"August 5, 1920. This pass was crossed from the Roaring River side, today, by a party of thirteen persons with thirteen animals (four saddle animals and nine pack animals). The pack trail was in charge of Ernest E. McKee of Badger and Onis I. Brown of Lemon Cove. There was no trail nor any indications of the previous passage of animals over the pass, except for the traces of a sheep trail. A trail was worked out by the packers and some members of the party in about eight hours on August 4 and 5. The passage was made without accident to any animals. The members of the party were: Mr. and Mrs. Duncan McDuffie, Berkeley, Cal.; Mr. and Mrs. Arthur Elston, Berkeley, Cal.; Mrs. Wm. Knowles, Oakland, Cal.; Mr. James Hutchinson, Berkeley, Cal.; Col. W. H. Williams, Oakland, Cal.; Mr. Chas. Noble, Berkeley, Cal.; Mr. Chas. Noble, Jr., Berkeley, Cal.; Mr. Fred Torrey, Berkeley, Cal.; Mr. Vernon Kellogg, Stanford University."

Ernest McKee tied into his brother Earl's marked trail on the east side of Colby and the party went down through the rough Kern-Kaweah Pass, to Junction Meadow, and on to the northwestern end of Big Arroyo as close as possible to the base of Black Kaweah. Black Kaweah, 13,752 feet elevation, had never been climbed, a foreboding, cracked, scarred, broken, ragged, black peak. Onis Brown, Duncan McDuffie, and J. S. Hutchinson made the difficult ascent, built a monument with a camera tripod and a white flag, and left this note in a tobacco can on the top:

"August 11, 1920: Left camp one mile below Nine Lake Basin at 5:40 a.m. Attempted to climb along N.W. ridge but impassable notches prevented. Then dropped down about 400 feet into the southern cirque and ascended the chimney which reaches the northwest ridge 100 feet N.W. of the summit. Arrived at summit at 1:45 p.m. – Duncan McDuffie, Berkeley, Cal.; Onis Imus Brown, Lemon Cove, Cal.; J. S. Hutchinson, Berkeley, Cal."

Onis Brown and others going up the Kern-Kaweah chute which connects to the trail my dad, Earl Sr. marked on the east side. With a mag-
nifying glass you can see Onis' light-colored horse below a large tree in
the notch. Photo 1920.

AUTHOR'S COLLECTION.

Using the Colby Pass route cut two days of trail time to Mt. Whitney. Another trail built to make a more direct route to the east was the High Sierra Trail from Giant Forest. I packed that trail many times.

On one of the Fuller trips in the 1950s, Leroy Maloy was one of the packers. From camp at Colby Lake they made it over Colby Pass to Kern Kaweah where they set up camp. In putting up the bedrooms, it was discovered that one bedroll was missing. It belonged to Jim O'Brien, partner in the paint company. He had nowhere to sleep. It was apparent that his bedroll didn't get packed; Leroy said he was the guy responsible, so he'd take a horse and mule and go back to find O'Brien's bed. Jim didn't want Leroy to go alone, so he rode with him up through Colby Pass and down to their previous camp at Colby Lake where they found the bedroll behind a rock. When they rode back through Colby Pass at midnight, a bright full moon illuminated the peaks, silent and beautiful, so they stopped for a drink from Jim's bottle of Old Forrester–his favorite, then had a few more as they relaxed in the moonlight near the top of the world. It was after 2 a.m. when they returned to camp and Mr. Fuller was waiting up to have another nightcap together.

Jim Livingston and John Grunigen built sections of the High Sierra Trail and the trail up to Kaweah Gap. For several summers starting in 1928, the two men directed work on the High Sierra Trail from Crescent Meadow in Giant Forest that crosses the 7-Mile Hill Trail, around the bluffs to Bear Paw Meadow and eventually to Kaweah Gap.

Another crew worked from the east from Mt. Whitney toward the Great Western Divide. In February 1933, John Grunigen was notified that he was beyond the age limit for trail foreman and was being replaced by a civil servant. They retired someone who knew what they were doing just so they could hire some young guy that'd get somebody killed while he was trying to learn the ropes.

Jim told some great stories about how they cut trails in steep granite cliffs. He and John Grunigen blasted the trail around the bluffs to Bear Paw Meadow. Jim showed me photos of him suspended on ropes over the bluffs using a single-jackhammer. It was the hand-crank kind that rattled into the rock, a real slow process drilling holes in the wall to set charges to blow out the trail. They used dynamite by the ton. Once they got footing, it was blasted to a comfortable width so no one would be afraid to ride it. The trail was built up to Hamilton Lake, and along the sheer granite walls towering above the lake they encountered a steep rocky chute which they spanned with a swinging bridge. Jim Livingston said he made his way up the steep chute of gravel, rock, and shattered granite (as you can see in the photo), and drilled and sulfured in some pins to secure the steel cables into the opposite side. It was an old process with a jackhammer. He anchored the pins and John threw a rope to him to pull the cable across. With that in place, Jim could traverse the ravine hand-over-hand on the cable to work on the opposite side. He was an agile guy, wiry, and hard as nails. He did some work and was coming back, hand-over-hand, when the pin came out and Jim fell into the canyon, he slipped down the cable picking up steel splinters through his gloves. He hung on the end of the cable, hit the cliff with his feet and swung back and forth until he was above a dirt area about twenty feet below. He was able to drop to the ground, just bucked his knees and escaped injury. Then they had to start all over again, climb, anchor the pins, pull the cable to finish off a platform, and cement the ends for the swinging bridge. They hauled hundreds of mule loads of material on those trail jobs. Trail construction continued on up Hamilton Gorge and over Kaweah Gap on the Great Western Divide and from there it was pretty easy to get to Chagoopa Plateau.

The swinging bridge was destroyed by snow slides a couple of years later and not replaced because it was really dangerous to send stock across. Instead, the trail was blasted deeper into the back wall of the chute. There was such a big overburden to remove, Jim said they drilled deeper and set extra heavy shots but instead of breaking the canyon wall loose, it blew a hole inward. So they just kept blasting until they cleared a tunnel that pack mules could get through. Cribbing and pins were placed to hold the overburden. The 2011 photo on page 137 by David Husted clearly shows the trail, tunnel and chute.

That bluff trail was wide enough to turn a string of mules around. I was packing bridges on the job across Bear Paw; the mules were loaded with decking and steel and Jim Harvey was swamping. I looked down the trail and there was a Park ranger leading two mules heading our way. He was a 90-day wonder. I hollered back to Jim, we need to turn around. (When you check out Husted's photograph, you can appreciate what a predicament an oncoming rider created here.) The mules carefully turned without scraping their loads on the cliff and headed back the way we came until we found a wide spot to let the ranger go by. All we could say was, "You don't know if another party is following you, do you?"

At Bear Paw there is another set of bluffs, spectacular, the trails are so good you couldn't knock a mule off of it.

This photo by David Husted of Fresno, California, shows the trail cut into the mountain above Hamilton Lake and the tunnel created when the initial dynamite charge blew inward, not outward.

Photo 2011, courtesy of David Husted.

www.panoramio.com/user/814238/tags/The%20High%20Sierra%20
Trail%20Sequoia%20NP

Bob and Joe Davis

Bob Davis (1921-1968) and his brother Joe Davis (1922-2001) lived across the road from us. Their mother was Fredrica (Maxon) Davis, a sister of Hat Maxon and a passel of other Maxon brothers and sisters. Though Bob and Joe were nine and ten years older than me, you might say we grew up together and wound up working on trails together in the Park in the late 1950s.

As a kid, Joe was roly-poly and in his senior year of high school, when all his buddies enlisted in the service for World War II, he found out he wasn't accepted. That was a terrible embarrassment to Joe and he was sensitive about that the rest of his life. So Joe spent the next winter in Greasy Cove, on Ban Freeman's ranch next to our ranch there, where he worked like hell repairing several miles of fences. My dad loaned him a horse and a couple of mules to pack posts and Joe roughed it building fence, mostly by himself. When Joe came out in the spring he was in top physical shape, weighed about 165 pounds, we hardly recognized him. He joined the merchant marine and was then able to join his friends in the war effort.

Joe worked for the Park in charge of roads and trails under Fred Walker, and when Fred retired, Joe took his place to supervise roads, and his brother Bob Davis, took over trails. I first worked with Joe when I started packing bridges for the Park Service in 1957, and later for Bob. Joe and I worked together to design the concave pack kyack boxes with lips on the outside to carry steel on the pack mules for which Joe received a park employee award.

Joe's wife, Sue, and my wife Gaynor taught dance arts together and Joe and I became close friends. He had a bouncy personality that people liked, always whistling so he was easy to find. We hunted together for many years, always opened the deer season somewhere around Three Rivers. We took a lot of trips to Montana and Utah, traveling a lot of miles together across the Midwest.

The Park transferred Joe from Sequoia to Zion National Park in Utah, and later to Mt. Shasta, California. We'd visit him in Utah, stay at a beautiful place above Zion and hunt on the rim there. Joe was the opposite of bow-legged so when he walked his Levis brushed at the knees–I remember when we went deer hunting he would be stalking somewhere out there, on a ridge above or in back, and I'd sometimes pick up that familiar scrish-scrish sound.

Joe retired from the Park and spent his final declining years in a care home in Fresno. Before he died, Joe called me one day to tell me he loved me. I told him my feelings for him were the same. I have since humbly regretted that I did not make time to visit Joe at the rest home before he passed away. To write these words brings a tear to my eye because it was an act of omission that I cannot repair. Joe, you were a very special person to me; I cherish all those happy times we spent together.

Bob Davis was in charge of Park trails and he oversaw all the trail bosses and crews in the different sections of the Park. Every season the trail crews repair the damage from winter snows, rock slides, avalanches and fallen trees, to make them safe for back country users.

Bob Davis was good because he was "old school" and he knew the old, practical ways, instead of a theoretical way printed in a how-to manual.

Bob Davis died young from a heart attack. His widow, Marguerite, gave me one of his possessions—a U.S. Army Canon stove. That story comes later.

Trail bosses had seasonal workers, young men who wanted to spend a summer in the Sierra, who were hired and packed in to a trail job and a lot of guys got their start in life working in the backcountry. They learned how to live in the camp, in the dirt, around the campfire, learned the basics of life, how to survive, what to do in a wild fire, how to start a fire in the rain, how to survive when cold or wet, more important than any college class. I knew a number of fellows who started out on a trail crew and they would say it was some of the happiest times of their lives, especially working for someone like ol' Ben Loverin. All the bosses were real characters, but they knew how to do everything.

Onis Brown

Onis Brown was a kind of hero of mine, much like my father, Earl A. McKee Sr., who I lost when I was 15, and maybe Onis was like a father figure to me for a time. Onis was a gentle man with a mind filled with the knowledge of the great truths about just about anything that had to do with training horses, packing mules, trails throughout the Sierra, about hunting, or any of his outdoor life experiences.

He was such an authority on stock trails throughout the Sierra mountain ranges, from the lower Kern River north through the Kings watershed and on to Yosemite. My dad packed through these same mountains all of his adult life, and died there at Sixty Lake Basin. He started in the packing business from here in Three Rivers in 1910 and knew Onis Brown very well. I said this before, but I've heard my dad laugh and say, "When I wanted to know something about a place I just discovered, I'd ask Onis, and Onis had not only already been there, but he knew a short cut!"

141

Onis used to come up to Greasy Cove ranch to work cattle with me and we'd spend all day talking as we rode and he would point out all the places he had hunted or tracked along the way. I will forever have a soft spot in my heart for Onis, because he was a humble little guy and such a good horseman. Onis was married to Mabel Lewis from around Naranjo, on the old Bill Lewis place. Onis and Mabel had three children, Lewis, Billy and Frances, and then were divorced. Billy died fairly young; Lewis died not too old–they both had cancer. Their daughter, Frances, married Willis Beutler at Onis' home on Red Hill in 1934, and she lived to be 97 years old.

Onis Imus Brown (see Colossians 4:9) was born at Mount Pinos, near Fort Tejon and Frazier Park, California. As I said before, Onis' mother died in 1902 and in 1905, his dad and their eight children moved to Lemon Cove. Onis took off in 1904, while in his teens, and rode over to the Chorizo Plains to trap wild horses. The infamous "industrial cowboys" Miller and Lux owned a million head of cattle and a million and a half acres of land covering the Chorizo Plain, a good part of the Tejon area, all up and down the coast range. They employed a lot of Mexican cowhands from old Mexico, called *Californios*, and Onis learned from them how to trap and tame a horse. Onis was a good horseman and would tell me, "This is the way the Spaniards did it." He caught five horses on the Chorizo Plain, then rode across the plains through east Bakersfield to Kern, took the Little Kern to about Grasshopper Arroyo, and rode up and over Farewell Gap into Mineral King. Onis told me he trapped wild horses up in Mustang up the South Fork soon after he arrived in 1904, there were quite a number of mustangs there. My dad used to own that land and I sold it a few years ago to the owners of the South Fork range.

Onis said he came to Mineral King because he wanted to see the mountains and he wanted to pack. Onis sold the horses he brought from the Chorizo Plain and packed for John Broder, taking people over into the Kern River from Mineral King. In the winters, Onis came down to Three Rivers and stayed at Broder's homestead on the South Fork. Onis showed me where he lived there; Broder Mountain is on the right, it is a small mountain and on the back side there is a little flat that was culti-vated and fig trees were planted. John Broder died in 1907.

In the off-seasons Onis stayed and worked around Three Rivers. He worked for Fred Ward on the Ward Ranch on Dry Creek. The Ward Ranch property is where my dad was born. Ward ran razor-back hogs all over that country, and Onis had some hog dogs that were the best. Onis always had good dogs. He told about one time he and the dogs got separated on the way into Greasy Cove to gather hogs; the dogs ran off in another direction, found the bunch of hogs Onis was after, herded them down to the corral and were sitting in the gate when he got back. These kinds of dogs are rare. The Hengst Ranch also employed Onis because he knew their ranch and he had good dogs to gather cattle in that dense brush.

Scrapper, his little white dog was always with him and Onis would demonstrate the dog's understanding of English. He said if you spend enough time with your dog or your horse, they will learn what you're talking about after a while. Onis would say, "Scrapper, go in the house and get my spurs." It might take a little while for the dog to find them, but he would bring out the spurs–if he didn't find both, he'd bring one and go back for the other. And Onis would say, "Scrapper, lead this horse over there to the hitching rail, would you?" and hand Scrapper the rope and that little dog would get the rope in his teeth and lead that horse to the rail. Onis could teach his dog to do anything.

About 1957, Onis and I went on our last hunting trip; we left the group and rode out of Mineral King over Farewell gap to the Rifle Creek ridge. Onis was riding his horse, Stormy, a real mountain horse that climbed over rocks like he was glued to them. Onis was a good judge of what a horse could or couldn't do. I'd lead my horse. Onis would say this horse has four legs and I only have two and besides, I can't hardly get on, so why would I get off? (He was talking this way because of his age then.) Onis was strong, but short, and had to stand on a rock to get on his horse–it was tough to reach the stirrups. Onis had a heavy saddle so he built a hoist, or in the mountains threw a rope over a tree limb, to pull his saddle up off his horse, tie it off. His horse was trained to stand while he lowered the saddle on him, so he didn't have to throw it. When you're older like me, getting on a horse ain't pretty. Throwing a 50-lb. saddle wrecks your back–I really don't want an audience now when I saddle and get on my horse because I saddle him from the wrong side so the cinches are already on that side and I don't have to sling it; then I step on a rock to get on. I can do this because my horse is dog-gentle. But when we were young we could do anything.

I wrote a poem about Onis Brown. I loved old Onis Brown. I thought the world of him, he was always good to me.

Another brother of Onis' was Rennie; Rennie took over their father's job as superintendent of Lemon Cove Ditch after Marcellus Sr. was killed in a ditch accident in 1914. Later Rennie became constable for Woodlake district.

Onis died of cancer November 7, 1959. He had asked me to sing at his funeral; it was tough–I sang through tears in tribute to Onis. I am so thankful for the time in my life that I knew him and spent time with this man. Onis Imus Brown is buried in Woodlake, California.

Marcellus Brown

Of Onis' brothers, I only knew Marcellus, Jr. Marcellus was a friend, a gentleman, built low to the ground and strong as a bull. He wasn't a horseman like Onis. He was muscle-bound, could lift things up as high as his waist, but from there on up his bulging muscles got in the way. He was great at shoeing mules though, just got hold of that hind leg and hung on. They couldn't kick him, maybe yank him a little bit, but he'd just hold firm and shoe it. Marcellus also knew the mountains well, and ran a trail crew.

It was fall and Marcellus had been working the trail crew and stayed late, so the Park sent a helicopter to fly him out. Marcellus had on his hard hat, thank God, or it would have killed him. He always walked a little hump-backed because of his over-sized muscles, and he was told to duck as he stepped off the chopper. With the blades whirring and dust and all, he ducked but became disoriented and walked to the rear, right into the tail rotor. It hit him, split his hard hat and knocked his head back and the blade cut him from the side of his eyebrow down his cheek, face and cut his shoulder bad. Marcellus survived and underwent a long repair and recovery in the hospital. The force of that blow did several thousand dollars of damage to the rotor gears, so his friends teased him that he almost totaled a helicopter with his head.

Marcellus used to run trail crew up around Tamarack and Hamilton Lake. He was a tough old buzzard. The crew made camp at Lone Pine creek right below Tamarack Lake one night. Bob Davis was there. Bob would stay up and argue with anyone until daylight. They were standing around the campfire when a big wind whipped the trees and then went quiet. All at once a tree fell–crash–right on Marcellus, right in the camp. Had him pinned. Luckily the guys were able to roll the tree off of him and radio for a helicopter that came in at first light.

After Marcellus retired from the Park, he spent his later years in a little rental house across from the Dinely Bridge in Alta Acres here in Three Rivers. His neighbor in the next little house was Skinny Kirk who was also retired from the Park and lived alone. They looked out for each other.

I sang at Marcellus' funeral, and at Skinny Kirk's as well.

Ben Loverin

Both Ord and Ben Loverin were great storytellers and they might stretch it a little bit but you never wanted to doubt too much because they'd done so many things. Ben was born in 1893, Ord about 1884. They used to hang out in Visalia's Chinatown at a notoriously rough and dirty tavern owned by an uncle. Ben said he never saw anyone whip Ord Loverin–called him "Red" because Ord had red hair. Ben said that if a tough teamster came to town to claim he was top dog, he hadn't run into Ord yet. You could look at Ord's nose and tell it had been moved all around.

I packed with Ben Loverin on trail crews when I was packing bridges in 1957 and 1958–that was over 50 years ago. Ben and Ord were old men then. Ben was a little old guy, always had a big grin on his face and, like the other Loverins I knew, his voice was a little rough and raspy. Ben had calluses on his lower lip from smoking Bull Durham and he rolled his own. He'd be smoking a half-burnt cigarette stuck to his lip and it would bounce up and down when he talked. Talk about a character. Every summer Ben lived and worked in the backcountry; at the start of the season, Ben would buy two new pair of Levis and two new chambray shirts. In the mountains, you didn't want to get downwind from Ben because he was allergic to water. When Ord told him he should take a bath in the river, Ben would say no, that water is too warm to drink and too cold to bathe in. When he came out in the fall, his shirtsleeves were rotted off, the Levis slick with grease, beard grown out all summer so he looked like Grumpy of the Seven Dwarfs.

Ben was particular about his coffee cup though–never washed it–and if it ever got washed it made him mad, said you take all the flavor out of it if you wash it. He'd just pour out the old coffee, maybe rinse it with a bit more hot coffee, and hang the cup on the limb right close to the stove. They sort of just lived like wild animals up there. But what a storyteller.

Ben was smart; all the Loverin kids were smart. I'd talk to Bob Davis about the bridges we were working on, and he said that Ben was about the smartest guy he ever saw. When Davis and everyone had pencils and paper trying to calculate how many board feet of lumber and materials were needed, old Ben would keep saying, "Well, write this down." While they were still figuring, Ben had the answer in his head.

Ben handled dynamite like a little kid plays with blocks. When you rode into his camp, he and his crew–usually Pappy, Dick Percival, and George Whitfield–would be sitting around the campfire on boxes of dynamite. Once you understood dynamite you didn't have any fear of it, because it takes the pressure of an explosive, the cap, to set it off. If dynamite is thrown in the fire, it will not blow up but it will burn big. The caps are dangerous; if there was an electrical storm, they made sure the dynamite caps were out of camp–an electrical charge in the air would set off the caps so they tied them all together and put them under a rock away from camp. I've never packed so much dynamite in my life; going over Bishop Pass, I had to bring back three mule loads of powder for Ben. If he didn't use it all, he'd hide it somewhere so he'd have plenty next season.

I packed steel and materials to Ben up Mehrten Creek in lower Buck Canyon and he wanted some eggs, powder, and some of the good stuff. The mules traveled loose and I put the eggs and dynamite on the gentlest mule that would pack it safely. I didn't know she didn't like rattles. The gas stove packed on top started to rattle and about a half mile up the trail she stampeded, got by my string leader and ran. We found pieces of this and that along the trail and I was waiting for a big boom. We caught her about two miles up with the load of scrambled eggs and dynamite.

Ben hid his camps out away from the trails; he didn't want the Park rangers or anyone to know were he camped. The Park would try to bring him provisions, but he didn't want the rangers around because when he needed meat, he'd shoot a deer. Year round he ate venison. It wasn't always legal, but he never wasted deer meat. It was dressed, quartered, and at night hung in the dry, cold air and in the morning a deer bag–a cotton sack–was slipped up over to cover it and it was put in the pack, or around camp it was put under his bed. I told Ben he was part mountain lion. Even if a ranger found his camp, to inspect the packs they had to have a search warrant. You could tell them you did not want them looking through your private property for whatever reason, and Ben could think of a million reasons.

Ben was an excellent cook, could cook a venison roast that was moist, which is hard to do because venison is a dry meat with little marbling. I'd eat dinner with him any time. It was his clothes and his hygiene that was awful.

Ben had his own trail crew. He was one of the best. He understood the art of dynamite carving. He could take an old sugary rock–there are certain kinds of granite that will shatter–he'd mud shots on that, roll it into the trail on a rough place to be flattened, and blow it down. Blast! and he'd have gravel and sand, just ready to rake around for a smooth trail. He would use dynamite to clear fallen trees across the trail or explode a tree into firewood–kindling and logs to last the whole job–a lot faster than sawing it.

Early in the season, Ben would work over on the Alta trails but when Granite Pass melted he would go over to the Middle Fork of Kings Canyon where he preferred to work.

The trail crews were supplied with radios and Ben would turn his on long enough to listen to where everyone was, then turn it off. He kept his radio hid with some dead batteries around so he could claim he couldn't answer because the radio was dead. Bob Davis would say that old son-of-a-bitch didn't answer his radio, especially late in the season, because he knew we needed to have him come out because we were running out of money. But Ben wanted to stay late until deer season and figured the Park would find money enough to pay him so he just kept working. Ben was always a hard worker and an expert on trails. At the end of the 1957 season, I was deadheading my stock back from the bridge job at Bishop, and Bob Davis asked me to go by and bring Ben out of there. We packed up his camp and headed out with Ben riding his horse, Charlie. Near a lake, right in front of us stood a big buck so Ben pulled his rifle from somewhere, levered a shell in his gun, but Charlie kept fidgeting, stepping sideways, while Ben tried to aim and he growled, "Goddammit Charlie stand still!" He shot the buck from horseback and Charlie hardly flinched. Ben packed out the deer for his winter larder.

One of Ben's crew was George Whitfield who packed for him. He was around here a long time; you didn't want to push him around but he was a nice guy and later alcohol became his too-close friend and it got him. But he was a good friend of mine, could do about anything, a good packer, horse shoer, good dozer operator and all. He packed with Old Ben several years on trail crew. About that time, Ben was living with Ruth. She was probably near 40 years or so when she became pregnant, they got married, and had a little boy they named Tommy. Looked just like Ben. Bob Davis was running the trail crews and he gave permission for Ruth to stay with Ben in camp and she'd help cook. Ben called his fuzzy-haired little boy Bacon Rind because he toddled around camp all the time chewing on a bacon rind.

Ben had a little short mule he called Stubby that had the body of a grown mule but real short legs, kind of funny, but he was a good, gentle little mule. When Stubby didn't have much of a load, Ben would put whatever Tommy weighed on the one side and stick Tommy in the pack on the other and it was so comical to see Tommy's head poking out of the pack as the mule bobbed along.

There was a place called Keyhole coming down to what was called Reload Flat, halfway down that long hill going to Simpson from Dougherty. Stubby the mule was short and couldn't make it through the keyhole–Ben kept him loose–so the little mule approached the Keyhole, looked at it and saw that he couldn't make it, so he just left the trail and made his way through the boulders and around and came back to the trail on the other side.

Ben's wife Ruth died fairly young when Tommy was still in high school. As it happened, we were leaving on a private pack trip that we took with three other couples several summers when Ben telephoned me to say Ruth had died and he wanted me to sing at her funeral. I said, "Well, Ben, we are leaving for Cedar Grove right now." He just said, well that's ok then. So we went over to Cedar Grove and I got to thinking about Ben, felt really bad for him, got in the car and came home for the funeral the next day. When I arrived at the cemetery, Old Ben teared up.

Ord Loverin

I knew Ord as a pretty sweet kind of guy, a good neighbor, and he lived to be "only" 91 years old, born in 1884 and died in 1976. I was almost related to Ord—his wife Maud was a cousin of Harry Britten, the husband of my dad's sister, Stella McKee Britten. Maud's father was Ernest Britten. Ord owned the Wolverton Pack Station in Giant Forest from 1924 until he sold it to my dad in 1929. Ord named some of the early day families in Three Rivers: ". . . on the South Fork were the Blossoms, the Busbys and the Alleses; on the Main Kaweah were the Carters, Mullinexes, Brittens and Bahwells; on the North Fork, the Purdys, Windsors, Taylors (formerly of Kaweah Colony), and the Bartons, Lovelaces, and Washburns." He said at one time in the early days there were 20 families and 23 bachelors; many of the bachelors were old codgers who preferred a remote and solitary life.

Ord drove the mail stage from Giant Forest to Kaweah Post Office on old Colony Mill Road. One day a lion jumped right in front of him. He grabbed a six-shooter off the seat, shot through the windshield, and hit the lion. It ran off but there was no blood trail and Ord couldn't see where he went so he kept driving. Around another turn he encountered another lion in the road. This time Ord took aim and shot that lion dead. He got out and looked at the lion—there were two bullet holes. It was the same lion. Now I thought that was just some malarkey because Ord told the story at Whisperin' Bob's mountain oyster feed where everyone was spiking each other's drinks. But later I mentioned it to Johnny Britten and he said oh no, it was true because he was with him; said he couldn't hear anything for three days from those gun shots.

Ord told about hunting lions with Jay Bruce, the California State Lion Hunter. Mountain lions feed only on deer, unless deer are scarce, then they go down to mice, or a skunk and raccoons. Jay Bruce hunted with four plain old hounds that would get a scent and tree the lion, then Bruce would come along and use his .38 pistol to kill it. He didn't track with horses because he didn't want a horse slowing him down. Even his hounds couldn't keep up with him. Ord hunted with Jay Bruce in this area for three winters. Ord explained that an average hunter or fisherman would never see a lion, but the lion would see him, always. They don't move, just slink down and watch—that's why you don't see them. In

1929, a party from Long Beach hired Ord and his trained lion dogs for a two-week lion hunt in the mountains of Arizona.

Ord was from Eshom Valley, Tulare County and was a teamster and cattleman. He said he drove a team for the Sanger Lumber Company, hauling supplies to a Hume Lake lumbering camp. In 1903 he drove the first freight team into Mineral King for Broder & Hopping. In early 1905 he drove a team of fourteen mules and two big 1600-pound horses, the wheelers, pulling a rig of three wagons with supplies to the desert mines in Panamint Mountains on the east side of the Sierra. Ord told me how they got those heavy wagons rolling–the mules couldn't pull it to start with, so the point man would herd the team to the left, then run them back to the right, then left, just to get the wheels to turn; when he'd run them back to the right and he'd hit them with all the leather he had to get those wheels rolling. He worked in Panamint for a year and then returned to the Three Rivers area where he was a Park ranger for five years during the War.

All three of Ord's sons were pilots: Wesley, Bud, and Orlen (nick-named Baldy). Orlen flew in WWII and was killed in a plane crash coming home from the War. One time Bud Loverin flew Forrest Homer and me up to Bieber, California to look at bulls, then up to Montigue where we both bought several bulls. Like his brother Wesley, Bud was sharp, a cool pilot. When Wesley was in the service he flew a P39 under the Golden Gate Bridge, didn't get quite low enough and had to eject after the tail hit one of the bridge struts.

Ord told me several stories about helping Guy Hopping gather cattle several seasons. The Hoppings were former members of the Kaweah Colony; Guy joined the Park Service in 1918. He lived on a homestead in Salt Creek where he ran some cattle. In the spring, Guy took his cattle to Chagoopa Plateau southeast of Big Arroyo for summer pasture. Ord said one year Guy waited too late to drive his cattle out of the mountains. Ord helped bring the cattle out, I believe he told me it was late in the season–October–of 1917. They drove the cattle to Big Five Lakes and heading to Black Rock Pass they were caught in a terrible blizzard, it must have been a record-setting blizzard at that time, so bad they couldn't see the cattle. It was freezing cold so they made camp at Pinto Lake that was out of the blast of the storm. It stormed all night. In the blinding snow, almost the whole herd drifted over a bluff, about 62 head. The cattle could not see, they were crowding and one followed the other over the edge. After it cleared off, Ord and Guy went back to see if there were any cattle left. There weren't. They found two or three that had frozen to death while being pushed against the rocks by the winds, frozen while standing up. Fifty years later, on one of the Soararsis trips, we camped at Pinto Lake and the horses grazed in those meadows and off that bluff the pile of the bleached bones of Guy's cattle were still visible.

Another time, my uncle Jesse Finch and Ord were helping Guy gather some of his wild cattle up in the Salt Creek country. Ord and Jesse were coming down a ridge, the cattle running wide open. Guy had ridden ahead, heard the brush popping behind him and hid behind a tree to get out of the way of the stampeding cows. Guy apparently thought he saw the last cow charge by and jumped his horse from behind the tree right in front of Ord, sent Ord's horse cartwheeling down the mountain. Guy looked over his shoulder at the wreck but just kept on going out of sight. Ord and his horse both had broken legs; Jesse had to destroy Ord's injured horse, then get Ord, who was in blinding pain, up on his own horse to lead him down out of there. The wild cows got away again!

Ord and Jesse Finch helped Guy bring some wild cattle out of Washburn Cove down to the old C. L. Taylor Ranch, the site of the old airport, now the catfish farm. A Holstein bull, owned by Taylor, was grazing peacefully in the field when the stampeding cattle came down the hill. The bull didn't realize the danger it was in, just stared at the cattle as they ran toward him at breakneck speed. The raging herd ran right over the bull and broke his leg. The bull had to be destroyed and Guy had to make restitution.

Archie McDowall

Mr. W. P. Fuller, Jr. always asked for Archie McDowall to be the cook on their annual pack trips. Archie was one of the reasons that made those years very special. We had a lot of wonderful, funny experiences. Archie was always thinking, gazing at the treetops, thinking, analyzing how things might be done better. On one of these trips, around the relaxed campfire setting at Thunder Lake at the head of Kern River, Archie explained to his audience–including one regent, and the Stanford University president, no less–how he, as an Englishman, would go about restructuring the entire educational system of the United States. Archie read classic works of literature and philosophy and appreciated any chance to discuss his favorite writers because the packers sure didn't know anything about classic works.

Archie was a character, a very proper, well-read character with an English accent who never said "yes," it was "yawse." And if you walked by his kitchen and he needed something, bacon for example, he would ask that the next time you go to the pack, "please bring some bacon across."

Archie McDowall was originally from England, but grew up in Alberta, Canada. He married Mary Alderson in 1926; Mary was born in Wilbur, Washington but moved to Calgary, Canada as a youngster, attended college and taught school for several years there before moving with her family to live with her cousin's family, the McCutcheon's in Exeter, California. (Her cousin Ray McCutcheon drove his home-made fire truck to my place and doused hot spots all night during the wildfire here in 1987.) Mary taught in two valley schools for several years before she was hired to teach in Three Rivers in 1930.

Archie bought property on North Fork in 1936 where he raised chickens, and in the summers he was the cook on my dad's pack trips. I could write a book about just the things that happened on those trips with Archie. He was a Ray Pinnell with an English accent when it came to catastrophes. Poor Archie made the news three times in 1937 for being run over by the truck he was helping a guy load with wood in the hills, a black widow spider bite, and sunstroke. Then of course there were the floods. In 1950, Archie was warned that huge floodwaters were due in an hour and he and his daughter Bobbie, then a junior in high school, went out at midnight to move the chickens to higher ground. The upstream bridge was dammed with debris and when the approaches to the bridge broke loose Archie and Bobbie were swept downstream in a wall of water and lodged in a barbed wire fence. They fought their way along the fence to the flooded road and safety. The flood of 1955 caused even more damage to their chicken ranch.

Archie McDowall was trail camp cook for the pack station when Ord owned it, and afterward Archie cooked for my dad. This story happened about 1928. Colonel White, the park superintendent, used to take rides in the backcountry and he was hell on horseflesh. He had been a cavalry man and he expected the horse to make up lots of miles, which is okay on flat country but not in the mountains, but wherever he could he would trot or lope. Archie told a story about going into the Kern River with Ord Loverin and they'd just arrived at a good place to stop for the night. Ord, like his brother Ben, ate deer meat, whether it was within the Park boundary or out. There was a nice buck standing close by, so Ord got his gun out of its hiding place and shot it. They were still setting up camp when Archie saw a horse galloping toward them and told Ord it looked like Colonel White. Ord looked up and said, "By God, that is Colonel White!" Archie said Ord just threw the camp gear, beds and equipment around the dead deer on the ground and covered it all with manties. Colonel White saw their camp and came riding over. According to Archie, Ord was a master at deception because he just exclaimed heartily, "Get off your horse, Colonel, we'll have something to eat here pretty soon." They didn't have any chairs, so the Colonel sat on the edge of the covered pile of equipment–he was sitting on the edge of the buck right there, while Archie cooked up some lunch. Archie would tell this story and almost shake. He would say, "Gud Low-rd," he talked with an English accent, "I just couldn't believe the man! I wanted him to get the Colonel the hell out of there, you know, and Ord just kept on making him at home!"

When Archie got excited he would exclaim, "Jesus Whept!" Archie rode an old bell mare named Shorty. Austin Lott broke her to ride and named her; she was an Army horse. The Army bought horses, branded the left side of the neck, had a dog tag and a file of army misinformation for each horse, in a word, useless. Shorty was a good traveler but had a mean streak; she would nip you when you cinched her up. The mules loved her and tried to get close but when they got too close Shorty would kick and bite. Wherever Shorty was, the mules were there too. If Archie was in the saddle when she'd get mad, she'd reach around with teeth bared and bite Archie's toe and Archie'd get mad and kick back.

One time we came down the Kern Kaweah, off of Colby Pass, through the chute–had to unpack the mules, lead them through and repack. All it would have taken was about six mule-loads of dynamite to blow out the chute, but it was just far enough away from one side and the other that the trail crews never quite got there. Years later, they did fix it. But it was hot and this time Archie was riding Old Daisy, another bell mare the mules loved. Daisy would not allow any of the mules to pass her, but they always tried to crowd close. I was behind trying to hold back some mules that were pushing to get around me. It was hot and Archie was thirsty, so he spurred Daisy ahead so he could stop and get a drink from the river before the mules caught up. He was down on hands and knees to drink, with his arm through the reins. Well, I couldn't hold my mules back and a couple of them jumped ahead and went around Archie's mare. She wasn't going to allow that, and bolted, dragged Archie under water down the river. He got his footing and stood up soaking wet. All he would say was, "You dutty bitch!" He wouldn't say "dirty," it was "dutty." English accent you know.

It was the same problem when Archie had to relieve himself; it was almost impossible to dismount and finish his business before the mules crowded the mare and she would bolt. So I noticed Archie riding kinda funny, sideways-like; he was going while he was going. Well, that was just the way it was for the guy on the bell mare.

On another pack trip with a group of guys on a hunting party over in the Woods Creek area–it used to be outside Park boundaries–Archie was cooking some beans on the stove and he put a large can of beans in a bucket of water–you can simmer the can in a bucket of water all day without opening it, then if you decide not to serve it, it can go back in the pack. But Archie got busy and forgot about the simmering beans and the pot boiled dry. He made a bread pudding, biscuits for every meal, just puttering around the kitchen and he tapped something to move it over on the stove and that is all it took. The can was just sitting there ready to blow when he tapped the bucket and it blew the pot lid up in a tree and the hot beans hit Archie across his forehead, seared his face and burned off his left eyebrow. Never did grow back and he always knit his brows in thought, but after that there was only one eyebrow to knit. His eye got burned, turned a little smoky but he didn't lose his eyesight. I wasn't on that trip. Archie told me about it.

Archie told me this story and said don't you ever repeat it because I will deny it. It happened when Archie was a young fellow in school in Alberta, Canada. There was a young lady he really wanted to court, but there was also another fellow who had eyes for her. One day as fate would have it, both came to call on her at the same time, and the gracious hostess invited both in, making a rather awkward scene of three teen-agers sitting very properly in the living room, twiddling thumbs trying to think of something to talk about. The family cat sauntered into the room, sat down on the rug and began to scratch its ear with its hind leg, typical cat behavior. Just to make conversation, Archie piped up, "I bet you guys can't do what that cat is doing," pointing at the cat. But the instant everyone turned to look at the cat to see what Archie bet they couldn't do, the cat was not scratching its ear, it was licking its butt. The fellow ran out one door, Archie bolted for the other.

I remember on one trip Archie and Jim Kindred got in a fight over how to cook biscuits in the Dutch oven. I liked to cook biscuits, cooked hundreds of biscuits to help Archie. There is a real trick to timing them, you can always lift the lid and peek and if they're getting too done, just kick off some ash.

The trick is a good hot fire of dead branches, let it burn down, and put the lid of the Dutch oven in the fire to pre-heat it, then when the coals are deep, dig a little hole and put a shovel full of coals into it and set the Dutch oven on them. Melt two spoons of Crisco, grease the cut biscuits both sides, place on a tin pie plate and put it inside the oven, and cover. Shovel coals around the sides, put some on top of the Dutch oven, make a little dirt berm and let them bake. Peek at seven minutes; if they are light, then fan the coals a bit and bake until golden brown.

Jim and Archie argued over which was the best method: hot and fast; or slower fire, longer bake. "I've had enough of your bulls__t!" Archie told him, and took his glasses off in a fighting gesture. Jim yanked his glasses off, too. Here was the packer and cook ready to go at it over biscuits.

On another trip Archie cooked for a bunch of guys who put ketchup on everything. Archie realized he was going to run out of ketchup and worried about what to do. Amazingly, he got a chance to send someone to the store for more ketchup, not easy from an 11,000-foot mountain range. Actually, another pack train came by, heading out to the east side, and mentioned they'd be coming back in a couple of days. Archie asked if they could do him a big favor and bring back two or three bottles of ketchup.

Meantime, Archie had some canned stewed tomatoes in the grub pack. So he told the guys, well, we are running out of ketchup but I'll see if I can make some. He started cooking the stewed tomatoes on the stove, and put an empty fruit jar nearby in which to pour the finished product. The guys saw that and waited for Archie's homemade ketchup to happen. A day or so later while the men were out fishing, the returning pack train dropped off Archie's order. He quickly took what was simmering on the stove and threw it over the grade, and filled the fruit jar with store-bought ketchup. At lunch the guys raved that Archie's homemade ketchup sure was the best they'd ever tasted.

I thought the world of Archie. He was honest with a heart of gold. Everyone loved Archie McDowall. I sang for both Archie and Mary's funerals in Three Rivers.

Asa (Ace) Peck

Ace Peck was a Park ranger. Colonel White told my dad that he regarded Ace as the best, a man he really respected. Ace had a reputation as a doer not a talker who used common sense as his guidebook. My dad said Ace had a temper, but that's it, when it was over, it was over. When Ace disagreed with the Colonel, he'd go face to face and yank his ranger badge off and throw it at the Colonel and invite him to perhaps put it where the sun don't shine. That would have cinched a retirement for most employees, but the Colonel respected a man who stood his ground.

This is the story Ace Peck told at a Pioneer Night dinner (c. 1960), about fighting a forest fire in 1926:

"As far as fire fighting was concerned back in the old days, all they took to the fire was tools to fight fire with–shovels, axes. We didn't–there was no thought of beds or food or water. If we got water, we got it where we could find it. They took a few canteens along but the idea was to get there and fight fire, not sit down and plan for two or three days for a 300-man camp and drive stakes and string lines and so forth for the dining room and sleeping quarters and so forth. If we slept, we slept out in the cold. We'd find a place where a log had burned and kick the hot coals away and sleep on the warm ground and ashes and so forth. Beds, blankets, there was no such thing as Simmons mattresses.

"But the biggest fire I was ever on was in 1926 and that burned over 80,000 acres, it was about 25 miles from where it started that we stopped it. I was in Redwood Meadow after the thing had been going for two or three weeks, and they called me over there to bring over some government stock that I had at Redwood Meadow. Said [to me] no, you won't go to the fire, just bring the stock over because they need them there.

"Well, I got over there in Giant Forest and they said, well, you'll help the packers take these mules down the Colony Mill Road where the Yucca Creek trail takes off and then you'll come back and go back to your station. Got down, it was after dark. We went down that road on a dead run, the dust was 6 to 8 inches deep and I was behind, I couldn't see anything but I'd let out a yell every once in a while. We got down there; I told them I'm from Giant Forest and they dumped the whole thing in my lap. Said, you're in charge.

"I started out to find the man who was in charge to relieve him, and they couldn't find him, and finally I was walking and found where 10 or 12 men had taken off up the hill and I tracked them down and they were sitting on the hill and the man in charge was sitting on a rock, crying! He'd broken down and gave it up. He didn't know where his men were, didn't know where his supply lines were, didn't know anything. So I said, all right, forget about it and go home. I'll take care of it.

"So I had it for about two weeks and the only sleep I got, I'd fall off my horse and say, wake me up in 10 minutes, and I was gone again. There were camps going in for four miles along the front. Had an average of 2000 men. I'd go by the camp–had a camp–two cooks, a hand to take care of the horses, saddle horses, and he'd have an extra saddle horse ready for me when I got there. Finally we stopped it [the fire] on that long ridge. . .I was black as that camera there, clothes and all, clothes burned full of holes and they called me back to Giant Forest. And the Secretary of the Interior was there! Colonel White was superintendent, said, "Come on in, come on in." Well, imagine how I felt after they'd seen me then, and after I'd cleaned up they wouldn't have recognized me! But that was fire fighting in those days. We worked."

The Park was desperate to get help to fight the fire Ace talked about, so Park superintendent Colonel John White phoned the Visalia newspaper to print an appeal for men to report immediately to Three Rivers.

Ace arrived in this area in 1908. Ace was born in Tipton, California in 1888. As a young man he had a life-time of adventures in a few short years–he worked in the back country as a packer and guide, was held captive in Mexico when he was there to help some Americans appraise a ranch, joined the army and was sent to Siberia. In 1924 he went to work as a Park ranger where he plotted the route for many of the trails in the eastern portion of the Park. He told some hair-raising stories about fighting revolutionaries in the miserable winter in Siberia. His favorite stories were of the Sierra country and one I remember was here on South Fork.

Ace was really a character. He was a Park ranger from 1924 until retirement in 1955, stationed in the Kern River canyon, Sequoia Park, and Hawaii for a short time. He and Ester Mires, who lived in Three Rivers as a child, were married in Los Angeles in March 1929. A daughter, Maile Jo, was born on April 16, 1936 in Hawaii. Ester's sister, Gladys Mires was married to my uncle Jesse Finch.

Ace and Ester Peck homesteaded west of Grouse Valley on Blue Ridge where they lived one winter under a rock, down on the lower side of the place. He owned a total of 1000 acres. Ace built a cabin down in the pocket by Pepperwood Ridge. I rented Ace's place for 40 years, my brother-in-law Lee Maloy had rented it before that, and I'd see Ace up there and he loved to talk and we'd sit there and tell stories. I wished I had recorded them because there were so many that I can't recall now.

Ace worked for the Park Service. Every week or so he'd ride horseback down to the Three Rivers store—the Britten Store—for canned goods and such. It was wintertime and all the old guys would come in the store and sit around the pot-bellied stove to get warm and reminisce, chew tobacco and hit the spittoon now and again. Ace had been missing some things out of his cabin and had an idea of who might be responsible. When he tied up at the store one day, he saw that the horse his suspect rode was tied up and the fellow was with the regulars around the stove. It was Forest "Hog Jaw" Busby.

(I called Dan Busby to ask if I could use his father's nickname, Forest "Hog Jaw" Busby, in my book. Dan said it was okay, that's what people called him, his dad knew it and always said that he wished he'd grown a beard to cover up his under-shot chin.)

Ace joined in and threw out a red herring that he was on his way up to Salt Creek to help Guy Hopping move his cattle. (Guy worked for the Park also in the early days and ran cattle on the ranch that I lease now for my horses.) Ace made it real plain that he was going to be at Salt Creek for several days gathering cattle. He got on his horse and rode up the road, just as it goes today, around the sharp turn above where the Mercantile Store is now. He hid out of sight, and peeked around to watch the hitching rail at the store. Pretty soon, Busby came out, got on his horse and took off in a lope heading towards the South Fork road. Ace said he waited a little while and then started tracking, followed him to Bolton Canyon, about eight miles up to a wagon road that went to Pepperwood Ridge. Ace took another trail and found his horse tied up in the trees. Ace said he took the bridle off and chased the mare off down the road, got his 30-30 and took up surveillance of the cabin. When Hog Jaw stepped out the door with canned goods and a tow sack, Ace said he put a bullet in the doorjamb right next to his ear. That fellow threw everything up in the air and took off running, and every time he picked up a foot Ace put a duster on his track. Ace said he could of shot him but he wasn't out to kill him, just wanted to scare him. Quite a story that took place when times were hard and people did what they had to do to feed their kids. I'm sure it is true because it is not something that Ace would lie about.

I rented Ace Peck's place up on Grouse for 40 years. He had his cabin up there, still there and one of these days I'm going to take a trip up there just to take pictures of it. It might be fallen down by now.

Ace died in 1981. His widow, Ester, sold the ranch to the condor people and it became part of the Blue Ridge National Wildlife Refuge. That is about the time they started capturing condors to breed in captivity because the California Condor was almost extinct. Condors liked to roost on Mt. Dennison and they could be seen soaring and once in a while would get down close to Ace's. I've seen them fly over and you can identify them because they have a white marking in the shape of a big 7 under their huge wings. Ester wanted me to buy their ranch, but I couldn't afford it. That was about the time my son, Earl, died.

Ben Harris

According to Ben Harris, a ninety-day wonder was bossing a trail crew working over Franklin Pass out of Mineral King. Ben was riding with Ord Loverin packing supplies up to their camp at about timberline, probably below Franklin Lake.

A lightning storm hit and the trail workers ran for cover under rocks or anything that might serve as shelter, but not the know-it-all trail boss. He climbed on a rock and shouted insults at the crew for being cowards, that there was nothing to be afraid of. Then he pounded his chest like Tarzan and let out a whoop just as a bolt of lightning struck him dead! That's the way Ben Harris told the story. So Ben and Ord, being the packers, put the guy in a sleeping bag and threw him over a mule and went out to find some authority to declare him dead. Doc Robert Montgomery and his wife, Nora, happened to be staying at their cabin in the Mineral King area so Ord and Ben rode over there and the Doc declared the trail boss dead–just a formality because the guy had been dead for a day or two by that time. So Ben goes on with the story. Ben had a big scab on the side of his face and the Doc looked at it and asked, "Ben, what did you do to your face?" "Oh," says Ben, "The goddam lightning–I've always been able to dodge that lightning–this time I seen it coming and I jumped aside but that lightning hit a rock and glanced over and got me!"

That's the kind of stories Ben told. Ben had a tent cabin down in the quaking aspens between Mineral King and the Cold Spring trail where he spent the summers. Ben said one time huge mosquitos swarmed his camp, they were so big he was afraid for his life so he crawled under his big dishpan. Those mosquitos bored holes right through the bottom of that dishpan, but being smart Ben had his shoeing hammer with him and when they'd run their bills through the hole, he'd just brad them over. Bent their bills over so they couldn't get loose and Ben said that in no time at all "there were so many mosquitos hooked on there they flew away with my dishpan."

Ben Harris had a team and buggy and he would haul supplies for people back and forth between Three Rivers and Mineral King. The kids used to hear him coming, he had bells on his wagon. They used lots of bells when they were going up Mineral King so other wagons could hear them coming up the hill. (Folks in Three Rivers recognized the chimes on Jason Barton's eight-horse freight wagons going through to Mineral King and Giant Forest.) Ben was a shirttail relative of Paul Huneke–the infamous voice at the Lemon Cove telephone exchange who shouted "lemonlemonlemon!" whenever you rang up central. Paul did not like Ben because he was "a stinkin' old man and never would take care of himself." My dad agreed with Paul on that.

My dad invited Ben to be the featured speaker for a Chamber of Commerce meeting held at the Three Rivers Hotel next to the Britten store and asked Ben to come and tell some lies. The hardest part was to get Ben cleaned up. Ben was a storyteller and seldom repeated himself, he had an unending supply of stories, absolutely crazy and some of his best ones were the ones you couldn't print. So at the Chamber meeting, my dad introduced Ben as "the biggest liar in the State of California." Ben stood up and said, "Well, folks, I used to tell some pretty tall ones all right, in fact I was so good at it I started believing them myself, but I finally decided I'm not going to lie anymore. So I'm going to tell you something that actually happened." So he told this story about growing corn in Kern River–already the story is suspect because that is a terrible place to try to raise corn–and his cornfield grew and the ears were large and full, so he picked a big sack of corn and here comes a mother bear and two cubs. "She attacked me, pulled me down and sat on me while her cubs took that corn, they shucked every ear right there and ate it right in front of me."

Joe Doctor, of Exeter, published a collection of Ben Harris stories, entitled *The Man Who Could Dodge Lightning.*

One of Ben's first jobs was in Lemon Cove trapping gophers in the newly planted orange groves. The U.S. Census of 1900 counted Ben Harris, (age 44) born in Texas March 1856, residing as a boarder with Henry Alles in Three Rivers. Tulare County Historian Annie Mitchell's files provided information that Ben Harris was adopted by the John Hambrights in Texas and arrived with them in Farmersville, a little town just east of Visalia, in 1859. John Hambright owned a couple of quarter sections on Lime Kiln Creek (Dry Creek) by 1892.

There was a story that Ben Harris fell in the main fork of the Kaweah River, got pneumonia and died; I remember overhearing the adults at my Grandpa Finch's card party saying that's what happened to Old Ben. However, another story by his nephew, Jack Huneke, speculated that Ben sneaked away from the old folks home in Visalia where he was forced by the infirmities of old age to reside–sneaked away to visit old cohorts in Farmersville. Whatever the story, the official record is he died in Lindcove, California, on June 22, 1934.

The Ben Harris historical marker was placed at the old Lemon Cove fire station. It reads:

"BEN HARRIS"

"Ben Harris, unwashed & profane, was known as 'The Greatest Liar in the Sierra.' He frequented Lemon Cove and the Mineral

King back country and became part of the folklore. His mule was the smartest, his dog the meanest, his gun the shooting-est and his eye the keenest for nigh on 75 years. He should be remembered when tall tales brighten the campfire.

"Dr. Samuel Gregg George Chapter No. 1855 E. C. V. September 18, 1976."

Walt Pratt

Walter Pratt was always an ornery character, a jokester. He thought everything was funny. He was a big fellow, on the portly side, with a big laugh. If you didn't know Walt Pratt, you really missed something. Walt was from Porterville and everybody knew he drank more whiskey than anybody over there, until he had to stop when he was diagnosed with diabetes. He was a big promoter of the annual Jackass Mail Run in Porterville, would let his hair grow wild and dress up in a buckskin outfit to advertise the event.

He and my dad were close friends; he had packed for my dad since he was almost a kid. Walt got a kick out of little ordinary things. Out on a pack trip my dad stabbed his thumb with an up-down can opener blade and let out a yelp. Walt mimicked that yelp constantly until my dad told him to just shut up.

He used to come up to Mineral King after the packing season was over and hang around the pack station there, he had a place to put his horse, and he'd ride back into the mountains for a few days at a time. I was out with him in the old days and he'd get up just about every day before dawn and walk down to the river, strip off his clothes, and dive in. He liked to wake himself–and everyone else–by jumping in the ice cold river and letting out a loud "Waa-Hoo!"

Walt was a good packer. He was there when my dad died and it was he who rode out to Cedar Grove, told everyone the news, then returned and rode out with my dad's body. The horse, he said, was so tired he was standing with his head on the ground. One of the best characters I could ever talk about is Walt Pratt.

Jim Kindred

Jim worked for my dad building fence in the 1930s and packed every summer for my dad, and later for Lee Maloy. At campfire time on the W. P. Fuller pack trips, Jim loved to sing, not on key, but he sure had the rhythm and knew a lot of funny songs. He was a great dancer too. For years he packed out of Mineral King for Phil Davis. I remember a story Bob Davis told about getting a ride down from Mineral King in Jim Kindred's old Chevy. Bob was just a kid and always wondered about a paint line on the side of the bank going down the grade until he got in the car and rode with Jim. Jim's Chevy had old mechanical brakes and they never worked too well, so he'd gear down as low as it would go, and even then it would get to going too fast, so Jim would run one fender along the bank to slow the car, sort of a friction brake. Jim was a character.

He lived at the Lovering ranch in 1933 chasing cattle in the mountains and he could tell stories about old Whisperin' Bob. He refereed the fight between Harry Hughes and Hog Jaw Busby. In the winters, Jim worked for Gill Cattle Company most of his life; he was a good cowboy.

Jim loved bronc mules and packed a string of our mules that were more outlaw than anything else. He was a man of small stature, never weighed over 145 pounds at his heaviest, but he was a hell of a worker and could get things done. Jim once packed a wood range to Bear Paw Meadow. The removable pieces went on one mule and the heavy stove, probably heavier than it should have been, close to 300 pounds, Jim loaded on Old Gus. He let Gus rest twice on the way. At Seven Mile Hill he stood Gus against some flat rocks and slid that stove off the saddle platform so Gus could rest, then later Gus stood still again while Jim slid that stove back on. It was way too much for one man, but nothing was too much for Jim. That stove is probably still in the cabin because wood stoves don't wear out.

At Woodlake High School, I really got in shape trying to keep up with Jim when we played football. I followed Jim all over the mountains hunting horses and I was never in front; I guarantee you, Jim was a tough mountain goat.

During WWII, in 1942, Jim was with the U.S. Cavalry stationed at Jolona in Monterey County where he packed mules for the army. (Cavalry regiments, anxious to fight in the War, wanted to be shipped out with their horses to the Pacific Theater. The war planners vetoed that idea but did station cavalry regiments along our southern border because of rumors that the enemy might land in Mexico to invade the U.S. mainland.) Jim was an expert cowboy and packer for my dad and convinced his superior officer that army pack saddles were bulky and too heavy, that a lighter saddle would work better, and they should consult with an expert he knew. So Jim and his commander and another guy showed up at our house in an army truck at 1 o'clock one morning to consult my dad about pack saddles. I remember we all got out of bed, and mother fixed a midnight supper for them while my dad explained the advantages of the lightweight pack saddle built on a Tehama tree. My dad loaned a pack saddle for them to try and at 3 a.m. they departed. But the army has their own protocol, their way and those who benefit from their way, the status quo, so nothing changed.

My dear friend, Jim Kindred. Photo c. 1946.
AUTHOR'S COLLECTION.

Jim came out of the Army in WWII as Lieutenant and we'd get sideways with each other once in a while and I'd salute him, "Yes, Sir!" to piss him off. Jim Kindred was a good man, hard working, probably got up every morning at three o'clock and got home after dark. He and Lucille resided in an adobe house on North Fork until he died. Jim got sick and my sister, Blanche Maloy, came by one day to tell me I had better go see him, because Jim was dying of cancer. I went to see him the next day. He always smoked Camels and ran on Old Crow. He was just like a piece of iron. I told Jim he needed to go to the hospital and he said he had an appointment the next Thursday. Well, he could be dead by next Thursday, so I called a Veteran officer and asked what to do to get him into the Veteran's Hospital. John Wollenman and Frances Brown, who ran the store in Three Rivers, drove the Three Rivers ambulance at that time and as suggested by the officer, we did not call ahead for permission to admit, just drove Jim straight to the Emergency Room. I sat in back to reassure Jim and we talked. He smoked cigarettes the whole 70-mile drive. He was admitted for tests to see what could be done for him. The commanding officer accused me of pulling a fast one by getting Jim admitted through the E.R. instead of telling them he was scheduled to be seen the following week. I told the commander I wasn't sure Jim would still be alive next week, and what would he do if his life-long friend needed care? He nodded his head, "I'd do what you did."

I paid a visit a few days later and Jim was in good spirits. We talked about old times. Ten days after admission, he died, with his wife Lucille beside him. This was 1966.

I sang at Jim's funeral. The next day I went to his house and picked up two six-month-old pups that he was so worried about leaving that he promised them to me on his death bed. They were weaned and Jim had named them Snip and Snap. Snip was a Blue Merle, but he just didn't have any cow in him, paid no attention to cows, but loved to chase birds. The fellow who had a milk route in Three Rivers, delivered bottled milk, wanted a good dog for his family, so Snip found a good home with them. Snap was black with a ring neck, longer hair and I almost gave him away too because at first I didn't think he would be worth a hoot with cattle. Snap proved himself and we became like blood brothers for thirteen years.

Tom Phipps

Tom Phipps grew up in Three Rivers. I just found his grave the other day in the Exeter Cemetery; I think he was born in 1893, the same year as my mother, and he died in 1967. He and my dad kinda grew up together because my dad was born in 1891. Tom's parents were the first owners of the store in Old Three Rivers on Alles corner. Tom later built a house across the river from the old Sequoia Hall on the huge bedrock that extends down into the river. He packed out of Three Rivers in the summers, as did my dad. Tom was in the horse business in the off-season and became a famous horse trader. You know the old saying, a good horse trader would sell his mother a blind horse. That was Tom. He took pride in buying a horse from another horse trader, doctoring him up and selling him back to the same guy without his knowing it. He'd laugh about it. He was sharp, had a quick mind, like Peanuts (Floyd) Carter. Tom Phipps had a pack station in Mineral King and sold it to Bart Ross in about 1927.

Clough's Cave

On the trail at Franklin Pass there is a plaque on the tree where William Clough (1852-1917) is thought to have died. His death remains a mystery. Clough spent the summer months each year in Mineral King, working his own mining claim and doing assessments for owners of other mines. He was also hired by the Mt. Whitney Power Company to close the valves at its storage lakes at the end of the season. Late each fall he stopped at a little cabin on the way to the lakes but in 1917 he didn't come out. Two different search parties set out to look for him, but the snow was too deep to continue. The next spring, Dan Alles, Hat Maxon and two others went back and found some of his clothing, his watch and his daybook in which the last entry said he had closed the Eagle Lake valves on November 2nd. The wrench he used for turning the valves was found on the trail. Another story is only his whiskers were found. It is likely that wild animals dragged his body off.

Billy Clough discovered the cave named for him on a mountainside of upper South Fork, at the west corner of Sequoia National Park. For visitor access, a footbridge was built across the river. (The same bridge I drove my cows across on the way to Cahoon Meadow in the '60s.) The *Sacramento Daily Union*, July 24, 1886, described the discovery as:

"A Natural Cave that Surpasses All Previous Subterranean Wonders. While prospecting lately W. O. Clough, of Three Rivers, discovered a large cave about a mile and a half from what is known as the Crabtree cabin, or Brushtown, and about thirteen miles from the postoffice at Three Rivers. There is nothing to show that any person, white or Indian, had ever entered or known of the cavern before. There are three small caves near the second crossing above Manzanita camp. But this cave discovered July 1st of this year is not any of these, as some have supposed. It was at first a difficult matter to find one's way back to this large cavern, but a trail has been made leading to it. . . .The first chamber is a long, narrow one, being four hundred feet in length by twenty wide, and eighteen feet high, and is very nearly straight. Beautiful crystals are numerous in this apartment, as are stalactites in every conceivable shape and of all sizes, from that of a lady's finger to the dimensions of a locomotive boiler."

A Fox News cameraman filmed the cave in 1929 and declared that if it was advertised properly thousands of visitors would visit the cave, as many visitors as go to see Carlsbad caves in New Mexico.

Everyone agreed that Billy Clough was an eccentric character. A story told at one of the Pioneer Dinners described Billy Clough as a good, mild-tempered man, a sort of a religious fanatic who believed that cutting his beard would rob him of his strength. It was easy to get him started preaching, very hard to get him stopped. One time he preached at Atwell's Mill and the lumberjacks said he should use the edger table, which was on rollers, as his pulpit. When he got on top of the table and started his sermon, they yanked the table from under him and chuckled at their joke. Clough didn't show any anger, just got up from the ground and continued preaching.

One time, while packing from one mine over to another, Bill noticed a hole that could possibly be a cave entrance. His companion, of slimmer stature, crawled in first and shouted a warning to Bill not to follow because the opening was too small and he'd get stuck. Bill tried anyway and got stuck; it took a lot of pushing to get Bill out of the shaft so they could both get free.

When they were together above Mineral King at Monarch Lake, Dan Alles commented on the clouds of mosquitos humming over the water. Bill corrected him, "Those aren't mosquitos. They are angels." (Remember that the next time you go camping.) Billy preached the funeral sermon for Alles's father, Conrad Alles, Sr. in 1891. Bill Clough's brother Fred Clough, who resided in the Gold Country (Amador County), met Dan's brother Henry Alles there and told him about the South Fork in Three Rivers after which Henry convinced his family to move here from Michigan in 1887.

Another story by a pioneer said, "Old Bill claimed to have special grace that not many people have, that the Lord had granted him 1000 years to live. Bill had some mining claims in Mineral King and was offered $40,000 for the claims, but he knew $40,000 would not be enough to last 1000 years so he asked for $100,000." Interestingly, the September 22, 1912, *San Francisco Call* newspaper reported that ". . .the mining claim known as the Annie Fox at Mineral Hill owned and worked for years by William Cluff [sic] has been sold to a mining company. The price was said to be about $40,000. This mine is situated on the mountain side overlooking Mineral King and is a combination of copper and gold, running about $10 to the ton of gold ore. . . .This summer mining experts, representing two different companies, tested the Annie Fox thoroughly and following this the sale was made . . . ."

MINERAL KING

ᏣᎳᎩ

The Mineral King valley, said to have only one known alpine counterpart on the planet–the Alps–is accessible by car in the summer via a narrow 22-mile dirt road with 300 turns–seems like 1000. There are three trails out–through Franklin Pass, 11,250 feet; Farewell Gap, 10,588; Timber Gap, 9400; and if you want to do some trail work, Sawtooth.

Sawtooth is the most recognizable peak in Mineral King and can be seen on a clear day from Hanford, 65 miles distant on the San Joaquin Valley floor. From Mineral King valley, Sawtooth looms clear, a ride of five or six miles to the summit, from which you can see Mt. Whitney, 14,494 feet; seven miles north of that is Mt. Tyndall, 14,386; another two miles north is Mt. Williamson, 14,300 feet.

Lee Maloy was running the pack trip when we took the Bill Crocker party out one year in Kern River and brought them home over Sawtooth Pass. No one had been over that pass for probably twenty years for the main reason that the pack station would have to send out a crew every year to clear the trail because it is heavy snow avalanche country. It just didn't make economic sense when there were three other ways out of Mineral King. Jim Kindred, Clarence Brown and Charlie Reece were the other packers, and we spent three days in Lost Canyon below Columbine Lake working to clear the old trail while the dudes relaxed and fished around Soda Creek. We figured if this plan didn't work, we could backtrack to Big Five Lakes and come out over Black Rock.

Columbine Lake is down in a granite basin, the shoreline is a talus field, so we had to come across in the water at the narrow end. We led the horses and mules on a granite bench in crystal-clear water about knee-high on the mules; the edge drops off into the dark green depths. One mule carrying a wide dunnage load–dunnage is bed rolls in canvas slings on both sides of the mule–bumped his pack on a boulder and went off into deep water. He swam to the other side and the load of about six bedrolls was soaked. I remember Mr. Crocker always took a heavy, oversized bedroll.

One of the dudes on the trip was Crocker's friend, Osgood Hooker, who behaved as if he'd been catered to all of his life, a big pear-bottomed fellow, a real pill at times who broke several of our folding chairs; he'd come in off the ride and exhale a heavy "O-o-oh, Gaawd" and fall in a chair and bust the corners out. He was a former colonel or something in WWII and insisted on riding English saddle but he sat like a sack of potatoes way back on the horse's loin and before the trip was over, the horse had a sore back. On the last day, Lee decided to put the guy on a mule–Old Gus–that was gentle but had never been ridden. Jim Kindred put the English saddle on Gus to do a little test ride. Gus was fine, but it didn't really matter because Lee was going to lead the mule anyway. Like a scene from a pageant, the dude on an English saddle was led over Sawtooth Pass into Mineral King sitting upon an ass–well, a half-ass, Old Gus the mule.

When we rode into Mineral King, Ray Buckman, owner of the Mineral King pack station, greeted us with disbelief because he hadn't seen anyone come over Sawtooth Pass in twenty years.

The Mineral King area encompassing 15,000 acres was added to Sequoia National Forest by President Teddy Roosevelt in 1908. There were numerous private properties in the valley that retained private ownership status. To extend protection over these lands the whole valley was designated Sequoia National Game Refuge.

Credit for discovery of Mineral King probably goes to a hunter who looked over the edge of the bowl and thought, "how beautiful," and continued to track his prey, this according to Thomas S. Porter's treatise. Porter identified the likely first non-native to behold Mineral King as Parole O'Farrell, a meat hunter for trail crews building a connecting trail from Hockett Meadows off of South Fork to the eastern slope of the Sierra to reach the mines in Fort Independence in Inyo Valley. The Visalia & Inyo Wagon Road Company pursued an ambitious plan to build a delivery route straight over the Sierra to Inyo in order to become the chief suppliers to the silver mines there. It was a race to finish their road ahead of a Porterville group that saw the same opportunity. The Visalia company completed a wagon trail in five years through Hockett. Porterville abandoned its plans when the Inyo mines gave out.

Mineral King Mines

Guy Hopping gave a talk in 1953 about the mines in Mineral King and said the first gold was discovered there in 1864 by a man named Lute, a hunter for a trail crew building the Hockett Trail from Visalia to Camp Independence in Inyo. J. A. Crabtree filed a mining claim in 1867 and a trail was built to Mineral King in 1873. In June 1875 the Pony Express started weekly service to carry mail to Mineral King, and at the same time bids were invited to run the postal route from Porterville by way of Pleasant Valley and Soda Springs to Mineral King, a distance of 65 miles. In 1879 the news reported that a new town named Beulah was being laid out at the Mineral King mines. Twenty-five years later it was reported the town was still growing fast. At one point the population reached 3,000, with 500 registered voters and 14 saloons. Hopping said there was plenty of fighting but no killings.

By 1874, so many silver and gold mining claims were being filed for Mineral King that the county recorder of East Kaweah District moved the recording office up from Plano (Porterville) to Silver City where he could process the rush of new claims locally, Silver City being about five miles down from Mineral King.

Orlando Barton recalled that there were so many greenhorn prospectors dynamiting on the mountain that the residents passed a law that miners had to keep their rocks on their own land because charges set by the amateurs sent barrages of rocks rolling through town. In 1876, a smelter was finished and tested. The day operators were Enos Barton and Horace Bivins; night shift was Orlando Barton and W. S. McCann. To prove that smelting could be successful, Joe Palmer and John Crabtree built a small furnace with blacksmith bellows to smelt several pounds of bullion

The sawmills made a lot of money due to the building boom. Avalanches created setbacks, one in April 1880 swept away the workers' barracks and injured twenty-one miners.

March, 1874 *Daily Alta* "The Visalia & Inyo Road Company have completed their wagon road from Visalia to within 15 miles of the new mines in Mineral King district, and a good trail connects with the mines. Work is pushed to open for travel by July. Several big companies are preparing to mine on a large scale." More road news in May 1874 *L.A. Herald*: "The Inyo & Visalia Wagon Road Company have a good trail completed from Mount Hope to within 2-1/2 miles of Harry's Bend near the center of the mines. Silver City, almost five miles due west from Harry's Bend, is fast settling up." Additional news said the present pack trail will become a wagon road within eighteen months of sufficient size to accommodate six-horse wagons to pass a larger team on a run at most any point. The only practical route is up the Kaweah [as opposed to the Porterville route]. Senator Fowler drove a buggy through to the mines for the first time in August 1879, declaring the wagon road to Mineral King to be open. On the same day, the first loads of machinery for the Empire Company's large stamp mill left Visalia en route to the mines.

Disney Divide

It was known as the great Disney Divide. The U.S. Forest Service actually decided that Mineral King in its village status of private cabins, store, post office, hotel, etc. did not meet the "highest and best use" test for the land. A joint survey in 1947-48 by the U.S. Forest Service, Tulare County, and California Ski Association concluded the valley was superb ski terrain.

Ray Buckman invited Walt Disney to come up for a look-see about 1950. Disney was enchanted and made many more visits. As his vision for a ski resort came into focus, Disney sent a secret buyer to secure 740 acres of private land; the rest of the land would be leased from USFS. Securing ownership of the 143 acres of Silver City was key to control of the area. In 1965, politics as usual wrecked Disney's plan when the California legislature jumped the gun and announced approval of 25 million dollars to upgrade the Mineral King road and that news sent land prices skyrocketing. The issue—a dream of profits and windfalls versus the nightmare of environmental destruction polarized the region. So here we saw neighbors and life-long friends turn into bitter enemies.

The original 1960s Disney plan was a $35 million development anticipating 2.5 million visitors per year via a new all-weather road, a tramway from a 10-story parking garage for 3600 cars to a 1030-room hotel in Mineral King valley; skiing with seven to ten chairlifts. Summer recreation would feature fishing, horseback riding, picnics, hiking, and camping. Walt Disney died in December 1966. In 1969, the Sierra Club sued to stop the Disney resort.

October 1882, Golden trout were transplanted from Little Kern River to two large lakes in Monarch Canyon at the base of Miner's Peak. It was considered a success when the Golden trout from rivers were found to do well in lake waters. On September 5, 1896, John Broder guided visitors from New York, William C. Harris, editor of the *New York Angler*, and John L. Petrie, the artist on *Angler's* staff, to Mineral King and over to Mt. Whitney Creek so they could catch, eat, study, and sketch the famous Golden trout. The New Yorkers were guests of the Visalia Sportsman Club.

Before that, in 1880, Joe C. Palmer and W. B. Wallace, both well-known mountaineers and prospectors, guided a group of four men over Sawtooth and up to the summit of Miner's Peak. One described the panorama: ". . . massive granite slabs of every form and size, piled in utter confusion. Immediately around us, yawning abysses, plunging precipices . . . the sudden crash and roar of loosened rocks that dashed down some deep chasm near us . . . in the deepest gorges nearest us, we counted nine emerald green lakes . . . we could faintly see the Tulare plains, the surface of Tulare Lake and the outline of the Coastal Range . . . ." These are the same scenic vistas our pack trips afforded guests all those many years.

A mail service and stage schedule was advertised in the San Francisco papers in 1908: "Leave Lemon Cove railroad terminal on Tuesday, Thursday and Saturday at 9 a.m. and arrive in Mineral King Wednesday, Friday and Sunday at 12 a.m. Write P. Alles for particulars . . . ."

Packing Out of Mineral King

The commercial packing business in the western Sierra was started by John Broder in 1898 when he guided a San Francisco attorney by the name of Thornton from Mineral King to Giant Forest. Two years earlier, as noted above, he had guided the New York party.

I was invited to give a talk about the history of the packing business in Mineral King, but most of my stories were about Giant Forest because that's where our pack station was. I have an article written in 1931 by my parents, Earl and Edna McKee, about the packing industry in Mineral King and Giant Forest. In addition, Bart Ross had a pack station, and he filled me in on some packers and dates that support my dad's article. Bart and I used to trade cassette tapes telling about our packing experiences.

In 1908, Chester Wright started packing in this district, had enlarged his outfit to about sixty animals when he sold out to the Kings River Park Company in 1919. Ord Loverin started a small packing outfit in 1916 and had about twenty animals when he bought out the Kings River Park Company in 1924. By 1931 he had about eighty head.

In 1909, Earl McKee and Clarence Britten started commercial packing, each with a small outfit of about ten animals and worked as partners for several years. Britten added to his outfit and had about thirty animals when he quit the business in 1918. My dad, Earl McKee, with eighty animals by 1931, operated his business continuously until he died unexpectedly in 1946 on a pack trip.

In 1920, Eugene Davis established a successful packing headquarters in Mineral King across the creek and upstream about a quarter mile from Roy Davis. He sold it in 1924 to his brother, Phil Davis, dba Mineral King Packing Company. Phil enlarged his outfit to 160 animals at one time; in 1929 he sold 84 head to Buckman and Eggers.

Photo 1986 at my talk in Mineral King.

AUTHOR'S COLLECTION.

Between 1914 and 1918, Fred Maxon, Onis Brown, Bill Canfield, and Tom Phipps each started doing commercial packing with about twenty animals each and were still in business in 1931, except Tom Phipps. Fred Maxon was one of the pioneer veterinarians of this country; he built up his tourist packing business, assisted by his sons Hat and Jack.

In 1927, Tom Phipps sold a half-interest in his outfit to Roland Ross with headquarters in Mineral King, and increased their stock to eighty head. In

October 1929, Phipps sold out his interest entirely to Ross and went into the family furniture business.

In 1923, Roy Davis started a packing business located on the slope across from the ranger station, with about twenty animals. There was no flat area to speak of to offer the horses shelter and they spent those cold nights on the steep hillside. Some said that when Roy had too many horses idle in the corral he could locate a trail over Sawtooth to Lost Canyon where the meadows are gorgeous. This was before the Park had helicopters. Roy was still in business in 1931.

Lawrence Davis bought a small outfit from Bert Smith in Mineral King in 1924.

Bart Ross bought into his brother Roland's outfit that took over the lease of the Crowley Store. Roland Ross, whose father-in-law was J. E. Buckman of Exeter, had business interests in Mineral King in 1933 because in early spring he snowshoed or skied in with Oscar Alles and Bart Ross to check snow damage to the cabins. Later that same year Roland drove his car to Atwell's Mill, from which point his party of three had to hike in through four feet of snow. I remember meeting Roland Ross at the pack station when I was a little kid.

Ray Buckman bought the Phil Buckman/Frank Eggers station in 1937 and acquired the Bart Ross pack station in 1939. Ray Buckman told the audience at a Pioneer Dinner that he was 13 years old when he packed for Broder and Hopping in 1903. The trail he used went out of Giant Forest to Mineral King, then over Farewell Gap to Coyote and on to the Kern. In 1904 and 1905 Ray said he drove the Broder & Hopping stage from Visalia to Giant Forest, two round trips a week. Ray Buckman had his own packing business in Mineral King for 28 years. I sang for the funerals of both Ray Buckman and later his wife, Gem Buckman. They each left a request for me to sing "Oh Sweet Mystery of Life, at Last I've Found You."

My mother remembered that Ray Buckman's father, Ray Sr., also drove the stage. It was memorable because of the bells, and the fact that Ray Sr. had lost an arm in the Civil War and handled the big team with just his one arm.

The last commercial packer mentioned in my parents' article was Craig Thorn who took out his commercial packer permit in 1929 for twenty animals and set up his headquarters at Silver City.

My parents' article compared the revenue from the beginning of the industry to the date of their report: Gross receipts for Broder's first trip in 1908: less than $600; 1931, operating with 480 animals, gross receipts for local packers exceeded $100,000.00.

Lee Maloy still had the pack station in Giant Forest when he bought Ray Buckman's outfit about 1954; he ran it about four years then sold to Bill DeCarteret who owned it at the time I packed the Big Arroyo bridge out of Mineral King in 1958. Dan Bidell bought Bill out sometime in the 1960s.

When I packed those steel bridges for the Park, I had to work from the road's end most of the time. I packed one bridge to Kern River from Mineral King and it is a real long ride to get there. We rode over Franklin Pass, down Rattlesnake Canyon to Kern River. The thirteen-mile Rattlesnake trail from Mineral King to Kern was built in 1909. From Kern we headed up to the mouth of Big Arroyo. Big Arroyo is a huge glacial valley like a freeway to the Kern. That was a long day. I trailed those mules every day and they were strong. We packed a lot of steel, cable and winches there–up, over and down, dumped it off, stayed over night, and the next day rode back. The following day we'd weigh out the loads, then get up early the next morning to hang the steel on the pack boxes and head for Kern River again, two round trips a week.

I asked for Troy Hall to be my swamper on that bridge job and he worked like hell. On one trip he "forgot" to pack a gallon of wine to take to Lon Maxon, trail boss of bridges, and said he'd just hang it in a nose-bag on his saddle. He was in front on a tough little pinto horse, a half-Shetland, that could eat up the mountain going up Franklin Pass. Riding down the other side, however, the saddle kept running up on the horse's neck and Troy would have to get off and adjust it. I started to notice that Troy was not too steady on his feet. We got down in the rocky part at the head of Rattlesnake and old Troy finally stopped and half bawled, "I can't keep my damn saddle on this pony and I'm too drunk to lead him." This really slowed us down and it was dark when we got to Kern River. The wine had control somewhere along about Cow Camp when a thoroughly frustrated and tired Troy took a wild swing and fell under his horse. When we finally got to camp on Kern River, Troy unpacked one of the steel mules–there were 10 mules–and the load fell and pinned him in the brush. I told him to get in his tent and sleep it off.

Late that season I had to leave the mountains early because I had some crews lined up for corral building at the ranch, so I couldn't stay to pack out the trail boss, Lon Maxon. It took some 40 mules to get that camp out, just before the snow flew.

A great pack trip from Mineral King to Mt. Whitney starts over Timber Gap, over Black Rock Pass (11,600 ft.) to Five Lake Basin–Big Five and Little Five. From Little Five you see Big Arroyo and over to Chagoopa Plateau. This is a panorama of contrasting color and terrain– Black Kaweah, Red Kaweah, miles of beautiful meadows surrounded by stands of timber. Chagoopa was wonderful cow country before it became federal land. The trail goes past Chagoopa Falls and Funston Creek where Big Arroyo slides into Kern Canyon. From the end of Big Arroyo, the trail goes up-canyon then eastward through Crabtree to reach Mt. Whitney.

Forester Pass (13,160 ft., the highest pass in the mountains) at the far north end of Kern Canyon provides a breathtaking view south down the length of this enormous glacial gorge, clear to Kernville. It is a picture no one can forget.

MC KEE PUREBRED QUARTER HORSES

∽ШШ∾

Fine Horsemen I Have Known

The horseman I admired most was my father, Earl McKee. He was a great horseman, broke many horses, I guess that's where I got my thoughts about the fine points of breaking horses, horses with a good mouth, that carry their head just a little higher than flat to make them look sharp. My dad was careful with the sensitive mouth, so when you picked up the rein it was like driving a Cadillac. Some heavy-handed guys could break a horse to gather cows and do the job but they didn't know sic 'em about a horse with a sensitive mouth. That's the difference between a bridle man and a horse breaker. My dad trained his horses to pivot, stop and slide, and turn. My dad had his own method to start a colt out, with light-faced horses started in the hackamore, worked in a confined area, until the colt understood what you wanted him to do, then put him in a snaffle bit, so when you picked up either to right or to left the first pull would be on the side that you wanted him to give to; the rein on the neck came next, but it was a matter of placing your body correctly, training with leg position and pressure.

My dad was good, he could break a horse to hackamore, he had a good hand. My dad taught me so much. When I finished breaking a horse, I could watch a gate for anybody, a horse that you could ride into a gate, part out the whole bunch of cattle and never lose a calf or cow. That's what you train for, to show him the job, and the horse knows how and when to turn the cow. Forrest Homer always wanted to buy the horse I rode. Truth be told, I could break a horse better than Forrest could, but I never argued this point with him. He really knew how to show a good bridle horse.

My father's favorite horse, Joker, was very well known around here. In the 1926 movie of the wagon train from Three Rivers to Woodlake, there were a lot of scenes of Joker pulling a fancy buckboard. My dad broke him to everything. In those days you needed a horse that was versatile, to ride, to pull a buggy to the dance or a day in Visalia. I heard Tom Phipps talk about Joker and what a good horse he was. He told me Joker would pull the buggy up the hill to the homestead and hold it while my mother got out and opened the gate, then she'd cluck to him and he'd pull the buggy through and wait while she closed the gate and got back on the wagon.

My dad was a member of the Tulare County Sheriff's Posse whose members used to play polo on their cow horses. There was a lot of friendly competition running stake races and horse races at community picnics and rodeos. Joker was a champ in the stock horse class where the horse runs, slides straight, does quarter turns, full turns, and spins to show how well he works. Joker could really turn the stakes and my dad was seldom beaten on that horse. I remember my dad telling about the times he was challenged to race a fellow named Cuff Burrell who rode a fancy reining buckskin mare, and my dad beat him every time. Cuff supplied rodeo stock, including his "tough Brahmas," for rodeos in Visalia and around the state in the mid-1940s. I used to see Cuff around the Visalia stockyards.

My dad started raising horses when he was a young man. My dad packed continuously since 1909; from 1929 on, he owned eighty head of horses and mules for his Giant Forest pack station. Half the horses were ones he bred and broke. The foundation of my dad's horse business was the stud, Mars Mouse.

The U.S. Army was in the horse business to supply its cavalry in WWI and after the war, studs, called re-mount studs, were offered for lease, not for sale, to horse breeders. They were blooded horses, registered thoroughbreds. There was no Quarter Horse registry then; a Quarter horse is just a short-running thoroughbred that was fast at a quarter mile, a sprinter. It was found that those horses would make great cow horses because they were fast and quiet-minded. In the 1920s, my dad leased a remount stud, Mars Mouse, and bred a stable of big powerful horses that became well known for their great disposition, excellent feet, bone and withers. Those horses were sought after around the Valley. A news item in 1937 read: "Fanciers of fine horses, William McDuffie and his son, of Pasadena, flew to Visalia on Saturday and from there motored to the home of Earl McKee at Three Rivers, bent on purchasing some of the McKee stock. Their ultimate goal was reached when they were leaving here they were owners of two fine horses sired by the well-known government stallion Mars Mouse. The horses were shipped to McDuffie ranch in Mendocino County."

My sister, Blanche, won the horse races at the Three Rivers picnic on her Mars Mouse sorrel, Bud, preliminary to competing in the Visalia Rodeo Sweetheart contest in 1933. She competed in several Rodeo Sweetheart contests, and raced and showed horses with the best of the cowboys.

In 1940, my dad bred a thoroughbred mare, a Mars Mouse mare, to a beautiful dark gold palomino stallion at Lemoore named Cameron, whose lineage went back to Plaudit, an early horse that could run. He named the colt Parmer (after W. P. Parmer Fuller, Jr.), trained that horse, and put a fine rein on him. I inherited Parmer when he was only six years old after my dad died.

W. V. "Bill" Smith

W. V. Smith was an exceptional horseman who broke horse and mule teams in the old days to work the fields and pull the wagons, but made his money in vineyards. He lived in Exeter. Bill and my dad were good friends, and after my dad died I used to visit and he'd reminisce about my dad. Bill broke fancy big hitch wagon teams–eight-up–and ride in parades. The crowds would watch in amazement as he turned his team of eight horses and a wagon around right in the middle of the main intersection of Exeter–Pine and E Street. He was famous throughout the Valley for his highly trained teams.

He worked with his horses everyday. His barn had stalls on each side. He could sit in a chair at the end of the breezeway and speak to his horses and they obeyed. In the afternoons he would send them out to the watering trough, one by one. The stall doors would all be rolled open, and when called a horse would come to the door and stand shoulder even with the door. He'd put on a halter with a 125-foot drag rope, and "cluck-cluck" to it and the horse would walk, not run, down the breezeway, around the barn to the trough and drink. The horse would return to the barn; stop, turn and back down the breezeway; stop, turn, and back into its stall as far as shoulder line, then wait for the halter to be taken off. When the next horse heard his name, he would perform the same drill.

Mr. Smith owned a big palomino named Gold Digger that he could signal to run a little ways out, then he'd yell "whoa" and the horse would slide; then he'd command "backup" and he'd back into the barn down to his stall, stop and back into his stall and stand and wait.

I enjoyed visiting with Bill who always had some training tricks of the trade that he would show me. He taught me many things I used throughout my life. In the round pen he rode a horse with a calm disposition to work alongside his colts. The colt was saddled and Bill held a lead rope as they moved around the ring side-by-side. If the colt wanted to buck, he'd just move with it around and around until it was tired. Bill used a buggy whip to reach over to either side of the colt's shoulders to give him a gentle tap to guide him as he wanted. It was never used as a whip. It wasn't long until his horses were trained to obey directions and then he'd put reins on them for finishing. He had a remarkable way with his horses.

I bought a nice, very well-trained horse from him once, and Bill cautioned me to be sure to ride him as soon as I got him home, don't get busy and put off riding for days. Also especially on cold mornings walk him around a bit before getting on. I forgot his advice and a week or so later when I saddled him for work one morning, that horse bucked me off.

Bill was still breaking colts at about 90 years of age when he lost some fingers. He was riding a filly and training her to pull. To do this you rope a stationary or heavy object, then let the rope slip, give a little, so the horse will keep pulling. The saddle horn needs to be wrapped with cotton so the dally can slip. The horse backs up until the rope is tight, then you slip the dally a little and he realizes he has to pull more. Bill was doing this. He roped a sturdy fence post anchored in cement and was teaching the horse to back up, letting the dally slip a little. Well, at 90 years he wasn't as quick as he used to be. The mare jumped around and the rope looped over his hand and crushed it against the saddle horn. He fell off and hung by his hand. No one heard his yells. The horse finally pulled loose, but Bill's hand was so broken and mangled, four fingers had to be amputated.

I went to see him in the hospital and joked that it's going to be kinda hard for him to write now. Naw, he said his writing was getting so shaky anyway, that when he writes with his left hand you can't tell the difference. He got healed up and lived another several years. I think he was 94 when he died. I sang a cowboy song at his funeral. He was a charter member of the Tulare County Sheriff Posse as was my dad. He always talked about playing polo with my dad.

Harry Rose

Harry Rose was a dear friend. He was a famous horse trainer who was part horse. He rode and broke some of the most famous reining horses in the world. He could show bridle horses like very few others. Harry had no fear of any horse and would have a green bronc doing amazing things in just a few days. I sent one of my athletic bronc horses to Harry for training. I learned a lot about horses from Harry.

Quarter Horses at My Stables

I've raised and bred Quarter horses most of my life. I started raising old foundation registered Quarter horses seriously here at my ranch about forty years ago.

In 1972, I bought the first of several studs to expand my horse business. Acres Cup Cake was the first stud, a Poco Bueno-bred horse, purchased from Frank and Mary Costa of Visalia. I won't name them all, but another beautiful stud was Docs San Peppy Go Man Go, a large stallion that sired some beautiful rope and ranch horses. Several in my band of mares are sired by Go Man Go. In 1995, I bought a King 234-bloodline stallion, Cue Berry King, from my good friend Ray Lindseth of Dupuyer, Montana.

In 1997, I purchased a red roan stud colt named Plenty Valentine, "Pinky," from another good friend, John Balkinbush of Conrad, Montana, a breeder of some of the finest horses in the northwest. Pinky matured into a great cow horse and breeding animal, all the while maintaining his kid-horse disposition. His colts have the same traits, are very easy to break and have lots of color. He is so dependable, I just lead him out of his stall, throw on a saddle, cinch up and step on. He's ready to go, no funny business and a real pleasure to ride. He takes good care of me.

I try to keep about thirty breeding mares. After foaling and breeding time in the spring, I run most of the mares in the foothills. This is where the foals learn from their mothers about rocky trails, how to go through brush, how to ford creeks, how to jump a draw and to respect barbed wire. This important exposure to the wilderness, with its dangers and challenges, educates the young mind of these horses. In my belief, these life-molding experiences are what separate the mountain horses from those that haven't been out of a paddock.

I have American Quarter Horses to sell and keep a number of horses at the home stable to train. When possible, a dear friend, Sommer Shannon, spends time with my colts and my stallions to develop their trust and accustom them to being handled. She is personable, thinks 'cowboy' and works hard like one. I mention this because Sommer's own horse had a misaligned gait, so I hauled him down to Ronald Georgi, D. C. for her. Dr. Georgi is a chiropractor in Woodlake who I thought might be able to help because, interestingly, he treats both humans and horses, (different waiting rooms). Dr. Georgi took a special course of study to treat the equine vertebrae with a stimulus device and a mallet, along with other methods. I've known Dr. Georgi for forty years; he was elected to the Woodlake elementary school board in 1972, about the time I was on the high school board. I remember his pork-chop sideburns.

Mules

I have a soft spot for mules. A mule is a true hybrid animal, the result of cross-breeding a jackass with a female horse (mare). A mule has one more chromosome than either the jack or the horse and it carries some of the best qualities of both. Mules are smarter in some ways than horses on the trail because they will not step where the footing is insecure. The trait isn't so much stubbornness as it is intelligence. There are two kinds of mules–hinnies and jennies. A hinny is a mule from a stud horse and a female donkey. A jenny is from a jackass and a mare horse. They are different because a hinny is raised by the mother donkey; a jenny is raised by a mother horse and tends to be calmer, more sensible and easy to work, more horse-like.

I raised a bunch of mules during the late 1980s and 1990s. Jacks are hard to handle and hard to breed. I owned three different jacks, one was an experienced breeder named Romeo Red that I bought from a friend who raised jack stock in Havens, Kansas.

There were some interesting mule trades when I first started raising mules. One mule breeder had a big black jack and his mares produced some fine mule colts. I wanted to buy two of them, but he'd only sell them if I also took one from the year before (1968), the ugliest mule, head like a barn, really out of proportion to his body. His name was Barney and he grew to become one of the best mules I ever owned. He lived to be 38 years old. Mules live longer than horses because they take better care of themselves, watch their step to save themselves, don't get rattled like a horse. They reason things out–if there's a bad place in the trail a mule will go around it, even if you tried to lead him through it, his head might be over the trail, but his feet are way off to the side, going around. Some other mules I raised were Helen, 1972; Lye (named for Adaline Fuller), 1973; GeeGee (named for George Fuller's wife), 1974; and Tammy Fay, 1978.

The Park Service bought mules from two mule traders I got to know named Willis Grumbine and his partner, Major Cokely, from Kansas. Major Cokely sold me a jack, one of the hard-to-breed jacks. I had decided to raise more mules and also put the jack at stud for other horse owners.

Here's a little lesson on animal husbandry just in case you're interested. When a stud horse–stallion–is introduced to a mare in season (heat), he moves in close with a lot of sweet nothings to tell in her ear to get her ready to go and then does his job. A jackass, on the other hand, is a real jackass. He'll just run up, bray EEE-AHHH loud enough to scare the mare out of heat, then wham. No class.

It takes preparation and patience to breed the jack. This is when you practice your profanity, brush up on your cuss words. You tie him a few feet away so he can see the mare, then you wait. You can't talk him into it. He'll study the sky or watch the birds on the telephone wires until he finally gets the idea in his head; then it takes time for the idea to get from one end to the other to make him drop (meaning his equipment is ready). When you see the drop, he is ready and you lead him to the mare. He has to wear a halter with a draw around his chin to keep his mouth shut so the only noise he can make is a hrrrr hrrrr, can't bite and terrify the mare with brays that start her kicking and fighting.

To hold the mare, I built a special breeding stock. Milton Savage was interested in learning to raise mules so he helped me lay out the pattern and weld the one I designed. We called it the rape machine, but its purpose was to keep the animals from hurting themselves and each other. It was a chute–a stock–as long as a large horse, made of welded pipe and plank sides, with a short, adjustable door to enter and a tall door to exit at the other end. Soft braided ropes went across the mare's back to rings along the side to keep her from rearing backward. The mare stood on a lower level than the jack to compensate for the height difference. The mare was led in, her head secured, and the short gate was closed below her tail end. When she was settled, you sat down and waited.

I had to be away with the band on the day a gal brought her two mares over to breed, so Scott Erickson, who worked for me at the time, was there to unload the mares into the corral and watch over the procedure. I showed Scott what to do and explained that this is going to take time because that jack will spend his time gazing at birds in the sky and seem oblivious to the mare, so here's a nice chair and some Westerns, funny books, and magazines. Just sit down and wait for the jack to do his job. When I got home I noticed the broken handle of a brand new shovel, looked at the mare and said, "Looks to me like you might have had a little trouble here." In that case, the mare was the problem, not the jack; she wouldn't stop kicking.

This first breeding jack died in an unfortunate, unexpected, accident. I then bought another jack from Major Cokely that I named Romeo Red. Romeo Red was my best jack. He was an ideal type–big boned, powerful build, a sorrel, and he produced beautiful mules. Sometimes he'd stand in the field like he was transfixed on some point on the horizon. Early in the morning, about the time the chickens would crow, he'd let the whole canyon know he was available with a long, long bray. He could hold his breath longer than any jackass I ever saw–heeeeeeeeeeee haw, haw, haw, haw, haw, haw. . . . We used to count his monotone haws and write down the long ones just for fun–one morning he hawed thirty-two times, he really must have been lonesome that morning. Old timers used to call mules "mountain canaries."

John Casey was a mule breeder in Fowler, California. He was from Missouri, a funny guy who wore bib overalls, and could bray like a jack. I took mares to be bred to his jack. I was late to one of my visits, so he and his friends had a few drinks, and when I got there Casey climbed on a haystack and demonstrated his braying talent for us. I told him he could win the Mule Braying contest at Mule Days but he never went. I hauled a horse and mule to compete in mule packing contests when Sacramento had Mule Days for several years, as did my friends Bill Wylie, Leon Craig, and Dave Wilson. Over in Bishop, California, the annual Mule Days is a premier mule event that has been going on now for forty years.

This is Romeo Red, a sorrel, 14-1/2 hands-high and 950 pounds, a great breeding jack that produced some beautiful sorrel mules. Photo c. 1990.
AUTHOR'S COLLECTION.

My dad groomed and "dressed" his mules for the trail; they always looked parade-ready. The mane was clipped short from the withers to ears, the middle section was left a little longer to create an arch on the neck, up to about 1-3/4 inches high. Each side of the mane was cut close and shaped to the center for a narrow, clean Mohawk look. The tail hair was trimmed close at the base and down six inches or so into a V. Handmade buckskin brow bands really made them look sharp. My dad thought his mules should look good and I followed his example because I wanted to be like him.

We washed the mules' backs every work day. Each mule was fitted with its own custom-made saddle, because mules have different conformations—some with high withers or wider backs. I made quite a few of the saddles myself. I preferred what's called a Tehama tree, the bars of which were made from Douglas Fir. Bars on the bottom of the saddle, front to back, are where the weight rests and that is what needed to be custom fit. This was done by wetting the mule's back and lightly setting the saddle on, then removing it and filing off the high spots that were wet, using a horseshoe rasp, repeat until it becomes wet all over when gently placed on the wet mule. Then you know the weight of the load sits evenly. The bars are then covered with sheepskin. Forks were cut to shape and bolted on. When the saddle fit, the mule's name was burned onto the saddle. I'd rig the saddle, cut the britching, spider and breast collar from a whole side of harness leather worked with liquid leather to make it soft and pliable.

This is Old Rube, foaled in 1969, died in 2003. I followed my dad's example and kept our pack mules parade-ready. The mane was trimmed close into a bowed shape; each halter had a buckskin brow band. Photo c. 1970.

AUTHOR'S COLLECTION.

Aluminum boxes—kyacks—with straight sides were sold all over to pack stations. These created a pressure point right in the middle of the mule's ribs and if it happened to be where a cinch came down, it would wear his hide off and be terribly uncomfortable. Fiberglass kyacks were better because they give slightly against the mule. Long pads and blankets kept the kyack off from the mule's hide. I helped Joe Davis, who was working for the Park Service, to design concave boxes. We cut these wooden boxes slightly concave so the pressure point wasn't all against the mule's ribs, the weight was evenly distributed. Joe received an award of several hundred dollars because the kyacks worked.

On our final pack trip with just guys we were at Deadman Canyon, camped at the lower end of Ranger Meadow, one of the prettiest places in the mountains. It was a pretty day and the stock were feeding in the meadow as I watched one mule, Gee-Gee, make her way back to camp; she favored one foot and walked up to the mule line and stood. She didn't move because she needed my help. I took a nose bag and rope over and saw that her nose was full of porcupine quills. Obviously she had pawed a porcupine because one foot also had quills embedded all around it. She let me pick up her feet while I removed all the quills.

When I started raising Quarter horses, I had to get rid of the mules because mules run the colts, or any small animals; they just can't be left together.

MY FRIENDS IN THE CATTLE BUSINESS

Cow Dogs

At one time, I raised cow dogs. I built a great kennel with three runs, all concrete, and even put in a below-ground septic tank so everything could be washed down, clean and odorless. I bred dogs and sold some pups and gave some away. When I left the cattle business, I got out of the dog business, too.

When gathering and moving cattle to summer pasture you really need good dogs. I had a great dog named Snap, and every once in a while I have a dream about him. He's like a part of me. He had the greatest voice; up in the timber his voice would echo. Forrest Homer said one day, "You know, Earl, that dog has the best bark." I could send Snap out front and know where he was when he barked. We worked together for 12 or 13 years.

The end was a sad story. Snap was old and retired and slept under my car. One day I didn't see him, so I don't have to tell you what happened. X-rays showed broken bones and a broken pelvis. He never wanted anyone but me to touch him, and at the Vet's office it was no different, so our Veterinarian John Magliori gave the injection and I held him until his breathing stopped. At home I carried Snap to the corral where he always sat and watched what I was doing. Snap was gun-shy and terrified by thunder–during a bad thunderstorm he was so panicked he broke some teeth chewing out of his dog pen. I buried him there at the corral, and as I was digging, the worst thunder and lightning storm hit. I'll tell you, it took me a week to get over that.

I wrote a poem in honor of Snap, about our life together. It is in the chapter of poetry.

The 1955 flood washed out most of the bridges in Three Rivers, the river changed course a couple of places and in Visalia people went to work in boats. It was just before Christmas and it rained 8-1/2 inches here and about 15 inches in the mountains in 18 hours. Fences were washed out in the valley, swamps were flooded and livestock, including Gill Cattle Company stock, were loose all over clear to Visalia. Gill's cowboys were sent out to gather the cattle and haul them to Sage Brush ranch at Horse Creek ranch so I went over to help them make room for the arriving cattle.

I really needed my dog, Slim, a McNab shorthair, all day there but Gill did not allow cowboys to use dogs in the open country, probably because of some bad experiences of untrained dogs running the cows, so Slim stayed home. Because the main bridges had been washed out in the flood, all the traffic was detoured from Hwy. 198 to the old road in front of my house. Later in the day, Slim heard my truck coming home and ran out to the road to meet me. But it wasn't my truck, it was one just like it owned by Kelly Ogilvie–a 4WD Jeep pickup. A car coming from the other direction hit Slim and ran over him.

Slim was a young dog and when he was six months old he could go get a bunch of cattle and bring them back to where he last saw me and hold them right there. The first time he did it I couldn't believe it. We were at Ace Peck's place to move out some of Gill's steers that had gotten in through the fence. I took Slim and his brother, they were just pups, didn't know sic 'em. But I thought I'd see what they would do, so I hollered at them to "Get ahead, Slim." The one came back in a few minutes, but Slim didn't. I kept yelling "Get ahead, Slim," and pretty soon I heard him bark maybe a half mile away, then coming closer on the trail along the fence line. I was on my horse on the hillside above the brush. I heard brush popping and Slim pushed those cattle right to where my horse was. But when they saw me the steers bolted and ran right over the top of Slim and headed back the way they came, through brush too thick to ride through. I thought, well, can Slim do it again? So I told him to "get ahead!" and pretty soon, the same thing happened–the steers came up through the hole in the brush, but this time Slim was trotting right by a steer's hock with its tail in his mouth. Those steers were so quiet I could have taken them anywhere.

I could send Slim after one cow. Snap and Slim were head dogs, herders that get on the other side to turn the cow back. A gripper, called a heeler, will just get behind and drive the steer in whatever direction it is pointed.

The night before the '55 flood I had shut some cattle in the corral at Greasy Cove. I was worried so a couple of days after helping Gill, I took my horse, Copper, in a one horse trailer to get across the South Fork Bridge–the center had collapsed in the high water so the road crew made it passable by putting planks across to make a one-way bridge. In Lemon Cove, the Iron Bridge had washed out so we couldn't get to Woodlake or Dry Creek that way. The St. Johns Bridge by Woodlake was the only way to cross the river, so I had to detour through Lemon Cove, west to Moffitt's Crossing, Cottage Post Office, to the road to Woodlake, then back up to the Dry Creek turn off.

I drove up to Dofflemyer ranch out on a little flat near Dry Creek and unloaded Copper close to the river. I knew of a long wide spot where the water wouldn't be too deep. I tried to cross there because it seemed that the river was receding, but it wasn't as low as I thought and the current was stronger than I expected. I was about half way out and could tell my horse was going to be knocked down, the water was crashing over his neck and he couldn't hold on. He went down, and I just went off the back. Luckily he turned towards the bank we came from. If he'd headed the other way, I'd a been stranded over there for a few days. I had a hold of his tail as he swam for the riverbank that the high water had cut out like an arroyo. The current was pushing us down. The horse was floundering trying to get his footing when I saw his right front shoe get caught in the bridle bit. That was grim, but by some miracle, the bar and the bit broke; if it hadn't, my horse would have drowned for sure.

It was just a miracle that the bit broke first before the leather did so my horse could get his hoof free, but even then he continued to struggle, and right then he grabbed his cinch–he was a little cinchy–which means he just froze and gave up. I paddled to a little eddy near a logjam and climbed out. I was wearing enough gear to drown me in that ice-cold river–had a slicker, chaps, boots, a thermos with some soup, and spurs. I stripped to my pants and swam back out to him. I pulled his head up and he'd get air and I managed to get him around in the little eddy which was about three feet on the bottom of the logjam and out of the current. He was laying there in the river just about four feet deep. But he wouldn't hold his head up. He just gave up. I thought, well, I'll save my saddle, so

I undid the billet on the off-side cinch and loosened it. It didn't come off but it went to the next hole; when that happened, he jumped up and had water running out of every hole in his body–he'd almost drowned, he'd swallowed a lot of water that was running out of his ears and rear end. He jumped onto the bank and took off bucking across the field. I gathered up my stuff and pretty soon I heard him nickering and he came back to me. Copper had needed help, he was just terrified. I was ever so thankful to put him in the trailer and take him home.

And just the other day I got that bridle out, still hanging on my wall, an antique of sorts. It is a Visalia Spade bit and I had my cousin, Norman McKee, braze that bit together right after the horse broke it in the flood. It is a good bridle, I took it out and polished it the other day and put it on a big roan stud and rode him, roped some calves with that bit. There're a lot of memories there. Never will forget that day.

I had to wait to check on those cattle in the corral for another couple of days until the river was lower and I knew we could get across. When I got there and let them out, they were just fine. Hadn't eaten for four days but they ate all the grass they could reach through the fence and they sure weren't out of water because it had been raining hard and pools of water were everywhere.

Copper was born in the spring of 1946, so my dad got to see that colt. W. V. Smith bought two studs from The King Ranch in Texas– Bueno Tempo and Doctor Red. Everyone liked Bueno Tempo. Copper was out of a fast mare and Bueno Tempo. Mr. Smith tried to buy Copper from me, offered me $750, very good money in 1946, but I refused to sell. My dad thought I was crazy. Copper made a fine gate horse, he watched the cow, and could really pull. I could rope full-grown cows off him–this was necessary to bell a cow, or to treat a cow for corns between its hooves. (Corns can develop and cause pinching and soreness so she won't move to graze.) Copper later had a dislocated back so I turned him out to pasture for the last five years of his life.

Gill Cattle Company and Spring Branding

Fred Gill founded the Gill Cattle Company in Exeter, California. He had a twin brother Ernest, and another brother, Levi. Fred's sister, Lottie, married Clarence Britten (half-brother of my dad's brother-in-law, Harry Britten) my dad's first partner in the packing business in the

1920s. Fred Gill was born in 1869 and died in 1954. He had three sons: Roy (1897-1983), Emmett (1900-1964), and Adolph (1905-1986). They were all smart kids but when they were old enough to carry a rope, Fred took them out of school and put them to work on the ranch; one finished third grade, another got through grammar school. This ranch covered 40,000 acres, all of Yokohl Valley to Frasier Valley. Gill also owned ranches in Wyoming, Texas, Arizona, and the fabulous Roaring Springs Ranch, 40 miles square, in Oregon. Sometimes my dad worked on cattle drives for the Gills in Oregon and Nevada.

For two or three years around 1949, I sold some of my cattle to the Gill ranch. Old Fred Gill came over with me to the Greasy Cove ranch to look over my cattle. He bought my yearling steers and heifers in 1949 and 1950. He was sharp-minded with a great sense of humor. At the gate he'd count the cattle by fours; we'd think we needed to slow the herd for the count, but he'd tell us to "come on, come on." I loaded and hauled one lot of steers to Gill headquarters at Yokohl ranch, where we ran them onto the scale. Fred held up his hand and stopped me, "You've got one too many there." I was confused. "Young man, we don't ever weigh 13 head of steers here." So I took one steer off and weighed it in the next batch. I remembered then I had heard that Fred Gill never allowed 13 of anything, in any form, anywhere; he avoided black cats and followed the *Almanac*. At one time, Fred Gill ran the fifth-largest cattle operation in the nation.

Along with cattle, the Gills had a herd of nice mares and raised a lot of good horses for sale. I remember three of their studs: Bear Hug, Old Mark, and Texas Tandy Jr. that set a world record for the quarter mile. Ollie Osborn trained all their colts, got them started for the finish trainer to put a rein on them. Ollie was a good cowboy who also worked cattle with Emmett and Adolph Gill and Ray Pinnell.

Our family singing group, The McKee Family, performed at a big BBQ at Adolph Gill's spacious yard to raise money for "Goldwater for President" in 1964. Senator Goldwater was represented that day by a marvelous, entertaining, western-garbed speaker named Ronald Reagan. I helped gather six big steers from their Yokohl ranch to be deep-pitted for the affair. With the help of Lee Maloy I barbecued two of those huge steers; we cut and wrapped the meat at Frances Brown's Three Rivers Market and locker. Richly seasoned with fresh onions, garlic and tomatoes, sealed in foil within layers of newspapers in burlap, bound with baling wire, it was cooked in the deep pit at the Lions roping arena. Leroy Maloy and I laid the brick for that BBQ pit to replace the old one that had been dug too close to the river–one high-water year the annual roping deep pit BBQ was on the rare side.

In 1966, I sang the "Star Spangled Banner" at an event for Ronald Reagan when he came to Tulare, California, during his campaign for governor. At another rally for Ronald Reagan, in Visalia at the Sons of Italy Hall, the Jazzberry Jam Band played music and Jimmy Stewart, the actor, was one of the speakers.

I was thinking about the first time I sang at a funeral; I was 23 years old and it was for Fred Gill. He died in 1954 and after that I sang at every Gill funeral, except one. Roy Gill came over to me one time at a funeral or something and said, "Earl, I want you to sing at my funeral. I'll be laying out here somewhere in Exeter, and I don't want anything pretty. I just want you to bring an old orange picking box and when they're throwing the dirt down on my face, I want you to sing "I'm Glad You're Dead, You Son of a Bitch, I'm Glad You're Dead." Actually "I'm Glad You're Dead" is an old Louie Armstrong tune, but it doesn't say "son-of-a-bitch." Roy was a character, a wild cowboy, but as it worked out, I could not sing at his funeral because Roy died when we were out of state at a jazz festival and I couldn't get home.

Emmett Gill was a dear friend of mine. He summered in the Klamath area of Oregon. He ran white-faced cattle. I liked to be around him because he was a good horseman. He broke good horses that would watch the cow. He competed in steer tripping in Montana and Wyoming. Emmett and Lee Maloy won the Champion Steer Roping Buckles at Three Rivers Lions Roping. Emmett died in 1964 after being hospitalized for a surgical procedure. He about went crazy being confined to bed, so he checked himself out of the hospital in the middle of the night and tried to walk home. A neighbor found him. He was re-admitted with a wound infection, went into shock and died. I sang at his funeral. Emmett Gill was a great honest-to-God cowboy.

Emmett trained Clay Carr, Elmo Carr, and Francis Appelby to ride broncs. They all competed in rodeos. Clay Carr was the Rodeo Cowboys of America (RCA) World Champion for two years running; just a kid from Exeter, California who worked summers at the Gill Ranch. They always had lots of horses, some of them were mares from the 3V Ranch in Arizona. Clay was an athlete, great calf roper, bulldogger, bronc rider, and all-around rodeo cowboy, and worked hard at it. J. B. Coffelt, who was in charge of the stock at Giant Forest when I was packing bridges, grew up with those boys and told me many stories about them.

Francis Appelby was a good bronc rider, could stay atop any bucking horse anywhere, but in competition his posture got him some goose eggs. He was fearless but rode a little humped over. One time, Francis didn't mark his horse out, meaning he didn't have his spurs high enough on the bronc's shoulders on the first jump out of the chute. Your knees have to be up on the bronc's shoulder line and you've got to sit tall and rake your spurs on the first jump, that's been the rule forever, to let the judges know you're not afraid to make him buck and you've got to prove you can ride him. So Francis didn't mark his bronc to suit the judges and the judge threw the yellow handkerchief which means the rider might as well jump off, he's zeroed, done. Francis ignored the kerchief and stayed atop the bucking horse while he put a cigarette in his mouth and lit it, just to show 'em he could ride him. The crowd got a kick out of that.

Emmett told a funny story about Francis at a branding. They were at Chicken Coop Canyon to the south of Oak Flat in Yokohl Valley, and Francis was in the corral trying to rope calves off a bucking horse that had only been ridden two days! Well, in the corral there are several pairs of ropers catching calves, and other guys branding, cutting, dehorning and so forth. Here was Francis getting wrapped up in his rope and bucked off, and finally Emmett told him to get out of the corral before he killed somebody.

Herman Colpien

Herman Colpien, what a marvelous man he was. I sold cattle to Herman for over 30 years. He was one of the most honest men I ever met; all we ever did was shake hands on a deal. He loved to argue weights and engage in some good-natured dickering, and afterward we'd go to breakfast and reminisce. We went to the livestock sales together and we'd guess weights as the steers came into the ring. He traded cattle with just about everyone but he was always waiting to deal with me; I considered that a compliment because he was of such means he could buy and sell anyone in Tulare County.

Herman had cattle stuck everywhere, leased land out in Tulare Lake bottom, rented pasture on the other side of Corcoran. In some bad feed years, he'd let me take cattle out to his pasture; in those situations he'd always say, "We'll figure it out." Herman had leased land connected to Carl Twisselman, a big cattle ranch on the West Side. Carl was a fine rancher and I can remember riding cattle with him.

One time I invited Herman Colpien, Jack Shannon, Ray Pinnell, and Don Miller on a pack trip along with Dave Wilson and my cousin Don Britten. Don Miller managed Colpien's feedlot and had worked for Swift Meat Company buying and selling cattle. That was a great trip. Jack Shannon loved the mountains; he was a fine gentleman as well. He had lots of business going all the time. Jack owned feedlots and hog farms that took in half of the county. He and Colpien had the two largest feedlots that amounted to anything at that time; they ran thousands of cattle.

We packed out of Horse Corral, up Ferguson Creek where there's lots of good horse feed. I remember we were riding out across Ellis Meadow and there was a big mother bear and her two cubs eating grass in the meadow. Herman thought that was the most wonderful sight he'd ever beheld. Herman rode horses around his feedlots, but he'd never been to the mountains, always too busy. Herman didn't know how to fish, but Jack liked to fish, so we cooked some great fish dinners. Every night there was music and tall tales around the fire. For Herman, this was the trip of his lifetime so we planned another one for the following summer.

After the pack trip, Herman surprised us with a gift–he had his shop guy make new light-weight stoves for Dave Wilson and me, fabricated from aluminum, much lighter, that he thought would pack easier. Herman stamped his initials on the stoves. Dave used his on a pack trip, but found that rimmed pots left an indented ring on the stove top–the metal wasn't tempered and warped in the hot fire.

That winter Herman suffered a stroke. After the stroke Herman could still drive to his feedlots and take care of business but it affected his speech so he'd talk gibberish sometimes. We'd be working out a deal and settle on a price and he'd say, ahhhh-noooo and wave his finger and get his words backwards, then write it on a piece of paper. Tears would well up. I'd say, ahhhhhh, I understand perfectly, don't worry about it, and shake hands. Herman knew I'd make any deal right with him; if one of my steers was sick or died, I'd replace it. I remember that steer the pack of dogs had chewed the ears and tail off of was in one lot, it looked funny but it didn't affect the quality of the beef. But I found another beautiful steer and hauled it over to replace it and Herman had a big smile on his face.

Herman was a fine old gentleman, I really loved Herman Colpien. I sang for his funeral. I was proud to be a friend of both Jack and Herman.

Branding

Branding takes place in the spring and all the ranchers try to coordinate because we need each other's help. I still go to several brandings every year for various ranch owners but now I have to step from a rock to get on my horse–he's a great horse that always takes good care of me. A lot of things can happen in the branding pens, especially if there are novices (or some fool like Appelby on a bucking horse).

Finishing up for the day at spring branding at Holland Meadow. Three tall guys in back row (l to r): Jim Wells, Leroy Whitney, Scott Erickson (can barely see his big mustache). Middle row (l to r): Jack Erickson (Scott's dad); Lyle Loveall, Gary Davis, Jr., Forrest Homer, Mehrten "Tookie" Homer, Ernest John Britten, Earl McKee. Kneeling in front (l to r): Clarence Holbrook, John Dofflemyer, Craig Thorn. Photo c. 1986.

AUTHOR'S COLLECTION.

The cattle—cows, calves, steers, maybe a neighbor's stray or a wild cow or two, are gathered into one corral in which the calves will be kept back for branding. The other stock are separated out to the adjoining corral. The gate between the pens is wide open and you and your horse become the gate. A couple of cowboys bring the cattle slowly along the fence, and by a touch you cue your horse to turn back the little ones and let the big ones through. This is watching the gate, or tending the gate. When you have a well-trained horse it is exhilarating to know it is eager to work with you, watches what you're watching, ears pointed, ready to jump in and cut off a calf, or move aside to let several cows through. The cows are experienced and know to go into the pen, but the calf doesn't know anything, just runs around looking lost. The horse jumps off his hocks one way, then another. It isn't like a cutting horse that is marvelous to watch but they only lock onto a single cow. In the second pen you might have to do more separating - parting cattle - cows, strays, a dry cow, one for the sale, into a third pen.

Thomas Davis could part out his cows faster than anyone, he and Forrest Homer, because they always had good mounts. Working the gate was enjoyable when you were on a good horse.

Corral ropers catch the calf for branding, one on the head, the other the back feet—I'm sure everyone has watched this event at rodeos. You need a horse that can work among a bunch of cattle, roping, or pulling, or cutting stock. Novices are dangerous in a corral. Sometimes they might let a calf run behind their horse and don't spin the horse to the calf, then the rope goes across their horse's tail end and he'll jump into someone who has a calf at the end of their rope. I've been bucked off because somebody dragged a calf up under my horse's tail end. You've got to watch everything that is going on, especially a new guy. I've seen ropers lose a thumb because they dallied upside down—thumb down instead of up (to dally is to wind your rope around the saddle horn to secure it quick after your lasso catches the calf).

One time at Gill's we were roping 400 to 500-pound bulls, and I roped a Brahma and had to gallop to keep ahead of him because he really took off. There were a couple of guys on horses sitting there waiting to heel, but we were near some kids wrestling a calf, so I headed to an open area where I could handle the rope's arc and one of those guys just threw an underhanded loop and dallied thumb-down. I didn't know he had heeled my calf, he wasn't in position, the rope snapped tight and cut off his thumb. Part of him he doesn't have anymore. An attempt was made to reattach it; it would have been successful in modern medicine. You hate this kind of thing.

Kenny McKee, grandson of Ernest McKee, my dad's brother, roping a calf at John Dofflemyer's ranch on Dry Creek. I took this photograph. I like to do photography at brandings because I know the action and when to shoot to get a loop like this one. Photo January 2013.

AUTHOR'S COLLECTION.

My old classmate, Leroy Whitney, ran a small herd on his family's original ranch property near the head of Horse Creek. His father, Dow Whitney, born in 1900, ran a successful cattle operation on that range. Leroy and I were the same age, were buddies all through Woodlake High School, were always involved in FFA and competed on the judging teams. Leroy was a great friend, we went buck hunting together. Leroy was always at my brandings. His ranch joined with Gill Ranch, Byron Allen and Lee Maloy. Leroy died in 2002.

I went up to help Leroy brand about 50 or 60 head of calves. There was one corral, four ropers, and a couple of other helpers—a small crew.

The fire pit to heat the irons is traditionally dug just outside the corral fence, out of the way of the stock. The fire is below ground level so it is out of the wind. While the tip is heating in the coals outside the pen, the handles lay flat on the ground just inside the fence to stay cool and be within reach. Some old timers would dig the fire hole underneath the fence rail, which works in a large corral. Leroy dug his fire pit all the way inside the fence. (By far, the favorite method to heat the irons is an oak fire inside a 50-gallon drum with a hole in one side for the irons.)

At Leroy's branding I think it was John Dofflemyer who roped a big bull. I was on my edgy horse, King, standing in the stirrups leaning in to throw a good heel loop at the same moment a calf ran along the fence toward the fire. With a loud yell, Chucky Fry jumped right in front of my horse to stop that calf. King whirled out from under me and in an instant I was on the ground, still had the rope in my hand but my foot was hung up in the stirrup. My horse dragged me through that fire. My first thought was I'd torn out my new knee that had just healed up after knee replacement. Chucky was afraid I was burned and hauled me out of the coals. All parts were ok so we all went back to work.

My friend Leroy Whitney taking a break at the Davis ranch branding. Photo c. 1972.

AUTHOR'S COLLECTION.

I remember the first time we took our grandchildren, Hillary, Katie, and Gracie, to spring branding. I guess we assumed they would know what grandpa was doing, but when the first calf started bawling, they joined in a loud chorus of boo-hoos, as most children would.

When she was older, Gracie really wanted to be my right hand cowgirl. She loved to ride and help me gather cattle up in Salt Creek BLM. One time I remember we came upon the largest, most beautiful bear I've ever seen. We were gathering cattle on Salt Creek ridge across the rim up above Skull Gap. There was a breeze up canyon and the bear didn't see us, just kept ambling toward us. He was very fat, sorrel red, with a big white diamond on his chest. We yelled at him and he went off in another direction.

The grandkids lived in Visalia and were busy with school activities that didn't leave much time for ranch life. When time permitted Gracie trained horses for me, and she rode the top-priced horse in the sales arena at my first Quarter Horse auction about eight years ago. It was a memorable moment for both of us.

Granddaughter Gracie at a spring branding. I taught her to cut bull calves and she was really good at it. Here she has just finished one, holding the knife in her teeth, clamping the emasculator with her left hand and handing the balls to the nut bucket. Photo c. 1986 by Rick Fraser.

AUTHOR'S COLLECTION.

I took this photo from horseback as we moved cattle across Dry Creek at the exact spot I nearly lost my horse in the raging floodwaters in 1955. The J. W. C. Pogue house where my dad was born stood about 400 yards straight west, behind me. This is now part of the Dofflemyer Ranch. Photo 2008.

AUTHOR'S COLLECTION.

Spring branding at the Cherokee ranch. I am riding my stud horse Plenty Valentine, "Pinky." The first branding I went to in my life was at Byron Allen's at Cherokee. Photo c. 2011.

AUTHOR'S COLLECTION.

Ray Pinnell

Ray Pinnell was foreman on the Gill's Yokohl ranch for fifty years, through dry years and good years. His sister Madgil married Emmett Gill. One year, about 1968, Ray and I took the Gill kids on a pack trip. There was Freddie Gill, the son of Adolph Gill–the only boy in the Gill clan; two sons of Gerold and Virginia Gill Howison, Adolph's daughter; the son of Chuck Morris, who worked for Gill for 30 years; and my boy, Earl III. The boys were all ten or twelve years of age. We camped in Cloudy Canyon at Roaring River, which was a quarter mile away from a little cabin where Park ranger Gordon McDonald was staying. Gordon rode up every evening and we sat around and told stories until long after the boys had gone to sleep.

The next day, while the boys went off to fish and explore, Ray and I rode down to see Gordon and were gone until late afternoon. The kids heard our horses coming back to camp, and when we rode in, they were huddled around a sleeping bag. To Ray's horror, there was Freddie, the male heir to the Gill empire, bloody and bandaged on his bed, one leg in a splint. "Oh, my God! Something's happened! What do we do!" Ray went ape-shit. The boys let the shock effect run a few more seconds before Freddie jumped up and the kids roared at their joke. No blood, just ketchup.

Chuck Morris's son, Chuck Jr., turned out to be a bull rider and bronc rider like his dad, and was one of several cowboys who posed as the Marlboro Man, and still is in cigarette ads. I saw Freddie Gill not long ago at a branding. Freddie's mother was very involved in the Riata Ranch Cowboy Girls, as was Freddie. He accompanied the Cowboy Girls famous trick riding group to England where they were invited to perform for Queen Elizabeth's Jubilee in 2012.

Don Britten, a cousin I grew up with, often worked with Ray Pinnell down at the Gill feedlots. Don told me this story about the feedlot. The pens were mounded to provide dry footing for the cattle when it rained but several low spots near the tail water could flood. Ray and Don were riding sick cattle before daylight–riding through the pens, moving any cow with runny nose or cough to the hospital pen for treatment. To reach one of the pens, they had to ride across the runoff–you can imagine what kind of run-off that was from a 1000 steers–on a cold morning, water up to a horse's belly after it had rained for days. Ray's colt was jumpy, felt that cold water up under his belly, bowed his neck and bucked Ray off. Don said Ray just sailed through the air like an old Mallard landing on the lake, hit the water and went out of sight. Just his hat was floating on top of the green soup! He came up resembling the Creature from the Black Lagoon that was playing at the time, raking the gunk off his bald head and out of his eyes. Ray was a tough old buzzard and lived through that, too. Ray recounted this story many times after this as only he could tell it, and everyone roared with laughter.

Ray supervised all the Gill ranges, including one called Sage Brush located over the ridge south of Horse Creek. I was driving home in my flat bed truck hauling a ton or so of hay from my haystack in Lemon Cove, coming down hill nearing the turnoff to the lake campground. To my right, at Dave Mehrten's driveway, I happened to see a guy sitting on the ground with a cast on his leg and he gave me a little salute, just a little wave, as I went by. I realized it was Ray Pinnell, so I turned around as soon as I could and when I got back to Ray I could see he had been there quite a while because there was a pack's worth of cigarette butts ground into the dirt around him. He said, well, he was checking on a spring up in Sage Brush in his 4WD Scout when he spun out and got stuck, so he hobbled down the hill with his leg in a cast and hoped someone would stop. I was headed to South Fork to feed some yearlings, so Ray came along, then we got my 4WD truck and we went back to pull out his Scout.

Ray had a crutch but wasn't too proficient with it, then I noticed his pants. "By golly, Ray, I see you've got a zipper on the side of your pant leg so it's easier to pull them on over your cast!" Ray had been busted up many times, bucked off, drug through the horse shit countless times and when he stood his knees would sort of lock together. Ray explained, "You know my wife, Bebbs! I have a whole stack of these zippered pants in the closet–I got zippers on the right leg, got zippers for the left leg, and whenever I have another wreck, I just go in there and get the zipper that will work on that leg."

Ray's daughter, Lucinda, reminded me of a story the other day, a bear story. Ray and his friend, Earl Weatherhead, often hunted together. Earl owned a large trucking business in Exeter. This time Ray drove them in his 4WD truck to the Grouse ranch up South Fork that Gill Cattle Co. had just bought. Ray's wife Bebbs went along .

In the hills, Ray spotted what looked like an orphan bear cub. Ray thought he could catch it with a rope, so he and Earl and the dog trailed the cub up a tree and watched it for a while. The cub started to bawl. Then they heard branches snap and mother bear came charging at them.

Bebbs also saw mother bear and was scared the bear was coming after her, so she put the truck in gear and floored it. Ray and Earl were left running in the dust yelling at her to "stop the goddamn truck so we can get in!" Ray always said, "You know I thought we was running pretty good because we passed the dog–outran that dog–to the truck."

Ray was always roping something. He roped a bear or two. Once he was galloping over a rise in pursuit of a wild cow, arm up with the loop. Ray forgot about the cow when a startled buck jumped right in front so he roped him instead. Ray had a supply of deer meat after that.

You might say Ray Pinnell was accident prone, but more than likely it was just that there were so many hazards out there he just couldn't avoid them all. Ray Pinnell was a master of cuss words. His vocabulary was fascinating because he could swear better than anyone I ever knew. He made four-letter words sound respectable even in mixed company, mostly horse people. He had a drawl, not a native Texas drawl because he didn't come from there. He didn't try to dress up his stories to protect his pride, just told it like it happened. Everybody loved to sit and listen to Ray tell stories.

Ray Pinnell with his Brahma steer, Charlie. Photo c. 1970s.
AUTHOR'S COLLECTION.

One time Gills bought a load of cattle from the Mexican border that included a big Brahma steer. Whenever Ray tried to drive it from one pen to another that steer thought it was a big game. It was obvious that it had been raised by a family because he was just so big and docile, so Ray named him Charlie. Ray had to use a feed bucket to coax Charlie from pen to pen. Ray grew attached to Charlie so when it came time to send steers to market, Ray would hide Charlie away in another corral. Ray really loved Charlie.

This ploy did not escape Adolph Gill's notice. He finally let Ray know that he knew he was keeping that Brahma back, and told him to go ahead and take that steer home. Charlie went home with Ray to Woodlake, where he continued to eat the feed Ray brought home to him from Gill's feedlots.

I dearly loved old Ray. We went duck hunting together, he was a sports-minded guy, loved deer hunting, fishing, and loved the mountains. I tried to arrange to have Ray go on as many pack trips as possible because he was the conversation corner—around the campfire he was an entertainer. On one trip I invited Jimmy Rivers, the guitar player, Ray Pinnell and his grandson Jason Hixon, Don Britten and his son, and I took my son Earl. Just music, story telling and laughter. One of Ray's favorite ballads around the campfire was "The Castration of the Strawberry Roan," which I always sang for him. When Ray told stories about being in some wreck, being bucked off or dragged, it was dead silence while he was center stage. It's a wonder he lived.

Ray retired from Gill Cattle Company about the time Adolph Gill retired and sold the Yokohl spread to J. G. Boswell. It is beautiful country where one of the Boswells has proposed a controversial plan to build a new town for 30,000 residents.

At his funeral, Ray's daughter, Lucinda, requested that I sing his favorite song about the Strawberry Roan, but there were too many young ears there, so I sang several other songs for my dear friend, Ray Pinnell.

Don Knudsen

My friend Don Knudsen was another cowboy from Strathmore-Porterville area, who was one of the nicest guys I've known. His brother, Slim, worked for the Park Service. I have a photo of Don and me together; he came to Three Rivers and we went with our wives to dinner together, and laughed and talked about old times. Not long after that he was up on a ladder in his barn, ladders are deadly, and fell on the concrete floor. He told his wife he was broke all to pieces and not going to last long. He died two days later. The funeral was south of Porterville and I went to the little cemetery to sing a cowboy song for my old friend Don. The family brought Don's dog to the funeral and he was watching everything. I started strumming my guitar and the dog went on alert, perked his ears and when I started to sing, the dog started howling. He barked and howled so loud I finally had to stop, and I told the folks that Don has to be sitting beside us somewhere slapping his thigh and laughing while his dog drowns out this song I'm trying to sing for him.

Don Knudsen (l) and Earl McKee, Jr. The photo was taken about four years ago (c. 2008), six months before Don died.

AUTHOR'S COLLECTION.

THREE RIVERS RANCHERS

⟨₰⟩

South Fork Ranchers
Whispering Bob and the Blicks

I could write a whole book about Whispering Bob Lovering.

Notice the name is L-o-v-e-r-i-n-g, Lovering with a "g," not the same name as Ord and Ben Loverin. In fact, Bob would take issue with anyone mistakenly pronouncing his name as "Loverin."

Bob Lovering's name was Roy Ingersol Lovering. His sister was married to Judd Blick, one of the owners of the 5000-acre La Cuesta Ranch on South Fork; John Blick and Major Frederick Burnham were the other owners. Bob and Nell Lovering of Orange County, California, bought 560 acres of ranch land on South Fork in 1908. It was a three-week trek to move to Three Rivers with two wagons, four horses, two mules, one milk cow. Bob and Nell Lovering were Gaynor's grandparents on her mother's side.

A year and a half later, Bob sold the ranch to take a job as foreman on a large wheat ranch in Mexico owned by the Blicks. The family, including their young daughter Norma, was in Mexico when the Mexican Revolution began and word reached the ranch that the local Indian tribe was on the rampage, seizing stock and food to feed the Army. Rumors also abounded about Pancho Villa raiding ranches from Mexico to Texas. Bob and Nell made plans to escape. One morning at 2 a.m. they abandoned the ranch with some belongings packed in barrels, two mules pulling a wagon, and one horse and headed for the railroad station 15 miles away. Nell and their daughter boarded the train for California. Bob made the long trip with horse and team. All arrived safely in Three Rivers.

Bob decided to raise cattle in Three Rivers where he bought a section of land up river from the Blicks. He divided his time between

Orange County citrus ranching and Three Rivers cattle business. He was a good cowman, had worked around feedlots and had also worked as a butcher part of his life. He was remembered for his loud voice and explosive temper. Bob would blow up over nothing.

In Three Rivers, he continued his close friendship with Bill Peterson who he knew in Mexico, and who got a lot of enjoyment in arguing with Bob just to set him off–they'd start cussing each other, then Bob would forget about it. Bill Peterson was a Park ranger at Hockett Meadows in those days. The Lovering family went on an annual pack trips to Hockett Meadows.

Gaynor McKee's parents, Norma (Lovering) and Sonny Hardison, enjoying early morning coffee on the annual Lovering family pack trip. Photo c. 1948.

AUTHOR'S COLLECTION.

When I was just a little kid, my dad took me along to see Bob about something and Bill was there. We drove up in the middle of one of their arguments. They were cutting up a freshly-butchered steer, faced off across a butcher block in the yard, calling each other sons-of-bitches and waving big knives. The knives and yelling scared me so much I begged to leave, but my dad reassured me that they weren't going to kill each other. In later years I noticed that when Bill Peterson would call Bob an s.o.b., he always had a smirk on his face because he was just agitating Bob so he could watch the explosion.

Bill always helped Bob gather cows in Salt Creek, as did Jim Kindred. Bob had a voice you could hear for miles; if he was in the next chair talking, the volume would be like a megaphone, so loud everyone would turn to see who it was. He was a short guy, but stocky–shorter than Gaynor and her mother (Gaynor is five feet one inch!) but you never thought of him as being tiny. He always had a cigar in his mouth and a little snap-brim hat on. He should have been in the movies because he would explode over nothing and five minutes later he was laughing again.

Bob, Bill, and some other cowboys were up Salt Creek drainage on the Case Mountain range in the late fall–they would go late so they'd be there at deer season. They camped high up to push the cows over the hill into South Fork and on home to Lovering's place. It was getting colder and when that happens the cows start thinking about going down lower. The guys were calling the cattle, had some salt along for a little reward so the cows would call in. They rode all that country for several days–it is a big area, about 4000 acres up into the pines and redwoods–looking for cows, and were just taking a last pass. Way down on the east side in Donkey Creek is a canyon with an overlook point, a really pretty place, so they rode down there, calling. They didn't hear or see any more cows, so they figured they were done and ready to go home. Bob called again, one more time, and an old cow bawled in answer from way over toward Eden Grove in the Park. What else could he do; Bob took his hat off and yelled "OH SHIT!" No one wanted to ride clear over there, it meant another whole day. So Bill Peterson named that place "Oh Shit Point." It still is known by that name; I've told most of the guys that story. I told Dave Cairns who actually owns that property and he said, oh, yeah, he'd been told that the place was called Oh Shit Point.

You can almost hear Whispering Bob yelling again in this story. He'd had a terrible time trying to gather his cattle out of upper Salt Creek in 1938 because, as usual, cows had scattered across the brushy ravines and glades making for days of searching and searching, like Oh Shit Point.

"By god, they're not going to hide from me next year!" So Bob stormed off and bought 54 cowbells–54! He cut bell straps from old car tires and used baling wire instead of buckles to fasten them on. That was probably one bell for every three cows, but by god those cows couldn't hide from him any more.

Bill Peterson told a story about deer hunting with Whispering Bob up Salt Creek one fall while gathering cattle. Bob had a dog, Pinto, he was really proud of, but Bill said the dog was just a deer chaser. Bob was trying to keep Pinto real close to him in case he wounded a deer the dog would find it. They had this all planned out–real early in the morning, be as quiet as possible, and wait, one on either side of the canyon. Well, the dog had caught the scent of a deer or something and run off. Bob, who was sitting on a rock across the canyon from Bill, couldn't see his dog, so he whispered, "Bill, oh, Bill," but Bill just looked away as if he didn't hear anything. Pretty soon, Bob whispered louder, "Bill. Bill! Is the dog there?" Bill made no response and didn't even look in his direction. Bill said that Bob finally got up on a rock, cupped his hands and yelled, "Bill!" as loud as he could, you know, "Bill! - Is - That - Dog - Over - There!" That pretty much ran all the deer out of that canyon. Bill said, "I just fell over backwards on the rock laughing so hard," because he saw that Bob realized that Bill had heard him the whole time.

There were always fights over water. Bob told the story about the time he was having words with Pansy Cahoon Kirk over ditch problems. Her ditch came out below Bob's. People will figure a way to get along on most things in the world but they'll all fight over water. Bob was riding down from checking cows near Clough's Cave in the evening and he saw Pansy Kirk on the hillside above, setting fence posts–she worked like a man, digging postholes, handling barbed wire barehanded. He called out cheerfully, "Hello, Pansy. What are you doing?" She didn't even waste a look in his direction but grumbled, "I'm digging postholes you old son-of-a-bitch," and he heard her. He said it was comical.

Bob's wife, Nell, was used to hearing Bob's outbursts. One time Nell heard him shouting into the phone about his car, ". . .car pissed and quit." She scolded him for cussing on the phone, but he wasn't cussing–a piston quit and he was ordering a new one.

Bob, called "Bronco" by his grandkids and family, was a fun-loving guy, and liked music, the same kind of opera music that I listened to in high school, vocalists like Mario Lanzo and Caruso. I never heard Bob sing. His daughter Norma (Gaynor's mother) had a beautiful soprano voice and was a well known vocalist in southern California where she graduated from high school in Fullerton. The Loverings went to the mountains about every summer. The ranch was the scene of great swimming parties and barbecues on the river.

On the Lovering South Fork ranch, just after a swim party in the river: (l to r) Whisperin' Bob ("Bronco" to the family, always wore cowboy boots), daughter Norma Lovering, unnamed friend, Nell Lovering, and Jim Kindred. Photo c. 1940.

AUTHOR'S COLLECTION.

Norma and Sonny, their two kids, Roy, 4 and Gaynor, 2, lived at the Lovering ranch in 1933 and 1934 before Sonny took a job in Texas where he worked in the oil fields for thirteen years, moving constantly. In 1948, just about the time electricity was finally brought up the South Fork canyon, they moved back here for good. Sonny started work as an electrician wiring houses and installing electrical appliances. Norma went to work at the Three Rivers school cafeteria as the school cook—cooking and washing dishes. Gaynor enrolled as a sophomore at Woodlake High School.

In 1961, Whispering Bob gave his ranch property to Norma and her sister. Sonny started doing ranch work, ran two Brahma bulls and fifty Hereford cows. One of the bulls was a mean one and Sonny wanted to haul it off to the sale. Johnny Britten came up to help load it. It took three hours just to get the bull into the corral but then it wouldn't go in the loading chute. Sonny's patience was worn thin about this point, so he jumped down into the pen to try and beat it in to the chute. The bull charged Sonny, blew snot all over him trying to hook him. Johnny saved Sonny's ass by throwing his jacket on the bull's head so it couldn't see. Sonny climbed to safety. He was so mad he threw rocks at the bull until it finally ran up the chute into the truck headed to market for his "last ride." One rock he threw with such force that it broke one of the corral boards in two.

Norma Lovering and children, Gaynor and Roy. Photo c. 1939.
AUTHOR'S COLLECTION.

The Blick Ranch

This is just some interesting background about the first owners of La Cuesta Ranch.

John Burnham, with his brothers-in-law Judd and John C. Blick, owned the 5000-acre La Cuesta Ranch on South Fork for thirty-eight years and sold it in 1947 to Walter T. Wells of Huntington Park, California. Whisperin' Bob Lovering's sister was married to Judd Blick. Judd and John Blick's sister Blanche married Frederick Russell Burnham, a world-renowned scout for the Englishman Lord Roberts. Both Blicks also served under Lord Roberts during the Boer War in South Africa. Burnham had come to Three Rivers from Pasadena in search of a healthy climate for his family. John C. Blick, associated with H. C. Frick, the steel magnate, was an archeologist and searched for fossils throughout the world. The Blicks also owned a silver mine and ranches in Mexico.

Frederick Russell Burnham was a scout, mining expert and adventurer, born May 11, 1861 in Minnesota. He grew up in California and loved the outdoors. He learned from the best scouts in the regions, learned riding, tracking, hunting, and wilderness survival. He worked as a mounted messenger for Western Union when he was 13, as a cowboy, big game hunter, and prospector. In 1893 when he read about the career of Cecil John Rhodes in South Africa, he took his wife and son to Africa where he worked as a scout for Rhodes and fought in two Matabele Wars. He was decorated for his service in the Boer War by King Edward of England.

He and the Blicks returned to Pasadena, California where he conducted his ranching interests, mining, archeological explorations, and co-founded the Boy Scouts. The *Los Angeles Herald* published letters from Judd Blick who wrote about their adventures in Africa. In 1896, it reported the "Pasadena people who are supposed to be en route from London for here include Mr. and Mrs. Fred Burnham, Mr. and Mrs. Ingram, Judd and John Blick and King Macomber." The Burnhams lived at La Cuesta Ranch on South Fork until 1923 when they struck oil in the Dominguez Hills and returned to Southern California.

Gaynor's mother had a 1910 photograph of Winston Churchill, Judd Blick, John Blick, Frederick Burnham and the Earl of Kent all mounted on camels at Giza, Egypt.

Frederick Burnham (1861-1947), Blanche Blick Burnham (1862-1939), Judd Blick (1873-1951), and John Blick (1875-1960), are buried in the Three Rivers Cemetery.

Byron Allen

Byron Allen ran Black Angus cattle on about 3000 acres on South Fork called Cherokee. He was built like a jockey, short and trim, and in fact had been one in his youth. His boots had to be custom made to fit his size-five feet. He rode big spirited horses that he trained, always said he'd never been bucked off a horse. My dad said Byron was an excellent horseman.

Byron smoked constantly and his hands were yellow because he smoked with his hand cupped around the cigarette like he was trying to hide it. Forrest Homer used to help Byron drive cattle to Silver City meadows for years and said he learned the art of driving cattle from Byron. Byron married into the Carter family homestead land that encompassed what is now Cherokee Oaks clear over to the main river. He also owned farmland northeast of Visalia, very rich soil. My dad's 1922 daybook has entries about going down with teams to plow or harvest at the Allen place in Visalia.

My dad and Byron belonged to the Visalia Masonic Lodge. Byron drove a 1942 tear-drop Ford. My dad told me one time he rode with Byron to Lodge even though he didn't like Byron's driving. Of course, everyone knew my dad was a terrible driver, he drove more horses than he had automobiles. I was with him one time when he wrecked the car. A couple of other times my dad ran off the road and hit a rock pile just because he was thinking about all the details of an upcoming pack trip and not paying attention to the road. That's fine if you're on a horse–it knows to stay on the road–but you can't forget to drive the car.

So my dad was riding with Byron and they got down on the other side of Lemon Cove somewhere and finally my dad says, "Byron, are you ever going to shift this car into high?" He was still in second gear just crawling along for twelve miles.

Sounds impossible, but a lot of those men knew everything about horses so to them a car was just something to get somewhere, didn't matter how it worked, but if it didn't work it wasn't worth a damn. They didn't become mechanics. Judge Walter Fry, Park superintendent, ordered his first car by mail and practiced driving in a pasture.

In 1926 Byron had the meat concession and operated the butcher shop at the market in Giant Forest, so he moved about 300 head of cattle from Three Rivers to the Cabin Meadow area a few miles northwest of Giant Forest to supply his business for the summer.

Byron would gather his cattle way late and there were always a few that would get away and go wild, and we'd tell him that there were some wild cows to gather before we quit, and his famous reply was, "Well, I tellya, we get 'em next year." He'd bring his cattle down to Cherokee. He wasn't a fence-mender, literally, his cows were always getting out. Johnny Britten was once asked where the cattle grazed the rest of the year after coming down from the mountains. He said, "Well, they went everywhere. Byron Allen said his long pasture was from Visalia to Three Rivers. . .he never had any good fences. . . ."

I knew Byron's fences weren't in very good repair. I was 17 years old when I courted my future wife, Gaynor Hardison, who lived five or six miles up South Fork on her grandfather Bob Lovering's ranch, beyond the Wells Ranch (formerly LaCuesta). I drove a 1942 DeSoto coupe, a heavy car, and I found I could start the car and leave the Hardison's driveway, downhill, then turn off the key and coast all the way home. But along a stretch below the Wells Ranch meadow I had to watch out for Byron's cows because they were often loose and might be bedded down in the middle of the road. One moonlight night there was a black cow in a black shadow that luckily I saw in time to stop, but then I had to restart the motor and try for some momentum to coast the rest of the way home. Saved gasoline and my generated batteries.

Wells/Seaborn Ranch

The ranch first known as LaCuesta, was called the Wells Ranch after Walter T. Wells of Pasadena, California bought it in 1947. Wells acquired more land from Byron Allen, including Cherokee, bought Tharp's Peak clear to Horse Creek, making a total of over 8,000 acres to run cattle. He was an inventor, patented an oil well drilling device that retrieved lost drilling rods, but he didn't know too much about the cow business so he hired Bill Graham to manage the ranch. Bill was just out of the army when he went to work for Walt and he didn't know cattle either but he could ride. We traded help a lot. Bill learned on the job and turned out to be a fine cowman who helped Walt improve his herd. He was a prince of a guy and we became close friends. Bill's father-in-law was Gus Waller who bought Spotts Cider Mill. After some years, Bill bought a ranch in Bieber, California, next to Johnny Britten's land, where he raised cattle the rest of his life. He passed away June 2009 at age 86.

Don Benchoff took over after Graham. After a time, the ranch name was changed when the Wells' swapped horses with the Seaborns:

Mrs. Wells married Mr. Seaborn and continued to live on the ranch that was thereafter referred to as the Seaborn Ranch. Mr. Wells and ex-Mrs. Seaborn moved to a ranch in Arizona.

Walt Seaborn was a teacher who knew more about the classroom than cows so he hired Tommy Welch to manage the ranch. Tommy and I traded help a lot. He was the only guy I ever crashed into on horseback.

Seaborn wanted to learn how to be a cowboy and struggled to pick up the skills needed to work in the corral. I know a lot of people who get to be competent riders, but just don't master the cow sense and horse sense needed to work cattle.

Early on at his corral, Walt decided to train his horse how to rope. There was a pretty calf standing alone, so Walt threw a rope on it, dallied–watched the dally instead of where his horse was going–the calf hit the end of the rope and ran under his horse's belly. The horse couldn't get away, just jumped and kicked back, struck the calf in the head and killed it. Tommy sat open-mouthed, wondering what was Walt doing. He did some completely unexplained things.

We always crossed the Wells/Seaborn Ranch to take our cattle to Ace Peck's range up on Blue Ridge. One time I left the home place at daybreak to get the herd going up South Fork Road before people left for work–always put a point man in front because we didn't want to meet some driver going wide open around those turns. At Seaborn's, Tommy Welch joined us for the ride up to Ace's. Walt wasn't up yet.

We had reached Berton Field quite a ways up in the hills when we heard a shotgun blast. Tommy looked at me and wondered if that could have been Walt. We rode on another hour to the top at Berton corrals where we stopped, unsaddled the horses, and let the cattle blow for a while–it had been a climb to get there. We were there when Walt finally caught us, came riding up on a buckskin horse–it was the horse that Emmett Gill had given to me, sired by my stallion, Parmer. The first thing I saw were the welts all over that horse's ass end. I was furious. I said, "Walter, you shot that horse didn't you!" It was obvious that Walt couldn't catch the horse in the pasture; he said he taught that horse a lesson, because it ran right to the corral after he shot it. Well, how do you keep respect after that? I will never forget that. He finally figured out that the horse was too much for him and retired him to better horsemen.

Walt Seaborn did take some advice on how to improve his herd, did business with Curly Thurber at Ft. Tejon Cattle Ranch where for several years running he bought a truck and trailer load of their black white-faced yearlings. He developed a real good bunch of cattle. It took years of hard work and struggle but Walt Seaborn turned out to be a good cowman.

At some point the Seaborns retired to Oregon. Peggy Wells Seaborn's son, Jim Wells, took over the cattle business, did a good job, worked hard, branded, roped, bought some expensive bulls to raise a certain Beef Masters variety. They sold the ranch in the late 1990s.

North Fork Ranchers

Walter Braddock settled on the North Fork in the 1886 and raised cattle in partnership with Alfred Hengst. Braddock took his cattle to the high mountains back of Mineral King for summer pasture. He died in the 1930s.

Alfred Hengst was born in 1868 in Saxony, Germany and arrived in the USA in 1890 and to Three Rivers in 1895. His brother, Frank, joined the Kaweah Colony; another brother, Harold "Shorty" Hengst also ranched on North Fork. Alfred raised bees; his apiary produced 400 to 500 gallons of orange and cotton honey each season that he sold in the Bay Area. Alfred was a carpenter and a construction superintendent on the redwood flume to Power House No. 1, the first hydroelectric plant in Three Rivers built by Mt. Whitney Power Company.

In 1905, Alfred Hengst brought two milk cans of Golden trout from Whitney Creek over the Great Western Divide to plant in Granite Creek and Granite Lake. Alfred was active in the community, served as president of Three Rivers Chamber of Commerce and headed up airport and bridge committees. He was a conservationist and a backcountry trail builder. In his honor an 11,127-foot Sierra mountain peak in the Mineral King area was named for him in 1980.

Alfred Hengst died in 1944.

Harold "Shorty" Hengst

Shorty Hengst and Alfred Hengst were brothers and neighbors but somewhere along the way they got sideways with each other and refused to speak. Shorty sold a half interest in his place to Walter Braddock.

They branded the cattle "HB" for Hengst-Braddock, on the left rib, or as Shorty and Alfred said in their heavy German accent, "HB on the wib." Alfred Hengst died first and brother Shorty did not go to the funeral. My dad mentioned this fact to Shorty, that he didn't see him at his brother's funeral. Shorty told him the reason was, he was there all right, but he waited until everyone left so he could go over and piss on Alfred's grave.

Shorty was a character, ran the trails barefooted, wore bib overalls with nothing underneath. He didn't wear shirts because running through all that brush they'd just get torn off. His hide looked like a piece of leather, brown from living out in the open and my dad said he went barefoot half the time, his soles were tough as iron. However, Shorty did dress up for special occasions. In the 1926 group photograph of the Three Rivers '49ers taken on stage at Woodlake, Shorty is in a vintage long coat holding the leash to his big pet possum perched on a stump.

Shorty rode a big stud horse with an army saddle. He said if that saddle was good enough for the army, it was good enough for him. Shorty was riding his big horse down the hill, probably to the Kaweah post office, and about Fingerpoint, he died and fell off his horse, or fell off his horse and died, no one knew. That was about 1950. A neighbor adopted Shorty's dog, Shep, a Blue Merle. Shep knew how to get steers out of the brush, he was a great dog that lived to be 21 years of age, loved to play and dive for rocks in the river.

I can never forget going to Shorty's house with my dad. Most people cut wood to fit the stove and stacked it outside the door within easy reach. Shorty cut tall skinny trees and trimmed them into poles for firewood. He poked the whole tree through a hole in the kitchen door and stuck the end in the firebox of his big wood stove that sat right off the kitchen. As it burned, he'd just shove the pole further into the firebox. To keep the pole from burning too far out and catching the house on fire, he wrapped the part next to the stove with wet sacks. The house was pretty smoky from that damp wood.

We put up our horses and mules overnight at Shorty's corrals on the two-day trip to trail our packing stock to Giant Forest. One time I remember, Shorty's stud horse jumped the fence into the corral with one of our mares. My dad asked Shorty, "You don't think he bred her, do you?" Shorty shook his head no, "He vant, but she no like." Next year the mare had a filly born in Rowell Meadow so my dad named her

Rowell. She became a great bell mare because the mules loved her and stayed close. She spent a lot of her life as a bell mare in the mountains.

Dave Wilson

I went to school with Dave Wilson, he was two years ahead of me. His dad, Herbert Earl Wilson was an author, lecturer, and Park ranger who could have been president because he could get up and make a speech anywhere about anything. Herb built the Lake Elowin resort on Dinely Drive in Three Rivers. Elowin is an Indian name. Prior to 1929 when he signed with Yosemite Park and Curry Company to take charge of the horseback riding concession, nature guides, and programs, Herb worked for two years in Sequoia National Park and wrote a book, *Lore and Lure of Sequoia*. Herb was raised in Yosemite with the Indians, studied their ways, and became a blood brother with Chief LeeMee, head of the Yosemite tribe, before he brought his family to Three Rivers.

When he was a little kid, Dave got a horse from Onis Brown he called Mars, he was a Mars Mouse horse, a real gentle horse and Dave used to ride him down to the store where the Shell station is now. I was a smaller kid and would really take notice of Dave because he wore a cowboy hat. He'd tie Mars at the post, about where Oscar Maxon used to tie old Daisy.

Dave went to work for Bisconer, who bought the Hengst-Braddock ranch on North Fork, and afterwards for Elliott Ranch. He married his wife, Laverne, and raised four kids in Shorty Hengst's old house. Dave traded help with us, and he packed for our pack station because he loved the backcountry life. He was a typical cowboy like you see in the movies, not quite as reliable close to the weekends because Friday nights were for good times on the town. Dave was a damned good hand, he worked on the ranch by himself, like I did, and when you spend a lot of time alone you really learn how to get things done by yourself. You know when you can part cattle out without disturbing the other cattle, to give them time, because if you're by yourself and get in a hurry and rush them, they get agitated so you have to wait a while and start all over again. That all teaches patience. Dave knew how to drive cattle and had helped Homer and me in the steep country up to Cahoon. Dave loved that place. He helped me so I let him take a dozen head of his own cows up with mine for the summer.

223

Dave Wilson at a Tom Davis branding. Dave helped me move cattle and didn't like the cold mornings so he'd make a fire in an old tree. If we couldn't find him we'd look for smoke. Photo c. 1973 by Bud Kilburn.

AUTHOR'S COLLECTION.

Kenneth Savage

Kenneth "Skinny" Savage and his brother Alan Sr. lived on the original Savage apple ranch on North Fork. They both packed and were trail cooks for my dad for many years. Their dad was Fred Savage who arrived here in 1896 and planted apple orchards.

Kenneth was nicknamed "Skinny" for obvious reasons—he was tall and slim. His brother Alan didn't have a nickname, but he made a jolly round Santa Claus at the school Christmas parties. Ken and Alan were students at the Sulfur Springs school in Three Rivers. They were the terrors of the local school teachers and it was said they caused at least one teacher to leave because of their pranks. They liked to hide gopher snakes, water snakes, and other scary things in the teacher's desk.

Skinny's son, Milton Savage, was in the service in WWII. He came up to help out at Giant Forest in 1946 after my dad died. He loved the mountains and managed the corrals for us at the Wolverton pack station for several summers after that. Gaynor and I stayed with Milton and his wife Carol at their Mineral King cabin the weekend I gave the talk there. Milton taped an interview of his own that evening for a book he was writing about horsemen and horse trainers. He was a career educator at Sierra High School in the mountains near Big Creek.

Alan Savage Sr. worked for Woodlake Hardware. He had a great personality. He would sell in the field, stopping by to shoot the breeze and to take orders for anything anyone needed. His son, Alan Jr. was incorrigible in school. We were in high school together and Alan set a record for being sent home–32 times. He was expelled several times and his poor dad had to use all his salesmanship to get Alan one more chance.

Alan Jr. would go out in the school hallway and yell "wow-O" just to make it echo, then disappear. Students and teachers would rush out to see what the emergency was. I remember one time he and Forest Busby or someone got in a fistfight in English class. They knocked over one whole row of seats–the desks were on rails. Our principal was Byron H. Conkle. The kids called him "B.H." Alan would draw silly pictures of Mr. Conkle and tape them up in the hall. Mr. Conkle would try to keep a straight face when he'd see the drawings; he'd say, "that looks to me like the work of Alan Savage." When pinned down, Alan would laughingly admit that yes, he did it.

Alan Jr. drove a 1937 Ford two door sedan as fast as it would go–probably not over 60 mph because it didn't have enough horses to go faster. He'd peel out and laugh and hoop and holler. Craziest guy you ever saw. But everyone loved Alan.

Alan Jr. worked at Horse Corral for Ernest Cecil and later bought the pack station. He ran it for two years. Business was pretty slow there because it was an out-of-the-way location between the Parks. Alan Jr. served as mayor of Woodlake at one time

OLD MOVIES AND HISTORY

⚬⚬⚬

Old Movies

My mother, Edna McKee, unpacked an old trunk years ago and found two celluloid movies of Three Rivers old timers, one made in 1926 and the other in 1933. There was also a photograph of another group of old timers taken in 1913, and I know the date because Fred Ogilvie was about twelve and he was born in 1901; my mother wrote a caption identifying each person there. I filmed that picture, zooming in for close-ups of each face as I narrated the name. That is one reason I am able to identify quite a few of the Old Timers in the two movies.

The oldest movie is of the 1926 wagon train from Three Rivers to Woodlake, entitled *Pioneers Rolled Back the Years*. There is quite an interesting history to this film. In 1926, several prominent Woodlake boosters, including Mr. Ropes, Mr. Goldman, Mr. Dinkins and Mr. Pugh planned an ambitious community entertainment to raise funds to benefit Woodlake High School. This Woodlake delegation met at my grandfather Finch's house with a dozen enthusiastic Three Rivers people including Mr. and Mrs. Jason Barton, Phil and Grace Alles, Phil Davis, Mr. and Mrs. Phipps, Earl and Edna McKee, Dr. and Mrs. Nice, and the Byron Allens. It was decided that Three Rivers would stage a reenactment of a 1849 wagon train to Woodlake as part of the Woodlake gala.

All the Valley newspapers had front page coverage of the wagon train, this from Visalia: "People are still talking about the great spectacle put on by the energetic residents of Three Rivers at Woodlake last Saturday, a '49 celebration staged as Three Rivers' contribution toward raising a fund with which to later produce a pageant to be given for the benefit of the Woodlake high school. Five thousand visitors were attracted to Woodlake by this event and visitors are unanimous in stating that it was the greatest thing of its kind. . . ."

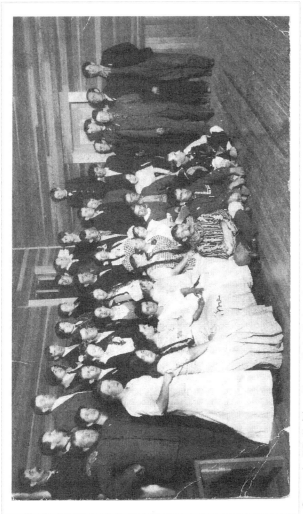

1913 gathering at Sequoia Hall. Top Row (l-r): John Grunigen, Clarence Dinely, Bob Carter, Rose Atwood, Roy Davis, Vera Davis, Daisy Hopping, ?man, Clarence Britten, ?man, Fred Ogilvie. 2nd row (l-r): Charles Blossom, Mrs. Blossom, ?man, ?woman, Bessy Fry, Laura Ogilvie, Frank Atwood, Merle Atwood, Tom Phipps, Ed Phipps, ?man, Loren Finch, Fred Blick, Jesse Finch, Bert Wells, ?man, Earl McKee. 3rd row (l-r): ?woman standing, ?woman seated, Edna Finch McKee, ?woman, ?woman, Rose Mullinex, Grace Mullinex, Opal Packard, Carrie Swanson, R. I. (Bob) Lovering, Nell Lovering. Seated on Floor (l-r): Bill Swanson, Ben Packard, Billy Austin. Photo 1913.

The wagon train arrived in Woodlake at two o'clock in the afternoon, February 6, 1926. Professor W. F. Dean, dressed as an Indian scout, led the parade; Jason Barton was wagon master. Jesse Finch drove a herd of cows; my dad drove his favorite horse, Joker, pulling a fancy buckboard; my Grandfather Finch in a cork hat, accompanied by Ida Purdy, drove a buggy; and grandmother Rhoda Finch, in a gown and biting a corncob pipe, was riding sidesaddle on the big roan mare. There were carriages, horseless carriages, dogs, mules, cattle, Indians–real Yokuts families and some fellows dressed up like Indians. Phil Davis, chief organizer, declared that 250 Three Rivers residents took part in that parade. It was an enthusiastic and fun-loving crowd. Jason Barton called the quadrilles danced in the light of the bonfire.

Manager J. Fred Miller of the Theatre Visalia was on hand with motion picture cameras, along with cameramen from Pathe, Fox, and Universal film companies, to take numerous movie views of the caravan, which was the big event of the day, along with incidental pictures. ". . .The films were rushed to San Francisco and Mr. Miller was notified over the phone today that they turned out exceptionally well. They will be developed at once and returned to Visalia, where they will be shown at Theatre Visalia at an early date, the exact date or dates to be announced later."

After an overnight camp-out in the wagon circle in the center of town, with music, dancing, cookouts, and stage show, the wagon train was cheered by almost the entire population of Visalia when it arrived there the next day, by special invitation, to receive the honorary Key to the City. One of the covered wagons was hauled up on the stage of the Theatre Visalia to set the scene for the '49ers performance accompanied by the Poison Oak Orchestra of Three Rivers.

The new gymnasium at Woodlake High School, made possible by the fundraising '49ers, was dedicated at a community turkey dinner in December 1929. Entertainment was by the Poison Oak Orchestra.

In the 1960s, my mother went to some trouble and expense to have this priceless celluloid 32mm 1926 wagon train movie transferred to 16mm film; Mervin Fulton of Tulare, California was the expert who did this. Sometime before the community split in the feud over the Disney development in Mineral King, I donated the 16mm version to the Three

Rivers Chamber of Commerce. At that time the Chamber was really active with a program of dinners and events to involve everyone and to promote the businesses in Three Rivers. Then came the great "Disney Division" in town, everyone at war–those in favor of the Disney ski development in Mineral King, versus those opposed. One group picked up their marbles and went off to form a second C of C–two Chambers of Commerce in the tiny hamlet of Three Rivers. Eventually both groups ceased to function.

When my mother died in 1986, both Chambers had been out of business a long time and I got to wondering who had gotten custody of that old movie. I tracked it to the last president of the break-away group, who had since moved to the coast, and told him that the movie needs to come back to Three Rivers. After it was eventually returned to me, I transferred the 16mm movie to a VHS and narrated it, naming the people I knew.

The 1933 film also has an interesting history. My Grandmother Finch originated the idea and chaired the Woman's Club committee that planned the first "Over Seventy" dinner party (later called Pioneer Dinner) in 1924 to honor the old-timers. She also was in charge of planning the annual Pioneer Dinner held on October 14, 1933 to honor old timers and 'Grandma' Christina Alles' 91st birthday. She arranged for Mr. Lindley Eddy, a photographer who had spent twenty years working in Sequoia, to film members and guests as they paraded outside the Club House. Eighteen guests over the age of 70 were honored. In this movie, I could identify Mr. and Mrs. Floyd Carter and his mother; Zola Finch, Ben Harris, Mr. and Mrs. Walter Fry, Mr. and Mrs. Maxon, Frank DeVoe, Enos Barton, Nellie Britton's mother Mrs. Sievertson, Carrie Swanson, Professor Dean, Clarence Fry and his wife. Native Yokuts, Joe Pohot, his wife Mary and family posed for a family shot, as did other family groups. Later Joe Pohot did a little Indian sashay with his wife, Mary, clapping the beat; then bowlegged Enos Barton joined Joe and tried to dance like an Indian. This is the movie with a final scene of four girls tap dancing–Earleen McKee, Alice Noreen Ogilvie, Virginia Thorn, Jean McComber–and two-year-old Earl (me) playing ukulele. I had the movie transferred to DVD at Mike's Camera, Visalia.

1926 Pioneer '49er Parade on stage at Woodlake, CA.

Front row, sitting (l-r): Maudie Lovern, Jason Barton, Will Rice, Grace Alles, Jude Walter Fry, Mrs. Butz–sister of Jason Barton, Shorty Hengst (with pet possum), Frank Finch (seated with fiddle).

Standing, (l-r): Marion Carter, Wes and Orland Lovern in wagon; Blanche McKee, Noel Britten, Philip Alles, Jim Mehrten, Ethel Grunigen, John Grunigen, Amy Mehrten, Phil Davis, Laura Jobe, Earl McKee, Rhoda Finch, Bert Nice, Jeff Davis, Legrand Ellis. Photo February 1926.

Quite a few movies or scenes have been shot on location in Three Rivers. Walt Disney productions came up to Three Rivers in 1968 to film an episode for the television show, Walt Disney's *Wonderful World of Color*. The locals cast in the movie were Kathy Thorn (now a judge); Jack Garrity as the sheriff; my wife, Gaynor, was dressed in a kimono; and I led the posse composed of Willis Beutler, Hat Maxon, and Don Benchoff that chased off a mean old rancher. It was filmed up South Fork on the Kenwood and Hat Maxon ranches and some scenes were shot in Redbanks, down past Woodlake, at an old filling station. It was Episode 18, Season 14 entitled "My Family is a Menagerie" and aired February 11, 1968. We watched the program and were disappointed that my posse and I didn't make it through the final edit, our brief movie career snipped out. Disney filmed two other episodes on the South Fork, "The Boy and the Eagle" and "Day on Beetle Rock."

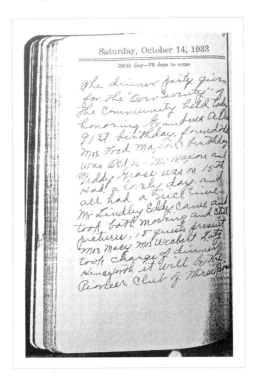

The October 14, 1933 entry in my Grandmother Rhoda Finch's daybook in which she describes the success of the dinner party to honor the "over seventy" Pioneers of Three Rivers.

AUTHOR'S COLLECTION.

Pioneer dinner, 1933. Honored guests were:

(back row, l - r) Enos Barton, Henry DeLong, Mr. Maxon, Mr. Pritchard, unnamed man, Bill Marrow, Uncle John Rice. (front row, l to r) unnamed lady, Mrs. DeLong, unnamed lady, Mrs. Griffeth, unnamed man, Mrs. Sivertson, Grandma Alles, two ladies from North Fork. Photo October 1933.

AUTHOR'S COLLECTION.

Photo taken on location of the 1968 Walt Disney production of "My Family is a Menagerie." My wife, Gaynor, posed with a mountain lion owned by Disney. Photo 1968.

AUTHOR'S COLLECTION.

THREE RIVERS LANDMARKS

Cemetery

I served on the cemetery board with Bob Barton and Ray Prichard for a number of years. Ray Prichard was president of the board longer than anyone else; Bob Barton served almost as long. Later Bill Wylie came on the board. I especially enjoyed the time I spent with Grace Alles who was the secretary because I loved to hear her stories of Atwell Mill and her beloved mountains. I wish I had recorded her stories, of how her son, Oscar Alles, used to ski that whole country to Mineral King. Every fall, Grace would almost have to be dragged away from her cabin at Atwell's Mill; she would not leave until the bucks went to the valley and the snows came. Grace's husband, Philip Alles, retired sawmill operator, was grounds keeper at the cemetery for years. Grady Nunnelly, who worked for the Park, also served as sexton for many years.

The board had to acquire more land to enlarge the cemetery and arrange re-sale of plots purchased in the early days by people who had since moved away. They might own two or three plots, each plot accommodated four graves, and we needed the space as the locals continued to pass on, so Grace spent time tracking absentee owners. Charles Blossom, Jr. came to see me one time because his wife was terminal and there was only one site left in the family plot. He wanted to be buried with the family when his time came, so he asked if we could dig deep and stack the vaults.

Bill Wylie and I were on the board when we made the deal with Portland Cement Company, owner of Blossom Peak at the time, to sell a few acres–actually we had in mind that they could be convinced to make "a charitable gift of two acres," so we appealed to the agent's civic mindedness and the tax advantage and received the property as a donation.

Portland Cement had estimated in 1927 that Blossom Peak contained some ten million tons of limestone and that was their reason for acquiring it. A small area of marble was quarried in the early days with high hopes that it could be used for tombstones, but it was laced with too much lime. It is a real problem digging graves in that hillside and we had to blast some of them. We pre-built one section of graves–Ray Prichard's idea– excavated the dimensions and used redwood to build boxes with lids and covered them with dirt for later use. It looked strong at the time but after four or five years a few fell in, so we filled the remaining excavations with new dirt so it could be easily dug out when needed.

I helped dig the grave for Clell Brewer's father who was 88 years old when he died. We had to drill and blast, set the vault in the grave, set the planks and cover the hard crumbly clay mound with imitation grass, ready for the funeral. Reverend Anderson officiated and it was time in the service for me to sing. When the Reverend stepped to the front of the casket on the plastic grass, the loose clay beneath gave way and the good Reverend fell in the grave up to his waist.

We always hired Larry Britten's company to do the backhoe work, and when I was on the cemetery board, Clyde Bradshaw was hired as the powder man, he was good at setting the right charge so as not to damage adjoining graves. It was a joke about the dynamite: "You'll rattle a lot of teeth around here if you load it too heavy," said Clyde.

Clyde Bradshaw had to excavate a grave right above the caretaker's shed, near Charlie Blossom Jr.'s grave. He used a borrowed compressor to operate the jackhammer. After the job was done with tent and grass in place, Clyde came down to my house and asked to borrow my 4WD pickup to tow the compressor out because a light rain was falling and the steep clay cemetery road was slick. All we needed to do was back my truck up to hitch the compressor. Clyde led the way in his pickup but lost traction and started slipping backwards. Trying to avoid rolling backward onto the terrace, Clyde cut the wheels short, spun out, knocked over the tent and his pickup went rear-end into the grave with his headlights shining into the sky. We had to get a tow truck to pull him out.

I served on the cemetery board for years, sexton was the title, and in that capacity I was often called to helped people select a grave site. Sam Pusateri called me. His dear wife Juanita had died. Sam had taken care of her for years after she was stricken with polio as an adult and she had spent years at home in an iron lung. Within that year, their daughter had died, Juanita's mother had died, and now Juanita was gone. Sam was in a bad way. He bought two lots near his daughter's grave and really broke down. I felt so sorry for him, couldn't change something like that, just happens to all of us; to me, too. That's what life's about—we live and we die.

Airport

At the June 1933 meeting of the Three Rivers Chamber of Commerce, fire protection was on the agenda. It was voted to petition the director of the National Park Service for an airport in Three Rivers so spotter planes could get in the air quickly. At that time Park personnel had to drive to Visalia, the site of the nearest airport, to take off on aerial reconnaissance.

There was some swift government action apparently, because a new field was completed under federal supervision on the C. L. Taylor ranch by September 1933 with the first landing on that date, followed by a half-dozen trial landings and take-offs for phase-one approval. The new Three Rivers Airport was designated by the government as an emergency landing field, a category that absolved the county of liability in case of plane crashes.

The landing strip, 4000 feet long and 400 feet wide, was declared suitable for any type of army airship; the army announced a plan to establish a base at the field with a squadron of planes and ground personnel to provide tactical air defense for the region. The community planned an extravagant program for the official dedication of the airfield on June 9, 1935.

The airport was officially named Jefferson Davis Field, in memory of young Lieutenant Jefferson J. Davis, Jr. of Woodlake, whose older brothers were Eugene, Lawrence, Phil, Roy, and Earl Jack Davis. He was a cousin of Thomas H. Davis II, who became my trusted friend in the cattle business. Lieutenant Davis had died two years earlier when his army airplane plunged into San Francisco Bay on its return trip to base from an aerial photography trip over Sequoia National Park.

The huge dedication event had stunt pilots, military fliers, parachutists, crop dusters and more. It was officially opened by Colonel

John White. The paper reported an audience of 15,000 people, many of whom watched from across the river along Highway 198. One of the more unusual events was a polo game played at one end of the field before the air show got underway. The riders, all mounted on regular western stock horses, were Girard and Tom Davis, Al Griggs, Jim Kindred, Lieutenant Nell, Bob Nyswonger, Clark Nyswonger and my dad, Earl McKee. Colonel White was the referee and Phil Davis and Byron Allen were managers. (My dad often played polo with his fellow Tulare County Sheriff's Posse members.) Next on the program after the polo game was a spectacular crop dusting demonstration. I was four years old and I remember it vividly. The crop duster plane clipped an oak tree and crashed right in front of us. I was so scared I couldn't cry.

The next month, a claim was filed against the Three Rivers Chamber of Commerce by Hal Squires, a part-time resident married to Hollywood stage star Edna Covey, who declared the plane crash damaged his yard. The Woodlake court dismissed the case.

At its October 1937 meeting, presided over by Frank Finch, the Chamber of Commerce passed a resolution to request the federal government to make improvements to the airport so it could qualify for a commercial designation, and to persuade a transcontinental airline to bring regular air passenger service to the Three Rivers. That would have been interesting.

May 19, 1938 was a national Air Mail Week celebration. Here in Three Rivers mail was flown out of Three Rivers in a plane piloted by J. M. Roland and delivered to the Visalia airport to connect to air routes around the country. There were special envelopes and stamp cancellations for the event. In June 1938 a large air show with dozens of stunt pilots and demonstrations again attracted thousands to Three Rivers.

A private twin-engine plane crashed at Three Rivers airport. Earl Jack Davis saw it approach down canyon, and ran onto the field trying to contact it on the radio. The pilot attempted a touch down, pulled up, then approached with the wind, stalled and crashed in front of the residence that used to be the Sulfur Springs schoolhouse. Four people were eating breakfast when the plane crashed and burned. The fellow who bought the Trinity Ranch was piloting the brand new plane and died in the crash.

The day after Pearl Harbor was bombed, the patriotic citizens of Three Rivers rallied to form a community civil defense association and just a week later sixty-one volunteers with pickup trucks, shovels and rakes converged at the airport to clear the runway of brush and rocks. They informed the government by letter that Three Rivers airport was available and fog-free for military planes to land when Valley airports were socked in.

After the War, Ray Prichard applied for a concession permit in 1946 to install amusement rides and stands off to one end of the airport. Ray was a very civic-minded individual who served on the cemetery board and chamber of commerce. Ray and his wife moved from San Diego to Three Rivers in 1938 and built a home just up the hill from us. His father-in-law was Jason Barton. Ray's son, Louis, was a former manager of the airport. Louis, a pilot and flight instructor, was killed in a plane crash in 1947.

Terminus Beach

Terminus Beach is included here, even though it is downstream ten miles next to Lime Kiln Hill, because of some interesting stories that concern some Three Rivers folks.

Terminus Beach was opened on the south bank of the Kaweah River in 1912 by Harry Ginner who arrived in Lemon Cove from England in 1905. Mr. Ginner planted oranges and built his popular recreation area with a dance hall and party facilities about the time Visalia Electric Railroad built a railroad spur to Terminus Beach to serve the orange packing houses. It connected Terminus to Exeter, Woodlake, Red Banks, Elderwood and Visalia. There were weekly dances with music such as the Harmonizers, a seven-piece orchestra, in the 1910s and 1920s.

All those guys were already old when I was a kid and they told stories about Terminus, the music, bands, dancing and, of course, drinking during Prohibition. The bar and a dance hall were near the river beach where sunbathing rafts were moored in the big swimming hole. During Prohibition, moonshine was plentiful, and one well-known supplier was Forest Hog Jaw Busby, Sr. from the South Fork in Three Rivers. The constable for Woodlake, Lemon Cove and Three Rivers was Rennie Brown, brother of my hero Onis Brown. Uncle Loren Finch said that Rennie was always after the South Fork moonshiner. The story goes that one night there was a near confrontation of the two at Terminus Beach. Rennie was sleuthing around in the dark among the trees between the building and the river, sensing that his prey was hiding there somewhere. He was right, someone was back there, hiding behind a tree, but Rennie didn't see him in the dark. Just as he crept by, that someone jumped out and shoved him off into the river. Rennie said he knew damn well who did it, but it was so dark he couldn't prove it. He was madder than a wet hen.

A nine-hole golf course was built on the Ward Ranch on Dry Creek across from Terminus Beach. Dry Creek–just like its name implies–can be crossed without a bridge in the summer. Harry Ginner built a swinging bridge from Terminus Beach across the Kaweah River to the course in 1922. My uncle Loren Finch talked about playing golf there on rocky fairways and greens that didn't stay green very long. In the spring, cattle were run on it to eat the grass down. Water to irrigate was going to come from the Kaweah River via a ditch with a take-out near the Thorn Ranch, which was the Griffes place then, close to the North Fork bridge in Three Rivers. One of the Carter family boys engineered the ditch, parts of which are visible today skirting the mountainside across the river from the present Three Rivers post office. The ditch got as far as Slick Rock where there was a problem getting it across bare granite. From the other end, Fred Ward started work on the ditch around to Bell Point. But before the routing above Slick Rock was solved, the landowner at the take-out point refused to allow water to be diverted from the river.

The 7000-acre Ward Ranch was sold in May 1929 to a Los Angeles developer who said he planned to diversify into a "high-class" cattle ranch, guest ranch, recreational facilities, and an airport. The buyer was a distributor for Ryan airplanes in Los Angeles. It doesn't appear his plans took off, because in August 1929 Woodlake and Lemon Cove businessmen offered the Ward ranch to the federal government for a "narcotic farm" that the government had 5 million dollars to spend on. It would be a working ranch for 200 to 4000 inmates and 500 employees. Los Angeles opposed the idea because they wanted the jobs. It is still rangeland, part of the Dofflemyer spread.

Bridges

The wooden bridge I saw swept downstream in 1937 was replaced and the new bridge dedicated in the spring of 1939 with a parade, picnic, games, and a lot of memories. Fred Savage, who came to the Kaweah district in 1896 remembers there was no bridge to North Fork before the wooden one was built. (After the bridge was built a three story hotel was erected on a beautiful point across the river in 1910, about where the Woman's Club house was.) Savage said there was a ford just downstream from the bridge site, and a rock on the riverbank was called "danger rock." When water was over the top of that rock it was not safe to cross. Professor Dean, a pioneer school teacher, once rode his horse into high water to rescue a man stranded midstream. A. V. Grunigen said that once he and his horse were washed downstream to the island.

About 1892, Mont Barton spent a year building a footbridge across the river about where the North Fork joins the main river. Another resident had a rowboat to help folks across to the school and store. Further up stream the Kaweah colonists had a ferry at one time. Savage said a group of young people forded the river on horseback to attend the dance at Redstone Park (located in Kaweah Colony). While they danced the night away, a hard rain caused the river to rise and the kids could not get home for over a week. And of course there were many stories of groceries lost in the current when fording the river. Floods have necessitated quite a number of new bridges on all the river forks. During high water and bridge wash outs the only way to bring supplies to North Fork residents was the wagon trail over the mountains from Ash Mountain, a rough day's drive by horse and wagon or by car.

Roads to Three Rivers

In 1918 the wagon road–Mineral King Road–that runs by my house was resurfaced with cement, parts of which are still used or visible along Slick Rock, Pierce Drive north to the old Cider Mill, a portion east of the Cider Mill, and the long stretch by my home through Old Three Rivers to Highway 198.

In 1929 the route for a new state highway was surveyed up the canyon with fewer curves and more cuts and fills. One of the most welcomed improvements was the 55-foot deep cut blasted through Lime Kiln Hill that eliminated the steep climb over the ridge. A lot of dynamite was also needed to build the new straightaway up Homer's grade. A construction superintendent declared that it was one of the best-aligned roads he had ever worked on.

Instead of following the curve of the hills through the Old Three Rivers, the new road went straight from what is now the end of Lake Kaweah to the North Fork bridge, by-passing the old business district.

The new state highway was finished in 1933. One of the celebrations for the new road was a moonlight dance held on the abandoned cement road at the Fannie Mehrten place near Horse Creek, where quadrilles, waltzes and modern steps were danced to the music of a live orchestra.

THREE RIVERS SOCIAL

⟨ww⟩

The Three Rivers Woman's Club hosted community card parties, fundraisers, and potlucks at their club house across the river from Sequoia Hall. It was built about 1910 by John Hunter and Dan Alles, both operators at the Edison hydroelectric plant, for an invalid girl, Elizabeth Maxwell, who passed away before the house was finished. A Mrs. Hays purchased the structure for $1200 and later bequeathed it to the Three Rivers Woman's Club for its first club house. I remember our school plays were put on at the Club House. The Woman's Club hosted the first "old people's dinner" in 1924–the dinner was renamed The Pioneer Club of Three Rivers in 1933. When I was four, I sang "Home on the Range" and "Pop Goes The Weasel" for the Pioneer dinner and my sister Blanche sang "Annie Laurie." At age 11, I accompanied Grandfather Finch, both of us played violins, Blanche sang and Mrs. Billy Swanson played the piano.

Sequoia Hall, built in 1909 about where the North Fork bridge is now, was the center for dances, school programs, socials, club meetings, Red Cross sewing groups, home defense lessons, and other civic activities. I remember one play staged at the hall. Carl Sweeney wrote it, and Thelma and Johnny Britten, Dick and Patsy Britten, Ted and Maricia Bartlett, Joe and Dot Carmichael, Lee and Blanche Maloy, Willis and Frances Beutler, all had speaking parts, the scene was a classroom, a privy (outhouse) served as a hilarious prop on stage, Carl was the teacher with silly glasses on the end of his nose, and he asked ridiculous questions. Willis made spitballs from toilet paper that kids threw at the teacher. Carl had done vaudeville and knew a lot of tricks so he rigged the teacher's chair to teeter on the edge of the stage and hang there so the kids would pull him up. But on cue, Lee Maloy shoved Carl too hard, the chair recoiled and hurled Carl across the set to the wall.

School plays were very popular fare, sometimes written by the teachers so every student had a part. About 1936 *One Midsummer's Day* operetta was directed by our principal Mrs. McDowall starring the entire student body. My sister Earleen had the leading role of Fairy Queen; cousin Sherman was a Honeybee and I was one of the Overall Boys.

Frank Finch founded the Poison Oak Orchestra: violin and banjo–Frank Finch; banjo–Freeman Walker, owner of a small store and gas station in Lemon Cove; piano and guitar–Ben Hardin, a rancher in Three Rivers; banjo–Al Brockman, bus driver at Woodlake High School; piano–Edna McKee; and Jeff Davis played bones like no one had ever played bones before. In later years, Fred Woods, high school bus driver, played banjo, while I played fiddle.

At one community potluck and dance, Grandmother Finch had the quadrille dancers dress up, men as women and women as men. Grandfather Frank Finch even wore fingernail polish and Grandmother wore overalls. It brought down the house. Quadrilles–later known as square dances–were very popular and there was a friendly competition between the Goshen quadrille dancers and the Three Rivers group. In 1933, Jim Rivers, "mayor" of Goshen, a little town on the railroad west of Visalia, challenged the Three Rivers quadrille dancers to a competition with his Goshen Gallopers at a big dance in Visalia. Three Rivers was recognized as having some of the best quadrille dancers in the state. In 1939, the Poison Oak Orchestra and quadrille couples were invited to entertain at Hotel California in Fresno to perform the dances they did at the 1926 Pioneer Days event. Frank Finch directed the orchestra; the dancers were Rhoda Finch, Phil Davis, James and Amy Mehrten, Mrs. Byron Allen, Earl McKee, Maud Hershberger, and Will Ogilvie.

Another musical group was the Calva Stewart orchestra that played for dances. Carney Franks played piano and violin.

The Three Rivers Hill Billies orchestra was composed of six women: Carrie Swanson, Grace Alles, Rose Vaughn, Mrs. Roy Tucker, Mrs. Ethel Grunigen, and Mrs. Fred McComber. They became quite popular in 1933 and performed their old fashion music on old-time instruments, wearing "hay seed" costumes.

For most of 1922, my dad worked the Saturday dance at Kaweah Park for which he was paid $5.00 a night. The C. L. Taylor apple packing house, built about 1933 on North Fork across from the airport, was also a favorite venue for dances.

I remember Roy Davis was the funniest guy; he'd drive up from Woodlake to the dances at Sequoia Hall, dressed in a tuxedo with an enormous diamond stickpin on his lapel. He was noisy, threw around funny quips like "My father claimed I was sired on top of Mt. Whitney," and he was the first to yell "Paul Jones" which meant everyone grabbed another partner. Another popular mixer was to put the ladies at one end of the hall and the men at the other, and at the yell "Go!" everyone would partner up. Either Roy or Earl Vincent would do the yell and get a head start across the room because they had an eye on someone they wanted to dance with, then they'd dance around to get near someone else and yell "Paul Jones." It was a lot of fun and could be a bit rowdy. Everyone danced the foxtrot and waltzes, then swing music became popular. Another mixer was Schottische.

In an old newspaper story about Three Rivers square dancers, Jason Barton was referred to as the unofficial mayor of Three Rivers ("his son Bob said he just mostly appointed committees") who always showed how old-fashioned dances should be called. Bob Barton learned to call square dances (quadrilles) from his dad; he was a good quadrille instructor and called the moves with a serious air.

Bob Barton drove the mail truck to Giant Forest and, of course, stopped at the Park check-in station at Ash Mountain every trip. Ford Spiegelmyer was the ranger at that check-in station and would inquire of every driver, "Is this your first trip to the Park?" Bob thought Spiegelmyer should at least look up and recognize him after so many check-throughs, but Spiegelmyer would not vary his script: "Is this your first trip to the Park?" "NO! NO! I drive this every day!" "And what is your name?" "You know damn well what my name is!"

Parades and Rodeos

My dad talked about the community picnics and horse races at the Carter farming fields–they called it Farming Field–what is now Cherokee Oaks. Local rodeos were staged there too. When we were kids we roamed the Farming Field, and sometimes played football or baseball there. In

May 1930, the first annual rodeo was held at the Craig Thorn Ranch. The following year improvements were made with a new quarter mile race-track and bleachers. A crowd of 1500 watched the bronc riding, cattle riding, bulldogging, racing and calf roping. The bucking horses were provided by Cuff Burrel and Happy Jack Hawn. Clay Carr, RCA All Around Champion, competed and took first in bronc riding. The 1933 rodeo advertised in the newspaper that "the meanest stock on the range" were being rounded up from the herd of Black Poles on the Byron Allen ranch.

Later, annual rodeos and team roping events were held at the Three Rivers airport grounds and always attracted hundreds of valley specta-tors and contestants. The attendance at one in 1947 topped 2000 visitors. Rodeo events were team roping, calf roping, horse reining and stake races, steer riding, along with a horse show. When I was ten years old, my sister Blanche had an 8mm camera and took a movie at the 1940 May Day picnic of my dad roping on Old Abe, a horse out of Mars Mouse.

The 1931 Fiesta Rodeo Parade in Visalia was reported as spectacular with attendance of 15,000 people. From Three Rivers, my dad, Onis Brown, Ord Loverin, Frank Eggers, and Phil Davis rode with a pack train of nearly 100 head of mules and horses. Fox and Universal filmed the parade and rodeo that year.

THREE RIVERS ENTERPRISES

❦

Redwood

H.C. Balch had a welding and woodworking shop in which he made beautiful redwood bowls, curios and candle sticks on his lathe, all from trees brought down by the great flood of 1867. He established himself as souvenir maker for Sequoia National Park in 1925. Colonel White ordered an oversize ceremonial redwood key to present to visiting dignitaries to the Park and named Mr. Balch the Park's official key maker. Mr. Balch was 69 years old when, after his shop burned, he relocated from Old Three Rivers to the main highway and called his new place The Redwood Shop. Mr. Balch's distant relative donated to the national forest the beautiful grove of sequoia trees above Springville that became known as Balch Park. H. C. Balch represented his family at the dedication of Balch Park because the donors were in Europe. Mr. Balch died in 1930 from injuries suffered when he collided with a train. Mr. Morris Macy bought the redwood shop and ran it for years.

Bill Case lived down where the Thorn Ranch was, across the main fork. His business was making shakes in the Salt Creek pines, quite a few miles distant up behind the BLM now, about 6500 feet elevation. He had some sort of road so he could haul the shakes in an old wagon down Salt Creek to the Kaweah River where he dumped them in the current then fished them out downstream to sell. That was his livelihood. Eva Pogue Kirkman wrote that in 1879 Bill Case drove a six or eight-yoke ox team to haul lumber from the Badger area for the miles and miles of fencing for her father J. W. C. Pogue's Dry Creek ranch.

Some of our forest redwood was shipped to France. From the *Pacific Rural Press*, Vol. 69, Number 8, 25 February 1905: "Big Tree Wood for Pencils: Times: Henry Alles, from Atwell's Mill on the Mineral King

Road, states that he is about ready to ship a carload of pencil wood from Exeter. The destination of the wood is France, where it will be used in the manufacture of lead pencils of a cheap variety. It is a big tree wood and is used as a substitute for cedar which is becoming scarce. The wood is shipped in boxes about 5 feet long and 3 feet wide and 18 inches deep. Shipments of pencil wood have been made from Sanger for several years but the shipment being made by Mr. Alles today is the first carload to go forward from this county."

In 1907, a journalist from San Francisco wrote about his trip by stage to see the Big Trees. In the mountains they met a six-mule team pulling a freight wagon piled high with new wooden boxes. The sides were stenciled with a city name and "France." He reported that Old Clate, the stage driver, explained to him "...them's wood pencils, anyway they will be when they get the lead put in them. Then they come back to this country marked 'Ribot, Paris; Siberian Graphite' and nothin's ever said about them redwoods."

In 1941, Carrol Barnes, sculptor in Three Rivers, carved his famous statue "Paul Bunyon and Babe the Ox" from one 20-foot long redwood log. It stood by Camp Sequoia across from Three Rivers Union School in the 1940s. Colonel John White officiated at the unveiling at this site. The statue is now at the Three Rivers Historical Museum. Photo c. 1947.

AUTHOR'S COLLECTION.

Jim Livingston Hardware

When I was talking about backcountry trails, I mentioned Jim Livingston and John Grunigen who built the High Sierra Trail. In the late 1930s, Jim Livingston was appointed superintendent at the Camp Potwisha CCC.

In the wintertime, I liked to visit Jim at his home or his hardware store in Three Rivers because he was a very interesting person. He opened a hardware store in a Quonset hut (across from The Redwood Shop, about where Barby's is today) where we liked to go on a cold winter's day to stand around the big heater and tell stories. He'd tell stories of the things he had done. In his younger days he was a halfback on the football team at University of California. He wanted to be a soldier and fought in the Spanish American War.

Jim suffered a shrapnel wound to the head in France in WWI where he was rescued and cared for by a French family named Terasse. His family back home had collected his death benefit because he was presumed KIA. Jim married the daughter of his French hosts, and returned to the U.S. By 1939, his wife's mother, Mrs. M. Terasse resided in San Francisco. Jim underwent more surgery for his head wound and as a result of the trauma had spells of forgetfulness.

Jim Livingston became scoutmaster of Three Rivers Boy Scouts in 1936. I joined the Boy Scouts when I was eight years old. The annual Jamborees were great fun, but sometimes our scoutmaster Jim forgot things: one year at the Thorn Ranch Jamboree, he forgot to bring us any food, so we made salad from watercress that grew beside a big spring up on the ranch. At the valley Jamboree on the Dofflemyer ranch on Dry Creek, my uncle Harry Britten was the guest speaker. Harry Britten was a Silver Beaver Scout, the highest award in Scouting.

Jim provided our transportation–six of us scouts–and dropped us off at Dofflemyer's but forgot to come back with our food and bedrolls, so Uncle Harry fed us and put us up in his tent. That's when Uncle Harry told us the story of Sontag and Evans, the famous train robbers. Uncle Harry said a long time ago a play about the train robbers was being performed at the school in Old Three Rivers. He was on his horse riding to the play when he heard voices in the night asking, "Who goes there?" He said he recognized the bandits' voices and told them that the play was about them and suggested that they come on over and make a surprise appearance on stage. Evans declined because they feared a gunfight might erupt if a Pinkerton man was hiding in the audience. Many locals liked the train robbers and some folks tried to help them out because most everyone hated the railroads.

In 1937, Jim built a Spanish style adobe house along the river on 20 acres he purchased from C. L. Taylor. He knew the recipe for making adobe bricks and two years later built an addition to his adobe home.

One day I went to Jim's hardware store because I needed some 3/4" pipe, the most common size that hardware stores always keep on hand. Jim said that he didn't have any in stock, but he was "expecting it anytime." He'd always say "expecting it anytime" and walk out front and look down the road like he was going to see that delivery truck drive up right then. I started to leave and he asked, "Wait a minute, what did you say you needed?" 3/4 inch. "Oh dammit, I've got all kinds of that in the back." Another blackout. And he was just so honest. Another time I needed to buy a pipe reamer or threader or something. He asked what I was going to do with it and I told him. He insisted, well, you don't need it very often, so here—just take this new one to use and bring it back when you're done with it.

Jim sold his hardware store to Fred Salmon who owned it at the time of the 1955 flood. Fred lived across the road from us and called me up to ask if I could bring a truck to help haul stuff from the store, the water was rising. I tried to help Fred out that night but the floodwater was as high as the headlights on my 2-ton truck when I parked in front on highway 198. The river was raging through the back of the store and half the building fell off into the current. Fred had hip boots on slogging around trying to save something. I yelled at him to get those things off, he'd drown for sure. He waded over and got in the truck and we backed down the road.

THREE RIVERS PERSONALITIES

There were many people I met or just knew of who were like background actors in any small town movie scene, a mix of curious manners or odd behavior, comedy and tragedy, shaped by choice or circumstance.

Ben Bennett

Ben Bennett was a jack-of-all-trades who lived in a little cabin up South Fork across the river and above where Dr. A. J. Rice lived in a teepee years ago. Ben had work in the valley, but also had time for jobs up here. He helped my father-in-law Sonny Hardison and me scatter a lot of pipe, helped us on ditch work, always had a winch on his truck and was good at highline jobs. Ben was always a friendly sort who liked to dicker, judging from the collection of old stuff stacked up around his cabin. Ben lived alone.

From his porch Ben could see the gate to the road that came up the hill to his house. The gate was across from Whisperin' Bob Lovering's place.

I got a call from Hat Maxon, a neighbor up the road from Ben, that Ben had probably had a slight stroke because he was acting strange and would not leave his place. He wasn't eating right and all day he sat on his porch with a 30-30 Winchester rifle in his lap and watched the gate below. The neighbors were half afraid someone might pull up at the gate and Ben would drill them.

I tried my turn at reasoning with him, that he should look out for his health and go to the hospital, but he didn't listen to me either. At that point it was decided for his own good he had to be carried off his hill. He was never able to return.

Monroe Spence

Frankie Welch's "Cactus Cabin" offered an affordable roof over the head of several interesting fellows over the years. It was a little shack by a big cactus patch on the old road not far from our house. Monroe Spence moved to Three Rivers in about 1947 and worked as "a specialist in general repairs, knife and saw blade sharpening and gardening," none of which guaranteed a steady paycheck. Walking down the road, Monroe had a peculiar gait sometimes associated with the fruit of the vine. He was born in 1887 in Mississippi and had been a peace officer and, as the "Meet Your Neighbor" item in a 1951 issue of *The Current* put it, ". . . through experience has a profound knowledge of civil and criminal law."

One time Sherman Finch and I were sitting on our grandfather's porch when we heard a car coming down the hill way too fast to make the curve, then–crack-crack-crack–the car snapped off about four fence posts in front of the house before it pulled back on the road dragging strings of wire off the back, and there was Monroe hanging on to the steering wheel like it was running away with him.

Jimmy Brockman

Jimmy Brockman was another resident of Cactus Cabin who arrived with a big old crank-start car. He was afoot much of the time because that car would not start. More than likely Cooney Alles could have repaired it, because he could fix anything. Jimmy wasn't a mechanic and I remember one day he cranked, and cranked, and cranked without so much as a turn-over, and he lost it. He took the crank and beat on the headlights, the fenders, the hood. Life was just overwhelming and his frustration had no damper. One night he kicked the boards off one side of his cabin.

Conrad Alles

The Alles family of six sons and four daughters homesteaded on South Fork in 1887. Conrad's mother, Christina Alles, was widowed in 1891. She was known as "Grandma Alles" to the whole community.

Conrad, called "Cooney" by most everyone, was an expert machinist, mechanic, designer, who had tools to build anything and fix everything. I had a Remington shotgun I used to hunt quail and the firing pin broke. It was during WWII and I figured I was out of luck because everything was rationed and no one could get parts. Cooney offered to take a look. The firing pin was steel, 4 inches long with camber on one side, it required precision to duplicate, but Cooney made a new firing pin for me. It is still firing in that shotgun. He did all kinds of machining on that lathe.

He had a great sense of humor and with his skill at design, built some outrageous parade entries. One can be seen in the 1926 wagon train movie. Cooney modified his wagon to look sort of like a horseless carriage with a vertical steering wheel in front of the seat and a cowling to resemble the front of a car. Behind him, the wagon bed had been removed, and hidden behind the driver, under curtains strung from corner posts, was the mule rigged up to push the wagon along somehow. As a kid, I remember seeing a Cooney entry in the Visalia parade. Cooney engineered some fancy gearing so the float was self-propelled by a horse on a treadmill on top of a flat bed trailer. Carl Sweeney was on the float flipping flapjacks and tap dancing. He'd give the horse a swat once in a while to make the float go faster.

During WWII, Conrad drove an old Buick that he wanted to paint patriotic red, white and blue, but he didn't have any blue paint, so his car was red, white and green. Tires were rationed, so for one of his old cars during the War–he had all sorts of old cars, motors, tractors–he cut circular slabs from a log and trimmed them precisely until he had four discs of wood about as wide as a tire of identical size, drilled for a center spindle just like a wheel for a car. For tread, he tacked on pieces cut from old tires. The ride on solid wood tires wasn't smooth or quiet–my dad would hear a "boom b-da, boom b-da" and say that sounds like Cooney. He'd drive by proud as punch. He made wooden wheels for his bicycle too.

Carl Sweeney

I've mentioned Carl Sweeney who worked for my dad at the Giant Forest corrals and entertained around the big campfires. Carl did a lot of vaudeville stunts to entertain at community affairs during the winter season in Three Rivers; my Grandmother Finch wrote in her daybook that Carl performed at the May 7, 1933 Three Rivers Board of Trade picnic.

Carl was born in Indianapolis, Indiana in 1887. In 1908 he was engaged to the daughter of a popular young lady, Miss Jeanne Wheeler, and her engagement and bridal shower were announced prominently on the society pages of the Indianapolis paper. But the wedding was described in one word: interesting. "An interesting wedding ceremony took place yesterday morning at 10 o'clock in SS Peter and Paul's Cathedral. . . ." leaving one to wonder what kind of stunt did Carl pull–vaudeville? ride a horse to the altar? tap dance on the kneeling bench? At any rate, Carl, his bride, their baby girl, and his brother-in-law arrived in the wilds of Hood River, Oregon in 1910. He made his way, alone, to Arizona, El Centro, New Orleans and then to Three Rivers by 1930. He lived in a cabin on South Fork and cared for old Henry Alles until Henry died in 1940. In 1941 and 1942, Carl worked winters for the exclusive Snake Tree and Smoke Tree dude ranches near Palm Springs, California. Carl's daughter Harriett Sweeney Dible came to see him from time to time. I remember her son Jimmy Dible worked in Giant Forest with us part of one summer in the mid 1940s. Carl helped me gather some steers in Greasy in 1950. Carl rode my big horse that about shook his liver loose because going down hill you swore he was bucking the whole way.

My mother received a telephone call from Carl Sweeney sometime about 1960. He was calling from Visalia to inquire about all his old friends in Three Rivers. He no longer could drive so he had hired a taxi to bring him up from Los Angeles area and had stopped to rest in Visalia. My mother told him that everyone he inquired about was dead, so he said he guessed he'd better get back in the taxi and go home.

Don Benchoff

Don Benchoff owned a horse boarding facility in Southern California in Surfridge that he sold or leased so he could move up here to work for Walter Wells at Wells Ranch on South Fork. Don's wife, Mary, was a very Irish lady with an Irish temperament and with my wife, Gaynor, taught dance. Mary went on her own and built a studio on the hillside above Pat O'Connell's station; it is vacant and falling down after all these years. Don's brother-in-law married my sister, Earleen, and they had four children, settling in Livingston, California before he was killed in a car wreck.

Don wasn't a cowman but he knew horses and we rode together a lot, and traded help just like I traded with Forrest Homer and Johnny Britten. He was a funny, likable guy. After Wells ranch, Don worked for Tommy Elliott's ranch before he decided to go back to his horse boarding business, taking care of the horses of the rich and famous, until he died.

Red Cannon

Red Cannon was a colorful soul with an unknown background. He worked at everything. He went to a Byron Allen branding one time on South Fork, where Johnny Britten remembered Red was in the corral just getting in the way. Byron kept saying, "Red, now ya better get back, ya better get back." The guys turned a bull loose that had just been cut, it raged around the corral and hit Red square in the chest, ran right through him, knocking every bit of air out of him. Someone rushed over and pulled on his belt, lifting and dropping him to get him to breathe, then dragged him out of the way, and went back to branding.

My mother never forgot the incident in the parking bay attached to our old shop. Dad and mother were going out for the evening, and when dad started the car and shifted in reverse he heard a loud shout, "Whoa!" Dad jumped out and found Red under the car where he had been sleeping off a binge.

Skinny Kirk

Everett "Skinny" Kirk was born in Porterville, California in 1893. He was about 40 years old when he moved up to Three Rivers on advice from his doctor because he had respiratory problems. He married the lady next door, Pansy Busby, a real hardworking mountain woman who often had charge of serving the rodeo barbecues. Skinny was a cowboy for Gill Cattle Company in the winters and worked in the backcountry in summer, packed a few seasons for my dad during WWII when all the young guys were away at war. In 1937 he was hired as junior foreman at the Maxon Ranch CCC camp.

Skinny worked for the Park Service as a backcountry ranger and he was one of the best, because he was part of the mountains, understood how things ought to be. He wasn't a handbook guy–he wouldn't give a Boy Scout a ticket for not having a fishing license; he'd remind him that he should have been prepared with one. On the other hand, if someone was abusing stock, he wasn't afraid to run them out of the mountains. He spent most of his time at Lewis Camp on the Kern River, but had a tent cabin at Chagoopa Falls, and travelled up and down the Kern. He was there for many years, packed in there as far back as 1910. Skinny was really a good man, and afraid of nobody. He kept the phone lines working over to Lewis Camp. He took Clay Carr and Elmo Carr when they were kids on a pack trip to Chagoopa Plateau and the kids hammered their initials and date in a scrap of sheet metal, like a tinsmith, then hid it in the rafters of a cabin at Moraine Lake. Years later Skinny retrieved that sign. He told me the story when I gave him a sign I found in Deer Camp when I was hunting horses. There were a couple of old deer hooks and the sign "Lou Davis 1921" on a tree in the old camp. Lou Davis used to own property on the Kern River, he was an old Park ranger too.

Skinny lived up South Fork and drove by my house on his way to and from work every day in his old Model A, the gears howling like a Model A did, a little coupe with a pickup bed on the back. He worked terrible hours, sunup to after dark, at Gill Cattle Company at Yokohl. He used to come to the brandings until he was up in his 80s, still could rope with the best. Well, I guess that's not so old, I'm still roping at brandings and I just turned 81 years.

Skinny Kirk at his homestead on Cinnamon Creek. Skinny is wearing Angora chaps, made in Montana, very popular in winter, not too practical in our summer weather. I always wanted a pair. Photo c. 1920.

AUTHOR'S COLLECTION.

I was at Yuet Sue's restaurant bar in Visalia when a fellow, seeing my cowboy hat, came up and asked if I was from Three Rivers, then introduced himself as Agent Pettyjohn, and proceeded to tell me what a great week he had spent with Skinny Kirk in the backcountry. The agent, head of the FBI office in Visalia, met Skinny on a case up in Kern River and told me he'd never met a guy like him who fed him so well; said Skinny didn't hide the fact that they were eating "camp meat," (Park venison) that was kept hid in a tree. He had such a good time fishing and talking to this character. The case for the FBI opened when my nephew, Billy Maloy, found a man's shoe, foot bones inside and leg bones sticking out, on some high, rocky bluffs when he went fishing out of Kern River, up Rock Creek.

Skinny Kirk and Marcellus Brown, both retired from the Park Service, lived next door to each other in a couple of rentals in Alta Acres across from the Dinely Bridge. They were widowers and looked after each other for a while, until a falling out over something, maybe because of health problems or old age. Skinny had eyes like an eagle, but lost his vision due to glaucoma. Packing in the mountains, he'd point out deer feeding on a mountainside in Big Arroyo that my young eyes thought were rocks, until he taught me to really "see." Skinny passed away in May 1978.

I was asked to sing at Skinny's funeral. I was riding on the South Fork ranch gathering cattle and someone mentioned what day it was. I thought it was another day, and I asked them today isn't Wednesday is it? Oh my God, I looked at my watch and said boys I am leaving you right now, you take my horse and truck, I'll take the car. I headed for Exeter, just time to stop at the house and grab a guitar. I had been in that funeral parlor in Exeter so many times that I knew the back door, so I hurried in that way and the organist saw me and said "whew." Luckily she knew the song I was going to sing because just minutes later the little light was turned on from the podium out front, which meant the director was ready for the music. I strummed my guitar and sang a nice cowboy song. I was filthy, just got off the horse, smelled like a horse. I should have gone out to the procession of mourners, but I stayed hid. Someone later on said, "Boy that sure was a good recording of you singing at the funeral." I felt bad about not seeing Skinny to the cemetery.

Clough and Cahoon

Skinny Everett Kirk married Pansy, daughter of Eva (Evelyn) Clough Cahoon, granddaughter of Julia Clough Blossom. Ira and Julia Clough Blossom were the first pioneers to make a home on South Fork in the mid-1860s.

George Cahoon was a hunter and some-time dairyman on South Fork. He came up from Linn's Valley northeast of Bakersfield. A news item in 1873 reported that George Cahoon had captured two bear cubs and sold them to T. J. Jones in Visalia who took the cubs to Sacramento to sell, or if he didn't get his price, he was leaving with them for Chicago. The next year, George Cahoon trapped with A. Everton in the area of Hospital Rock where Everton was injured and cared for by the Yokuts.

Blossom and Cahoon hunted and ran cattle between Clough's Cave and Hockett Meadow where many landmarks bear their names: Cahoon Meadow (where I ran cattle), Cahoon Lookout, Blossom Lakes, and Evelyn Lake. About seven miles from Clough's Cave to the east is South Fork Meadows, 7000 to 8000 feet elevation, a favorite area where Blossoms and Cahoons camped, ran cattle, and hunted for many generations. An old-timer said that George summered milk cows there and made salted butter, packed in tins, and in the fall took pelts, smoked meat and butter by pack train to market in Stockton. Three miles southeast of South Fork Meadow is the Quinn Ranger Station. A counter-clockwise loop takes you 1-1/2 miles northeast to Blossom Lakes, west 3 miles to Hockett Meadow, 3 miles to Cahoon Meadow, then along the back side of Homer's Nose and back to Clough's Cave. It is a beautiful area of forests, meadows and streams.

In 1877, George Cahoon, age 41, married Julia Clough Blossom's 16-year-old daughter, Evelyn (Eva) Clough. A daughter, Daisy, was born in 1879, a son George born in 1880, a son James born in 1882. (It is likely that Daisy was enumerated on the June 1880 U.S. Census as "David, age 1," because the record shows Daisy Cahoon DeBois, beloved wife of John W. DuBois a San Francisco businessman, died and was buried in San Francisco at age 18 years, 16 days, on October 24, 1896, survived by her mother Eva Busby, brothers George Cahoon and James Cahoon.) Eva Cahoon's next daughter, Pansy, was born in 1887.

George Cahoon was well known and respected by the residents of Three Rivers and Lime Kiln. They were shocked when they heard that on September 16, 1887 Cahoon was shot and killed. He was buried on his old home place on South Fork.

Daniel Boone Busby (grandfather of my classmates, Dan and Forest Busby), who had worked for George Cahoon for two years, claimed he shot Cahoon in self-defense. On December 22, 1887, a jury returned a verdict of not guilty after a two-week trial. There were many stories about the shooting, published and unpublished. Not long ago when I talked to Dan Busby, grandson of Daniel Boone Busby, he recounted to me his family's version of the 1887 incident and said not everything reported in the newspapers was correct.

A marriage license was issued to Daniel Boone Busby and Eva Cahoon on January 16, 1888. Subsequently, Eva and Daniel had four children, girls named for flowers, the boy for trees: Zinnia Mae (1889); Rose Bella (1890); Violet Evelyn (1893), Forest Wiles (1895). Pansy Cahoon Kirk wrote an autobiographical snapshot in 1960 when she was 73 years old in which she remembered they were all raised in the wild isolated South Fork canyon. They lived off the land, raised chickens, beef, and hunted game; a large flat area was planted to fruit trees and garden. She said she first wore shoes at age five when she was sent to Cinnamon School, enrolled so young because she was needed to make the minimum class size.

In 1900, Daniel Boone Busby left the family and returned to Kansas where he remarried. Eva married John W. Menteer that same year; three years later she married George Joseph Long. By 1910, she was widowed and lived with her four children on South Fork. Her daughter, Pansy Cahoon, married Richard Wells in Fresno, and a daughter, Muriel, was born July 23, 1910. Muriel was our bus driver for years when I was in grammar school. She drove the South Fork bus and Fred Ogilvie drove the big bus on the main route. Pansy had another daughter, Evelyn, who still resides in Three Rivers. Pansy's mother, Eva Kathleen Clough Cahoon, died May 22, 1938 at age 77. Pansy passed away in 1962.

I sang for the funeral of Forest Wiles Busby, son of Eva Cahoon Busby. I didn't really know him personally, but had heard stories about him. He lived through some tough times. He wrote some nice poetry; one poem was a favorite of an Exeter preacher who read it at several funerals that I sang for. As I mentioned before, I rode the school bus with his two sons, Forest and Dan.

Hat Maxon

Hat Maxon was born Harrison Darwin Hattfield Maxon January 29, 1891 on a ranch north of Exeter owned by his parents, the Fred Maxons. His grandfather, Erasmus Maxon, homestead 160 acres in 1873 where Exeter is now located and farmed wheat and fruit trees. Erasamus's wife Hannah died in 1875, whereupon Mr. Maxon donated land for the Exeter Cemetery. Maxon family members are buried in Exeter. The Maxon Ranch on South Fork was the site of a large CCC camp in the 1930s. Hat was chief engineer for an oil company and lived much of the time on the West Side to oversee the pumping stations from the oil fields around Taft and Bakersfield. Hat married Violet Busby in 1910.

Hat retired to South Fork where I used to visit with him a lot. Hat was an old fellow, and we were the greatest of friends. He loved to sing and wanted me to sing his favorite song at his funeral, "Dear Old Hills Of California, My Home Sweet Home." He told stories about Joe Palmer who was much older than Hat; in fact, Hat had an old pistol that belonged to Joe, supposedly the one used by Joe to hit an Indian over the head.

Hat loved to hunt. Joe Davis and I were driving out of Grouse after a day of hunting and ahead of us was Hat driving his truck. He obviously saw something because he stopped in the middle of the road, pulled out a rifle and laid it across the hood—worked fine because he was left handed—and shot a buck. The buck rolled off the hillside into the road and we helped clean and load it.

Hat Maxon's brother, Don Maxon, was a carpenter and stonemason. Don was one of two carpenters who built the Silver City store and living quarters in 1929. He was famous for his beautiful brick and rock chimneys in the early days. Don had retired up in Springville. I remember the day when I heard that Don Maxon had died. I was going through the Seaborn ranch on the way to Ace Peck's place and had stopped to talk to Walt Seaborn. Hat was working for Seaborn at the time and drove an old red 1956 Ford ¾-ton pickup. He pulled up beside me and said well, he guessed we'd heard that his brother died. He told us that Don hadn't been able to drive his open jeep with the oversize tires for several years because he was near blind and the family had taken away the keys. One day when he was left alone Don decided he could *so* drive and went out to prove it. Drove out on a mountain road where he lost control and rolled his jeep down a canyon. He was killed. So Hat told us this story and said, "You know, I told him he couldn't drive that damned jeep but he showed 'em. He showed 'em all right, and by God, he'll never do that again!" He was just so emphatic, "By God, you know what. He'll never do that again."

Hat and Don Maxon's sister, Tilly Maxon, married Ed Bryant. In the early 1930s Ed and Tilly ran a goat ranch on South Fork, over 1000 head of Angoras, raised for wool. I'd see Till out there once in a while when we ran cattle just above her house. One evening she was outside with a rifle in her hand trying to find some "camp meat." You know they lived off the land and shot a deer once in a while. I rode up and she didn't see me, it was getting dusk, about the time you'd look for camp meat. I said, "Hello, Till!" She dropped that rifle in the weeds and moved away from it like she was just admiring the sunset. I told her she could go pick up that rifle before it gets wet or full of mud, I knew what she was doing but sure didn't care, and she said, "Oh, is that you, Earl?"

Clyde Bradshaw

Clyde Bradshaw, along with Leroy Maloy and Duane Brewer, worked for Dick Lang building the original St. Anthony's Retreat compound at Salt Creek. These foothills are all granite so the whole building site had to be blasted. To hold down flying rock, a set of old bedsprings was laid over the shot; a lead wire from the dynamite cap was run back to Clyde's pickup where he used a car battery to detonate it. His mistake was to bring the lead wire across the top of the bedspring. The rule is to yell, "Fire in the hole" three times and before the third time, you'd better be behind some cover. When Clyde set it off, the blast sent the springs flying over a nearby power line and draped the trailing lead line across the high voltage wires. Duane said he could see fire shooting down that lead line over to Clyde's car. Clyde fell over, got up, shook, fell again, shook, tried to get up, then collapsed and stayed down. The lead line couldn't carry the full 60,000 volts but the jolt threw Clyde against the side of his car, burned his ass end and burned his feet, even melted some of the tacks in his shoes. He was rushed to a hospital and managed to live through it.

The big flood of 1955 took out the back end of Huffackers Candy Store (now Reimer's) and Millie Huffacker called on Clyde to replace the rock stairs that went from the rear of the store down to the river. Clyde did nice rockwork, and for the handrail he found a long piece of driftwood which he sanded and polished. Millie was so pleased with his handiwork and exclaimed how beautiful and natural it was. Clyde nodded in agreement, "You know, I thought it kinda breaks up the contrast." That line has become a classic in our jazz repertoire.

Phil Davis

Phil Davis lived across the road from us for quite a few years. He was a big promoter, came up with all sorts of schemes to solicit investors to join and then sometimes he would be away for a while afterwards. Phil was the committee chairman of the 1926 '49er parade to Woodlake, and the reunion party years later. Phil put on several rodeo events at his place and was quite involved in planning community celebrations–bridge dedications, picnics, parade floats, in the early years. Phil advertised plans to develop a 6000-acre dude ranch in Arizona, and cattle businesses in Mexico. In 1929 he opened a riding camp here in Three Rivers to train the sons of movie stars and tycoons. Phil's wife was never seen outside their house unless they were going off to a shindig. My mother always wondered, because every couple of weeks a big black car pulled up to their house late at night for a short time, then disappeared.

Phil really wanted to be in the packing business like his brother, Roy, and my dad, so he opened his own pack station across and up a ways from his brother's pack station in Mineral King, but he wasn't in business long. In the early '20s he had a running tab with my dad for alfalfa hay because he was always short. Phil made some colorful threats when he'd get worked up. One time he told my dad that he would just fence the five acres around his house and raise hogs to stink us out, forgetting that the twenty acres that encircled Phil's five acres were part of the McKee ranch. My dad told Phil he just might start raising hogs over there too. Phil moved away and eventually wound up in Guatemala where he died.

Oscar Alles

Oscar Alles bought the house that Phil Davis lived in. By the 1950s he was living alone. He suffered from emphysema. Oscar couldn't drink anymore for health reasons, maybe a nip now and then, he had apnea and had to sleep sitting up and use an inhaling device of some sort. I'd see Oscar trying to walk to the road to get his paper. There were several fence posts along the driveway and he'd walk to one, hang on to it and pant to get oxygen, then make his way to the next post, breathe, and then the next. Dick Britten would drive his little Volkswagen to Oscar's every day, pick up his paper for him, then sit and drink a pint of his own Sunnybrook booze he bought by the case and kept hid at Oscar's place. Then he'd leave on the back roads, because he was usually pretty well lit much of the time.

I was working cattle somewhere and when I returned, Gaynor told me that Dick had come over that morning absolutely bug-eyed to tell her that he had just found Oscar dead in his chair and asked her, "You don't have anything to drink do you?" Gaynor said she told him, oh, sure. She said he looked at it real funny when she handed him a glass of water. I had to laugh when she told me because Gaynor didn't really know what he meant.

Veterans

There were quite a few WWI veterans in Three Rivers who lived in cabins scattered in the hills, or in the case of Walter Ben, a tent-cabin. At least until 1939, there was housing for war veterans at the Maxon Ranch CCC camp on South Fork under command of Captain Lee Goff. According to my school friend, Dan Busby, one old Vet named Sharpy snapped, came down the road toward–then past–their house shouting and wildly firing one of his two six-shooters at trees and bushes. Dan's father, Forest Busby, wanted to shoot the fellow, but his mother wouldn't let him because he might just be drunk. Dan and his brother were sent to Skinny Kirk's place for safety. Skinny Kirk hid in the brush and when Sharpy retraced his steps, Skinny called to him by name–psst, Sharpy, I'm on your side, but I don't have a gun. Sharpy said okay and gave Skinny one of his revolvers that Skinny then used to hit him over the head and hold him for Constable Rennie Brown to show up.

My Grandmother Finch was on the Welfare Committee of Woman's Club and picked up food and clothing from Visalia Red Cross to distribute to many needy people in Three Rivers during the early 1930s. One of her Club reports noted 3000 pounds of flour and many dozen pieces of clothing had been distributed.

263

Walter Ben

An old veteran lived in a tent-cabin just east of Cobble Lodge (now in the Kaweah Lake bottom). His name was Walter Ben–had two front names–and he lived with his faithful old dog on the hillside between Highway 198 and the old cement road. Walter Ben was the guy who drew the first alligator on the rock on the right side of the highway coming up Lime Kiln Hill. (Someone later changed it to a fish; the alligator was better.) Walter Ben was a little different, but harmless. One day Lee Maloy was driving from his place headed for 198 and Walter Ben stopped him. "Hold it! Don't go any further. I saw someone planting mines in that road ahead last night so you better go back." Lee said he just thanked him kindly and turned around and took another way. Walter Ben ate a big pan full of fried onions every day and said that is why he lived so long. Onions were probably the only staple he could afford on a WWI army pension.

Oscar Maxon

On the South Fork between the Conley Creek bridge and South Fork bridge is a narrow road that was the original wagon road and legal right-of-way to the first Britten home and ranch, and my South Fork ranch–still is. Oscar Maxon built a tidy one-room cabin near the river a short way up this road. Everyone called it the Maxon cabin, and later, the Yellow cabin. Oscar pastured his horse, Daisy, there. Daisy was a big old mare with a little feather on her feet, maybe had some draft horse back there somewhere, just big with the heavy joints. Oscar rode Daisy to get his mail at the post office near the Three Rivers market on the main river. Oscar was old, little, and dried up, and he carried a little switch to keep Daisy moving along on the 45-minute ride. I'd see Daisy tied to the telephone pole right there while Oscar would be inside to get his mail. This was probably in the early 1940s. Oscar was the brother of Hat Maxon's father. Oscar is probably buried with the Maxons in Exeter.

Bill Smith, the Bootlegger

Another old cabin stood just to the east of Oscar Maxon's cabin, probably built by Henry DeLong, near the point where our right-of-way crossed Conley Creek to reach our South Fork ranch. I didn't know DeLong but my mother and dad said he owned the flats above the Maxon cabin. I knew his face from old photographs, he was a big Mussolini-type guy, a nice fellow they said. Back in the late 1940s when I was working up on our ranch, I used to ride by the cabin and talk to the old veteran who lived there, Bill Smith. The cabin was just a little weather-beaten shack with an outhouse to the side. One day as I was closing the gate on the way out, I said hello to Old Bill and mentioned that whatever he was cooking sure smelled good. He invited me to come on over and have lunch with him. It was a very tasty stew with carrots, potatoes and white meat. I cleaned my plate and asked him if that was pork? "No, it's raccoon. I shot him out of that tree last night."

Charlie Reese, who used to work for us, said that during the depression Bill Smith ran a still in the swamps down by the St. Johns River, north of Lindcove, where they used to go swimming as kids. Bill ran several stills and sold bootleg whiskey. He lived nearby with his best friend, a hog. A pet pig is smarter than a dog and can be housebroken and makes a good pet—feed them good food, just don't have mud holes around. Pigs are very clean animals. One really hot summer day, Old Bill jumped in the river to cool off and his pig followed him in and was dog-paddling when his sharp little hoof cut his jowl; he bled to death. Charlie said Bill cried and cried.

Bill the bootlegger wasn't a preacher but he was very serious when he told me how he helped straighten out Adam Alles who had been acting despondent. Adam owned the field next door to Bill's cabin. Bill said he just told Adam there's a lot of things to be thankful for, it isn't all bad, that he needed to just sit down there and read some out of the Bible. One day I took Charlie Reese with me to visit with Old Bill. Bill lived there for years, but how and where he went from there I don't know.

Dan Brown, the Shooter

Just west of Oscar Maxon's place, before you get to the little lime kiln on the south side of Blossom Peak, Daniel Theodore Brown lived in an old cabin near the river on Cooney Alles' property and got his water from a spring across the road in the lush thicket of grape vines and sycamore trees.

February 2, 1945, Visalia was underwater and it was still raining hard in Three Rivers. That evening, Dan Brown, Ord and Ben Loverin, and Martin Vertrees, had a poker game at Vertree's place adjacent to

Edwardsen's store near the bridge to North Fork. Vertrees owned the motel cabins across from the filling station (now Pat O'Connell's). Bill Jones was there but wasn't in the game. The story my dad told was that Dan Brown got mad and accused Martin of cheating because when Dan had a good hand, Martin always dealt Ord a better one. Dan figured they had signals. So when Dan lost another hand, he stormed out, and drove home to South Fork and returned with a shotgun which he poked through the door and fired one shot, striking Vertrees in the neck. Bill Jones grabbed for Dan but he got away to his truck and drove off. It was still raining, the road was muddy and his Model A Ford truck slid off and got stuck. He took off on foot and at the Old Three Rivers Y he stopped at Rose Vaughn's place and told her what he'd done. She made him a cup of tea and called Constable Rennie Brown in Woodlake. Fred Ogilvie came over and sat until Rennie arrived. The Visalia Sheriff's office dispatched two deputies, but because Visalia was under water they couldn't get to their cars or find gas. Roads were passable to Exeter, so Rennie delivered Dan Brown to deputies there.

My dad drove over to the shooting scene; I was old enough to ride along, but he wouldn't let me get out of the car.

Vertrees, age 59, was buried in Woodlake. Brown admitted to the shooting but pled insanity. He said the shotgun was in his truck, he grabbed it in anger and shot Vertrees. The other three men said Brown stormed out, sat outside awhile before he drove away, then returned an hour later and shot Vertrees. A jury found him sane whereupon the judge declared Dan Brown, age 70, guilty of first degree murder and sentenced him to life in San Quentin. My dad said Dan Brown had served time in prison for murder before he came to Three Rivers.

One-Eyed John

Then there was old one-eyed John Higgins. I remember exactly where his cabin was, just off the North Fork Bridge going toward Pat O'Connell's and on the east side of the highway was a little flat with an oak tree and a cabin. John was a trapper but I don't think he trapped with Shorty Lovelace or Sam Brown. He had a coyote for a pet, trained it as a pup to walk on a leash and he'd take it up and down the road. He kept it tied in the yard, probably afraid it would kill somebody's chickens if he turned it loose. I heard that he lost his eye in WWI, eked out an existence on a little pension.

Jack West

Another WWI veteran was Jack West. He was married to or just stayed with Lucy Lutz, the cat lady, who lived on North Fork close to where Christy Wood's Wooden Horse Stables is now. Lucy was referred to as the cat lady because she believed in reincarnation and every stray cat in the county she thought was probably a friend of hers so she'd keep it and feed it. You never smelled such a place in your life with all the tomcat pee, sometimes forty cats everywhere. Jack West lived up South Fork at a Veteran's camp and would walk down to Lucy Lutz' place and stay for a week or so, then he'd walk back. We'd see him walking on South Fork, probably in the 1940s, and if I was in my truck I'd give him a ride. He was a big, tough old fellow and talked gruff out the side of his mouth with a cigarette hanging on his lip. I bet he was a tough soldier.

Chief Land Elk

Chief Land Elk was a member of the Paiute tribe of Bishop on the east side of the Sierra. Tribes traveled an ancient foot trail across the Sierra from Owens Valley on the east, up Bubbs Creek, across Kearsarge Pass and down to our west side to trade. Generations before, Paiutes competed in running contests across the Sierra from LaVining above Bishop to Yosemite. The Chief said he had lived on a reservation north of Bishop, and how he happened to settle on South Fork at the Wells Ranch, I don't know. He really wanted to be a cowboy and would go with us to Friday night team roping down at Norman McKee's place in Elderwood. Once in a while the Chief would catch a calf and we'd brag on him. He was a good guy. Bill Graham lived on the Wells Ranch and brought home a gallon of cider from his father-in-law's place, Spotts Cider Mill. It was a hot summer day so Bill offered Chief a nice tall glass of cold cider. The next afternoon about the same time, Chief knocked on Bill's door and held out his glass and said, "Cider."

Chief Land Elk was a talented artist and some of his paintings were at the Noisy Water Cafe downtown for a long time. One of his paintings was of the backside of Homer's Nose and I would love to have that painting. I wonder what happened to his artwork.

I don't know what happened to Chief Land Elk, if he returned to the Bishop reservation, or not. He was a good person.

FIRST PIONEERS

ᗰᑌᑌᑲᓿ

The first pioneer family to settle in the canyons of the Kaweah River was Ira and Julia Blossom who hauled their household goods to the South Fork by sled via Big Oak Flat in the early 1860s. Their first home, "built more like an A-frame hen house," was across from the old Henry Alles (later Siodmak) place about where Troy and Laura Hall used to live. Ira planted an apple orchard. Their next place was about 500 feet east of my front door. Later Ira Blossom moved further up South Fork across from Joseph C. Palmer.

An old timer at a Pioneer Dinner in the 1960s said that the first two families to settle in Three Rivers proper were the Blossoms and the Works. The Work family planted an apple orchard in what is now Cherokee Oaks and built their house close to the mouth of the South Fork. They took out a ditch to irrigate the orchard.

Ira and Julia Blossom moved away a few years after my dad and mother were married. There weren't too many people left who could remember stories about Ira and Julia Blossom or knew where they came from.

Ira Blossom (b. 1832) and his wife Julia, two years younger, were both born in New York State. In 1850 Ira resided in Hinsdale, Cattarauger County, New York.

The photograph of Ira and Julia Blossom in their yard with Blossom Peak in the background is courtesy of the great-great-grandson of Ira Blossom, William Holden Jr.

We are so fortunate that, just a few weeks ago, William Holden, Jr., the great-great-grandson of Ira Blossom, came to my home with a box full of Blossom family photographs, just in time to insert his story in this book. Mr. Holden—Bill—has traced the Blossoms to their arrival in Massachusetts in 1629, and as far back as the 1500s England.

Ira and Julia Blossom sit for a photograph in their yard, which was about500 feet east of my front door. Blossom Peak, the heart of Three Rivers,is in the background. Photograph c. 1910.

Bill smiled as he told the intriguing story of why Ira Blossom came to California. It seems that Orson and Julia Clough and their three children resided in New York State and Ira Blossom lived in the same vicinity. Ira became smitten by Julia whom he pursued as the woman of his dreams. Mr. Clough did not take kindly to Ira's attentions toward his wife, so he moved his family away as far as possible from the perceived home-wrecker, across the continent, in fact, to the Gold Rush country near Stockton, California.

Undaunted, Ira chased after Julia to her new home where, in 1860, he persuaded her to leave her family, marry him, and move south 200 miles to what became known as Three Rivers.

We had a wonderful visit with Bill and his wife, Sharon. I showed Bill where Ira Blossom's last home had stood about 500 feet south of my place. I appreciate Bill's permission to use the above photo of Ira and Julia Blossom in this book.

So to continue with more details, Ira married Julia Maraschelleaux Clough in Stockton, California on September 10, 1860, where Julia and her first husband, Orson Clough, were residing with their four children: William Orson Clough (Billy), born 1852; Ida May Clough, born 1854; Frederick (Fred) Warren Clough, born 1856; and Evelyn (Eva) Kathleen Clough, born 1860. The Clough children stayed with their father in Amador County while their mother and her new husband established a home in Three Rivers.

An old timer interviewed in 1953 said that Ira teamed between Visalia and Stockton prior to 1860 at which time he was living in Sacramento area. In the summer of 1860, Ira and Julia lived in Scottsbury—today's Centerville, Fresno County—and had no children in their household. By mid-1860s the Blossoms were living here on South Fork. In the 1860s, Ira Blossom carried root stock by trail before there was a road to his homestead and planted an apple orchard. Daughter Emma Viola was born October 1864; son, Charles, was born November 27, 1866. The following year was the great flood of 1867 on South Fork, details of which will come later. Ira Blossom was a registered voter in 1867.

The 1870 census counted Ira Blossom, age 37; his wife, Julia, age 36, children Eva (Clough), 9; Emma, 5; and son, Charles, 3. The next neighbor listed was Joseph C. Palmer, age 35. (Billy Clough was prospecting and Fred Clough was still in the gold country.)

Ira worked at the flour mill in Visalia in the early days and later drove the mail stage to Three Rivers. Julia Blossom made friends with the Indians by giving them baked bread and desserts. Her little daughter, Eva (Evelyn), became close friends with the Indian children and one time ran off to the Indian camp to eat with them from the tribal dinner pot.

By 1880, the Blossom household consisted of Ira and Julie Blossom, son, Charles, 13; twin daughters Anna and Lottie, age 8. By then, Julia's daughter Eva Clough (Evelyn) resided separately with her husband, George Cahoon, a dairyman, and daughter Daisy, age 1.

Ira Blossom planted fruit trees from the State Experimental Agricultural Station. His pears were exhibited in the Visalia pavilion at the 1889 State Fair and were mentioned for their large attractive size. (A few of the old abandoned pear trees were still producing in the 1950s near his first home on South Fork; we called them horse pears.) He also made cider and apple vinegar for sale. Ira owned deeded land on the south side of Blossom Peak in 1892.

In 1910 Ira and Julia, then in their mid-70s probably resided in the home that stood across from my place with their son, Charles, age 42 and stepson, Bill Clough, age 57. (Billy Clough had discovered Clough's Cave twenty years before; he died in 1917.) By 1918 Ira and Julie had moved to San Francisco and lived with their daughter Emma and her husband Christian Buttman, age 65, and Emma's offspring, Robert and Hattie Sherman.

Ira Blossom died in San Francisco on May 5, 1924 and was buried in Colma, San Mateo County. He was 92. Julia died two years prior at age 90 and was also buried in Colma.

It is fitting that the first pioneer resident in the Kaweah canyons is memorialized by the distinctive landmark that is the heart of Three Rivers–Blossom Peak.

1860s Horse Creek and Yokuts

Many talks on the history of Three Rivers start with the arrival of Hale Tharp at Horse Creek but skip the pioneers on the rivers for which the settlement was named. After one such talk was reported by the newspaper in 1948, Frank Atwood (pictured in the 1913 group photo and owner of one of the large orange ranches in Lemon Cove) wrote a letter to the editor questioning the accuracy of their story about the earliest pioneer to Three Rivers. He explained: "I believe you are mistaken when you state that Hale Tharp was the first resident of Three Rivers. In the early days you were not considered in the Three Rivers District until you had passed Homer's Grade, and the Tharp Ranch is situated at Horse Creek canyon about half way between Three Rivers and Lemon Cove."

Homer's Grade was the long climb east of Slick Rock to what is now the Lazy J Ranch Motel—the motel site marked the entry into Three Rivers.

Frank said his grandfather had sailed around the Horn during the Gold Rush to California, then went back overland to Ohio to get his family and returned by covered wagon. Frank's father, Lou Atwood, was

14 years old when his family moved to Three Rivers in 1872 and he said there were people living there at that time who had seen the flood of 1861 and 1862. The Work family lived in the old adobe house near the first South Fork bridge and Joe Palmer was higher up in the canyon.

A history reference noted that because other white men had come to his area by 1860, Tharp took cattle to Giant Forest in 1860 to claim it for his own summer pasture. An old timer, speaking at a Tulare County Historical Society meeting in May 1953 is quoted as saying the Work family moved to South Fork in 1858, built a house and planted an orchard. Three Rivers, in the minds of the old time speakers, was the Kaweah canyon country and the first pioneers to settle here were Ira Blossom and Hopkins Work.

Hale Tharp settled at Horse Creek in 1856. He was born in Ohio in 1832 (some records show his birth year as 1830, or 1835). He was hired by Chloe Swanson, age 30, widow of Edward Swanson, to take her and her four sons by covered wagon from Illinois to California. John Henry Swanson, an uncle of Chloe's deceased husband, also traveled with them. They arrived in Placerville, California where Hale decided to marry Chloe because good women were in short supply. They married in El Dorado County, California, December 24, 1854. Hale worked in the mines in El Dorado County for a couple of years, then left to explore south along the Sierra foothills. In 1856, he following the Kaweah River east and stopped at Horse Creek, a few miles upstream from Lime Kiln (Lemon Cove) where he decided to stay. He built a home a short ways down from the present Horse Creek bridge. Billy Swanson, son of John Swanson who was Hale's stepson, showed me a few boards where the Tharp house stood just below the Horse Creek bridge near the point, north of the present-day campgrounds.

Hale Tharp died November 5, 1912 and is buried at Hamilton Cemetery outside of Exeter, California. His son, Norton Hale Tharp, sold the family's original homestead on Horse Creek to a Mrs. B. Meade of Los Angeles in 1936. Billy Swanson often said he was the first white child born in Three Rivers—in 1875. However, Charles Blossom was born in 1866.

Yokuts, the Indigenous People of Our Valley

The local Indians are known as Yokuts, the word is both singular and plural and means "peoples." The first Indians encountered by the white man in this area were Yokuts of the Wutchumna tribe who made their home in the area for 1000 years or more. It was idyllic; plentiful water, game, acorns, berries, grasses, and places for shelter. J. C. vonWerlhof's report in the "Environmental Impact/Antiquities Report" prepared prior to construction of Terminus Dam concludes the Yokuts were along the Kaweah after 1000 A. D., but one of the National Park Service reports says the Native Americans inhabited the area for at least 3000 and possibly 5000 years. There were about 2000 Yokuts living along the rivers and up into the Kaweah canyons.

Dixie Clarkson Ballew arrived in Lime Kiln with her family in 1904 when she was about seven years old. Her family also became friends with the Yokuts, and socialized with them, spending many summer days swimming in the river together. Dixie said that Blind Indian Molly taught Dixie's mother to swim. Sometime around 1980, Dixie gave me a copy of the Yokuts history she had gleaned from their stories and personal experience. Wutchumna hill, with its flat top and gentle slopes, now skirted with orange groves, sits like an island in the midst of the protected cove surrounded by the foothills on three sides, opening to the valley via Allen's Gap to the south. The Wutchumna villages were on the periphery of the east side of the cove, along the Kaweah River and up Dry Creek (also known as Lime Kiln creek). The villages were known as: Buckeye, to the east near Lipsey Creek; Buckeye Place, Bell Cove, and Lime Kiln Hill, to the north; Sand Flats and Bell Point near Terminus beach. At the northern base of Wutchumna, on the Kaweah River was their central village for Yokuts affairs called Sho No'Yoo. Where Dry Creek comes into the Kaweah, there was a village and several miles up stream was the home of Joe Pohot.

I recognized Joe Pohot in the 1926 movie *Pioneers Rolled Back the Years* mentioned earlier. I knew some of the younger Pohots. Joe Pohot was born about 1874 near the site of the Three Rivers Memorial Building. He was of Potwisha and Wutchumna tribe descent. His wife, Mary, was born about 1865 and they had nine children; I knew their daughters Refa, Mary, Leah, and Susie Pohot, and son Ray Pohot who played banjo and guitar in Print Stokes' band, The Rocky Mountain Cowboys back in the 1940s. Ray was killed in a car wreck. The Pohots lived about three miles up the Dry Creek Road and Joe and Mary are buried there in the family cemetery.

Johnny Valdez, wearing his angora chaps, worked for my dad in 1938 and during WWII at the Wolverton Pack Station. Johnny married Leah Pohot, daughter of Joe and Mary Pohot of the Yokuts Wutchumna tribe. Photo c. 1938.

AUTHOR'S COLLECTION.

Harrington Jim was Mary Pohot's uncle and his half-brother was Hathaway Jim. The 1933 movie made at the Three Rivers Club House shows Joe Pohot doing an Indian shashay like they did at the Rancherias when all the tribes joined together for a fandango. Mary Pohot claps her hands in time to the song. Enos Barton joins them for an encore.

Mary and Joe Pohot's daughter, also named Mary, married a Fredericks; her son, Loren Fredericks, was a great cowboy as well as a fine artist whose paintings were sold for income after he suffered a stroke.

Leah Pohot married Johnny Valdez who worked for my dad during WWII at our Wolverton pack station where he trained mules and took care of the stock. Leah and Joe lived in a little cabin at Wolverton during those summers. He wore a pair of black angora chaps.

Johnny Valdez also worked for my dad during deer season in Greasy Cove right after my dad bought the ranch in 1938. So many friends of previous owners were in the habit of hunting in Greasy that my dad had Johnny and Leah stay at the old Huntley house at the sulfur spring so Johnny could patrol the ranch on horseback. My dad declared he was going to put a stop to hunters. I think he deputized Johnny. I found one of my dad's No Hunting signs on a tree down by the road–it was wood, painted white, and my dad had lettered it in black, "A DEPUTIZED RIDER IS LOKING FOR YOU." He only had one "o" in Looking.

Johnny was a great horseman, soft-handed, finished horses for a lot of people. He talked to the horses and mules all the time in the Yokuts language. Johnny also worked for Tom Davis at times.

I remember Leah was such a good cook. She made the most delicious enchiladas–lots of onions, garlic, ground beef, and her great sauce; she'd bring pans of them for us to eat, and we'd always eat too much. I remember sitting in the kitchen watching Leah make her corn tortillas. She'd sit by her table, pull her dress up above one knee, roll a little ball of dough between her palms, and pat it flat on her large thigh. She said it worked better to pat them on bare skin because the tortilla didn't stick. Every tortilla was the same size.

A Yokuts named Tupino related many stories to Dixie Clarkson and her family. Tupino's daughter Maggie Tupino (1878-1966) married Henry Icho, the last Chief of the Wutchumna tribe and a cousin of Joe Pohot. Henry and Maggie Icho had four children: Bob Icho (1893-1975), Lonnie Icho (d. 1940), Felix Icho, and Katie Icho (1894-1970). I knew some of the Icho family also. Henry Icho's rancheria was on the road as you start up Dry Creek, where the China Berry trees are. Henry Icho's grandfather Chechin was a Rattlesnake Doctor.

Dixie remembered Blind Indian Molly Ogden who was married to Henry Lawrence Wah-hun-cha (1861-1959), parents of Henry Icho. Indian Sally Ned was a friend of Blind Molly Ogden and they rode a horse together to the Lemon Cove general store to do shopping. Blind

Molly would sit on the floor while Sally made the purchases. Sally was one of the tribe's expert basket weavers. Bob Icho, grandson of Henry and Maggie Icho, died in 1951 in the Korean war.

Hospital Rock

The Yokuts tribe on the upper Kaweah River rendered aid and cured the injured John Swanson, stepson of Hale Tharp, using hot applications of crushed Jimson Weed leaves and bear fat. He had hurt his leg on the trail near Kings and it was so swollen he could not walk. By the third day he was well enough to continue on home. There is another account of the Yokuts healing another injured white man. In about 1874, A. Everton and George Cahoon were hunting and trapping in that area. They had several set guns for bear. One morning, they found blood on the trail and assuming a wounded bear, Everton went back to get the dogs and accidentally tripped one of the set guns which shot him in the leg. He was carried to camp and the Yokuts women treated the very serious wound with herbs and nursed him back to health. After this, the place was known as Hospital Rock.

Although the early white men made friends with the Indians, the Yokuts lands and lives were changed forever–the white man's concept of 'owning' lands was foreign to the Yokuts; fences prevented free movement across what suddenly became 'private property' and of course the deadliest uninvited newcomers were smallpox and measles. Dixie Clarkson wrote that in 1902 there was a smallpox epidemic near the Pohot's, and another in 1905 on the Sand Flats. Dr. Robert Montgomery, Nora Pogue Montgomery's husband, treated, or quarantined the victims as best he could.

J. W. C. Pogue and his wife were always good to the Yokuts, according to their daughter, Eva Pogue Kirkman, who wrote about attending a tribal fandango when she was about five years old. The Yokuts trusted Mr. Pogue. Eva wrote in her family memoir that soon after her family moved to Dry Creek after the 1867 flood, Indian "Hog-eye" said to her father: "What's a matter, Jim Pogue? LONG time Indians got PLENTY deer, PLENTY fish, PLENTY grass, PLENTY everything. White man come. Indian got no deer, no meat, no got nothing. What's a matter, Jim Pogue?"

1861 and 1867 Floods

There is a lot written about the great 1867 flood, but the 1861-62 flood covered the whole valley. It was caused by a series of storms strung together in an "atmospheric river," not just one big storm, and a normal snow melt, not a huge one. The Central Valley was inundated from Sacramento to south of Bakersfield. Newspapers on the East coast had bold headlines; "California Washed Away; Great Flood of 1862!" From the western Sierra slopes one hundred foot tall pine trees with roots and all were carried by floodwaters down the San Joaquin, Kings, Kaweah, Tule, and White Rivers. The devastation was more severe north of Fresno, with huge losses of cattle, homes, and businesses. In Kern County many sawmills and quartz mines were swept away.

Byron Allen's mother, Marjorie Houston Allen Oakes, described The Big Flood of 1862 at a meeting in 1929 of Three Rivers residents who were worried about lack of rain as of mid-December 1929. Several Three Rivers pioneers tried to encourage hope by telling about other years when rain did not come until late, but then very wet seasons followed. Marjorie Allen Oakes said she was a young girl in 1862. She said there was no rain until January 2, and then it rained continuously for 35 days and nights. The water was the highest the white man had ever seen in this region. She said looking west from the foothills the whole valley seemed to be one sheet of water.

In 1861, the transcontinental telegraph service became operational, the Pony Express ended, and Abraham Lincoln was president, just to keep the happenings in Three Rivers in perspective.

Joe Palmer, Witness to 1867 Flood

Joe C. Palmer was born about 1836 in Missouri and is listed in the 1880 U.S. Census for Kaweah and Mineral King (Three Rivers). He served in the Union Army during the Civil War under Lieutenant Colonel George S. Evans. He was later stationed at Camp Babbitt, at Visalia. It's been said that he went to sea on a windjammer and returned with a fig tree from The Holy Land, a peach tree from Chile, and a grape vine from somewhere, and there were starts from his original plantings on the old Blossom place on South Fork.

I have a copy of a photograph taken before 1885 of several folks posing in an apple orchard west of where I now live. Pictured is Joe

Palmer, Charles Blossom, Frank DeVoe, Mac Dungan and Adell Curtis. Hat Maxon told me that Palmer had property either where my house is now, or where Ray Prichard had property. Palmer had a homestead on South Fork; Hat Maxon showed me the property up near Clough's Cave. There were a few old boards left of Joe's little cabin. Hat talked a lot about Joe Palmer, said Joe collected guns, also loved plants and surrounded his cabin with flowers. He called his place Rose Bud.

Joe Palmer was the only eye-witness to the December 1867 flood on the South Fork. On October 9, 1890, Palmer was interviewed by Judge Walter Fry. The story he told was that in late December 1867, heavy rain had fallen for 41 days straight.

Palmer is quoted as saying the snow was low, down to 5000 feet, the rivers were high and on December 20 the weather warmed. He went to bed and before midnight heard a terrible rumbling sound that lasted over an hour. Then everything was quiet, even the sound of the river. The next morning he saw that the river was dry and figured there had been a landslide upstream. The following night shortly after midnight Palmer heard a tremendous rumbling and thundering that "made his hair stand on end." The dam had given way. He ran for safety up the mountain. He saw the flood, 40 feet deep, carrying broken trees crashing down the canyon.

A geologist report in 2002 gave the dimensions of the landslide that caused such devastation: a half-mile-wide swath of dense forest of giant sequoias, pine, and fir rooted in 6 to 12 feet of saturated sandy loam slid from near the granite crest of Dennison Ridge (7500 feet elevation) down over a mile into the South Fork of the Kaweah River, forming an enormous earthen dam a half-mile across and 400 feet high. Twenty-five hours later the dam failed, ". . . and thousands of tons of timber and rocky debris went down the Kaweah River, past the small community of Three Rivers, and farther into the small town of Visalia . . . ." (U.S. Geological Survey, 2002).

Mr. Fry interviewed several residents of Visalia for his report on the flood; in June 1906 he talked to Ira Blossom who related that he was working at the grist mill in Visalia when the flood arrived prior to midnight of December 23, 1867. The water was about six feet deep at the mill. Many sequoia logs and driftwood were scattered for miles around.

The 1867 wall of water swept away the Work home and orchards at Cherokee Oaks and the family left in discouragement. Downstream, the flood damaged the J. W. C. Pogue home and those of his relatives in Stringtown on the way to Woodlake, so Pogue relocated to Dry Creek (Lime Kiln) the next year.

There are still redwood logs on the property I used to own down in the creek by Lovering's old place. And that's why, in all the old photographs taken around Three Rivers, you see lines of tall redwood picket fences, miles of them, bordering everything–yards, pastures, roads. The folks retrieved redwood trees out of the flood path–hundreds of them–cut the logs into rings and made shakes, or split 4 or 5-foot long sections for pickets, got a roll of wire and made a picket fence. There are still some portions of redwood picket fence over at the Barton's where I run a few horses. An old newspaper clipping about the 1867 flood says, ". . .great redwood logs can be found buried in the sand in Visalia. . . .Above Three Rivers are great redwood logs lying on top of boulders twenty feet high. In other places the reverse is seen–huge boulders resting on fallen Sequoias."

In 1880, while tracking deer, Joe Palmer discovered a cave (now named for him, Palmer Cave) situated near Putnam Canyon on the South Fork. The entrance he found was 25 x 30 feet and descended nearly vertical for 80 feet, then extended more level for 100 feet into a large chamber 100 x 200 feet with walls 100 feet high, containing stalactites of great splendor.

The *San Francisco Call* newspaper of January 22, 1899 reported a list of pensions granted by the federal government, one of which was to Joseph C. Palmer of Three Rivers, California, in the amount of $8 to $10 per month; that was about the time he lived with Emma Blossom Buttman and husband Christian on South Fork.

In 1901, Joseph C. Palmer moved from Three Rivers to the Home for Disabled Volunteer Soldiers at Sawtelle, California. He was 65 years old; at age 74 he lived at the Disabled Veterans home in Malibu. I don't know how long he lived after that.

PLEASURE PACK TRIPS

⌒⫘⫘⫘⌒

Probably twenty years ago was the last pack trip I went on. I really miss the sounds of riding in the backcountry, the echo of steel horse shoes striking rocks above timberline, hooves padding along on trails of soft dirt through quiet forests, plod, plod, plod, along at the mules' pace.

A bunch of guys got together–Leroy Whitney, Jesse Cox, Bill Wylie, and Scott Erickson and his friend–for some backcountry fishing and relaxing in Deadman Canyon. We did all our own packing and cooking, fished a lot, relaxed, and played guitars and sang. Dinnertime in the high country is without equal, everything tastes better, cook some steaks or fresh fish, sip a cocktail or more. It was memorable. Scott Erickson was my son's age, a little moody at times and didn't talk very much. His mustache would get longer and when he talked he refused to move his lips and I used to say "Huh?" all the time, then he'd shout at me and I'd say, "Don't shout at me, just pull that mustache up!" I'd kid him a lot, but he could talk to me about anything. Scott was a real good cowboy when he worked for me, and still is.

On this trip I had planned to scatter Harry Hughes' ashes in Ranger Meadow in Deadman Canyon but I forgot to bring them along. I should have sent someone back to get the box from my barn, but I didn't think of it in time. Harry Hughes, one of my dad's packers, used to describe Ranger Meadow as one of his favorite places in the Sierra where the stands of pine trees sweep out into the meadow below the lofty peaks. I wanted to return Harry to God's country.

Harry Hughes

Harry Hughes' nickname was "Slim" because he was tall and slim when he was younger, a tough guy and a confirmed bachelor. He liked the tough, outdoor life and he used to pack for my dad. One time he told me a story about a fight he had in Three Rivers at the Sulfur Springs Saloon, a bar located near the old North Fork Bridge, about where Chump's movie rental place is today. An argument grew heated between Harry Hughes and Forest "Hog Jaw" Busby, a life-long South Fork denizen—some called him a character—but before it turned physical, Harry told Busby that he had seen him in a barroom fight or two and did not want to get in a free-for-all. Harry said, "We're going to have a referee."

Jim Kindred was selected as the referee and everybody interested in the spectacle got in their cars and followed Slim and Busby up to the flat at the Lime Kiln on South Fork. A ring was drawn, just like a Clint Eastwood movie, you know, and Jim was the referee who laid down the rules—no kicking in the testicles or anything like that, it was going to be a fist fight. As Harry's story goes, they started sparring and Harry knocked Busby down and he laid there a minute, then got up and made a lunge and hit Harry in the chest with both fists, knocking Harry down. Harry got to his feet and delivered a blow that flattened Busby. He was on the ground for quite some time, then sat up and looked around and said, "You know, Harry, you're just a better man than I am." It was a good story because I heard it from both Harry and Jim, the referee. It happened in the 1920s, I think.

Harry packed for my dad in 1946. Harry and Jim Kindred were in the service in World War II and were both discharged in 1946, Harry shortly before Jim so Harry started the season packing for my dad. As soon as Jim was released from the army he met up with our pack trip in the Kings at Wood's Creek Junction. My dad didn't need both Harry and Jim, and didn't want to tell Harry that Jim was replacing him, so he resorted to a coin flip. Jim lost and rode out; Harry stayed and was there when my dad died six days later in Sixty Lake Basin.

Harry had worked for Byron Allen in Three Rivers in the old days. Harry helped me when I was just learning to pack, just a nice guy and I got to know him well. He came for Christmas with us and always carried a collection of rifles in the back of his old truck, maybe a new one that we'd go out and shoot somewhere. He was a great outdoorsman.

Harry moved to Merced where he worked as a state brand inspector for thirty years, a job that kept him out on the roads and in the wilds. His home base was a rented kitchenette suite in the old Tioga Hotel. Not long before my mother died, Harry came to see her at her apartment in Three Rivers when I happened to be out of town. He had let his beard grow so my mother didn't recognize him and was scared to death. Harry didn't leave a card and didn't telephone later.

I got a phone call one day, (about 1988, I believe, because my mother died in 1986) from his friend who told me Harry had died and his last wish was to be buried in Three Rivers and he was to call me. I told him, okay, have Harry's ashes shipped to my house. I contacted the Veteran's Administration to request a headstone for Harry in the Three Rivers Cemetery, but Harry's records cannot be located, perhaps because a fire destroyed many old VA files years back. Until we figure it out, Harry is safe in my barn.

Another time, I took Al Smith, Don Britten, and Jess Cox on a pack trip in early October in the 1980s, very late in the season. We were in Granite Basin when it stormed, dropped the temperature that night to zero. To keep the stock warm, we put a blanket covered with a manty on each one, then strapped on the saddle. We made fires in old stumps around the horses for warmth while they were tied to the picket line. It was snowing so we huddled in the tent. The next

morning there were icicles hanging inside the tent and my hat was frozen solid; it would have shattered if I'd dropped it. The creek froze over running water so you know it was cold. We had plenty of food, but couldn't risk staying. It was still cloudy and I thought we had better go home because Granite Pass is 11,000 feet and if there was a big snow we might still be there.

Irascible Order of Soarasis Club

I think Ord Loverin was the first packer to guide the Irascible Order of Soararsis (a respectable way to say Sore Asses) Club out of Cedar Grove, a group of men from opposing sides of a dam issue there in the Kings. In the late 1930s several businessmen from Fresno proposed to build a dam and hydropower plant at Cedar Grove for the benefit of Fresno. Kings is a deep canyon–the deepest, most beautiful in the country–a very large dam would have been required and spectacular country would have been lost under water. When it was all National Forest Service land, my dad took many hunting parties into the Kings Canyon clear up to San Joaquin country. The opposition successfully campaigned to transfer the Kings Canyon from private ownership to federal park land, obviating any dam. Those from both sides went on a "bury the hatchet" get-together pack trip and formed what is known as the Soararsis Club. The pack trip was an annual event. The Irascible Order of Soararsis incorporated as a non-profit group in the 1940s for the purpose of educating the Valley's business and political community to support the national parks and forest service. It continues to grant forestry scholarships to valley students.

On a pleasure trip to Kings River, in upper Tent Meadow. I am in front, riding old King, the best horse I ever owned. The first mule is Barney, followed by Helen. My brother-in-law Lee Maloy is in the back. Photo c. 1980s.

Seventeen years later, in 1957, it was going strong. Maynard Munger was the Head Soar. I was invited on five Soararsis trips: Simpson Meadow; another to Simpson from Cedar Grove; Ferguson Creek out of Horse Corral; Giant Forest over Kaweah Gap; and Kern River out of Mineral King.

On the Kern River pack trip were Congressman Bernie Sisk; John Davis, then current Park superintendent; Chief Ranger Peter Shuft; most of the Park ranger brass stationed at Kern River; a representative from Harvey Company that had just bought Giant Forest concession from George Mauger; and Bill (Mac) McCool, a trail boss. The Soararsis members kept a well-stocked bar in camp with everything they wanted for a relaxing cocktail hour in the chilly air. I always took my guitar and occasionally offered up a bawdy tune or two along with anything they wanted to sing or hear between stories around the campfire.

The Kern River Soararsis ride went out of Mineral King, over Franklin Pass, down Rattlesnake and camped at the Chagoopa Falls Ranger Station. Mac McCool was stationed at Kern River and went along with the powers-that-be because the Park was planning to install a prefab outhouse in the area of Kern Hot Springs and needed to scout a location. There had been a cabin there at Hot Springs with a privacy screen around an outside bathtub. A pipe from the hot springs ran to the tub; just pull the cork and it filled with very hot water. You always needed to add some cold river water. The cabin had burned some years before; the tub was fine, just left sitting out in the open. Don Biddel and I were the packers, so we took the horses up the canyon above camp for the night. I was in front, riding bareback and leading the bell mare, Don was in back driving the stock. Earlier that day when we were coming in, we had passed a couple on the trail with a big white dog on a leash—a setter with a long feathered tail—and I looked up the trail and saw them again, in that nice hot tub bath, a big embrace going on in front of God and everybody. So I started whistling, and yelled back to Don to hold up, don't drive the horses over me, we've got to stop a minute. When it appeared the bathers were dried and covered we continued up the trail and waved as we rode by. They made camp a little higher on a flat.

The next day, several Park people, including McCool, went up to map a site for the new outhouse. When McCool got back, I could tell by the look on his face that he was itching to tell us something. He gave us the raw story about how they rode through the hikers' camp just as they were engaged in what comes naturally. Mac said he insisted that something had to done about their conduct, but the rangers couldn't find anything in the regulations that says you can't make love in broad daylight, so they wrote them a warning ticket for a loose dog. We had a lot of laughs about this story back in camp.

I remember the Soararsis ride to Ferguson Creek in the Kings. I left the main party and took George Mauger, Chet Warlow (California state commissioner of highways for whom the rest stop Hwy 99 at Kingsburg is named), and another fellow on a little private side trip to Scenic Meadow. Chet was 73 years old, about 6' 6", 270 pounds, a big guy that took a stout horse to pack him. He had a lot of camera gear and took hundreds of photographs. That day he had the time of his life.

I took them out to a rocky point where you can see all of Cloud Canyon, Palmer Mountain, Brewer Creek across the way, then look right down into Ranger Meadow and Deadman. Ranger Meadow is one of the most beautiful places in the mountains, just the right elevation for lush vegetation. I had a mule along with provisions so I cooked a little lunch in a quiet glen by a stream full of Golden trout. We were sitting quiet and relaxed when here came a coyote like he was unaware of another living being in his glen; came up close and sat down just as quiet, cocked his head and just looked at us, maybe waiting to see if we would speak Coyote. The guys thought that was the most wonderful encounter, it was just one of those special days.

My dad always said you can't really tell about a man until you get him off in the woods for four or five days, then his real character will show. George Mauger was dedicated to his business running the Giant Forest and Bear Paw Meadow concessions. He wore a business suit and tie every day and I thought he was another dude. But he proved himself to be no phony when he was back in the mountains in his boots and Levis. Mauger went on the annual Soararsis trips and I remember one time we got down to Simpson Meadow on a long ride from our first camp at Granite Pass down to Granite Basin. On the trail, all down hill, we got into some yellow jackets and one of the riders— a partner in Jensen & Pilegard of Fresno, can't remember if he was Jensen or Pilegard—was thrown off when his horse got stung by yellow jackets. It broke the guy's collarbone so a helicopter was called to fly him out–it was 1957 and we had radios then. A mantie was laid out for a landing target.

Meantime, George Mauger had been having heart symptoms and had spent the day in his tent. We had come over that Pass and he didn't party much. The Park superintendent insisted that the chopper can pick up Mauger also and get him to a doctor. Mauger declined the offer and said he would be okay. He was a man whose business depended on him, who was in the backcountry with heart symptoms, but he was not going to be a quitter. The next day he felt better and rode out; it is a tough ride of thirty miles in two days. I respected Mr. Mauger for that. He was a dear friend. He eventually sold the Giant Forest concession to Harvey Company.

I have a photograph of one of the Soararsis groups at Bear Paw Meadow with John Davis, Park superintendent at the time; Lee Maloy; Tex Cook; Dave Wilson; George Mauger; former Park superintendent Eivind Scoyen; and myself.

Guitar Wreck on Franklin Pass

Four of us cowboys–Jimmy Rivers, Don Britten, Ray Pinnell, and I–went on a pack trip just to have a good time, go fishing, play music, and joke around the campfire. So we packed out of Mineral King, over Franklin Pass, a spectacular area, beautiful and not too tough, but down on the other side on the lip of the ridge the pack slipped on old Barney mule. Barney knew his pack was way over to the side so he laid down and when he did, the weight of the pack rolled him over on top of it. Two guitars, one on each side, were tied on the top of his pack. He was close to the edge there, so I slid out to him and got the pack loose to unload and one of the guitars just shot out like a sled right off the head of Rattlesnake Canyon. I had to go down about 300 yards to retrieve it. The case was battered up but the guitar was safe. The weight of Old Barney crushed the other case but only broke the little wood bridge of the guitar. At camp, Jimmy found a piece of wood and whittled out a little bridge and notched it so it worked good enough.

We had a great trip in there. Ray Pinnell was so funny, he had a fore-man position for Gill Cattle Company, lived in the Yokohl Ranch head-quarters and seldom got a day off. But he was with us. We sat around the fire and played guitars at night, told jokes, enjoyed our whiskey. It was a fine trip. Jimmy Rivers was the world-class guitar player.

On a pleasure pack trip at Lewis Camp, Kern River. (l to r) Billy Maloy, Leroy Maloy and Lee Maloy. Photo 1968.

Tug's Lost Trail on the South Fork of the Kings River

On another pack trip in 1978 we followed a map Tug Wilson drew from memory of a trip he made to Arrow Creek forty years before. Tug was an old timer from Woodlake who told me about hunting there in 1937 before the Kings became a national park. Oren Ruth and Paul Krabell, original owners of the Woodlake Hardware, went hunting with him.

I took Dave Wilson, Johnny Britten, Don Britten, Tokie Elliott, and a friend, and we followed Tug's map to Arrow Creek. It was remarkably accurate. The trail went out of Castle Dome Meadow which is up the South Fork of the Kings, actually beyond South Fork and the Rae Lakes branch of the South Fork. We found the iron markers where they had made a duck or two on the way up toward the top of Pyramid Creek.

The first night out is always steak night, with stories and cocktails around the fire. We were camped at Paradise and there was a bear robbery while I slept like a rock next to the food pack; the hairy thief slipped out a roast or two, apples and other groceries which he ate right there, leaving shredded wrappers all over. That bear reduced our menu choices considerably, but it wasn't the end of the world. The next day we located Tug's lost trail. On the way, a mule slipped a load and while we were repacking, I looked down the hill and saw something shiny. It was an old chromed Coleman lantern and we figured there was a story to it. Out on top of the mountain in Arrow Creek, we found Tug's old camp on a flat area in the granite. Arrow Peak, a spectacular painted mountain, towers above the campsite. This was right at 10,500 feet elevation with very little wood. There were places with evidence of horse manure because little broken pieces of hay and feed were laying in a flat place out in a meadow. We were the first people to take stock into that country in forty years.

We found the two old fish cans there that fit in a kyack. Forty years before, Tug and his friends had planted fish in the big beautiful deep upper lake there; they had caught fish in the river and packed them up in water cans to the lake. We stayed there several days, the bunch grass was thick for the horses and mules, and the fishing in the river just below the lake was marvelous. We never caught any fish from the lake, but there were some huge ones in there. I threw a lure way out in the lake and reeled it in and here came an alligator—well, it was a huge fish that looked like an alligator. He followed the lure, but was too smart to take it and when he saw me he took off.

On one of our pleasure pack trips in the 1960s, Don Britten, my second cousin, and I spent all night tracking horses up in the Kings. For several years running, four couples—Don and Wannie Britten, Jim and Barbara DuPratt, Wilson and Carol Pendery, and Gaynor and I packed into the backcountry. This was the trip delayed a day when I went back to sing for the funeral of Ben Loverin's wife. We rode over snow at Granite Pass to Horseshoe Lakes where we camped for two nights. The horses were loose in the meadow above us and on the second night while we were enjoying drinks and dinner around the fire, we heard horses crossing in the rocks below the camp and I told Don that we'd better grab a nose bag and run down there. We were using Lee Maloy's mountain stock, except for our two horses that were valley horses that tend to want to go home. We didn't hear the bell mare by the river and figured only a couple of horses were by the river and would be easy to catch. I grabbed a couple packages of paper matches and we took off in the dark without a flashlight. We saw two sets of tracks down the trail, and we set off in pursuit. Sure enough, the tracks went into Dougherty Creek and from there the trail was quite a climb up to where the horses would be stopped at the drift gate near an old Shorty Lovelace cabin, so we built a bonfire and rested a little bit before going on.

It was a cold, black night in late summer. We didn't have a flashlight, were getting short of matches, but we kept hiking; sometimes you lose the trail in the timber but after a while your feet work as little eyes to feel the difference in the trail; we bumped and tripped on a rock here and there but just kept going until we reached the drift gate about ten o'clock that night. There were no horses and the gate was open! I knew immediately what had happened. A trail crew had followed us in–Kelly Ogilvie and Troy Hall–headed for trail work over at State Lakes–no doubt dead drunk, had opened the gate and decided "ah, dere's no way ahm goin ta close dem damned gate" and rode on. The next time I saw Troy I really gave him a piece of my mind.

We knew right then we'd never catch the horses, they were heading home, and wouldn't stop until they reached Cedar Grove. So we had to turn around and hike back the way we'd come. Instead of climbing down and then out of Dougherty Creek, I told Don we could just go up canyon and cut across, but that turned out to be a bad idea because we got into thick brush. We got back to camp, dead tired, at three o'clock in the morning and of course everyone had worried that we were dead and the women were crying.

We camped another few days and then Don and I rode two mules back to Granite Basin where we got a couple of saddle horses to ride and found our horses above the drift gate at Tent Meadow–that gate was closed properly–grazing on the hillside. Back at camp my horse that was a little bit crazy anyway reared back when I went to untie him in the dark, and tore the meat off my hand–got my hand caught over the rope. If I'd a had a gun, I would have walked home.

Beer Drop

My guests on one pack trip were Herman Ziegler, Bud Lovering, Dave Wilson, Bill Ferry, and the son of old Doc McBratney. The Greenhall pilots were flying helicopters for the Park, keeping tabs, ferrying supplies to fire crews. One great pilot was Don Sides and we told the crew if they were anywhere in our area, over around Horseshoe Lakes, to bring us some beer. Doc's kid ordered some snuff. Ray Murray was working for the Park when I was packing and shoeing for the Park in the early '60s, so against official protocol he let me take a radio for use in an emergency, and told me to be careful on the air, don't say anything or give our location except for when he's coming in. There was a network of radio towers throughout the backcountry and the transmissions were continuously recorded.

There was a small wildfire burning in the area so they were flying in our vicinity. We were camped and lounging about, I was in the lake having a leisurely bath when I heard the "zoot-zoot" buzzing signal trying to locate us on the radio. I was running around there buck naked, trying to find the radio and turn it on, but couldn't get an answer. Nothing. I could hear them talking, "Where are you? Where are you?" One of the other guys came back from fishing and wondered what was going on. I said those guys are trying to find us, but this son-of-a-bitch radio doesn't work. And a voice comes out of the speaker, "Yes, it does, Earl."

Don set that helicopter down just as easy and unloaded our beer and he and Ray enjoyed a real nice fish dinner with us. When we put Ray back in the helicopter he was feeling no pain, but the next morning he was up early at headquarters to run the tapes back and blip my radio conversation, rather against regulations. It was only ten minutes by air from Ash Mountain, just over the hill, but by trail we were 50 miles away. It worked out that they could deliver supplies to the fire camp, then drop in for a visit and bring us a beer. Maybe I can get away telling this story after forty years.

FINCH AND MC KEE FAMILY STORIES

Tom Phipps was a kid when my Grandfather Finch traveled by team to tend to his orange ranch in Lemon Cove. He told me about the time Grandfather Finch's young team of horses ran away with the wagon. Mr. Finch fell off and the horses stampeded down the road, through an orange orchard where the wagon caught in a tree and the tongue was yanked loose. The horses were still hitched together and kept running right through Lemon Cove. Someone yelled "Can we corner them here, Frank?" and he shouted back, "Naw. Let the sons-of-bitches go!" That was funny, because everyone knew Frank Finch never swore in his life! Grandfather and Grandmother Finch never swore (well, Grandmother might say 'damn' when she was telling a joke), didn't smoke, didn't drink; that's just how they were raised in Iowa. They were just very fine people possessed of great humor and musical talent.

Grandfather Finch was a good businessman and very civic-minded. He served as president of the Chamber of Commerce and was a member of Woodlake High School board for three years starting in 1929. He loved radio programs. He lobbied Sacramento on behalf of his orange grower association and served on the Tulare County Grand Jury.

Frank Finch's twin brother, Fred, made his first visit to California in 1938 to celebrate their 71st birthday together in Three Rivers. About 1941, his niece, Nina Darr and her husband, Frank, came to visit from Iowa and then moved here about 1943. Their son, Clinton, had joined the naval reserves and was stationed on the West Coast. Frank Darr had just retired from the railroad as an engineer. Nina was retirement age when she started teaching 1st and 2nd grade class here about 1944. Frank used to talk about trains and how he enjoyed smoking a good cigar when he was driving trains all over the Midwest. When I smoked a cigar Frank would sigh that he wished he could join me, but just couldn't anymore. However, all those years he secretly carried a little square of tobacco in his pocket to enjoy the aroma on the sly. After Frank died, Nina was shocked when that bit of tobacco was discovered in his pocket.

Grandmother Rhoda Finch's brother T. H. Rice made several visits to Three Rivers; brother H. H. Rice visited in 1936. Rhoda's nephew Laurence Rice (son of her brother Grant Rice) worked for Walter T. Wells in 1938 at Wells' property in Silver City and in San Fernando, California. Grant Rice had stayed in California two years before 1889 but went back to Cherokee, visited again in 1938. There was always an outing to Giant Forest to see the Big Trees. One uncle was so nervous about driving in the mountains he tied a rope around the hand break in Grandmother's Maxwell car.

Rhoda's sister Opal Rice married Ben Packard of Cherokee, Iowa and eventually moved to Three Rivers where Ben worked for the Park Service and Opal worked at the post office in Ash Mountain. Opal was quieter, more conservative, than Rhoda who was full of mischief, always had a joke up her sleeve, something to pull on everybody. Opal and Rhoda often played Pedro at parties or at the Woman's Club and Rhoda loved to bluff her sister at cards, would bet on anything and always played wild to win. My cousin Sherman and I played Pedro with our Finch grandparents and cooked up a scheme of signals. When our strategy seemed to fail, we began to notice that Grandmother Rhoda would touch her nose or rub her knuckle–they were on to us and we were out-foxed.

Ben Packard was the nicest guy in the world. He died not long after retiring from the Park Service. Everyone liked Ben Packard. Ben and Opal had two sons and a daughter–Hal, Byrne and Polly. One son, Hal and wife Rosemary, had four children, Clifford, Bennie, Janie, and Kay. Kay Packard lives in Three Rivers.

Frank and Rhoda Finch gave portions of the Three Rivers place to their children, Jesse, Loren and Edna. Ten acres with river frontage in back of the current Post Office went to his son Loren Finch. The next ten acres he gave to his son Jesse and wife Gladys Mires Finch. Gladys died fairly young, having "enjoyed" poor health for most of her life, something of a hypochondriac. Glady's sister was Ester Mires Peck who was married to my good friend Asa Peck. Iva Tingley later bought Jesse's ten acres. To his daughter, Edna Finch McKee, he deeded ten acres. He sold the north end of his property to Jenkins and Les Dixon where the golf course and market complex is now located. Mr. Finch retained the twenty acres with their home along the Old Three Rivers road and later bought and remodeled the old school house across the road into a beautiful home where they moved in 1930 and lived their remaining years.

Zola Finch, their next to the youngest daughter, married John Kloth, a dairyman who farmed alfalfa and almonds in Visalia. Marjorie Finch, the youngest child, was born in 1914. She attended Fresno State College. The popular social scene for young people, including the CCC guys, in Three Rivers in the 1930s was the Saturday night dances. Marjorie got acquainted with a CCC fellow from Mississippi named Bob Pevey. He was the nicest fellow, sensitive, with Southern manners. They married just before he was sent to war. Bob ran a Chevron filling station in Visalia and it wasn't long before he was the manager of the Tulare fuel distributorship where he worked until retirement. Marjorie and Bob had a son and a daughter.

The first time I saw Bob he was busting up rocks on the highway to the Park when the CCCs were building the beautiful rock walls along the shoulders. Each rock was carefully sculpted to fit. There were some master stonemasons in that group and the beautiful bridges at Marble Fork and Clover Creek prove their artistry.

Bob loved to go quail hunting over on my Greasy Cove ranch and he'd bring a couple of friends along and make it an annual event; one of the friends was a Japanese fellow named Switch Yashida, and we'd exchange visits and I bought hay from him. Bob's brother-in-law, my uncle Loren Finch, usually joined in and I would hunt with them if I had time. Besides hunting on the ranch they always cut up a pickup load of dry oak firewood to take home.

Late in the day on what turned out to be the last hunt in Greasy, Bob's son Gary Pevey called me from Exeter Hospital. Loren filled me in later with the details. They were cutting wood, Bob was down the slope sawing a dead oak and all at once he set the saw down and fell over. They ran to help but his heart had stopped. They were way up Greasy so all they could do was haul him down to the hospital for the doctor's pronouncement.

Uncle Loren Finch was a builder and worked out of town for extended periods of time. His son, Sherman, and I were close to the same age–I was two years younger–and grew up like brothers doing everything together. Sherman lived with our Finch grandparents nearby because his mother deserted the family when he was very young. Sherman loved the mountains like I did and worked in Giant Forest with us for years. He was Sergeant First Class in the Korean War with the 5th Army for over a year, commanding an artillery and eleven men. He was awarded the Bronze Star for heroism. After returning to civilian life, Sherman completed his forestry school major at the University of Idaho. Sherman died in the Spring of 2012 and his ashes were buried in the Three Rivers Cemetery.

My uncle Jesse Finch raised cattle on two other parcels off the Ward ranch plus 670 acres that was part of the old Nort Tharp ranch lying south of the Kaweah River behind the Cobble Lodge up over the old Nort Tharp mountain to the Cherokee range owned by Byron Allen. Jesse's home, built by Loren Finch, was just back of Cobble Lodge, close to the Nort Tharp place. Jesse drove cattle transport trucks. He quit ranching to go into trucking full time when he decided that the cattle business wasn't all that profitable. Jesse was a good roper, a left-handed roper. He helped me at Greasy roping calves many years after he'd worked cattle, and he hadn't forgotten anything. Back when Jesse was working for Blicks gathering cattle in Hockett Meadows he roped a bear that was too close to the herd. He had a grown bear on the end of his rope on the other side of a rock, so Jesse tossed the rope over a tree and pulled it tight so the bear couldn't move, tied the rope off on his saddle horn and dismounted. He had a lot of confidence in his horse to stand still and keep that rope tight and that big bear immobile while he climbed on the rock and dispatched the bear with a knife.

Talking about Uncle Jesse Finch reminds me of several stories. In 1939, Jesse moved the family to Visalia where they eventually bought a little grocery store on South Conyer Street. His neighbor and good friend there was Harry Kulik. It was the good fortune of Three Rivers that Harry bought the land just west of the South Fork bridge on Highway 198 and built a hardware store. Harry, his wife Rose, and sons George and Mike, ran the store. You could find anything and everything you needed, from jeans to junction boxes. If Harry didn't have it, he'd get it within days because he had a great supplier representative who spent a lot of time there. Harry was the kind of citizen we appreciate, solid as the rocks in this canyon, a good, honest, hardworking American entrepreneur who gave so much to our little town. Harry Kulik retired years ago and sold his store, and it has never been the same since. Harry retired to his home in Cherokee Oaks. Harry's wife, Rose, is buried in Three Rivers Cemetery.

The buyer of Jesse Finch's ranch was Josh Hadley, the county coroner, undertaker, and owner of Hadley's Funeral Home in Visalia, which his son, Dud Hadley, took over. Hadley made money and decided to diversify into cattle. My dad helped Josh on his ranch all the time and they became good friends.

Josh Hadley was in charge of my dad's funeral. I remember his kindness so well. I was fifteen years old, had never seen a dead person before, and here I was viewing my own father. Josh stood quietly with us by the casket, then thoughtfully commented that just looking at Earl lying there, it seems he is about ready to ask, Hey, how 'bout bumming another one of your "tailor-mades." Josh thought the world of my dad and knew that he rolled his own, but also smoked a Lucky Strike once in a while, cigarettes he called "tailor-mades." My dad smoked Bull Durham. The tobacco came in a little cotton sack with a tag on the end of the drawstring, the wrappers on the side. I can still see my dad pull out a paper, open the sack and shake some tobacco into a paper, then bite the tag and pull the drawstring tight with his teeth. Later he bought a cigarette roller and would roll a day's worth to put in the little sack in his pocket, but that proved too unhandy for him so he went back to Bull Durham.

Sometimes my dad would have a pack of Lucky Strikes at home, and one time my mom and I went to a trick store and I bought a bamboo gizmo to sabotage a smoke–it would insert a toothpick up the center so when the toothpick burned it would explode the cigarette. I loaded one of dad's cigarettes. On cold days, dad would come in tired from working cattle and lay down on the floor in front of the fireplace to have a cigarette and sometimes fall asleep. He smoked the loaded one and it blew half the cigarette across his chest. He gave me a stern glare. I got only a few paddlings from my dad, but my mother wore her hand out on me. When I really asked for it, I got it–sometimes it would be with a willow switch that stung my bottom. I loved her for it later because it taught me respect.

Josh and Dud Hadley called on me to sing for dozens of funerals, some people I knew and some I didn't know. Brooks Funeral Home also called me to sing. I have stacks of those little memorial programs saved from funerals clear back to Fred Gill, the first one I sang for in 1954. I got acquainted with Rufus Connelly back then. I used to ride to the funerals with him in the hearse–Ruf would preach and I would sing. Ruf was always writing poems and songs and wanted me to sing his songs, but our styles really didn't match. He did publish quite a few, though. Ruf was postmaster in Visalia for years and preached hundreds of funerals. Folks really liked Ruf's plain talk because he'd reminisce about the old days, about the good–and sometimes even the bad–deeds in the life of the departed.

McKee

My dad had four siblings: Ernest, Lena, Maud, and Stella. His sister Stella married Harry Britten in Three Rivers. Harry was a Park ranger, and later was appointed as a judge in the Exeter court. Their son, Clyde Harold Britten was born in 1905. Clyde Britten did the usual packing and cowboyed for a time for both Fred Gill and my dad. Clyde graduated from Stanford University in 1927 with a degree in chemical engineering. He was employed by Shell Oil Company as chief technician. In 1939 he and two other scientists were granted a patent for Acid Oil Recovery system. He had a very successful but short life. He died of heart disease at age 53 and was buried in the Exeter Cemetery in 1958. Clyde's son, Don Britten, and I were as close as brothers; Don also died at a very young age.

My dad's sister Maud married Claude Hershberger, whose family came to Porterville in 1888. Claude was an engineer in the oil fields, and they first lived in west Fresno county and then Fullerton, California. They had two children, a daughter Lois M., born about 1912 and a son Willard born in 1910, in Lemon Cove. On November 21, 1928, Claude, despondent over financial matters, rigged a pistol and killed himself, at home, in the bathtub. Young Willard made the horrible discovery and was never quite the same.

My dad paced off a five-acre parcel across the road from our house and gave it to Maud. Her son, Willard, and her brother-in-law started construction on her new home in December 1939 on that beautiful knoll. Willard was an outstanding athlete at Fullerton High School where he was called "the greatest little catcher to ever put on the Fullerton uniform." He wasn't very tall, 167 pounds, could run, and hit the ball. Willard played on the west coast league then signed with the Yankees, and in 1938 played for the Cincinnati Reds. The Reds won the Pennant but lost the World Series in 1939.

His baseball roommate recalled Willard's insomnia. The Reds' manager, Bill McKechnie, talked to Willard about his depression.

In 1940, the Reds were in the playoffs against the New York Giants. Cincinnati won the first game, then lost the second game, and Willard hung the total blame for that loss on himself. Before game-time the next day, Willard, "Hershie" to his teammates, slashed his jugular, at the hotel, in the bathtub. The Reds went on to win the pennant and the 1940 World Series. The team members reportedly sent a portion of their championship money to Willard's mother, Maud Hershberger. The mail carrier in Three Rivers took time off to go to Cincinnati to bring back Hershie's new custom Ford Mercury he had just bought.

Maud's daughter, Lois Hershberger married Robert Walter Finch of Fullerton in 1935, no relation to the Frank Finches. Bob was a buyer for Swift Meat Company. Bob and Lois retired to St. Joseph, Missouri where they were neighbors to the old man J. C. Penney. Bob played golf with the president of Stetson Hat Company and one day Bob called me up to ask what size hat I wore because after hearing Bob talk about me, the guy wanted to send me a Stetson. Well, good, my size is 7-1/2. That Stetson is in my closet, it is pure chalk white, I've worn it a few times with a white tux and it really looks sharp. Some years back on a jazz trip, we drove through St. Joseph, I looked up Stetson on my iPhone and went to the store. My story that the president of Stetson had personally sent me a hat didn't impress anybody; the clerks just said "huh."

Maud passed away in 1947 after which her daughter, Lois, sold the property back to my mother. The house was newer with more modern conveniences, so my mother chose to live there for the next twenty years, after which time we convinced her to move to the brand-new Three Rivers apartments. She had first choice of the units as they had just been completed.

My dad's older brother Ernest is pictured with Onis Brown on Colby Pass (page 132), the first ones through it in 1920 when they packed for James Hutchinson. My dad and Ernest grew up on the Ward Ranch and both liked to ride bucking horses. If a horse wanted to buck in the morning, that was fine by them, they just stayed on. Onis Brown said that Ernest was the finest rodeo bronc rider that he'd ever seen, stayed on in perfect motion with the horse. Ernest moved to Woodlake around Elderwood and raised cattle. Ernest's son, Norman, was raised there. Norman's son, Kenny McKee, is a good cowman, runs cattle up in Eshom Country, has some orange land, and grows hay. He married Virginia Graves, a real nice gal. We see each other at brandings.

Gaynor Hardison studied ballet under Princess Pontiac in South Gate, California where she was raised. Gaynor taught dance at her own studio in Three Rivers after we were married. Photo 1946.

AUTHOR'S COLLECTION.

Sweethearts on Parade

Spring 1950
Woodlake Rodeo Parade

Earl McKee
riding "Copper"

Gaynor Hardison
riding "Buckie"

The 1950
Woodlake Centennial
featured covered wagons, bug-
gies, horseback riders, etc. in
the parade. A rodeo, dance and
BBQ made a fun weekend for
these sweethearts.

Earl and Gaynor were
married the following
December 28, 1950.

September 1950 Woodlake Rodeo Parade Sweethearts. Gaynor is riding
side saddle on Buckie. I am on my horse Copper. We were married the
following December.

I played football at Woodlake High School and as a reward for
winning district championships in both 1947 and 1948, our team
attended the Rose Bowl Game in Pasadena—we were volunteered as
ushers and if we found an empty seat we could sit in it or on the step.
The one year I was so surprised to see Colonel John White walking
up my aisle. I extended my hand, "Colonel John R. White!" "Young
Ull, that's you!" (in his English accent). The Colonel had retired to
Southern California.

Gaynor and I were married December 1950 in the Community
Presbyterian Church in Three Rivers. The quaint steepled church was
built on a knoll in 1939 with knotty pine paneling and exposed beams
that glow in the light from stained glass windows. My sisters, Earleen
and Blanche, both sang and Earleen played the wedding march. That was
the year Lee kept me out on pack trips until late October. It was 62 days

before I saw a road. Gaynor was getting worried that I might not make it to our wedding.

I am just four months older than Gaynor and our families were well acquainted because my dad had helped Gaynor's grandfather, "Whispering" Bob Lovering, gather his cattle for many years. Back in 1933, Gaynor and her parents lived for two years with the Loverings. One day my mother took me to visit and Gaynor's grandmother Nell commented that wouldn't it be funny if the little tykes grew up and got married.

After Gaynor and I were married we made our home in the house where I was born. We have lived there now for 62 years.

Gaynor, my loving partner and best friend, imparted her strong feelings about love, honesty and integrity to our children and their families. They've exhibited the best of all the creativity and talent from our McKee, Finch and Lovering lineage, so evident in their love of music, poetry and appreciation of the mountains.

Linda Nell was our first child, then Chearl, and Earl III was born in 1957. In my poem about Blossom Peak, I describe my wife Gaynor as a trainer. Gaynor was indeed a trainer who founded Our Gym in 1974 for dance arts instruction for 40 to 50 kids, kindergarten through 8th grade. Gaynor choreographed their annual Extravaganza presented by her students at the Memorial Building, a stage show enjoyed by the whole community. Her artistic talents included the design and sewing of the costumes. Gaynor owned Our Gym for ten years, and also served as a teacher's aide at the school for 24 years. Daughter Linda made dancing her profession also as an instructor and performer of dance arts at College of the Sequoias for the past 36 years. Chearl has a phenomenal ear for music, perfect pitch and when our family sang harmony she knew where that third note goes to make the chord. We still get together from time to time to harmonize. Chearl is a Zydeco dancer, enjoys traveling to band gigs across the country including New Orleans for the swamp beat–cajun beat music. She has a career as a massage therapist in her own business. We lost Earl III in 1984.

Gaynor taught dancing for a short time with Sue Davis, Joe's wife. Mention of Joe Davis reminds me of the story about the wood stove in our house.

After the road was finished to Giant Forest in 1903, the Army shipped in a lot of potbellied wood stoves. "U.S. Army Canon Stove" was cast in the iron door. When George Mauger sold the Giant Forest concession to Harvey Company, the stoves were in storage so he gave stoves to long-time Park employees like Joe and Bob Davis, and superintendent Eivind Scoyen. Joe took his stove with him when he transferred to Zion National Park in Utah but sold it there before he moved back to Three Rivers.

Bob Davis and his wife, Marguerite, were living in Park housing at Ash Mountain when Bob died unexpectedly. Joe and I cleaned up my cattle truck to move Bob's widow to a home in Cherokee Oaks. Of course I refused Marguerite's offer of pay, so she asked if I would like to have Bob's old wood stove in the yard. I was thrilled. It was one of the pot-bellied U.S. Army Canon Stoves. Bob had turned it into a flower planter. I dumped the dirt out and took it all to Randall's shop in Woodlake to be sandblasted and stove blacked. It looked brand new. But the most important part—the door—was missing.

So I took the stove to Gary Davis, whose father was Thomas H. Davis, II, one of my good friends in the cattle business. Gary was a fine cowboy who worked with his father on their ranch and we traded help. Gary was also a heck of a welder in Woodlake, who said he could make a door. At the time Gary was fabricating special racks for pickup trucks and sold a lot of them. His next ad in the paper had a photograph of his custom racks on his pickup taken when my stove happened to be in the back end of his truck. He got a flood of calls wanting to buy that stove. Gary said no one even noticed his racks, he sure wouldn't use that picture again. Gary crafted a door and we still use that army stove for central heat in our house.

About that time, Johnny Britten knew I was looking for a new bathtub for our house, and said there was a new one, still in the crate, in the basement of Frankie Welch's house, and did I want it. Frankie Welch (1886-1978) was the first librarian here and a regular contributor of feature articles to the valley newspapers. I said yes, thank you. Johnny used bathtubs to put salt in for his cattle, but didn't want to use a brand new one. The tag on the crate indicated it had been purchased by Frankie from the Woodlake Hardware in 1933. I installed it at home, but it was really too small, I could barely fit in it. Later, I found a larger bathtub at an antique shop on West Mineral King in Visalia. I always enjoy stopping at antique stores to look around and sometimes bring home some real finds—brass Hames bells, for instance. When I returned to pick it up, sitting beside the tub was a U.S. Army Canon Stove in perfect condition, had just come in for sale. I asked how much for the door and was told $300, so I asked how much for the whole stove, and again was told $300. I didn't buy it, but thought about it and went back, but a dealer in Bakersfield had bought it, and, as luck would have it, had just sold it. It was a dumb thing not to buy that stove when I first saw it. George Mauger and Eivind Scoyen, as well as other Park employees, had lived in Visalia. Chances are one of their families had consigned that stove.

When my sister Blanche married Lee Maloy in 1933, my dad gave them the parcel just west of our house where they built their first home. They had three kids, Leroy, Billy and Virginia, who all helped on the ranch and pack stations. In 1946, Lee sold the place to Joe Davis and bought Jesse Finch's old ranch behind Cobble Lodge from the owner Josh Hadley. Lee and Blanche lived in Jesse's old ranch house where they raised cattle, along with running the pack station in Mineral King. I helped him gather cows there.

Blanche was a trouper—capable, nervous energy like our dad. When they were running two pack stations—Giant Forest and Mineral King—and things were tight and not enough help—Blanche did everything. She'd drive their old 1-1/2 ton Ford horse truck, paneled off for grub and stuff, with a load of pack stock from Three Rivers clear over to Bishop, alone. She'd just get in and go. She raised a family, looked after the pack station, hauled horses and drove hay trucks to Mineral King; whatever had to be done, Blanche did it.

Lee and Blanche sold out and went to Reno not long after their son, Bill, moved there in 1959. Bill opened his first saddle shop in downtown Reno on Virginia Street. For 50 years he built handcrafted saddles, including silver-engraved trophy saddles for the Cow Palace and Salinas Rodeos. His work was honored with many awards including the Will Rogers Saddle Maker of the Year from the Academy of Western Artists, and the Canada's Cowboy Festival in Calgary as a Hero of Western Art and Craftmanship. In April 2011, I sang at Bill's funeral at the Catholic Church, and later at the celebration of Bill's life at the Silver Legacy in Reno. The songs I was asked to sing at Bill's wake probably shouldn't be printed here, but we gave Bill a great send-off!

Lee opened a saddle shop with Bill in Reno. Leroy joined his dad's business in Reno for a few years and then moved back to Woodlake. Lee Maloy died in 1991, after which Blanche and Gaynor's mother, Norma, moved to our ranch in a home we built for them.

I am seated beside my mother, Edna McKee, at her 90th birthday celebration. My mother was my biggest jazz fan. She sat in the front row at all our programs with her recorder and taped a million feet of music. Photo 1982.

AUTHOR'S COLLECTION.

Rice and Marx Orange Ranch

Just up from Terminus, and across from the mouth of Greasy Creek, now under Lake Kaweah, were the orange groves owned by my Grandmother Rhoda Rice Finch's relatives, the Charles Marx and Rice families. They were known for producing the sweetest oranges in these parts.

Rhoda Finch's aunt was Clementine Rice (Mrs. Charles Marx) whose daughter Cora Marx married Jacob W. B. Rice, Rhoda's brother, which made them first cousins. The 1900 census listed Cora and J. W. B. Rice and their children Charles Rice, 9; Clem Rice, 9; Pearl Rice, 7; Royal Rice, 5; Villa Rice, 4; Elmo Rice, 1; and Robert I. Marx, 13. The census noted they had been married for ten years. It seems J. W. B. Rice came from Iowa to Lemon Cove to visit his aunt Clementine and Charles Marx and their daughter, Cora. Well, there was a scarcity of daughters and J. W. B. and Cora took some liberties out of school and the first thing you know, Charles Marx said, "You will marry my daughter!" The first-born was probably Robert, and then they had a half dozen more, some of whom had peculiar traits owing to their parents being first cousins. J. W. B. was known to the family as "Uncle Will Rice."

In visiting with Wally Rice, a generation away from that family, he filled me in on the family with facts and stories about my lovable Rice relatives. Wally and his wife are in a retirement home in Visalia now. One of Wally's uncles, named Elmo, was a real character, a bit different, but he cowboyed around here, helped Joe Chinowth at Dofflemyer ranch. He was a great hunter, and when he was young he could out-walk or out-run a horse. I would find Elmo's track all over Greasy Cove, on Sulfur Peak, or Broke-Up Mountain where he hunted deer, he was a buck-hunter, that's all he thought about, always asked have you seen any big bucks up there, Earl? He looked like a character in the movies with an old straight cowboy hat, tuft of hair sticking out in the middle of his forehead, didn't comb it, just rubbed it up in the morning to pull it out of his eyes. He smoked an old Hawkshaw pipe, curled like a Sherlock Holmes pipe, and his shirt usually had a few chewing tobacco stains down the front. He saw himself as one tough cowboy. One time he came up to my house to see me about a horse, and while he was talking away he just reared back in the chair, pursed his lips and leaned forward, ready to spit a mouthful of tobacco juice on my hardwood floor. I guess he suddenly realized that he shouldn't do that in someone else's house, because he quickly clamped his hand over his mouth. That was Elmo Rice. There's a poem I wrote about him in the back of the book.

Elmo's sister, Clemmie married John Card. I met a fellow at jazz who had stayed with them years ago to go to high school. He said that one time Clemmie fell off her horse and broke both wrists. She went to some quack doctor—one who everyone called "the Vet"—who cast the bones crooked. Another physician said he needed to re-break and reset the bones so her wrists would heal correctly. Clemmie refused anesthetic when they re-broke her wrists; the doctor said he never saw a more stronger-willed person in his life.

Elmo's brother, Charlie Rice worked for my dad at the riding corrals in Giant Forest for about two summers during WWII. The sign said our corrals closed at 5 o'clock in the afternoon, and by God that's when Charlie closed them, even when tourists would hurry over a few minutes late wanting to ride. There could be ten customers with cash in hand, but Charlie would tell them, "We're closed," and cut off their pleading to rent horses with a gruff "Goddammit, I said we're closed," especially if the dudes were rude. He was a comical old boy, but he definitely lived by his own set of rules.

When the dam went in, the Marx and Rice families had to abandon their memories and fine orchards to the waters of Lake Kaweah.

MUSICAL TRADITION

⟨∞⟩

My grandfather Frank Finch played the fiddle and won fiddling contests, accompanied on the piano by Al Brockman, and sometimes by my mother. He also played fiddle in the Poison Oak Orchestra. My uncle Jesse Finch played piano. My oldest sister Blanche had a beautiful voice, with no formal training, and was asked to sing at community gatherings as well as weddings and funerals. She starred as Queen of Tarts in the Woodlake High operetta, *Prince Charming*. She made her "very successful singing debut" in 1937 on the valley KTKC radio. My sister Earleen also sang beautifully. She used to put on concerts in Three Rivers with Verna Bartlett, a flutist. Earleen studied at Juilliard and earned a Masters at Columbia University in music.

Earleen sang in New York City and performed in a recital at Carnegie Hall. She sang in stage productions where she became acquainted with Meredith Wilson, composer of *Music Man*, with whom she discussed the tough realities of Show Biz in New York. Earleen preferred to return home with her teaching and music credentials and pursued a life-long career as a high school music instructor. She married and raised four children at the family home near Merced.

Music then was certainly nothing like today's singers who take a breath in the middle of a word, can't hold a note, are obviously untrained because no one could train anyone that improperly. I call American Idol the "Coyote Call." Very little of that is talent, it is just amped-up screaming or yodeling.

As a youngster I could play hoe-down fiddle. Appalachian music fascinated me. My mother taught me to play the piano, chording mostly. When I was 11 years old, I played several violin numbers, accompanied by my sister Blanch and Mrs. Bill Swanson, for the Pioneer Party. I sang and played guitar, played trombone in high school, but didn't devote a lot of time to music after high school because the cattle ranch was my priority.

Print Stokes and the Rocky Mountain Cowboys was a local band. The Stokes were old timers from Woodlake. Joe Pohot's son, Ray Pohot, played banjo in that band. Another band member was Max Denning, a great musician. Max, who prefers to be called "Doc," started up his own band, the Sage Brush Symphony, and invited me to join because I could harmonize and played bass. I didn't stay with Max, however, because about that time I joined the Jazzberry Jam Band that was just forming. Max was so talented he was hired to join the Sons of the Pioneers with whom he toured for a year. Max is in his late 80s now and resides in Klamath, Oregon. He is my very dear friend.

McKee Family Singers

I started our family music group, The McKee Family Singers, when Earl was about ten years old. Earl liked music and was a talented guitar player. Linda, our oldest daughter, sang melody; daughter Chearl sang alto mostly, she had the ear, an amazing ability to sing harmony. Gaynor sang tenor and melody and I sang bass and tenor. Our music was inspired by the Sons of the Pioneers, we did a lot of their tunes, played for programs around Three Rivers and entertained the old folks at rest homes. We were invited to perform at the Exeter Emperor Grape Festival for five or six years, the Chamber of Commerce, the rodeos and roping. The Woodlake Rodeo put us out in the arena in the dirt in front of the bucking chute. We were guests on the Shirley Tow radio show on January 1, 1971, where we did an hour-long interview and performed several songs.

Gaynor inherited her mother Norma Lovering's voice. Norma was a professional vocalist who grew up in Fullerton on Orangethorpe Avenue. In 1925 she starred in *The Belle of Barcelona* at Fullerton High School. She sang at Carmelita Gardens on the same program with Dennis Day who complimented her voice and predicted a brilliant singing career in her future.

Norma married Sonny Hardison, her male lead in their high school operetta. Sonny chased the oil booms in Arkansas and Texas until 1948, at which time the family moved to the ranch owned by Norma's parents on South Fork, and Norma went to work at our school cafeteria. Gaynor had always been involved in music, band, choir and stage productions. We sang pretty good together.

The McKee Family Singers - (l - r) Earl III, Linda, Gaynor, Chearl and me. They set us up in the dirt in front of the bucking chute. Johnny Jackson is in the announcer booth, 2nd from left. Photo May 1971.

AUTHOR'S COLLECTION.

Three Rivers has always been a wildly diverse collection of folks whose connection to the outside world makes for some interesting encounters. The Blicks, I always thought, was a good example; Captain Kirk is another. But on the subject of music, for me there was one really memorable night.

It was in the early 1970s that I was invited to the North Fork home of Melvin and Belle Jones to meet their guests, singer, songwriter, actor, politician, and lion-hunter, Stuart Hamblin and his wife. What an evening. The older crowd reading this will remember Stuart Hamblin, and his famous hit song "It is No Secret What God Can Do," and others, but I've got to tell you about that evening.

Stuart loved to chase mountain lions and that's why he was visiting on North Fork, to go higher up on the Elliot cattle ranch with his lion hounds. He didn't chase mountain lions to shoot them, only to tree them and take their pictures! Then he'd gather his dogs and let the lions go. Stuart had his guitar and I had mine and we sat until the wee hours as he played and sang his hit songs and recounted his amazing life story. Stuart was a marvelous songwriter and great showman on stage, television and movies. He made movies with Roy Rogers, Gene Autry, and John Wayne in the '40s and '50s.

I asked Stuart about his running for president. Because he had refused to accept booze commercials on his syndicated Christian radio program back then, his show was cancelled. All of the publicity surrounding his stand against alcohol led to his nomination for President of the United States on the Prohibition Party ticket in 1952. He accepted the nomination and hit the campaign trail. I remember hearing my mother say, "What's that old drunk doing on the ballot?" General Dwight D. Eisenhower was elected president that year.

Stuart had gone through some serious drinking days and was rescued by "The Duke"–John Wayne–who looked him in the eye and told Stuart he'd be dead in six months if he didn't get his life straight with his God and stop drinking. Stuart told me that night there was no question in his mind that John Wayne saved his life. Stuart described his life-change to Wayne, saying "Well, it's no secret. . ." and Wayne told him that was a catchy phrase and he should write a song about it. He told about traveling with the Reverend Billy Graham crusades around the country and the many hymns and religious songs he wrote on tour that became hits. We talked and sang into the wee hours of the morning, an unexpected encounter with an amazing man.

Stuart Hamblin's song "It is No Secret What God Can Do" was the number one hit on all the charts–Gospel, Country and Popular.

Jazz

Jazz started in my living room with Leuder Ohlwein, the banjo player from Ireland who married Gaynor's cousin, Terry Sullivan. Terry had visited Ireland to trace her family's roots and there she met Leuder playing music at the pubs. On her second trip to Ireland Terry and Leuder married and lived there about two years and had a daughter, Diedra. Leuder was Irish by heart and loved their music, but he was actually from East Germany from where he and his family made a daring escape across the Elbe. Tragically, one of his sisters was shot and killed by the East German guards as the family swam for freedom.

Leuder and Terry arrived in Three Rivers in 1969, and I was working with Leroy Maloy on the flume job, replacing the wood scaffold and footings that hold up the seven miles of flume from Oak Grove to Power House No. 1. I took the job just to keep it open so Leuder would have work when he got here, but they didn't arrive until the job was over. They moved into the Lovering house on South Fork.

Leuder and I played music together for fun or maybe for dinner at the Pizza Pub (now known as The We Three restaurant) on Hwy. 198. I played guitar, Leuder on banjo. We played the White Horse dinner house and lounge. He really knew music but didn't know how to care for a family or hold on to his money, so their cupboards were often bare.

Leuder picked up on talk that there were other local musicians who would like to form a band. My sister, Earleen, a fine pianist, gave us the name of Vic Kimsey in Visalia. I had heard Doc Ropes of Woodlake play saxophone at the old dances; Charlie Castro of Three Rivers was a drummer playing in a country band in Exeter; and Bruce Huddleston played piano for various dinner houses. I played string bass. We got together and started practicing and our first rehearsal was in my living room.

That was the first time I had met Vic Kimsey. He owned instruments of all kinds, all kinds of horns and could play anything with a valve in it, didn't matter what key, or he could play by ear, had it all in his head and he had perfect pitch. You could belch and he'd tell you if it was in E flat, just a genius that way. Leuder liked New Orleans style jazz and wanted me to play tuba instead of bass. Well, I'd never played a tuba before, but Pete Sweeney found a sousaphone to borrow that someone in Visalia had made out of several old junkers. I practiced in the barn or locked myself in the bathroom and sat on a chair or on the lid of the john and played along to the tapes of jazz bands until I figured how to play the progression. That is how I learned to play the tuba.

Leuder named our group Jazzberry Jam Band and we got to be pretty well known locally. We played at the Matterhorn restaurant at the early Three Rivers golf course, in Visalia at the Depot Restaurant, and even at a store opening in Bakersfield. I found a used tuba at a music store in Fresno that played so perfectly and bought it for $200 and that is the horn I still play. In 1974, we played a big barn raising party at my new shop. One time we played at the Woodlake Rodeo where the stage was furnished with a piano that was so out of tune, the piano player had to go down a half step and play in another key—a tune in E-flat had to be played in D-natural.

The Jazzberry Jam Band at the dedication of my shop at the home place in 1974. The original band (l to r) Doc Ropes on saxophone; Charlie Castro, drums; Vic Kimsey, trombone; Earl McKee, sousaphone; Don Franscioni on trumpet; Leuder Ohlwein, banjo. Photo 1974.

AUTHOR'S COLLECTION.

Jimmy Rivers, the great guitar player who spent so much time with us when Earl III was sick, had a houseboat at Rio Vista, on the Sacramento Delta, and Leuder and I went to visit. Leuder played banjo, I played tuba and Jimmy on guitar, we went to the famous Moore's River Boat west of Stockton, an old paddle wheel steamboat remodeled as a restaurant. Mr. Moore, who looked like Col. Sanders in a white suit and bow tie, invited us to play because the regular band was off that night. We started playing, Leuder played the kazoo and the place went nuts. The rowdy crowd bought us drinks all night long. No one remembered leaving—talk about feeding the fish. This was about 1973, forty years ago.

Wearing my trademark black Stetson performing a vocal number. Photo c. 1988 by Doc Lawless.

AUTHOR'S COLLECTION

We took another trip to the Bay Area in Vic Kimsey's motor home to hear Turk Murphy play in Oakland and after that we went over to Ghirardelli Square to an Irish Pub. Vic Kimsey with his coronet, Charlie Castro snare drums, Bill Smith with his guitar, and me–I was carrying that big bass viol all over the hills of San Francisco. We set up on the sidewalk and played old jazz tunes and the crowds blocked the whole street. The cops said we were a traffic hazard and had to move. Bill set out the open guitar case in front of us and I never saw so much money. There was enough money for dinners all around at Spenger's in Berkeley, and steaks at Point Richmond the next day. There were quite a few Jazzberry adventures in Vic's motor home–Point Richmond, Jack Tarr in Hotel San Francisco, with lots of spontaneous jazz everywhere.

In 1976, Leuder quit the band for other endeavors and he said, with charming German accent, "I take the name mitt me." It was just as well because without Leuder the sound was different. We got Stan Huddleston on banjo and renamed ourselves High Sierra Jazz Band (HSJB). That is when HSJB put Three Rivers on the jazz map, almost forty years ago. Most any mention of the High Sierra Jazz Band expresses amazement that such a small, remote foothill town had the talent–working guys–at

315

the right time, right place, with a unique sound, to make music around the world.

The first Jazz Affair, where a half dozen guest bands joined us for three days of constant music, was held in 1973 when Leuder was still our leader, and 2012 was our 40th Anniversary of Jazz Affair. The thirty-six years of High Sierra Jazz Band has been written about many times. We've travelled to Europe–Ireland, England, France, Belgium, Germany. On the other side of the world, we played in New Zealand, Australia, China, Japan, South Korea, Thailand, Hawaii. I've had that tuba straightened many times, it has been wrecked in airplanes; about a year ago when we were in China it was just about demolished. It cost $600 to put the braces back in and get the dents out.

Our first jazz cruise was hosted by Carol and Bob Neuman, originator of jazz cruises, out of Florida. We toured Australia, New Zealand and Tahiti three times, the Far East, Alaska and Hawaii. We started small, we all had jobs, stayed close to home until our popularity propelled us literally around the world.

A Few Jazz Stories

Stories about the forty years playing and touring with High Sierra Jazz Band would fill two books and will have to wait for someone else to write it, but there are several stories pegged in my memory that I will include here.

In 1982, an enterprising young lady, Carol Neuman organized a cruise company out of Florida to feature Dixieland jazz music and the first band booked was the Oregon Jazz Band founded by Bill Borcher in 1947. Bill played trumpet. Reservations for the cruise were slow, so Bill called to ask if our band would go along. We agreed. The promotional brochure was headlined, "Oregon Jazz Band and another fine band" will perform. We got more razzing about that so we had "Another Fine Band" T-shirts made one time. The cruise was a sell-out. We flew to Florida for our first cruise in the Caribbean. A decade later Carol presented HSJB a plaque to celebrate our tenth cruise with her.

Our first cruise with Jazz Daagen Cruises was to Alaska in 1985 with the Nightbloomin' Jazzmen from Los Angeles. Jazz Daagen is owned by Peter Meijer's wife, Aleda Meijers, and has booked HSJB cruises since 1985.

316

A day or so into that Alaska cruise, we became aware that there was a nut on board, a goofy-acting guy, maybe with a drug problem? How did they let him on a cruise ship? One evening we were performing in the big ballroom and the nut-guy climbed onto the stage in the middle of a tune and started opening our instrument cases looking for something to play. We ran him off. Unbelievably, an evening or two later we thought he was back when an "Arab" wearing a turban made a noisy entrance on the dance floor with a trombone and started blowing off-key. I growled to Vic, "If I see that guy again, if he gets on this stage again, I'm going to deck him." As I often do, I had a recorder on between Vic (the trombone) and myself that picked up everything I said. Well, it turns out this "nut" was one of the Nightbloomin' Jazzmen, Peter Meijers, our future bandleader, acting out.

Peter Meijers joined HSJB in 1998 and has been our bandleader now for fourteen years. Someone sent him the tape from that night and he still has it, and jokes that it happened just the way it happened.

For six or eight years, I played with the The Three Riversmen, a trio composed of three guys from the HSJB–Stan and Bruce Huddleston and myself. It was around the time that our HSJB leader, Al Smith, decided to semi-retire from the band in order to be home with his family, so the band stopped traveling and only played local gigs. We had a lot of free weekends and decided to play; Stan was on banjo or guitar, Bruce on piano, and I played string bass and sang solos. Sometimes we sang trios. We did some nice crooning songs, some Bob Nolan songs, pretty music. We played for some small parties, a few festivals, and on a couple of cruise ships. After the HSJB became so popular with a busy tour calendar again, we never went back to our trio. I have a few tapes of practice sessions, and we did record one cassette called, *We Three*.

Traveling to jazz festivals, we make many dear friends with other band members from all over. Fred and Anna Whaler in Maryland staged the forerunner of jazz festivals at a hotel there and invited four traditional jazz bands to play at the same venue, one big place so the audience stayed put and the bands rotated sets. The host band, the Buck Creek Jazz Band, got its start in 1977 playing Sunday afternoons at Fred and Anna Whaler's house on Buck Creek Road in Temple Hills, Maryland.

We first met the Buck Creek Jazz band when both bands played at the Sacramento Jubilee. The HSJB went on cruises with the Buck Creek

Jazz Band, played just about all the same festivals. Gaynor and I were guests at Fred and Anna's home there at Buck Creek Road. Anna was a secretary at the White House since the Kennedy years and we were given a guided tour of the White House and the basement where high security meetings are held and she told us about being down there during the Bay of Pigs crisis.

Anna always called to invite the HSJB, and either the Black Eagles from Maine and the Grand Dominion from Canada and another band from Toronto. One year we went back and we decided to dress up like the Buck Street Jazz Band members, only our shirts said, "Buck Wheat Jazz Band" with wheat stalks. Each member of the band had something distinctive about him; for example, the trumpet player had curly blond hair, so our leader and trumpet player, Al Smith, wore a kinky blond wig; I mimicked their tuba player, John Woods, a dear friend of mine, by wearing half-glasses on my nose and borrowed a tuba instead of a sousaphone. We were announced as "The Mystery Band" and mimicked their style. It was a pretty good joke and they all got a bang out of it.

We were playing in Denmark on one of our jazz tours and were told that Walter Cronkite and his wife might be in the audience that evening. They were there, seated several rows back. Cronkite liked jazz and came back stage to visit with the band. Cronkite was very familiar with Wild Bill Davison and we had a lot of laughs together about him. Wild Bill Davison was a great coronet player from Chicago, a famous jazz player in the 1930s. I first met Wild Bill in Chicago about 1980 when the High Sierra Jazz Band was playing there. Wild Bill collected hats and admired my trademark black Stetson that I always wore on stage. He said that he would really like a Stetson. I was able to surprise him with a fine Stetson at the Sacramento jazz festival the next year. I shaped that hat myself. Wild Bill looked great with it on.

I called Wild Bill in Santa Barbara just the day before he went in for surgery, kidding him about leaving the nurses alone. He had an abdominal aneurysm and died in surgery in November 1989.

Today the musicians of the HSJB are Pieter Meijers, leader and reedman; Charlie Castro, drums; Stan Huddleston, banjo; Bruce Huddleston, piano; Howard Miyata, trombone; Bryan Shaw, cornet; and me on sousaphone.

Jazz festivals are facing higher expenses and lower attendance now because the crowds that have been fans for decades are declining–either they are not there, or in a cemetery somewhere, or need wheelchair or a walker. Let's face it, we're not kids anymore. The High Sierra Jazz Band has played longer than just about anybody as a band in all the circuits. The most distant festival, in Florida, invited us as usual in 2012, then had to cancel due to the high travel expenses. That was the first time we missed that festival in years, but we have our plane tickets already for 2013.

Australia

The HSJB entertained in Australia on three trips.

The first two tours were organized by Harold Parsons who did business in Australia selling gypsum products he produced on his Central California Coast Range properties. He knew all the interesting out-of-the-way places and wore us out with his jam-packed itinerary. I really enjoyed our gig at a huge barn at one of the remote sheep stations. We spent the day there and performed that night. It smelled like sheep, the loading dock was shiny from sheep's wool, the walls still had posters of the famous sheep shearers. (The most famous sheep shearer in Australia was Jackie Howe who set a record in 1892 for hand blade shearing of 321 sheep in 7 hours 40 minutes. He would have shorn more but they ran out of sheep. His medals were auctioned off for $360,000. By 1915, sheep shearing was mechanized using Wolseley shears driven by steam or combustion engines.) Several busloads of fans came to hear us and the locals put on a huge barbecue for us. A sheep and herd dog competition was going on also and I was really interested in shipping one of those dogs home.

The cultural highlight was performing in the Sydney Opera House. We staged quite a dramatic opening to the tune of "Hiawatha." The spotlight was on Charlie Castro wearing his genuine Indian feathered headdress, starting the drum beat intro, and then I came in wearing my black cowboy hat playing bass line rhythm on the tuba as the rest of the band took their places. It is really something to be able to say you played the Sydney Opera House. The acoustics are superb. The house wasn't sold out, of course, but Harold had put out flyers in the city and there was a nice crowd.

We travelled to the capital city, Canberra, and played at a bar on a long strand which was the hangout of all the foreign embassy people on Saturday nights. We played Melbourne; the memorable moment there was getting stuck in an overloaded elevator–everyone was scared to death, the ladies screaming. I saw a lot of nice cattle around Melbourne, English breeds as you would expect. On the coast there was a tour of the penguin nesting reserve, countless little penguins marched like little soldiers in a long row from the water up over the little hill to the nesting areas to feed their babies.

Then it was on to New Zealand. Before we took off to Christchurch, we went to a fair that I will never forget because I bought a big roll of cheese–about 3 inches thick and 12 inches across. Gaynor asked why on earth I bought such a thing–we'll never be able to eat it. I just thought it would be nice to have with wine during our week in Christchurch. At the airport we boarded with my cheese round and then sat for hours on the runway. There was a labor strike; they were always having strikes, like Italy. (Milan's airport was closed half the time due to strikes.) The captain finally announced that there would be no food service on the flight because the caterers were on strike. No food; however, there would be plenty of booze. That was one of the funniest airplane rides I've ever been on–two-thirds of the passengers were jazz fans and most everyone, including me, got snockered because we didn't eat, except for my wheel of cheese which was passed around and devoured. Even the stewardesses were tipsy. Some of our band members had their instruments on board and played wild jazz in the aisle.

Jazz has been a large part of my life. My wife, Gaynor, always says, "You know, if you hadn't learned to play the tuba, we'd a never got out of the front yard."

GRATITUDE

◯⟋⟍◯

I was a student at Fresno State in 1949-1950, taking agricultural classes the first semester at Hammer Field. I played football on the frosh team and got acquainted with two guys from Riverdale, over on the west side of Kings County, Bill Robinette and Gilbert McClure.

I hadn't thought about this for sixty years, until I got a long e-mail from Bill reminiscing about the old days. E-mail makes for great reunions. A mutual acquaintance had put us in touch via e-mail. The second semester in 1950, Bill asked if I would like to room with them at an aunt's house on Olive Avenue, downtown Fresno. There was Bill Robinette, Gill McClure, Henry Ramirez and myself at Aunt Ruth and Uncle Jody's house and she cared for us like sons. Aunt Ruth had very poor eyesight and held the newspaper two inches from her face and turned her head back and forth to read. She had red chickens in a coop in the back yard and gathered eggs every morning for our breakfast. I was always the one who got the feather in my eggs because she couldn't see; if there was a hair in the soup it would be in my bowl. She and her husband kept a clean house and were fine people; she just couldn't see.

Bill and Gill were friends from grammar school, both went to work for Challenge Creamery where Bill retired as a CEO. They both reside in Southern California and meet for lunch every day. We all marvel at the memories of sixty years ago.

I left the cattle business in the late 1990s and I always said that my selling out made beef prices go way up the next year. But just for fun I keep a little herd of Angus cows at the home place. A couple of years ago I bought a young Belted Galloway bull–black with a wide white belt around his middle. The Galloway is a hearty beef breed native to Scotland. My neighbor asked to have a wedding under a spreading oak in

321

my cow pasture, a pretty setting with Blossom Peak in the background, so I moved the herd to the adjoining pasture well in advance so we could mow and make sure there wouldn't be any cow pies in the aisle. At the wedding when everyone was seated, the Belted Galloway and his cows pushed up to the fence that was just a few feet from our chairs. When the music started, I whispered to Gaynor, oh no, I know what's coming. The cows started bawling in a loud chorus that drowned out everything else until they realized there was no feed connected to all these people and went off to graze. This year there were five calves, belted "Oreos"–as Gaynor calls them–Belted Galloways.

I am very grateful to have been born and raised here in Three Rivers at a time in history when the world was changing in so many ways. I grew up as a cattleman and horseman like my father, and I was very lucky to have known personally many old timers and characters who taught me how things really happened back then. Men like Tom Homer, his son Forrest Homer, Ernest Britten, Ord and his brother Ben Loverin, Thomas H. Davis II, R. I. (Whisperin' Bob) Lovering, Asa Peck, Everett (Skinny) Kirk, Judd Blick, Byron Allen, William (Bill) Wylie, Fred Gill and his three sons, Roy, Emmett and Adolph; Frances Appleby, Caryl Homer, Dow Whitney, Bob Barton, Clarence Britten, Jesse Finch, Elmo Rice, Charley Rice, Guy Hopping, Harry Hughes, Jim Kindred, Ray Pinnell, Lee Maloy, Robert Dofflemyer, Bill Graham, Dave Wilson, Dr. Don Britten DVM, Tommy Ray Welch, Walter Wells, and Walt Seaborn. These are the early cattlemen and horsemen that I knew who are no longer with us but are still very vivid in my memory.

My heart is in the backcountry and Giant Forest as I knew it, when it was welcoming, echoing life. I am thankful I knew it then, those are the memories I call upon with pleasure. I wish everyone could see the backcountry as I saw it, that there could be pack trains and facilities or a mode of alpine transport to open this wonderland to oldsters and youngsters. Current thinking has made the High Sierra a young-athletes-only park.

Sorting through trunks and my office files crammed with history, I find so many more items that have a story of their own. Just reading old news clippings from the '20s and '30s remind me of another book's worth of tales. Just before this book's final draft, I found an envelope from Toni Fuller, a daughter-in-law of W. P. Fuller, Jr., postmarked 1961. She had mailed me the words to W. P.'s favorite song, "Mike McCarty's

Wake." I looked up Adaline Fuller's number online—Adaline is W. P.'s daughter—and called her up. She is 88 years young now and we reminisced about pack trips, and the one I guided for them and Jim O'Brien in the early 1960s, after W. P. had retired from backcountry vacations.

You never know how lucky you are when you have your health and you're happy. Yeah, of course you may get out of sorts and everything, but you sit around and think a little bit—so damned lucky just to be in this country, where I grew up and where I live here, and the people I grew up with. I've sung at just about all my friends' funerals and some of them it is hard to even talk about because they were my friends.

Riding in the backcountry, the sound of steel horseshoes on the rocks, the rhythmic padding on the soft dirt trails, I really miss those sounds. I loved the packing and the mountains and saw the backcountry in the good times. I can tell you every trail, I can describe any itinerary over the great ranges and name everywhere you want to go.

I've been privileged to travel and it teaches you a lot, whether just following a bunch of cattle around, or touring forty years with the band. I think I've seen all the world I need to see.

POETRY AND MORE

I wanted to include a couple of poems here by our son, Earl A. McKee III. There are also several poems I wrote, including one about my soul-mate, Snap.

THOUGHTS
by Earl A. McKee III, December 25, 1976

Dew upon the ground has frozen,
The hallow of The Night has captured
Each and every crystal, and placed them in bondage.
And alas, among the leaves of crumpled brown
and tall grasses of a chilled gossamer blue,
Shuffles a very small being
Determined to keep his presence unknown.
Tis only the smoke of his breath
That has given him away.

And far away, perhaps the horizon, formations are
    beckoning.
The skies once hidden behind space,
Join The Trees and their branches, so many yet so
    alone.
And rays of light cast out their lines, not to capture
But to free a frozen Kingdom.
The window begins to blur with warming waters,
and the world is abstract for a moment.

But now pictures are being painted,
Pictures not remembered by the eye.
The oranges and the blues, the colorless colors
all contributing, all creating—exhilaration!
and the crystals begin to dance in the Meadow
and the glistening of drops as they fall
From the tops of the Johnson grass
Bring drops from the eyes of Man;

Those of Man who have taken time to concentrate
and they who have considered their existence.
For he who cares little for small things
Finds tomorrow simply another day.
But for the dreamer and his imagination
The dew will Freeze again.

PACK TRIP IN THE SIERRA, SOMETHING TO REMEMBER
Earl A. McKee III

Standin' up to your knees in a cold creek.
Tears or no tears, dammit it's cold as hell.
Swing those feet and keep 'em warm.
Baths at 9000 feet really wake you up in the morning.
Smell breakfast smoke along with the pine starter
Brother's carvin' his name on a tree, sure for all to see.
The mules at the end of the meadow
are grab assing in the morning sun—
paintin' the grass a bright but cold green
Just how does that old sun make that
windin' creek sparkle and glow a silver gleam?

Dad cut himself shavin' and the
paper on his chin looks like hell,
but I guess it helps stop the bleeding.
Sure hate to have him bleed to death.

The old lady's wakin' up. Dad loves
to cook in the mountains anyway.
My sister won't get up til noon.
Why she destroys her day I'll never know.

Baths in the creek are all right.
The rocks are talkin' to the water.
Hell of an argument they're having.
Always screaming at each other.
I like the way they talk tough.
Makes you feel like screaming with 'em.
To get it out of your system, it seems you gotta scream.
Better not though. I might wake the world from its
sleep and maybe scare the mules.

Better dry off now. Wished to God
I could feel my body so I could know if its dry or not–
On second thought, I like this old creek.
I might miss something' if I move.
There's a lot a person could miss,
if you know what I mean!

SNAP, my faithful old friend.

OL' SNAP
Earl A. McKee, Jr., August 13, 2012

In the year of nineteen sixty five,
Life seemed much simpler then.
'til the day I went to say my goodbye
to Jim Kindred, my life-long friend.

As we talked of those great days gone by,
Where he'd taught me a lot of the rules,
'Bout trailin' the "long ears" over mountains so high
Back when we were packin' those mules.

He said, "The Doctor has told me, 'it won't be very long
'Til I'm ridin' in much greener fields.'"
"Could you do me a favor before I am gone,
Just to help out my dear wife, Lucille?"

"I just bought a couple of young cow-dog pups,
And before I go take my long nap,
Would you please come and get 'em, before they're grown up,
I've gave 'em their names–SNIP and SNAP."

So I kept my promise, to take home the pups,
As I shook Jim's old gnarled hand, goodbye,
Then a mist seemed to blur my vision all up
I guess from knowin' old Jim would soon die.

Well, I brought the pups home the very next day;
They both were a sharp lookin' pair.
Snip was dark Blue Merle speckled grey,
While Snap's coat had black wavy hair.

As they started to grow and develop their traits,
Their difference was soon seen and heard.
While Snap's natural herding instincts were great,
Snip's instincts saw nothing but birds!

I knew Snip would be a great family pet,
But a Cow-Dog he ain't, God forbid!
So I traded him off to a milkman I met
Where Snip's life was then spent, herdin' kids.

Well, here's where the story of 'Ol' Snap' begins,
He spent thirteen long years by my side.
He was envied by most of my cow-punchin' friends
No matter which ranch we would ride.

I've raised and I've trained some good dogs in my day,
But Ol' Snap has to top off the list.
Between age two and ten he was in his heyday
Those great years with him, I sure miss.

For fifty years I drove cattle out of Old Greasy Cove,
Up the trail, 'til we crossed Rayme Gap.
Then down Homer Canyon, with great cowboys we drove,
But my handiest cowhand was Ol' Snap.

That dog seemed to know, long before I would speak,
When an old cow was leavin' the trail.
I'd just give him the nod, 'nd 'round the mountain he'd streak
And he'd soon have her back without fail.

We trailed them on down, east of Old Rayme Gap,
Like my Dad did when I was a kid.
With the best damn cowboys that ever wore chaps,
Who were proud of the hard work they did.

We'd each take a small bunch when the goin' got rough,
With those cows mothered up with their calves.
"Always give them some time, and make sure they don't puff,
And ride proud with the bunch that you have."

With Ol' Snap by my side, I'd ride point up in front,
Out ahead of the leaders we'd stay.
Roundin' up the neighbor's cattle, that Ol' Snap and I'd hunt
And we'd push them, all out of our way.

With cows strung for a mile, as they trailed single file,
The cowbells rang, crystal clear, as they'd clap
The calves hugged their mothers' glancing back all the while,
'Cause my cows all respected Ol' Snap.

In those years I drove cattle to the High Mountain Crest,
O'er "The Pass," east of ol' Homer's Nose.
Down to Cahoon Meadow, where the calves could all rest,
While the cows ate green grass, as they dozed.

It was here I have memories I treasure and keep
Where Snap pawed out his bed by my side

As I crawled in my bedroll, I'd soon drift off to sleep,
While he guarded my being, with pride.

If a cowboy was up for relief in the night,
Or a bear might pass by on the prowl,
Snap's presence was clear, and was soon brought to light,
He warned all, with his deep, throaty growl.

I might ride checkin' cows up by Evelyn Lake
Or Hockett Meadows, where my cattle might stray.
I'd put Snap on their tracks, soon the timber would shake,
With his voice as he brought them my way.

Well, it's forty years later, but only days now it seems
Since those days with Ol' Snap were at hand.
It was not long ago, I awoke from my dreams
By his unmistakable bark, only I understand.

As the masters of old said "All good things must end,"
So it felt, without Snap by my side.
His dimmed eyesight and deafness I couldn't amend
How that crushed me - the day that he died.

I was upset that morning as I jumped in my car,
I sped back to drive to my corral.
But his "yelp" stabbed my soul, with its unending scar
I had just driven over my Ol' Pal.

Filled with hate for myself, at the deed I'd just done,
Wild-eyed, I drove blind to the Vet.
After X-rays they said, "His chance of walking are none,"
I had but one choice, that Oh! How I regret!

I held him close in my arms, as only I could,
His wise old eyes seemed to know of my blunder.
I then felt his soul pass through me for good.
As John carefully pressed down the plunger.

I placed Ol' Snap there beside me as I slowly drove home,
Knowing, God's lessons are hard to accept.
All those years spent together, and the places we'd roamed,
Only God knows how hard that I wept.

I made up my mind where I'd bury my friend,
'Neath the young oak tree where I'd asked him to stay,
By the corral, where he watched me, for hours on end,
Hoping I'd give him my smile and O.K.

As I pulled in to the ranch, very soon I could tell
That God wasn't through with me yet.
Dark clouds crashed above me, thunder boomed straight from Hell
Lightening blazed, like I'll never forget.

Still there's more to this story that I haven't told,
Snap was gun-shy from the day of his birth.
Be it thunder or gunfire, no dog pen would hold
His fear, chewed, climbed or tunneled through the earth.

And that day by that oak–It's a mighty Oak now,
Where I buried my friend in that storm
The thunder seemed louder than my ears would allow
While God's Almighty Presence, Transformed!

Soon dark clouds started parting and were drifting away,
A soft breeze came with peace on its brow
Distant thunder still told me, "Remember this day!"
God! How could I forget! Even now.

So this ends my story of my faithful old friend,
Of his life and his wisdom and love.
And the lessons he taught me right up to the end
Where he still watches me, from above.

I still say a few words there, by that mighty oak tree
At his grave, never marked on a map.

Where I laid his remains, no one knows where, but me.
And God knows of my love for Ol' Snap.

Life's been filled with surprises, I now must concede
No matter which trail I rode, there's a bog
I've met friends by the hundreds, who've filled my heart's need
But no friend on this earth like that old dog.

THE COWBOY KING FROM HAWKEYE BEACH

I wrote "The Cowboy King From Hawk Eye Beach" just like Elmo talked. He didn't have a "g" on anything, everything was "n"–ridin', ropin', punchin'. He had some rough edges, certainly wasn't a valedictorian, but good-hearted and a skillful hunter. Elmo really did show us how his old Bay horse could slide. There was a funny story behind that last line in the second verse. I took Bill Wylie and Billy Maloy with me to gather a half dozen of my steers that had crawled through the fence and were down on the flat with cattle that belonged to Charlie Rice and Clemmie and John Card. There was no corral, so we gathered the cattle and held them against the mountainside while I slowly moved in to part out my steers and push them over in a little canyon until we had them together to take back up the mountain to my range. We were holding the cattle as I worked my steers out when we saw a rider coming at us across the flats at a hard gallop. We watched him as he charged by us full-tilt into the little herd and knocked over a couple of cows. He was leaned way back in the saddle trying to stop his horse, but that horse didn't have any stop in him.

Elmo rode back to us and says, "By God, Earl, what do you think of that stop!" He really wasn't a horseman, had only been riding the Bay two weeks. He thought he'd done a pretty fancy cow horse move–slide to a stop.

THE COWBOY KING FROM HAWK EYE BEACH
A Tribute
Earl A. McKee, Jr., 1993

I rise early in the mornin' and cut myself a chew,
And while I'm pullin' on ma boots, I'm a figgerin' what I'll do.
I grab ma thirty-thirty, from the hook above ma head
Then I kick ma damned old Shepherd dog fer pissin' in ma bed.

But before I go to ketch ma horse, I'm thirstier than hell.
So I pour maself a waterglass of lukewarm Muscatel.
Then I grab a rope and ketch Ol' Bay, 'cause I figger I'll take a ride,
He's the one I rode the day I showed Bill and Earl how he could slide.

So I slams ma kack on Ol' Bay's back, then I stops to take a pee
And I slides ma thirty-thirty in the scabbard 'neath ma knee.
Then I fills ma tapaderos, and I settles in the seat.
And Ol' Bay goes to buckin' and a shit'n in the street.

I raked him with ma gut hooks, as we flew down Lime Kiln hill.
He bucked plumb to Pace's Beer Joint where I showed the folks ma skill.
I finely yanks his head up 'cause my ass was a gettin' sore.
Al Pace handed me a cold beer as I rode him through the door.

I slid him right up to the bar and I steps off with a thud.
There sat Emma and Ol' Bill Cooper, just a soppin' up the suds.
Well, I finally bums a round or two and I says as I lit ma pipe,
"I gotta get goin' to kill a buck or I won't get back 'til night!"

So I leaped in the saddle and whirled away with a mighty rebel yell.
We roared through Freeman Walker's yard and tore it all to hell.
We flew like the wind back through the cut so fast I couldn't spit,
Rode straight to the ford at Hawk Eye Beach where I stopped to take a shit.

As I sat there a strainin', with ma ass between two rocks,
I scanned ol' Broke-up's rocky face with ma twenty power binocks.
Then all at wonst I seen him! Near the top all bedded down!
It looked as though his horns alone might dress two hundurd pounds.

He looked to be a mile away, as I squinted through the glass.
I could also see he was watchin' me, so I quickly wiped ma ass!

334

Then I reached for my model ninety-four, and yanks it from it's quiver.
Ol' Bay sets back and broke the reins and rolls plumb to the river!

I lays ma rifle over a rock as I levers in a shell.
When you're shootin' a buck that's a mile away, ya gotta hold steady as hell.
Well, I raised the back sight all the way, and aimed ten inches high
Then I slowly pulled the trigger and watched the bullet fly.

Then I lit ma pipe an takes a puff, and I gently settles back
In just five seconds by ma watch I heard the bullet smack.
That ol' buck bugled as he got up and with one last mighty leap
He cleared the bluff and sailed through space at least five hundred feet!

Then I jumped in the saddle and headed up, for as near as I could tell
It'll take at least an hour and a half to get to where he fell.
When I finally reached that awful scene, it made my poor heart shiver,
For during the fall that ol' buck's horns were smashed to a thousand
slivers.

Well I damn near cried as I turned to ride away on my Ol' Bay nag
He's illegal as hell and I can't pack him in, 'cause there's no horns left to tag!
So we slid off the mountain to the Hawk Eye ford where Ol' Bay trips
and falls.
I was slammed to the bottom right over his head and he stepped right
on my balls!

I was soaked to the skin as I got back on that stumblin' ol' son of a bitch.
There stood Charlie, Clemmie and Johnnie Card still arguin' over the
ditch.
Well I'm home again and the stock's all fed, and the fires are stoked as
well.
I settle back in my easy chair, with a fresh glass of Muscatel.

Then I open ma tin of Grainger, and I tamp some in ma pipe.
I light 'er up and watch the smoke go driftin' in the night.
My thoughts drift back to the day just spent, and the memories are nice.
I'm still the Cowboy King from Hawk Eye Beach, or my name ain't
Elmo Rice.

ONIS
My Tribute to Onis Brown
Earl A. McKee, Jr., March 18, 2003

There are men that I've known in my lifetime
That in my memory will always be missed.
Of the men I was privileged to work with
One man stands high on the list.

He never stood tall in his stature
He stood maybe five foot six.
But a stronger man you would seldom meet
With a chest heavy, muscled and thick.

He was born near the base of Mt. Pinos
Near the coast in the Caliente Range,
He grew up not far from the old Fort Tejon
And he rode on the Carrizo Plains.

He grew up in the saddle as folks did then
And when his lifelong dream set its course.
He'd be spending the rest of his wonderlust days
Just breakin' and trainin' a horse.

His early teachers he often told me
Were called the "Californios."
They were the Spanish Vaqueros from Miller and Lux
Who came here from old Mexico.

They taught him what the Mustangs were thinkin'
And how they could run o're the plains;
How to trap them, throw them and saddle them up
How to teach them to give to the reins.

At eighteen he packed his belongings.
On his horse he struck out on his own

With a small band of Mustangs that he'd broken to ride
Heading North through the valley alone.

He'd heard of the mighty Sierra
And their beautiful snow covered peaks,
So he headed Northeast of old Bakersfield
Up the Kern with its bubbling creeks.

He took the trail up the Little Kern River
Where the Foxtail Pine branches swing,
And over a pass they called Farewell Gap
Then down into Mineral King.

He'd heard of this mining town "Beulah"
Settled twenty five short years before.
He made friends with a man named John Broder
The year was Nineteen Hundred and Four.

He soon went to work with John Broder
Packing people and groceries and gear
Over Franklin and down to Kern River
And all points beyond far and near.

It was here in the Sierra Nevada
Where this man spent most of his time.
There was hardly a place in these mountains
That he hadn't discovered or climbed.

He was the first man to travel cross-country
Over passes like Colby and Glen.
He was the first man to climb Black Kaweah
And gaze from where no man had been.

He was always ridin' good horses
That were bridled so light and so free.
When he stepped off and the reins hit the ground
They'd stand if tied to a tree.

But horse training wasn't his only talent
And God's animals need to be led.
He would talk to his dogs without raising his voice
They would mind everything that he said.

His little white dog he called Scrapper
Seemed to know every trick in the book,
He'd bring him his boots, his gloves and his spurs
And his tail wagged with each step he took.

God knows this man was a hunter,
He'd hunted these mountains for years,
He knew all the country and where the bucks were.
When I think of those days it brings tears.

He shot a Winchester rifle with a hexagon barrel
With its accuracy seldom exceeded,
With a grip like a vise he could shoot with the best
And open sights were all that he needed.

Whether rifles or pistols he could sure shoot a gun.
There were very few men that out shot him;
And I heard him say: "There's one man I can't beat
That's my youngest son Bill, and I taught him."

I was with him the last time he went hunting
In the fall of Nineteen Fifty Seven.
Soon after the Lord came to gather him in
And I'm sure he's now ridin' in Heaven.

I knew early on of his sickness.
He fought hard till the day he went down.
I cried when I sang at his funeral,
And God knows I miss Onis Brown.

RED LEAR

Red Lear is a well-known tuba player and he owns a big butcher shop in New Athens, Illinois. That's Athens with a 'long A', not pronounced soft like the Athens in Georgia or Greece.

I talk to Red frequently. We've known each other 25 maybe 30 years since we met in Chicago at a jazz festival. Red plays with the St. Louis Rivermen band. Red is a guy who plays great solos and is a funny show-man, a lovable fellow with a smile that beams. He has red hair, so he's known by his friends as "Red." His name is David. We both buy and sell cattle and Red often says on stage that we both have cow manure on our boots. The crowd always enjoys our numbers done by two old cowmen; I usually sing and Red plays along, then he'll take a solo for a touching rendition of "My Mother's Eyes" or a light-hearted tune.

Red's butcher shop is full of hanging beefs and they wrap meat almost around the clock. Red gets up before 4 a.m. to wrap meat every day, then usually goes to bed with the chickens. At the butcher shop he always has something good cooking on the stove.

The St. Louis Rivermen were featured at a couple of Jazz Affairs here in Three Rivers and of course we've played in St. Louis, so Red and his wife Carolyn have stayed with us and we've been guests at their home several times.

Our band was playing somewhere so I had to miss Red Lear's 70th birthday bash so in his honor I wrote a poem and emailed it to his friend and fellow musician, Jean Kittrell, to read at the party. She said Red really appreciated the sentiments.

A DAY IN THE LIFE OF RED LEAR
by Earl A. McKee, Jr., September 19, 2007

If you're down in the town of old New Athens,
And in search of some steak or some good sausage rations,
There's a shop on the strand of this Illinois town
That will tickle your palate as your gut growls around.

And as you approach this busy meat store
A big red headed butcher you'll meet at the door.
He might try to tell you, "Your entry's forbidden!"
But the gleam in his eyes tell you–he's only kiddin!

Then he'll stick out his hand and his handshake ain't tame,
"We're real glad to see you, Red Lear is my name."
With a hundred one-liners, he'll split both your sides;
It's a barrel of fun where this big guy resides.

He don't even care if you're there to buy meat.
He'll stop you and say, "How 'bout something to EAT!"
"Grab a chair and sit down, you've got nothing to do.
I'll slip in the kitchen and I'll bring you some stew."

"While your stew's coolin' off and your hunger awakes
Grab some of that paper and we'll wrap a few steaks.
By now you've met Caroline, and all of the crew,
You've wrapped meat 'till you're numb and there's ice in your stew.

Still the laughter goes on as you yearn for relief.
Your hands say you've wrapped up a whole side of beef!
When you finally are done–friend, you won't be the same,
You've spent the day with great people and you're glad that you came.
He says, "Here's some steaks, but your money can't buy 'em.
Here's a couple smoked pork loins. Just take 'em and try 'em.

You try to recall, what it was you came after
But your mind is still filled with red meat and laughter.
Now your life's filled with memories you will always hold dear.
Cause you've just spent a day in the life of Red Lear!

A PACK STORY

※※※

This story from the *Visalia Times Delta,* September 9, 1935 illustrates the thousand details of itinerary, logistics, animals, packers, and supplies that had to be coordinated to provide an unforgettable, relaxing pack trip for the dudes. More than once my dad was so wrapped up thinking about the thousand things for an upcoming trip that he ran his car into the rocks.

The newspaper story had no by-line, but it sounds to me like W. P. Fuller's writing. After 32 trips with us, he'd been just about everywhere you could go in the mountains. We'd have to decide where he hadn't been, and after that many years, there're only so many canyons to go up to find a nice camp with good horse feed. Mr. Fuller was well aware of that when he planned the itineraries with my dad.

Mr. Fuller kept a journal of every trip and often would bring an old journal to the campfire to read aloud the events of a previous pack trip, maybe one 25 years before. He jotted notes every day, but on layover days, he'd be at the table writing everything in his journal, whistling under his breath as he scribbled. We joked privately that he had dysentery of the pen. He had served as secretary to President Herbert Hoover and you could almost see his mind working; it was like a clock. He was a stickler about time, laid down the law about meal and departure times. He'd say we'll eat breakfast at 8:10 a.m. and if you're not here at 8:10, you will eat lunch. That was for the benefit of the cook. It was seldom that any of his party was late, but if one was, he'd be good-natured but firm in enforcing his rule. In his diary, he recorded the precise minute of departure, for example: "At 9:05 we mounted up and headed out to . . . ." as well as arrival time and all the incidents in between. This item says the annual play was from 10 to 11 p.m. Sounds like W. P. Fuller to me. Here is the article.

"Three Rivers, September 9, 1935: Completing their annual pack trip through the Sierra with the usual overnight stop in Three Rivers, the W. P. Fuller party broke up with a dinner at the Three Rivers lodge Friday night for members of the party and packers alike. Then Mr. Fuller and two others went on to Fresno to take the 1 a.m. plane for Mills field, the balance of the party remaining to return to their homes by auto the next morning.

"This makes the seventh summer that W. P. Fuller, of the Fuller Paint Company, and family have gone into the Sierra with Earl McKee, local packer and guide and concessioner of packing in Sequoia National Park. It is the eighth trip with McKee, one summer including two trips.

"In the party this summer when it took the trail August 3rd, at Parchers camp, 20 miles west of Bishop, which had been reached by airplane, were Mr. and Mrs. W. P. Fuller, Jr., Mr. and Mrs. W. Parmer Fuller III, Mr. and Mrs. George Fuller, John M. Fuller, Robert Fuller and Jack Kuhn, all of San Mateo; Miss Betty Leigh Wright, Pasadena, Alfred Benson Page of Topeka, Kansas. McKee conducted the party personally. His packers were Walter Pratt, Ernest Britten, Jr., and Onis Brown; cooks, Alan Savage and Norman Ju, the latter a Chinese cook brought by the Fullers. Twenty-two pack mules and seventeen saddle horses were used.

"Traveling south via the Middle Fork of the Kings River, the party split, going over Mather Pass and the others via Cartridge creek, to join again at Marian Lake. The trip was taken very leisurely, stops of from one to four days being made in each camp. At the South Fork of the Kings River, 1500 pounds of groceries were packed in to the outfit from Independence. Then the party moved on via Woods Creek, Sixty Lake Basin and Forrester Pass to Milestone Creek where a five-day stop was made. Ten of McKee's mules were taken to Independence for another ton of supplies.

"Robert Fuller left the party here August 24th to return to school. He was met in Independence by his father's airplane.

Mt. Whitney Scaled

"Climbing Mt. Whitney was the next event of importance. Leaving the outfit at Crabtree, all of the party but three packers made the ascent, Maggie, the lunch mule, was taken along with wood as well as food in her pack and at the crest snow was melted and a hot lunch served deluxe at the top of the United States.

"From Mt. Whitney the outfit made its way on down the Kern Canyon to Moraine Lake, where the party was joined by Joseph S. Thompson, brother of Kathleen Norris, the writer, and his wife, from San Francisco. Lee Maloy, McKee's son-in-law, packed them out from Giant Forest with six more animals, augmenting the outfit to forty-five head of stock. The Thompsons continued with the party the remaining ten days out.

"Some startling experiences were had with electrical storms during the trip. Parmer and John Fuller, Jack Kuhn and Onis Brown climbed the Black Kaweah, reaching the top in an electrical storm. Lightning struck all about them and the air was so full of electricity that their hair literally "stood on end" actually standing straight up. Going up, a loose rock hit Brown between the eyes, blacking both of them. The day the outfit left Moraine Lake lightning struck a big pine tree on the rim of the Big Arroyo after McKee had passed it and before the following pack train reached it.

"The last camp was made at Big Five Lake Basin. Here was given the annual play, in which every member of the outfit is called upon to do something. Clever burlesques and take-offs on each other, skits and songs furnished an entertaining program from 10 to 11 p.m.

"Mineral King was reached via Sawtooth Pass on September 6th. Here the autos awaited to bring the party to Three Rivers for the last dinner before disbanding."

REFERENCES

❦

PHOTO OF TUNNEL ON HIGH SIERRA TRAIL:
A special thanks to David Husted for his photograph of the tunnel on the High Sierra Trail.
http://hikenhi.smugmug.com/Davids-Hiking-and/Tripple-Divide-Peak-Trip-2010/11267155_8sKTXM#!i=1460363246&k=KjRCrjG

http://hikenhi.smugmug.com/Davids-Hiking-and/The-Nine-Lakes-Basin-August/7951056_Ov4cnf#!i=5205033856&k=A2kxU
http://hikenhi.smugmug.com/Davids-Hiking-and/The-Nine-Lakes-Basin-August/7951056_Ov4cnf
http://www.panoramio.com/user/814238/tags/The%20High%20Sierra%20Trail%20Sequoia%20NP

David Husted of Fresno, California, posts stunning color photographs of the panoramas seen from each trail that he hikes, and he's hiked nearly all of them. Visit his website to view many of the same trails we packed through the magnificent Sierra.

Newspaper articles on the shooting incidents in 1887 and 1946 can be found in the Annie Mitchell History Room, Visalia Main Branch of the Tulare County Library, for reference.

ADDITIONAL PHOTOS

1910 portrait of Edna Finch two years before she was married to Earl A. McKee, Sr.

STAPLES

25#	Flour
5#	Cornmeal (Yellow)
10#	Flap Jack Flour
2 pkge	Coarse Wheat Cereal
2#	Baking Powder
2½#	Salt
1 can	Pepper
1 bot.	Celery Salt
15#	Sugar
6#	Shortening
6 pkges	Cookies
3#	Crackers
2#	Rice
3#	Cheese
4	1 Quart cans Syrup-Log Cabin
6 pkge	Matches-1 doz. small to pkge
6 bars	Soap -Crystal White
3-6	Loaves Bread(White)To be used on
	(Rye)first days out
	Catsup or Woncestershire Sauce

VEGETABLES & FRESH FRUITS

25#	Potatoes
10#	Onions
1	Garlic
1 doz	Grapefruit
1 "	Oranges
1 "	Lemons

CANNED VEGETABLES

3 cans	Sweet Potatoes
3 "	Asparagus
8 "	Corn
3 "	Succotash
8 "	Peas
8 "	Tomatoes
3	Spaghetti (bulk?)
3 "	Spinach
3 "	Dill or Sweet Pickles
6 "	Sauerkraut (Heinz, cooked)

COFFEE AND TEA

10#	Coffee
1#	Tea

MEATS - CANNED AND SMOKED

3 cans		Roast Beef
12 "		Pork and Beans
1		Ham
1		Bacon
3 cans		Clams
6 "		Vienna Sausage

MILK, BUTTER AND EGGS

1½ doz		Tall cans Milk
1 "		Small " "
12#		Butter (in cans)
1/2 case		Eggs

FRUITS - CANNED

6 cans		Pineapple
6 "		Pears
3 "		Fruit Salad
3 "		Grape Fruit
6 glass.		Jams or Preserves
6 cans		Peaches
3 "		Apricots

FRUITS - DRIED

5#		Peaches
5#		Prunes
3#		Puffed Raisins

A grub list folded inside Earl A. McKee Sr.'s 1922 day book.

EASTMAN KODAK COMPANY

ROCHESTER, N.Y.

March 30th, 1917.

Mr. Earl A. McKee,

Lemon Cove, Cal.,

Dear Sir:-

Your name has been given me by Mr. William E. Colby as that of a competent guide for the Kings and Kern River country. I have some intention of making another camping trip in the Sierras this fall, starting say the latter part of August or early September, and shall be glad if you will let me know whether you can supply the equipment which I require, and also your terms. There would probably be a party of four persons and the duration of the trip about four weeks. We have our own complete camp equipment, including tents, beds and cooking outfit. The outfit requires twelve pack horses, in addition to the four saddle horses. We do our own cooking but the guides' cook is expected to wash the dishes, and the guides to supply wood and water, and of course to pack, unpack and set up the outfit. We furnish our own food. To handle our party it usually takes four guides, a cook, and one or two extra men as wranglers and packers; and altogether twenty-eight or thirty horses. If this kind of an affair appeals to you I shall be glad to know what route you would recommend for such a trip.

Yours very truly,

March 30, 1917 letter from George W. Eastman to my father, Earl A. McKee, Sr. to arrange a pack trip. My father was recommended to Mr. Eastman by William E. Colby.

349

This is one photo from a stack of old negatives found in an Oregon attic; the new homeowner noticed the "Blossom Peak" sign on the left and through the Internet located Three Rivers and sent them to me about 2010. This is the old Phipps (later Alles) store at the Y in Old Three Rivers. Notice the Bell Telephone logo on the entrance post. The building burned to the ground in 1939.

AUTHOR'S COLLECTION.

Another photo from old negatives (pre-1939) found in an Oregon attic. Mules are packing odd loads, some long pipe, sheets of plywood, steel frame, across a bridge over the Kern River. The rider is off his horse, probably climbed in the rocks to take the picture while his mules stood still on a bridge over the river.

AUTHOR'S COLLECTION.

A photo from old negatives (pre-1939) found in an Oregon attic. Mule loads of lumber and cots, probably in the bottom of Kern River canyon.

AUTHOR'S COLLECTION.

A photo from old negatives (pre-1939) found in an Oregon attic. It shows 21' long pipe sections packed across two mules. The mules must be real gentle to stay in line; a rolling hitch allows the pipe to move a little bit to get around switchbacks. On real bad trails like Bishop Pass, the pipe would have to be cut to 10' lengths. On the hillside, dwarf sage looks like this was taken in Onion Valley on the Bishop side of the Sierra.

AUTHOR'S COLLECTION.

This is the westerly view of property that has been in this family for 110 years. I designed the Bar O horse ranch with eight pastures, return lanes, breaking pens, roping arena, hay barn, a first class horse barn with 12 stalls, each with a 40' run attached, and a regulation round pen. The top rail of the pipe and cable cross-fencing is charged with water at 100 pound pressure. It is a beautiful 20-acre spread adjacent to my home place where I still raise American Quarter horses. Photo 2013.

AUTHOR'S COLLECTION.

Made in the USA
San Bernardino, CA
10 April 2017